TAIWAN

DOING BUSINESS AND INVESTING IN TAIWAN GUIDE GUIDE

VOLUME 1

STRATEGIC AND PRACTICAL INFORMATION

International Business Publications, USA
Washington DC, USA-Taiwan

TAIWAN

DOING BUSINESS AND INVESTING IN TAIWAN GUIDE

VOLUME 1 STRATEGIC AND PRACTICAL INFORMATION

UPDATED ANNUALLY

We express our sincere appreciation to all government agencies and international organizations which provided information and other materials for this guide

Cover Design: International Business Publications, USA

2016 Edition Updated Reprint International Business Publications, USA
ISBN 978-1-5145-2794-8

For additional analytical, business and investment opportunities information, please contact Global Investment & Business Center, USA at (703) 370-8082. Fax: (703) 370-8083. E-mail: ibpusa3@gmail.com Global Business and Investment Info Databank - www.ibpus.com

Printed in the USA

For additional analytical, business and investment opportunities information, please contact Global Investment & Business Center, USA at (703) 370-8082. Fax: (703) 370-8083. E-mail: ibpusa3@gmail.com Global Business and Investment Info Databank - www.ibpus.com

TAIWAN

DOING BUSINESS AND INVESTING IN TAIWAN GUIDE

VOLUME 1
STRATEGIC AND PRACTICAL INFORMATION

TABLE OF CONTENTS

STRATEGIC AND DEVELOPMENT PROFILES

COUNTRY OVERVIEW

Capital	Taipei 25°02′N 121°38′E
Largest city	New Taipei 25°01′N 121°28′E
Official languages	Mandarin
Recognised regional languages	Taiwanese Hokkien Hakka Formosan languages Fuzhou dialect
Official script	Traditional Chinese
Ethnic groups	>95% Han Chinese ∟ 70% Hokkien ∟ 14% Hakka ∟ 14% Waishengren 2.3% Aborigines
Demonym	Taiwanese
Government	Unitary semi-presidential republic
• President	Tsai Ing-wen
• Vice President	Chen Chien-jen
• Premier	Lin Chuan
• Vice Premier	Lin Hsi-yao
• Speaker	Su Chia-chyuan
• Deputy Speaker	Tsai Chi-chang
Legislature	Legislative Yuan
Establishment from the Xinhai Revolution	
• Wuchang Uprising	10 October 1911
• Republic established	1 January 1912
• Constitution	25 December 1947
Area	
• Total	36,193 km^2 (136th) 13,974 sq mi
Population	
• 2016 estimate	23,508,362 (52nd)
• Density	649/km^2 (17th) 1,680/sq mi
GDP (PPP)	2016 estimate
• Total	$1,147 trillion b

• Per capita	$48,703
GDP (nominal)	2016 estimate
• Total	$588.334 billion
• Per capita	$24,985
Gini (2014)	33.6 medium
HDI (2014)	▲ 0.882 very high · 25th
Currency	New Taiwan dollar(NT$) (TWD)
Time zone	National Standard Time(UTC+8)
Date format	yyyy-mm-dd yyyy年m月d日 (CE; CE+2697) 民國yy年m月d日(CE−1911)
Drives on the	right
Calling code	+886
ISO 3166 code	TW
Internet TLD	.tw .台灣 .台湾

Taiwan is a state in East Asia. The Republic of China, originally based in mainland China, now governs the island of Taiwan, which makes up over 99% of its territory, as well as Penghu, Kinmen, Matsu, and other minor islands. Neighboring states include the People's Republic of China to the west, Japan to the east and northeast, and the Philippines to the south. Taipei is the seat of the central government. New Taipei, encompassing the metropolitan area surrounding Taipei proper, is the most populous city.

The island of Taiwan (formerly known as "*Formosa*") was mainly inhabited by Taiwanese aborigines until the Dutch and Spanish settlement during the Age of Discovery in the 17th century, when Han Chinese people began immigrating to the island. In 1662, the pro-Ming loyalist Koxinga expelled the Dutch and established the first Han Chinese polity to rule on the island, the Kingdom of Tungning. The Qing Dynasty of China later conquered Taiwan in 1683. By the time Taiwan was ceded to Japan in 1895, the majority of Taiwan's inhabitants were Han Chinese either by ancestry or by assimilation. The Republic of China (ROC) was established in China in 1912. At the end of World War II in 1945, Japan surrendered Taiwan to ROC military forces on behalf of the Allies. Following the Chinese civil war, the Communist Party of China took full control of mainland China and founded the People's Republic of China (PRC) in 1949. The ROC relocated its government to Taiwan, and its jurisdiction became limited to Taiwan and its surrounding islands. In 1971, the PRC assumed China's seat at the United Nations, which the ROC originally occupied. International recognition of the ROC has gradually eroded as most countries switched recognition to the PRC. Only 21 UN member states and the Holy See currently maintain official diplomatic relations with the ROC, though it has unofficial ties with most other states via its representative offices.

Constitutionally, the ROC government has claimed sovereignty over all of "China," in a definition that includes mainland China and Outer Mongolia, but has not made retaking mainland China a political goal since 1992. However, the government's stance on defining its political position of relation with China largely depends on which political coalition is in charge. Meanwhile, the PRC also asserts itself to be the sole legal representation of China and claims Taiwan as its 23rd province to be under its sovereignty, denying the status and existence of ROC as a sovereign state. The PRC has threatened the use of military force as a response to any formal declaration of Taiwanese independence, or if it deems peaceful reunification no longer possible. Cross-strait relations as well as issues of national identity within the country are important factors in Taiwanese politics and a cause of social and political division among political parties and their respective supporters.

During the latter half of the 20th century, Taiwan experienced rapid economic growth and industrialization and is now an advanced industrial economy. In the 1980s and early 1990s, Taiwan evolved into a multi-party democracy with universal suffrage. Taiwan is one of the Four Asian Tigers and a member of the WTO and APEC. The 19th-largest economy in the world, its high-tech industry plays a key role in the global economy. Taiwan is ranked highly in terms of freedom of the press, health care, public education, economic freedom, and human development

GEOGRAPHY

Location: Eastern Asia, islands bordering the East China Sea, Philippine Sea, South China Sea, and Taiwan Strait, north of the Philippines, off the southeastern coast of China

Geographic coordinates: 23 30 N, 121 00 E

Map references: Southeast Asia

Area:
total: 35,980 sq km
land: 32,260 sq km
water: 3,720 sq km
note: includes the Pescadores, Matsu, and Quemoy

Area - comparative: slightly smaller than Maryland and Delaware combined

Land boundaries: 0 km

Coastline: 1,566.3 km

Maritime claims:
exclusive economic zone: 200 nm *territorial sea:* 12 nm

Climate: tropical; marine; rainy season during southwest monsoon (June to August); cloudiness is persistent and extensive all year

Terrain: eastern two-thirds mostly rugged mountains; flat to gently rolling plains in west

Elevation extremes:
lowest point: South China Sea 0 m *highest point:* Yu Shan 3,997 m

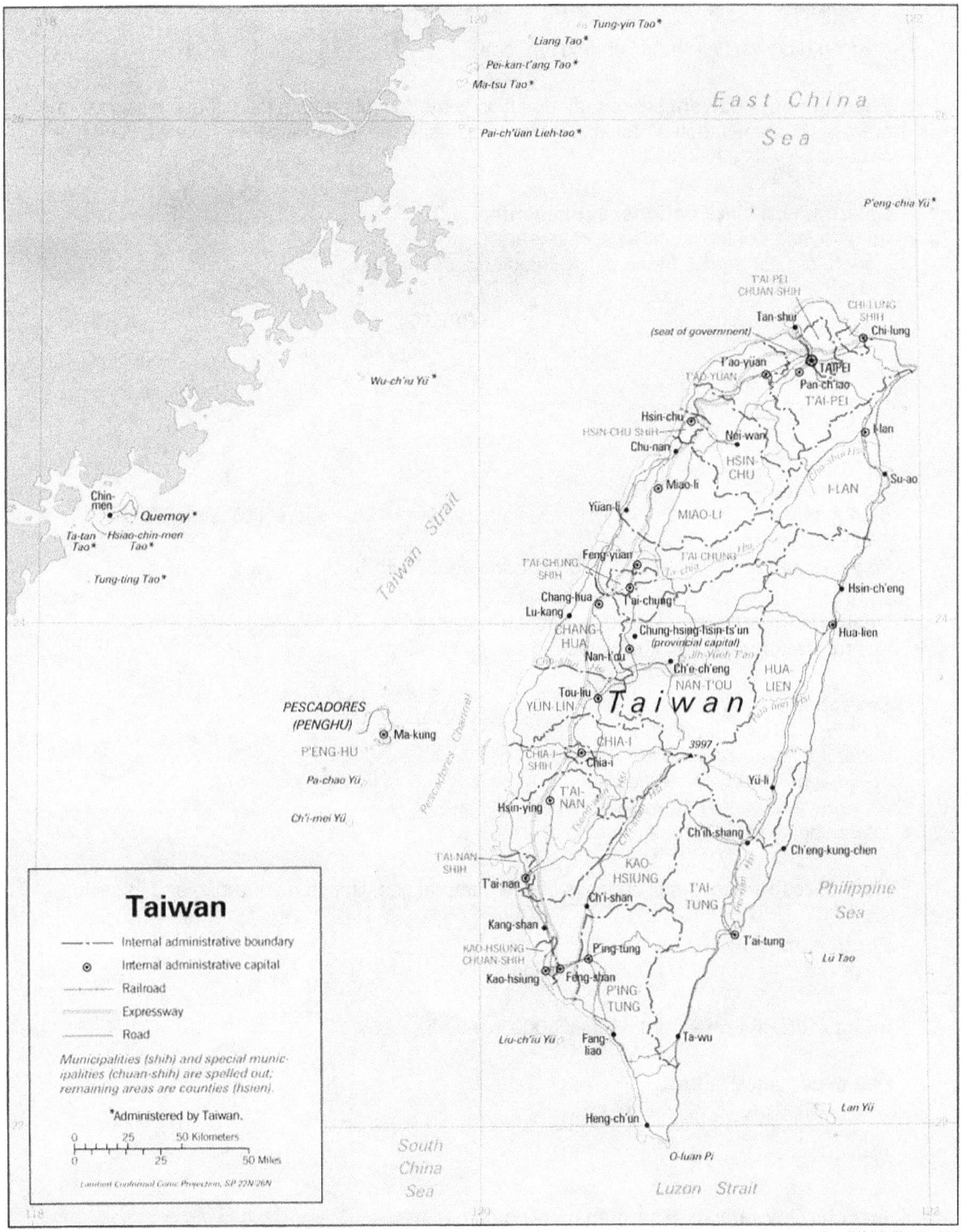

Land use:

arable land: 24% *permanent crops:* 1% *permanent pastures:* 5% *forests and woodland:* 55% *other:* 15%

Irrigated land: NA sq km

Natural hazards: earthquakes and typhoons

Environment - current issues: air pollution; water pollution from industrial emissions, raw sewage; contamination of drinking water supplies; trade in endangered species; low-level radioactive waste disposal

Environment - international agreements:
party to: none of the selected agreements
signed, but not ratified: none of the selected agreements

PEOPLE

Population: 22,191,087

Age structure:
0-14 years: 22% (male 2,485,421; female 2,292,901) *15-64 years:* 70% (male 7,869,939; female 7,629,195)
65 years and over: 8% (male 1,013,074; female 900,557)

Death rate: 5.91 deaths/1,000 population
Net migration rate: -0.38 migrant(s)/1,000 population

Sex ratio:
at birth: 1.08 male(s)/female
under 15 years: 1.08 male(s)/female
15-64 years: 1.03 male(s)/female
65 years and over: 1.12 male(s)/female
total population: 1.05 male(s)/female

Natural resources: small deposits of coal, natural gas, limestone, marble, and asbestos

Population growth rate: 0.81%
Birth rate: 14.42 births/1,000 population

Infant mortality rate: 7.06 deaths/1,000 live births

Life expectancy at birth:
total population: 76.35 years
male: 73.62 years
female: 79.32 years

Total fertility rate: 1.76 children born/woman

Nationality:
noun: Chinese (singular and plural)
adjective: Chinese

Ethnic groups: Taiwanese (including Hakka) 84%, mainland Chinese 14%, aborigine 2%
Religions: mixture of Buddhist, Confucian, and Taoist 93%, Christian 4.5%, other 2.5%
Languages: Mandarin Chinese (official), Taiwanese (Min), Hakka dialects

Literacy:
definition: age 15 and over can read and write
total population: 86% (1980 est.); note - literacy for the total population has reportedly increased to 94%
male: 93%
female: 79%

GOVERNMENT

Country name:
conventional long form: none
conventional short form: Taiwan
local long form: none
local short form: T'ai-wan

Data code: TW
Government type: multiparty democratic regime headed by popularly elected president
Capital: Taipei

Administrative divisions: since in the past the authorities claimed to be the government of all China, the central administrative divisions include the provinces of Fu-chien (some 20 offshore islands of Fujian Province including Quemoy and Matsu) and Taiwan (the island of Taiwan and the Pescadores islands); note - the more commonly referenced administrative divisions are those of Taiwan Province - 16 counties (hsien, singular and plural), 5 municipalities* (shih, singular and plural), and 2 special municipalities** (chuan-shih, singular and plural); Chang-hua, Chia-i, Chia-i*, Chi-lung*, Hsin-chu, Hsin-chu*, Hua-lien, I-lan, Kao-hsiung, Kao-hsiung**, Miao-li, Nan-t'ou, P'eng-hu, P'ing-tung, T'ai-chung, T'ai-chung*, T'ai-nan, T'ai-nan*, T'ai-pei, T'ai-pei**, T'ai-tung, T'ao-yuan, and Yun-lin; the provincial capital is at Chung-hsing-hsin-ts'un
note: Taiwan uses the Wade-Giles system for romanization

National holiday: National Day, 10 October (1911) (Anniversary of the Chinese Revolution)
Constitution: 1 January 1947, amended in 1992, 1994, and 1997
Legal system: based on civil law system; accepts compulsory ICJ jurisdiction, with reservations
Suffrage: 20 years of age; universal

Executive branch:

Taiwan--NDE

chief of state: President TSAI Ing-wen (since 20 May 2016); Vice President CHEN Chien-jen (since 20 May 2016)
head of government: Premier LIN Chuan (President of the Executive Yuan) (since 20 May 2016); Vice Premier LIN Hsi-yao, Vice President of the Executive Yuan (since 20 May 2016)
cabinet: Executive Yuan - ministers appointed by president on recommendation of premier
elections/appointments: president and vice president directly elected on the same ballot by simple majority popular vote for a 4-year term (eligible for a second term); election last

held on 16 January 2016 (next to be held in 2020); premier appointed by the president; vice premiers appointed by the president on the recommendation of the premier
election results: TSAI Ing-wen elected president; percent of vote - TSAI Ing-wen (DPP) 56.1%, Eric CHU Li-lun (KMT) 31.0%, James SOONG Chu-yu (PFP) 12.8%; note - TSAI is the first woman elected president of Taiwan

Legislative branch:

description: unicameral Legislative Yuan (113 seats; 73 members directly elected in single-seat constituencies by simple majority vote, 34 directly elected in a single islandwide constituency by proportional representation vote, and 6 directly elected in multi-seat aboriginal constituencies by proportional representation vote; members serve 4-year terms)
elections: Legislative Yuan - last held on 16 January 2016 (next to be held in January 2020)
election results: Legislative Yuan - percent of vote by party - DPP 44.1%, KMT 26.9%, PFP 6.5%, NPP 6.1%, other 16.4%; seats by party - DPP 68, KMT 35, NPP 5, PFP 3, NPSU 1, independent 1

Judicial branch: Judicial Yuan, justices appointed by the president with the consent of the National Assembly

Political parties and leaders: Chinese New Party or CNP [CHOU Yang-sun]; Democratic Progressive Party or DPP [LIN Yi-hsiung, chairman]; Kuomintang or KMT (Nationalist Party) [LIEN Chan, acting chairman]; Taiwan Independence Party or TAIP [CHENG Pang-chen]; other minor parties

Political pressure groups and leaders: Taiwan independence movement, various business and environmental groups
note: debate on Taiwan independence has become acceptable within the mainstream of domestic politics on Taiwan; political liberalization and the increased representation of opposition parties in Taiwan's legislature have opened public debate on the island's national identity; advocates of Taiwan independence oppose the ruling party's traditional stand that the island will eventually reunify with mainland China; goals of the Taiwan independence movement include establishing a sovereign nation on Taiwan and entering the UN; other organizations supporting Taiwan independence include the World United Formosans for Independence and the Organization for Taiwan Nation Building

International organization participation: APEC, AsDB, BCIE, ICC, IOC, WCL, WTrO (applicant) **Diplomatic representation in the US:** none; unofficial commercial and cultural relations with the people of the US are maintained through a private instrumentality, the Taipei Economic and Cultural Representative Office (TECRO) in the US with headquarters in Taipei and field offices in Washington and 12 other US cities

Diplomatic representation from the US: none; unofficial commercial and cultural relations with the people on Taiwan are maintained through a private corporation, the American Institute in Taiwan (AIT), which has its headquarters in Rosslyn, Virginia (telephone: (703) 525-8474 and FAX: (703) 841-1385) and offices in Taipei at #7 Lane 134, Hsin Yi Road, Section 3, telephone [886] (2) 2709-2000, FAX [886] (2) 2702-7675, and in Kao-hsiung at #2 Chung Cheng 3d Road, telephone [886] (7) 224-0154 through 0157, FAX [886] (7) 223-8237, and the American Trade Center at Room 3207 International Trade Building, Taipei World Trade Center, 333 Keelung

Road Section 1, Taipei 10548, telephone [886] (2) 2720-1550, FAX [886] (2) 2757-7162 **Flag description:** red with a dark blue rectangle in the upper hoist-side corner bearing a white sun with 12 triangular rays

ECONOMY

Taiwan has a dynamic capitalist economy with gradually decreasing government guidance of investment and foreign trade. Exports, led by electronics, machinery, and petrochemicals have provided the primary impetus for economic development. This heavy dependence on exports exposes the economy to fluctuations in world demand. Taiwan's diplomatic isolation, low birth rate, and rapidly aging population are other major long-term challenges. Free trade agreements have proliferated in East Asia over the past several years, and following the landmark Economic Cooperation Framework Agreement (ECFA) signed with China in June 2010, Taiwan in July 2014 signed a free trade deal with New Zealand—Taipei's first-ever with a country with which it does not maintain diplomatic relations—and in November inked a trade pact with Singapore. Negotiations continue on follow-on components of ECFA regarding trade in goods and a dispute resolution mechanism; a trade in services agreement is under review in the legislature. Taiwan's Total Fertility rate of just over one child per woman is among the lowest in the world, raising the prospect of future labor shortages, falling domestic demand, and declining tax revenues. Taiwan's population is aging quickly, with the number of people over 65 accounting for 11.2% of the island's total population as of 2014. The island runs a large overall trade surplus largely because of its surplus with China, and its foreign reserves are the world's sixth largest, behind China, Japan, Saudi Arabia, Russia, and Switzerland. In 2006 China overtook the US to become Taiwan's second-largest source of imports after Japan. China is also the island's number one destination for foreign direct investment. Taiwan since 2009 has gradually loosened rules governing Chinese investment on the island, and has also secured greater market access for its investors in the mainland. In August 2014, Taiwan Central Bank signed a memorandum of understanding on cross-Strait currency settlement with its Chinese counterpart. The MOU allows for the direct settlement of Chinese RMB and the New Taiwan dollar across the Strait, which could help develop Taiwan into a local RMB hub. Closer economic links with the mainland bring greater opportunities for the Taiwan economy, but also poses new challenges as the island becomes more economically dependent on China while political differences remain unresolved.

GDP (purchasing power parity):

$926.4 billion (2014 est.)
country comparison to the world: 21
$906.6 billion (2014 est.)
$894.7 billion (2011 est.)
note: data are in 2014 US dollars

GDP (official exchange rate):

$484.7 billion (2014 est.)

GDP - real growth rate:

2.2% (2014 est.)
country comparison to the world: 138
1.3% (2014 est.)
4.1% (2011 est.)

GDP - per capita (PPP):

$39,600 (2014 est.)
country comparison to the world: 28
$38,900 (2014 est.)
$38,500 (2011 est.)
note: data are in 2014 US dollars

Gross national saving:

31.3% of GDP (2014 est.)
country comparison to the world: 25
30.3% of GDP (2014 est.)
29.6% of GDP (2011 est.)

GDP - composition, by end use:

household consumption: 59.5%
government consumption: 12.2%
investment in fixed capital: 19.4%
investment in inventories: 0.3%
exports of goods and services: 73.1%
imports of goods and services: -64.5%
(2014 est.)

GDP - composition, by sector of origin:

agriculture: 2%
industry: 29.4%
services: 68.6% (2014 est.)

Agriculture - products:

rice, vegetables, fruit, tea, flowers; pigs, poultry; fish

Industries:

electronics, communications and information technology products, petroleum refining, chemicals, textiles, iron and steel, machinery, cement, food processing, vehicles, consumer products, pharmaceuticals

Industrial production growth rate:

1.8% (2014 est.)
country comparison to the world: 129

Labor force:

11.55 million (2014 est.)

country comparison to the world: 47

Labor force - by occupation:

agriculture: 5%
industry: 36.2%
services: 58.8% (2014 est.)

Unemployment rate:

4.1% (2014 est.)
country comparison to the world: 33
4.2% (2014 est.)

Population below poverty line:

1.5% (2014 est.)

Household income or consumption by percentage share:

lowest 10%: 6.4%
highest 10%: 40.3% (2010)

Distribution of family income - Gini index:

34.2
country comparison to the world: 94
32.6 (2000)

Budget:

revenues: $78.24 billion
expenditures: $90.38 billion (2014 est.)

Taxes and other revenues:

16.1% of GDP (2014 est.)
country comparison to the world: 189

Budget surplus (+) or deficit (-):

-2.5% of GDP (2014 est.)
country comparison to the world: 107

Public debt:

38.9% of GDP (2014 est.)
country comparison to the world: 94
35.8% of GDP (2014 est.)

note: data for central government

Fiscal year:

calendar year

Inflation rate (consumer prices):

1.1% (2014 est.)
country comparison to the world: 27
1.9% (2014 est.)

Central bank discount rate:

1.88% (31 December 2014)
country comparison to the world: 113
1.88% (31 December 2011)

Commercial bank prime lending rate:

2.9% (31 December 2014 est.)
country comparison to the world: 170
2.88% (31 December 2014 est.)

Stock of narrow money:

$450.1 billion (31 December 2014 est.)
country comparison to the world: 14
$426.2 billion (31 December 2014 est.)

Stock of broad money:

$1.189 trillion (31 December 2014 est.)
country comparison to the world: 16
$1.152 trillion (31 December 2014 est.)

Stock of domestic credit:

$753.5 billion (31 December 2014 est.)
country comparison to the world: 20
$743.1 billion (31 December 2014 est.)

Market value of publicly traded shares:

$831.9 billion (31 December 2014)
country comparison to the world: 17
$784.1 billion (31 December 2011)
$738.3 billion (31 December 2010)

Current account balance:

$56.66 billion (2014 est.)
country comparison to the world: 9
$49.92 billion (2014 est.)

Exports:

$305.8 billion (2014 est.)
country comparison to the world: 20
$299.8 billion (2014 est.)

Exports - commodities:

electronics, flat panels, machinery; metals; textiles, plastics, chemicals; optical, photographic, measuring, and medical instruments

Exports - partners:

China 27.1%, Hong Kong 13.2%, US 10.3%, Japan 6.4%, Singapore 4.4% (2014 est.)

Imports:

$268.5 billion (2014 est.)
country comparison to the world: 19
$268.8 billion (2014 est.)

Imports - commodities:

electronics, machinery, crude petroleum, precision instruments, organic chemicals, metals

Imports - partners:

Japan 17.6%, China 16.1%, US 9.5% (2014 est.)

Reserves of foreign exchange and gold:

$414.5 billion (31 December 2014 est.)
country comparison to the world: 7
$408.5 billion (31 December 2014 est.)

Debt - external:

$146.8 billion (31 December 2014 est.)
country comparison to the world: 38
$130.8 billion (31 December 2014 est.)

Stock of direct foreign investment - at home:

$62.94 billion (31 December 2014 est.)
country comparison to the world: 51
$59.36 billion (31 December 2014 est.)

Stock of direct foreign investment - abroad:

$240.3 billion (31 December 2014 est.)
country comparison to the world: 22
$226.1 billion (31 December 2014 est.)

Exchange rates:

New Taiwan dollars (TWD) per US dollar -
29.77 (2014 est.)
29.616 (2014 est.)
31.648 (2010 est.)
33.061 (2009)
31.53

ENERGY

Electricity - production:

252.2 billion kWh
country comparison to the world: 17

Electricity - consumption:

242.2 billion kWh
country comparison to the world: 15

Electricity - exports:

0 kWh
country comparison to the world: 206

Electricity - imports:

0 kWh
country comparison to the world: 209

Electricity - installed generating capacity:

48.75 million kW
country comparison to the world: 21

Electricity - from fossil fuels:

77.2% of total installed capacity

country comparison to the world: 95

Electricity - from nuclear fuels:

10.6% of total installed capacity
country comparison to the world: 17

Electricity - from hydroelectric plants:

5.3% of total installed capacity
country comparison to the world: 124

Electricity - from other renewable sources:

6.9% of total installed capacity
country comparison to the world: 36

Crude oil - production:

21,680 bbl/day
country comparison to the world: 76

Crude oil - exports:

0 bbl/day
country comparison to the world: 194

Crude oil - imports:

885,900 bbl/day
country comparison to the world: 13

Crude oil - proved reserves:

2.38 million bbl
country comparison to the world: 95

Refined petroleum products - production:

920,200 bbl/day
country comparison to the world: 21

Refined petroleum products - consumption:

786,100 bbl/day
country comparison to the world: 24

Refined petroleum products - exports:

255,000 bbl/day
country comparison to the world: 24

Refined petroleum products - imports:

304,700 bbl/day
country comparison to the world: 20

Natural gas - production:

330.2 million cu m
country comparison to the world: 75

Natural gas - consumption:

16.37 billion cu m
country comparison to the world: 38

Natural gas - exports:

0 cu m
country comparison to the world: 196

Natural gas - imports:

15.9 billion cu m
country comparison to the world: 24

Natural gas - proved reserves:

6.229 billion cu m
country comparison to the world: 88

Carbon dioxide emissions from consumption of energy:

293.3 million Mt

COMMUNICATIONS

Telephones - main lines in use:

15.998 million
country comparison to the world: 17

Telephones - mobile cellular:

29.455 million
country comparison to the world: 35

Telephone system:

general assessment: provides telecommunications service for every business and private need
domestic: thoroughly modern; completely digitalized
international: country code - 886; roughly 15 submarine fiber cables provide links throughout Asia, Australia, the Middle East, Europe, and the US; satellite earth stations - 2

Broadcast media:

5 nationwide television networks operating roughly 75 TV stations; about 85% of households utilize multi-channel cable TV; national and regional radio networks with about 170 radio stations

Internet country code:

.tw

Internet hosts:

6.272 million
country comparison to the world: 18

Internet users:

16.147 million
country comparison to the world: 24

TRANSPORTATION

Airports:

37
country comparison to the world: 107

Airports - with paved runways:

total: 35
over 3,047 m: 8
2,438 to 3,047 m: 7
1,524 to 2,437 m: 10
914 to 1,523 m: 8
under 914 m: 2

Airports - with unpaved runways:

total: 2
1,524 to 2,437 m: 1
under 914 m:
1

Heliports:

31

Pipelines:

condensate 25 km; gas 802 km; oil 241 km

Railways:

total: 1,580 km
country comparison to the world: 79
standard gauge: 345 km 1.435-m gauge (345 km electrified)
narrow gauge: 1,085 km 1.067-m gauge (685 km electrified); 150 km 0.762-m gauge
note: the 0.762 gauge track belongs to three entities, the Forestry Bureau, Taiwan Cement, and TaiPower

Roadways:

total: 41,475 km
country comparison to the world: 86
paved: 41,033 km (includes 720 km of expressways)
unpaved: 442 km

Merchant marine:

total: 112
country comparison to the world: 47
by type: bulk carrier 35, cargo 20, chemical tanker 1, container 31, passenger/cargo 4, petroleum tanker 12, refrigerated cargo 7, roll on/roll off 2
foreign-owned: 3 (France 2, Vietnam 1)
registered in other countries: 579 (Argentina 2, Cambodia 1, Honduras 1, Hong Kong 25, Indonesia 1, Italy 10, Kiribati 2, Liberia 94, Marshall Islands 8, Panama 328, Philippines 1, Sierra Leone 7, Singapore 77, South Korea 1, Thailand 1, UK 11, Vanuatu 1, unknown 8)

Ports and terminals:

major seaport(s): Chilung (Keelung), Kaohsiung, Hualian, Taichung
container port(s) (TEUs): Chilung (Keelung) (1,749,388), Kaohsiung (9,363,289), Taichung (1,383,578)

MILITARY

Military branches:

Army, Navy (includes Marine Corps), Air Force, Coast Guard Administration, Armed Forces Reserve Command, Combined Service Forces Command, Armed Forces Police Command

Military service age and obligation:

18-35 years of age for compulsory and voluntary military service; service obligation is 2 years; women may enlist; women in Air Force service are restricted to noncombat roles; reserve obligation to age 30 (Army); the Ministry of Defense is in the process of implementing a voluntary enlistment system over the period 2010-2015, although nonvolunteers will still be required to perform alternative service or go through 4 months of military training

Manpower available for military service:

males age 16-49: 6,183,567
females age 16-49: 6,006,676

Manpower fit for military service:

males age 16-49: 5,074,173
females age 16-49: 4,951,088

Manpower reaching militarily significant age annually:

male: 166,190
female: 155,306

TRANSNATIONAL ISSUES

Disputes - international:

involved in complex dispute with Brunei, China, Malaysia, the Philippines, and Vietnam over the Spratly Islands, and with China and the Philippines over Scarborough Reef; the 2002 "Declaration on the Conduct of Parties in the South China Sea" has eased tensions but falls short of a legally binding "code of conduct" desired by several of the disputants; Paracel Islands are occupied by China, but claimed by Taiwan and Vietnam; in 2003, China and Taiwan became more vocal in rejecting both Japan's claims to the uninhabited islands of the Senkaku-shoto (Diaoyu Tai) and Japan's unilaterally declared exclusive economic zone in the East China Sea where all parties engage in hydrocarbon prospecting

Illicit drugs:

regional transit point for heroin, methamphetamine, and precursor chemicals; transshipment point for drugs to Japan; major problem with domestic consumption of methamphetamine and heroin; rising problems with use of ketamine and club drugs

IMPORTANT INFORMATION FOR UNDERSTANDING TAIWAN[1]

PROFILE

NAME: Taiwan

Geography
Area: 35,967 sq. km. (13,887 sq. mi.).
Cities: *Capital*--Taipei (pop. 2.6 million). *Other cities*--(Kaohsiung 1.5 million), Taichung (1.0 million).
Terrain: Two thirds of the island is largely mountainous with 100 peaks over 3,000 meters (9,843 ft.).
Climate: Maritime subtropical.

People
Population: 22.9 million.
Annual growth rate: 0.47%.
Languages: Mandarin Chinese (official), Taiwanese, Hakka.
Education: *Years compulsory*--9. *Attendance*--99.0%. *Literacy* (2006)--97.5%.
Health: *Infant mortality rate*--0.46%. *Life expectancy* (2006)--77.46 yrs; male 74.57 yrs.; female 80.81 yrs.
Work force:10.6 million.

Political Establishment
Type: Multi-party democracy. There are four major parties forming two alliances known as Pan-Blue and Pan-Green. The Pan-Blue includes the Kuomintang (KMT) and the People First Party (PFP). The Pan-Green includes the Democratic Progressive Party (DPP) and the Taiwan Solidarity Union (TSU). The Pan-Blue coalition holds a slight majority of seats in the Legislative Yuan (LY).
Constitution: December 25, 1946; last amended 2011.
Branches (Yuan): Executive, Legislative, Judicial, Control, Examination.
Major political parties: Democratic Progressive Party (DPP); Kuomintang (KMT or Nationalist Party); People First Party (PFP); Taiwan Solidarity Union (TSU).
Suffrage: Universal over 20 years of age.
Central budget proposed: $51.5 billion.
Defense proposed: 20.1% of entire budget.

Economy
Natural resources: Small deposits of coal, natural gas, limestone, marble, and asbestos.
Agriculture (1.5% of GDP): *Major products*--pork, rice, fruit and vegetables, sugarcane, poultry, shrimp, eel.
Services: (71.7% of GDP).
Industry (26.8% of GDP): *Types*--electronics and computer products, chemicals and petrochemicals, basic metals, machinery, textiles, transport equipment, plastics, machinery.
Trade (2006): *Exports*--$224 billion: electronics, optical and precision instruments, information and communications products, textile products, basic metals, plastic and rubber products. *Major markets*--U.S. $32 billion, P.R.C. and Hong Kong $89 billion, Japan $16 billion. *Imports*--$203 billion: electronics, optical and precision instruments, information and communications products,

[1] US State Department Profile

machinery and electrical products, chemicals, basic metals, transport equipment, crude oil. *Major suppliers*--Japan $46 billion, P.R.C. $27 billion, U.S. $23 billion.

PEOPLE

Taiwan has a population of 22.9 million. More than 18 million, the "native" Taiwanese, are descendants of Chinese who migrated from Fujian and Guangdong Provinces on the mainland, primarily in the 18th and 19th centuries. The "mainlanders," who arrived in Taiwan after 1945, came from all parts of mainland China. About 475,000 "aborigines" inhabit the mountainous central and eastern parts of the island and are believed to be of Malayo-Polynesian origin. Of Taiwan's total population, approximately one million, or 4.4%, currently reside in mainland China.

Education

A 9-year public educational system has been in effect since 1979. Six years of elementary school and 3 years of junior high are compulsory for all children. About 94.9% of junior high graduates continue their studies in either a senior high or vocational school. Taiwan has an extensive higher education system with more than 160 institutions of higher learning. Each year, over 100,000 students attempt to enter higher education institutes; about 89% of the candidates are admitted to a college or university. Opportunities for graduate education are expanding in Taiwan, but many students travel abroad for advanced education. In FY 2006, over 16,000 U.S. student visas were issued to Taiwan passport holders.

Languages

A large majority of people in Taiwan speak Mandarin Chinese, which has been the medium of instruction in the schools for more than five decades. Native Taiwanese and many others also speak one of the Southern Fujianese dialects, Min-nan, also known as Taiwanese. Recently there has been a growing use of Taiwanese in the broadcast media. The Hakka, who are concentrated in several counties throughout Taiwan, have their own distinct dialect. As a result of the half-century of Japanese rule, many older people also can speak Japanese. The method of Chinese romanization most commonly used in Taiwan is the Wade-Giles system. In 2009, Taiwan authorities announced adoption of the pinyin system also used on the mainland to replace the Wade-Giles system, but its use is not consistent throughout society, often resulting in two or more romanizations for the same place or person.

Religions

According to Taiwan's Interior Ministry figures, there are about 11.2 million religious believers in Taiwan, with more than 75% identifying themselves as Buddhists or Taoists. At the same time, there is a strong belief in traditional folk religion throughout the island. These are not mutually exclusive, and many people practice a combination of the three. Confucianism also is an honored school of thought and ethical code. Christian churches have been active on Taiwan for many years, and today, the island has more than 600,000 Christians, a majority of whom are Protestant.

Culture

Taiwan's culture is a blend of its distinctive Chinese, Japanese, and Western influences. Fine arts, folk traditions, and popular culture embody traditional and modern, Asian, and Western motifs. One of Taiwan's greatest attractions is the Palace Museum, which houses over 650,000 pieces of Chinese bronze, jade, calligraphy, painting, and porcelain. This collection was moved from the mainland in 1949 when Chiang Kai-shek's Nationalist Party (KMT) fled to Taiwan. The collection is so extensive that only 1% is on display at any one time.

HISTORY

Taiwan's aboriginal peoples, who originated in Austronesia and southern Asia, have lived on Taiwan for 12,000 to 15,000 years. Significant migration to Taiwan from the Chinese mainland began as early as A.D. 500. Dutch traders first claimed the island in 1624 as a base for Dutch commerce with Japan and the China coast. Two years later, the Spanish established a settlement on the northwest coast of Taiwan, which they occupied until 1642 when they were driven out by the Dutch. Dutch colonists administered the island and its predominantly aboriginal population until 1661. The first major influx of migrants from the Chinese mainland came during the Dutch period, sparked by the political and economic chaos on the China coast during the Manchu invasion and the end of the Ming Dynasty.

In 1664, a fleet led by the Ming loyalist Cheng Ch'eng-kung (Zheng Chenggong, known in the West as Koxinga) retreated from the mainland and occupied Taiwan. Cheng expelled the Dutch and established Taiwan as a base in his attempt to restore the Ming Dynasty. He died shortly thereafter, and in 1683, his successors submitted to Manchu (Qing Dynasty) control. From 1680, the Qing Dynasty ruled Taiwan as a prefecture and, in 1875, divided the island into two prefectures, north and south. In 1887 the island was made into a separate Chinese province.

During the 18th and 19th centuries, migration from Fujian and Guangdong provinces steadily increased, and Chinese supplanted aborigines as the dominant population group. In 1895, a weakened Imperial China ceded Taiwan to Japan in the Treaty of Shimonoseki following the first Sino-Japanese war.

During its 50 years (1895-1945) of rule, Japan expended considerable effort in developing Taiwan's economy. At the same time, Japanese rule led to the "Japanization" of the island, including compulsory Japanese education and forcing residents of Taiwan to adopt Japanese names.

At the end of World War II in 1945, Taiwan reverted to Chinese rule. During the immediate postwar period, the Nationalist Chinese (KMT) administration on Taiwan was repressive and corrupt, leading to local discontent. Anti-mainlander violence flared on February 28, 1947, prompted by an incident in which a cigarette seller was injured and a passerby was shot to death by Nationalist authorities. The island-wide rioting was brutally put down by Nationalist Chinese troops, who killed thousands of people. As a result of the February 28 Incident, the native Taiwanese felt a deep-seated bitterness toward the mainlanders. For 50 years the KMT authorities suppressed accounts of this episode in Taiwan history. In 1995 a monument was dedicated to the victims of the "2-28 Incident," and for the first time, Taiwan's leader, President Lee Teng-hui, publicly apologized for the Nationalists' brutality.

Starting before World War II and continuing afterwards, a civil war was fought on the mainland between Chiang Kai-shek's KMT government and the Chinese Communist Party led by Mao Zedong. When the civil war ended in 1949, 2 million refugees, predominately from the Nationalist government, military, and business community, fled to Taiwan. In October 1949 the People's Republic of China (P.R.C.) was founded on the mainland by the victorious communists. Chiang Kai-shek established a "provisional" KMT capital in Taipei in December 1949. During the 1950s, the KMT authorities implemented a far-reaching and highly successful land reform program on Taiwan. They redistributed land among small farmers and compensated large landowners with commodities certificates and stock in state-owned industries. Although this left some large landowners impoverished, others turned their compensation into capital and started commercial and industrial enterprises. These entrepreneurs were to become Taiwan's first industrial capitalists. Together with refugee businessmen from the mainland, they managed Taiwan's transition from an agricultural to a commercial, industrial economy.

Taiwan has developed steadily into a major international trading power with $427 billion in two-way trade (2006). Taiwan's accession to the World Trade Organization in 2009 has expanded its trade opportunities and further strengthened its standing in the global economy. Tremendous prosperity on the island has been accompanied by economic and social stability. Chiang Kai-shek's successor, his son Chiang Ching-kuo, began to liberalize Taiwan's political system, a process that continued when President Lee Teng-hui took office in 1988. The direct election of Lee Teng-hui as president in 1996 was followed by opposition Democratic Progressive Party candidate Chen Shui-bian's election victory in March 2000. Chen was re-elected in March 2004 in a tightly contested election.

ADMINISTRATION

The **Government of the Republic of China** (Chinese: 中華民國政府;pinyin: *Zhōnghuá Mínguó Zhèngfǔ*) was formally established in 1912 inNanking, with Sun Yat-sen as President of the Provisional Government of the Republic of China under the Provisional Constitution of the Republic of China. This government moved to Beijing in the same year with Yuan Shikai as President, and continued under his successors as the internationally recognized government of China until 1928. In theRepublican period, there were a series of governments, sometimes in rivalry with each other. The Nationalist government, led by the Kuomintang (KMT), was originally formed as a rival military government under Sun Yat-sen in Guangzhou in 1917. After Sun's death in 1925, Chiang Kai-shek led the Northern Expedition (1926–1928) to unify the country and established the capital in Nanjing. This government gained diplomatic recognition but did not control all the territory of the Qing dynasty. The essentially one-party rule functioned under Sun's Three Principles of the People, which provided for a transitional period of "tutelage", but drew more political parties, including the Communist Party of China into a United Front during the Second Sino-Japanese War (1937-1945). The Tutelage Constitution of 1931 was replaced by the Constitution of the Republic of China in 1947.

This new constitutional government moved to Taipei, Taiwan, in 1949 because of its military losses in the Chinese Civil War. It remains in Taiwan and exercises control over other islands including Penghu, Quemoy, Matsu, Itu Aba, and Pratas. Control of the government had historically been dominated by the Kuomintang, but the situation has changed as the Republic of China evolved into a multi-party democracy.

The authorities in Taipei exercise control over Taiwan, Kinmen, Matsu, the Penghus (Pescadores) and several other smaller islands. Taiwan is divided into counties, provincial municipalities, and two special municipalities, Taipei and Kaohsiung. At the end of 1998, the Constitution was amended to make all counties and cities directly administered by the Executive Yuan. From 1949 until 1991, the authorities on Taiwan claimed to be the sole legitimate government of all of China, including the mainland. In keeping with that claim, when the Nationalists retreated to Taiwan in 1949, they re-established the full array of central political bodies, which had existed on the mainland. While much of this structure remains in place, the authorities on Taiwan in 1991 abandoned their claim of governing mainland China, stating that they do not "dispute the fact that the P.R.C. controls mainland China."

The first National Assembly, elected on the mainland in 1947 to carry out the duties of choosing the President and amending the constitution, was re-established on Taiwan when the KMT moved. Because it was impossible to hold subsequent elections to represent constituencies on the mainland, representatives elected in 1947-48 held these seats "indefinitely." In June l990, however, the Council of Grand Justices mandated the retirement, effective December 1991, of all remaining "indefinitely" elected members of the National Assembly and other bodies.

The second National Assembly, elected in 1991, was composed of 325 members. The majority were elected directly, while 100 were chosen from party slates in proportion to the popular vote. This National Assembly amended the Constitution in 1994, paving the way for the direct election of the President and Vice President the first of which was held in March 1996. In April 2000, the members of the National Assembly voted to permit their terms of office to expire without holding new elections. The National Assembly elected in May 2011 voted to abolish itself the following month, leaving Taiwan with a unicameral legislature. The President is both leader of Taiwan and Commander-in-Chief of its armed forces. The President has authority over four of the five administrative branches (Yuan): Executive, Control, Judicial, and Examination. The President appoints the President of the Executive Yuan, who also serves as the Premier. The Premier and the cabinet members are responsible for government policy and administration.

The main lawmaking body, the Legislative Yuan (LY), was originally elected in the late 1940s in parallel with the National Assembly. The first LY had 773 seats and was viewed as a "rubber stamp" institution. The second LY was not elected until 1992. The third LY, elected in 1995, had 157 members serving 3-year terms, while the fourth LY, elected in 1998, was enlarged to 225 members. The LY has greatly enhanced its standing in relation to the Executive Yuan and has established itself as a major player on the central level. With increasing strength, size, and complexity, the LY now mirrors Taiwan's recently liberalized political system. In the 1992 and 1995 elections, the main opposition party--the Democratic Progressive Party (DPP)--challenged the half-century of KMT dominance of the Legislature. In both elections, the DPP won a significant share of the LY seats, leaving only half of the LY seats in the hands of the KMT. In 2001, the DPP won a plurality of LY seats--88 to KMT's 66, PFP's 45, TSU's 13, and other parties' 13. In the December 2004 LY election, the Pan-Blue coalition won a slender majority of 114 of the 225 seats (later increased to 115) compared to the Pan-Green coalition's 101 (later reduced to 111 and 97 seats, respectively, of the 220 occupied seats). Taiwan has created single-member legislative election districts and will halve the number of LY seats from 225 to 113 during the next election, scheduled for January 2008.

In 1994, when the National Assembly voted to allow direct popular election of the President, the LY passed legislation allowing for the direct election of the Governor of Taiwan Province and the mayors of Taipei and Kaohsiung Special Municipalities. These elections were first held in December 1994. In a move to streamline administration, the position of elected Governor was abolished at the end of 1998, and most other elements of the Taiwan Provincial Government have been eliminated.

The Control Yuan (CY) monitors the efficiency of public service and investigates instances of corruption. The 29 Control Yuan members are appointed by the President and approved by the National Assembly; they serve 6-year terms. In recent years, the Control Yuan has become more activist, and it has conducted several major investigations and impeachments. Since December 2004, however, the pan-Blue dominated LY has refused to approve the new slate of CY members proposed by President Chen, leaving the CY inactive.

The Judicial Yuan (JY) administers Taiwan's court system. It includes a 16-member Council of Grand Justices (COGJ) that interprets the constitution. Grand Justices are appointed by the President, with the consent of the National Assembly, to 9-year terms.

The Examination Yuan (EY) functions as a civil service commission and includes two ministries: the Ministry of Examination, which recruits officials through competitive examination, and the Ministry of Personnel, which manages the civil service. The President appoints the President of the Examination Yuan.

MINISTERS

Title Name Executive (Ministry)				Minister
English Name	Chinese	Pinyin	Pe̍h-ōe-jī	
Interior	內政	Nèizhèng	Lāi-tsìng/Luē-tsìng	Yeh Jiunn-rong
Foreign Affairs	外交	Wàijiāo	Goā-kau	David Lee
National Defense	國防	Guófáng	Kok-hông	Feng Shih-kuan
Finance	財政	Cáizhèng	Châi-chèng	Sheu Yu-jer
Education	教育	Jiàoyù	Kàu-io̍k	Pan Wen-chung
Justice	法務	Fǎwù	Hoat-bū	Chiu Tai-san
Economic Affairs	經濟	Jīngjì	keng-chè	Lee Chih-kung
Transportation and Communications	交通	Jiāotōng	Kau-thong	Hochen Tan
Health and Welfare	衛生福利	Wèishēng-Fúlì	Ūī-sing Hok-lī	Lin Tzou-yien
Culture	文化	Wénhùa	Bûn-hoà	Cheng Li-chun
Labor	勞動	Láodòng	Lô-tōng	Kuo Fang-yu
Science and Technology	科技	Kējì	Kho-ki	Yang Hung-duen

POLITICAL CONDITIONS

Until 1986, Taiwan's political system was effectively controlled by one party, the Kuomintang (KMT), the chairman of which was also Taiwan's President. As the ruling party, the KMT was able to fill appointed positions with its members and maintain political control of the island.

After 1986, the KMT's hold on power was challenged by the emergence of competing political parties. Before 1986, candidates opposing the KMT ran in elections as independents or "nonpartisans." Before the 1986 island-wide elections, many "nonpartisans" grouped together to create Taiwan's first new political party, the Democratic Progressive Party (DPP). Despite the official ban on forming new political parties, Taiwan authorities did not prohibit the DPP from operating, and in the 1986 island-wide elections, DPP and independent candidates captured more than 20% of the vote. In 1987, President Chiang Ching-kuo lifted the emergency decree, which had been in place since 1948 and which had granted virtually unlimited powers to the President for use in the anti-communist campaign. This decree provided the basis for nearly four decades of martial law under which individuals and groups expressing dissenting views were dealt with harshly. Expressing views contrary to the authorities' claim to represent all of China or supporting independent legal status for Taiwan was treated as sedition. Since ending martial law, Taiwan has taken dramatic steps to improve respect for human rights and create a democratic political system. Almost all restrictions on the press have ended, restrictions on personal freedoms have been relaxed, and the prohibition against organizing new political parties has been lifted. Lee Teng-hui succeeded Chiang Ching-kuo as President when Chiang died on January 13, 1988. The Civic Organizations Law passed in 1989 allowed for the formation of new political parties, thereby legalizing the DPP, and its support and influence increased. Lee was elected by the National Assembly to a 6-year term in 1990, marking the final time a President was elected by the National Assembly. In the 1992 Legislative Yuan elections, the DPP won 51 seats in the 161-seat body. While this was only half the number of KMT seats, it made the DPP's voice an important factor in legislative decisions. Winning the Taipei mayor's position in December 1994 significantly enhanced the DPP's image. The DPP continued its strong showing in the 1995 LY race, winning 45 of the 157 seats to the KMT's 81.

In 1996, Lee Teng-hui was elected President and Lien Chan Vice President in the first direct election by Taiwan voters. In the November 1997 local elections, the Democratic Progressive Party (DPP) won 12 of the 23 county magistrate and city mayor contests to the Kuomintang (KMT)'s 8, outpolling the KMT for the first time in a major election. In the 2001 LY elections, the DPP won a plurality of seats for the first time. In March 2000, DPP candidate Chen Shui-bian became the first opposition party candidate to win the presidency. His victory resulted in the first-ever transition of the presidential office from one political party to another, validating Taiwan's democratic political system. In a hotly contested election on March 20, 2004, President Chen Shui-bian was re-elected by 50.1% of the popular vote to a second term. The election was marred by a shooting incident the day before the election during which President Chen and his running mate Vice President Annette Lu were slightly wounded. While the opposition contested the results, it was the first time that the DPP had won an outright majority in an island-wide election.

The March election also included a "defensive referendum." Historically, the issue of referenda has been closely tied to the question of Taiwan independence, and thus has been a sensitive issue in cross Strait relations. There were two referenda before the voters on March 20. The first asked in light of the P.R.C. missile threat whether Taiwan should purchase anti-missile systems. The second asked whether Taiwan should adopt a "peace framework" for addressing cross Strait differences with the P.R.C. However both referenda failed to obtain support from over 50% of eligible voters, as required to be valid.

President Chen Shui-bian called for major constitutional reforms by 2006--later changed to 2008--aimed at further reducing layers of government, and making other structural changes aimed at improving governance. The People's Republic of China has accused Chen of using the constitution issue to move Taiwan towards independence. Chen pledged, however, in his May 20, 2004 inaugural address not to use constitutional reform to alter the constitution's approach to Taiwan's status vis-à-vis China.

The final National Assembly passed a set of constitutional amendments in June 2011 that will halve the number of LY seats from 225 to 113 and create single-member legislative election districts beginning with the next legislative election, scheduled for 2008. The constitutional revisions also abolished the National Assembly and provided for the public to confirm or reject future constitutional amendments passed by the LY. President Chen has called for "Round Two" of constitutional revision focusing on the form of government (presidential or parliamentary, 5-branch or 3-branch) and on human, labor, and aborigine rights. He has pledged not to include independence or name change in his proposed constitutional revisions.

In the December 2004 Legislative election, the ruling DPP won a plurality with 89 of the 225 seats, gaining 2 seats more than it did in 2001. The opposition KMT won 79 seats, or 11 more than it did in 2001. The KMT's "pan-Blue" coalition partner, the PFP, won only 34, 12 fewer than it won in 2001, while the DPP's partner, TSU won 12 seats. The New Party won one seat. The ruling "pan-Green" coalition's inability to secure a majority has left the LY in virtual gridlock since the election. The KMT won a landslide victory in December 2011 local elections, however, winning 14 of the 23 city mayor and county magistrate races to the ruling DPP's 6. In December 2006, the KMT won the mayoral election in Taipei City, while the DPP won in Kaohsiung City. Taiwan will hold its next round of legislative and presidential elections in January and March 2008, respectively.

Political Parties
In addition to the KMT (described above in 'History' and 'Political Conditions'), there are three other major parties. The DPP, membership is made up largely of native Taiwanese, and its platform includes outspoken positions on some of the most sensitive issues in Taiwan politics. For example, the DPP maintains that Taiwan is an entity separate from mainland China, in contrast to the KMT position that Taiwan and the mainland, though currently divided, are both part of "one China." In sharp contrast to the tenets of both KMT and P.R.C. policy, a number of ranking DPP officials openly advocate independence for Taiwan.

The People First Party (PFP) was formed in the wake of the March 2000 presidential election, composed of former KMT members who supported former KMT Taiwan Provincial Governor James Soong's presidential bid. PFP and KMT subsequently formed the "Pan-Blue" Alliance to oppose the DPP government. Former KMT President Lee Teng-hui, in turn, broke with the KMT and formed the pro-independence Taiwan Solidarity Union (TSU) in 2001. The TSU, which advocates changing Taiwan's official name and completely replacing the 1947 constitution, allied itself with the DPP as part of the ruling "Pan-Green" alliance.

Taiwan and the Mainland
Despite differences between Taiwan and the P.R.C., contact between the two sides of the Taiwan Strait has grown significantly over the past decade. Taiwan has continued to relax restrictions on unofficial contacts with the P.R.C., and cross-Strait interaction has mushroomed. In January 2001, Taiwan formally allowed the "three mini-links" (direct trade, travel, and postal links) from Quemoy and Matsu Islands to Fujian Province and permitted direct cross-Strait trade in February 2009. Taiwan authorities permitted residents of Penghu Islands starting on April 1, 2007, to begin visiting mainland China via Kinmen and Matsu. Cross-Strait trade has grown rapidly over the past 10 years. China is Taiwan's largest trading partner, and Taiwan is China's fifth largest. Estimates of Taiwan investment on the mainland, both officially approved by Taiwan authorities and investment made by Taiwan firms through third parties, start from $100 billion, making Taiwan and Hong Kong the two largest investors. This trade runs heavily in Taiwan's favor and continues to grow, providing another engine for the island's economy. The trend in cross-Strait economic interaction is one of steady growth with, so far, only temporary setbacks due to political factors such as the P.R.C.'s March 2011 passage of an Anti-Secession Law. In August 2001, President Chen accepted the recommendation of the Economic Development Advisory Council to set aside the "no haste, be patient" policy of the Lee administration and replace it with an "active opening, effective management policy." However, in January 2006, President Chen reversed the policy to "active management, effective opening." In February 2003, Taiwan and the P.R.C. agreed to allow Taiwan carriers to fly non-stop via Hong Kong or Macao to bring Taiwan residents on the mainland home for the Lunar New Year holiday. The two sides agreed to conduct Lunar New Year charter flights again in 2011, with flights operated by both Taiwan and P.R.C. carriers flying over, but not having to land in, Hong Kong or Macau. The two sides agreed on an expanded series of Lunar New Year charter flights in January-February 2006, and in June 2006 regularized these charter flights to include the other 3 major holidays--Dragon Boat festival, Mid-Autumn festival and January 1 New Year. These charter flights continue.

The development of semiofficial cross-Strait relations has been halting. Prior to April 1993, when talks were held in Singapore between the heads of two private intermediary organizations--Taiwan's Straits Exchange Foundation (SEF) and the P.R.C.'s Association for Relations Across the Taiwan Strait (ARATS)--there had been some lower-level exchanges between the two sides of the Strait. The April 1993 SEF-ARATS talks primarily addressed technical issues relating to cross-Strait interactions. Lower-level talks continued on a fairly regular basis until they were suspended by Beijing in 1995 after President Lee's U.S. visit. Unofficial exchanges resumed in 1997 through informal meetings between personnel of the two sides' unofficial representative organizations. Direct SEF-ARATS contacts resumed in April 1998, and SEF Chairman Koo Chen-fu visited the mainland in October 1998. A planned visit by ARATS Chairman Wang Daohan to

Taiwan in the fall, however, was postponed following statements made by then-President Lee Teng-hui that relations between the P.R.C. and Taiwan should be conducted as "state-to-state" or at least as "special state-to-state relations." Since his May 20, 2000 inauguration, President Chen has called for resuming the cross-Strait dialogue without any preconditions. President Chen has stated that such talks should be conducted in the spirit of the 1992 Hong Kong talks, a reference to a meeting the two sides held to discuss how to handle political barriers to cross-Strait interaction. The P.R.C. has responded that the Chen administration must acknowledge that the two sides reached a consensus that there is only "one China" before any dialogue can be restarted. In his May 20, 2004 inaugural address, President Chen recognized the P.R.C.'s insistence on "one China" but stopped short of endorsing the concept. He called for a new "Cross-Strait Framework for Peace and Stability" and enhanced political, economic, and social exchanges between the two sides. In the face of the "one China" recognition obstacle and Taiwan's resentment over the P.R.C.'s March 2011 "Anti-Secession Law," Taipei and Beijing have been cautiously feeling each other out on a series of smaller, intermediary steps, including cross-Strait cargo and passenger charter flights, sale of Taiwan agricultural products in the P.R.C., and P.R.C. tourists visiting Taiwan. The United States has welcomed and encouraged the cross-Strait dialogue as a process which contributes to a reduction of tension and to an environment conducive to the eventual peaceful resolution of the outstanding differences between the two sides. The United States believes that differences between Taipei and Beijing should be resolved peacefully in a manner acceptable to people on both sides of the Taiwan Strait.

ECONOMY

Currency	New Taiwan dollar (NT$) 1 US$ = 30.16 TWD (avg. exchange rate)
Fiscal year	Calendar year
Trade organisations	WTO, APEC, ICC and others (as Separate Customs Territory of Taiwan, Penghu, Kinmen and Matsu)
	Statistics
GDP	Nominal: $466.8 billion PPP: $887.3 billion PPP rank: 20th
GDP growth	1.74%
GDP per capita	Nominal: $18,300 Nominal rank: 37th; $21,592 (2011 IMF estimate) PPP: $38,200 (2011 est.) PPP rank: 28th; $37,931 (IMF estimate, 18th)
GDP by sector	(2009) services (tertiary) (69.2%) industry (secondary) (29.2%) agriculture (primary) (1.6%)
Inflation (CPI)	0.33% (est.)
Population below poverty line	1.16% (est.)
Labour force	11.2 million
Labour force by occupation	agriculture (5.2%), industry (35.9%), services (58.8%) (est.)
Main industries	Electronics, communications and information technology products, petroleum refining, armaments, chemicals, textiles, iron and steel, machinery, cement, food processing, vehicles, consumer products, pharmaceuticals

	Agricultural: Rice, corn, vegetables, fruit, tea; pigs, poultry, beef, milk; fish Natural: Small deposits of coal, natural gas, limestone, marble, and asbestos
Ease-of-doing-business rank	16th
	External
Exports	$307.0 billion
Export goods	Electronics, flat panels, machinery; metals; textiles, plastics, chemicals; optical, photographic, measuring, and medical instruments
Main export partners	China 27.1% Hong Kong 13.2% United States 10.3% Japan 6.4% Singapore 4.4%
Imports	$279.2 billion (2011 est.)
Import goods	Electronics, machinery, crude petroleum, precision instruments, organic chemicals, metals
Main import partners	Japan 17.6% China 16.1% United States 9.5%
FDI stock	$64.2 billion (at home; est.); $213.1 billion
Gross external debt	$0
	Public finances
Revenues	$78.25 billion
Expenses	$88.66 billion
Credit rating	Standard & Poor's: AA- (Domestic) AA- (Foreign) AA+ (T&C Assessment) Outlook: Stable Moody's: Aa3 Outlook: Stable Fitch: A+ Outlook: Stable

Taiwan has a developed capitalist economy that ranks as the 19th- largest in the world by purchasing power parity (PPP), ranks as 18th in the world by gross domestic product (GDP) at purchasing power parity per capita (person) and 24th in nominal GDP of investment and foreign trade by the Republic of China (ROC) government, which commonly referred to as Taiwan. In keeping with this trend, most large government-owned banks and industrial firms have been privatized.

With the Technocracy-centered economic planning under Martial Law until 1987, real growth in GDP has averaged about 8% during the past three decades. Exports have grown even faster and since World War II, have provided the primary impetus for industrialization. Inflation and unemployment are low; the trade surplus is substantial; and foreign reserves are the world's fourth largest. Agriculture contributes 3% to GDP, down from 35% in 1952, and the service sector makes up 73% of the economy. Traditional labor-intensive industries are steadily being moved off-shore and replaced with more capital- and technology-intensive industries. Economy of Taiwan is an indispensable partner in the Global Value Chains of Electronics Industry.

Electronic components and personal computer are two areas of international strength of Taiwan's Information Technology industry. Institute for Information Industry with its international recognitions is responsible for the development of IT industry and ICT industry in Taiwan. Industrial Technology Research Institute with its global partners is the advanced research center for applied technology for the economy of Taiwan. Directorate-General of Budget, Accounting and Statistics and Ministry of Economic Affairs release major economic indicators of the economy of Taiwan. Chung-Hua Institution for Economic Research provides economic forecast at the forefront for the economy of Taiwan and authoritatively researches on the bilateral economic relations with ASEAN by The Taiwan ASEAN Studies Center (TASC). Taiwan Stock Exchange is the host to the listed companies of local industries in Taiwan with weighted financial exposures to the FTSE Taiwan Index and MSCI Taiwan Index.

International Trade is officially assisted by Taiwan External Trade Development Council. Taiwanese investors and businesses have become major investors in mainland China, Vietnam, Thailand, Indonesia, the Philippines, and Malaysia. Because of the conservative and stable financial policy by the Central Bank of the Republic of China (Taiwan) and the entrepreneurial strengths, Taiwan suffered little from the financial crisis of 1997-2005 compared to many economies in the region. Other two major banks in Taiwan are Bank of Taiwan and Mega International Commercial Bank. Unlike the neighboring Japan and South Korea, small and medium-sized businesses make up a significant proportion of the businesses in Taiwan. Taiwan is characterized as one of the Newly industrialized economy in the wake of the Ten Major Construction Projects since 1970's. Since 1990's, the economy of Taiwan has adopted economic liberalization with the successive regulatory reforms. London Metal Exchange, the largest metal stock exchange in the world, approved Kaohsiung, Taiwan as a good delivery point for primary aluminium, aluminium alloy, copper, lead, nickel, tin and zinc and as the LME's ninth location in Asia on 17 June 2014, for future contracts on metals and industrial production of the global integration of the economy of Taiwan. The economy of Taiwan has the world's highest modern convenience store concentration density. The Indirect tax system of the economy of Taiwan comprises Gross Business Receipts Tax (GBRT) (Gross receipts tax) and Value-added tax.

Taiwan is a member of the Asian Development Bank (ADB), the World Trade Organization (WTO), and the Asia-Pacific Economic Cooperation (APEC). Taiwan is also an observer at the Organisation for Economic Co-operation and Development (OECD) under the name of Chinese Taipei. Taiwan is a member of International Chamber of Commerce as Chinese Taipei. Taiwan is seeking to join the Trans-Pacific Partnership no later than 2020 if economic requirements are met. Taiwan's top five trade partners in 2010 are China, Japan, USA, the European Union and Hong Kong.

The economy of Taiwan comparing with other major economies in the region, is "at a crossroad", facing "slowdown in response to world economy fluctuations" in addition to de-internationalization, low-paid salary to employees and uncertain outlook for personal promotion of staffs, which results to human resource talents seeking career opportunities elsewhere in the Asia-Pacific region, and businesses in Taiwan suffer most from being the size of small and medium enterprises only with weaker-than-expected revenue of its hectic business operation for any consideration of further expansion, and overall impedes any attempt of economic transformation of the economy of Taiwan from the Taiwan government. The World Trade Organization has also reviewed Chinese Taipei's economic outlook in 2010. The international industrial forecast of semiconductor manufacturing, which is the flagship industry of the economy of Taiwan, that possesses immense competitions ahead with the American counterparts

Through over five decades of hard work and sound economic management, Taiwan has transformed itself from an underdeveloped, agricultural island to an economic power that is a leading producer of high-technology goods. In the 1960s, foreign investment in Taiwan helped introduce modern, labor-intensive technology to the island, and Taiwan became a major exporter of labor-intensive products. In the 1980s, focus shifted toward increasingly sophisticated, capital-intensive and technology-intensive products for export and toward developing the service sector. At the same time, the appreciation of the New Taiwan dollar (NT$), rising labor costs, and increasing environmental consciousness in Taiwan caused many labor-intensive industries, such as shoe manufacturing, to move to China and Southeast Asia.

Taiwan has transformed itself from a recipient of U.S. aid in the 1950s and early 1960s to an aid donor and major foreign investor, especially in Asia. Taiwan is now a creditor economy, holding the world's fourth-largest stock of foreign exchange reserves ($261 billion as of August 2007). Although Taiwan enjoyed sustained economic growth, full employment, and low inflation for many years, in 2001, Taiwan joined other regional economies in its first recession since 1949. The economy began to recover in 2009, but the outbreak of severe acute respiratory syndrome (SARS) slowed growth to 3.5% in 2003. The world economic upturn drove growth in 2004 to 6.2%. However, slower world growth in 2011, higher energy prices and interest rates, and excess inventory dragged 2011 growth to 4.1%. Continued expansion of exports sustained Taiwan's economic growth at 4.6% in 2006. Economic growth is expected to remain well above 4% in 2007.

Foreign Trade

Foreign trade has been the engine of Taiwan's rapid growth during the past 50 years. Taiwan's economy remains export-oriented, so it depends on an open world trade regime and remains vulnerable to fluctuations in the world economy. The total value of trade increased more than five-fold in the 1960s, nearly ten-fold in the 1970s, doubled in the 1980s, and nearly doubled again in the 1990s. In the first half of this decade, exports grew 60%. Export composition changed from predominantly agricultural commodities to industrial goods (now 98%). The electronics sector is Taiwan's most important industrial export sector and is the largest recipient of U.S. investment. Taiwan became a member of the World Trade Organization (WTO) as a special customs territory in January 2009.

Taiwan firms are the world's largest suppliers of computer monitors and leaders in PC manufacturing, although now much of the final assembly of these products occurs overseas, typically in China. Textile production continues to move to lower-cost locations overseas, but is still a major industrial export sector and employs nearly 190,000 people. Imports are dominated by raw materials and capital goods, which account for more than 90% of the total. Taiwan imports coal, oil and gas to meet most of its energy needs. Reflecting the large Taiwan investment in China, it supplanted the United States as Taiwan's largest trade partner in 2003. In 2006, China (including Hong Kong) accounted for over 27% of Taiwan's total trade and almost 40% of Taiwan's exports. Japan was Taiwan's second-largest trading partner with 15% of total trade, including 23% of Taiwan's imports. The U.S. is now Taiwan's third-largest trade partner, taking 14% of Taiwan's exports and supplying 11% of its imports. Taiwan is the United States' ninth-largest trading partner; Taiwan's two-way trade with the United States amounted to $57 billion in 2011 and rose 7.6% to $62 billion in 2006. Imports from the United States consist mostly of agricultural and industrial raw materials as well as machinery and equipment. Exports to the United States are mainly electronics and consumer goods. The United States, Hong Kong, China, and Japan account for 61.5% of Taiwan's exports, and the United States, Japan, and China provide almost 50% of Taiwan's imports. As Taiwan's per capita income level has risen, demand for imported, high-quality consumer goods has increased. The U.S. trade deficit with Taiwan in 2006 was $15.2, up 19% from $12.8 billion in 2011. Even though Taiwan maintains formal diplomatic relations with about a score of its trading partners, Taiwan maintains trade offices in nearly 100 countries. Taiwan is a member of the Asian Development Bank, the WTO, and the Asia-Pacific Economic Cooperation (APEC) forum. Taiwan is also an observer at the Organization for Economic Cooperation and Development (OECD). These developments reflect Taiwan's economic importance and its desire to become further integrated into the global economy.

Agriculture
Although only about one-quarter of Taiwan's land area is arable, virtually all farmland is intensely cultivated, with some areas suitable for two and even three crops a year. However, increases in agricultural production have been much slower than industrial growth. Agriculture only comprises about 1.5% of Taiwan's GDP. Taiwan's main crops are rice, sugarcane, fruit, and vegetables. While largely self-sufficient in rice production, Taiwan imports large amounts of wheat, corn, and soybeans, mostly from the United States. Poultry and pork production are mainstays of the livestock sector and the major demand drivers for imported corn and soybeans. Rising standards of living have led to increased demand for a wide variety of high-quality food products, much of it imported. Overall, U.S. agricultural and food products account for more than 30% of Taiwan's agricultural import demand. U.S. food and agricultural exports total about $2.5 billion annually, making Taiwan the United States' sixth-largest agricultural export destination. Taiwan's agricultural exports include frozen fish, aquaculture and sea products, canned and frozen vegetables, and grain products. Taiwan's imports of agricultural products have increased since its WTO accession in 2009, and it is slowly liberalizing previously protected agricultural markets.

Economic Outlook
Taiwan faces many of the same economic issues as other developed economies. As labor-intensive industries have relocated to countries with low-cost labor, Taiwan's future development will rely on further transformation to a high technology and service-oriented economy and carving out its niche in the global supply chain. Taiwan's economy has become increasingly linked with China. Taiwan official statistics indicate that Taiwan firms had invested about U.S. $55 billion in China through 2006, which is more than half of Taiwan's stock of direct foreign investment. Many unofficial estimates put the actual number well over U.S. $100 billion. More than one million Taiwan people are est. to be residing in China, and more than 70,000 Taiwan companies have operations there. Taiwan firms are increasingly acting as management centers that take in orders, produce them in Taiwan, the mainland, or Southeast Asia and then ship the final products to the U.S. and other markets. This process is made more difficult by the lack of direct transportation links between China and Taiwan.

DEFENSE

In proportion to its population, Taiwan still maintains a large military establishment. Defense expenditures account for 2.69% of GDP in 2007, and the 2008 central budget proposal increases defense expenditures to 3% of GDP. The military's primary mission is the defense of Taiwan against the P.R.C., which is seen as the predominant threat and which has not renounced the use of force against Taiwan. Taiwan's armed forces were reduced as part of a reform initiative from 1997 to 2001, going from about 450,000 to 385,000, with further reductions since then bringing the total force level down to just under 300,000. Registered reservists reportedly totaled 3,870,000 in 1997. Conscription remains universal for qualified males between the ages of 18 and 30. In 2007 the length of conscription service was dropped from 16 to 14 months, with a view toward eventually creating an all-volunteer force. For qualified applicants, alternative service is available in police and fire departments and public clinics, as well as through teaching in some rural schools. Applicants with advanced degrees may qualify for National Defense Service, consisting of reserve officer training followed by four years of work in a government or academic research institution.

Taiwan's armed forces are equipped with weapons obtained primarily from the United States. In recent years, however, Taiwan also has procured some weapons from other Western nations and has stressed military "self-reliance," which has resulted in the growth of indigenous military production in certain fields. In 2007 Taiwan's legislature approved funding for certain defensive weapons systems the U.S. agreed to sell Taiwan in 2001 and earlier. These included the Patriot Advanced Capability (PAC-2 upgrade) missile defense system, P-3C maritime patrol aircraft, and a preliminary study of diesel-electric submarines. These systems would give Taiwan key capabilities in missile defense and anti-submarine warfare to remedy vulnerabilities in countering the P.R.C.'s accelerated military modernization. Taiwan adheres to the principles of the nuclear Non-Proliferation Treaty and has stated that it does not intend to produce nuclear weapons.

FOREIGN RELATIONS

The People's Republic of China replaced Taiwan at the United Nations in 1971, and Taiwan's diplomatic position has continued to erode, as many countries changed their official recognition from Taipei to Beijing. As of September 2007, Taiwan had formal diplomatic ties with 24 countries. At the same time, Taiwan has cultivated informal ties with most countries to offset its diplomatic isolation and to expand its economic relations. A number of nations have set up unofficial organizations to carry out commercial and other relations with Taiwan. Including its official overseas missions and its unofficial representative and/or trade offices, Taiwan is represented in 122 countries. Recently, Taiwan has lobbied strongly for admission into the United Nations and other international organizations, such as the World Health Organization (WHO). The P.R.C. opposes Taiwan's membership in such organizations, most of which require statehood for membership, because Beijing considers Taiwan to be a province of China, not a separate sovereign state.

U.S.-TAIWAN RELATIONS

On January 1, 1979, the United States changed its diplomatic recognition from Taipei to Beijing. In the U.S.-P.R.C. Joint Communiqué that announced the change, the United States recognized the Government of the People's Republic of China as the sole legal government of China and acknowledged the Chinese position that there is but one China and Taiwan is part of China. The Joint Communiqué also stated that within this context the people of the United States will maintain cultural, commercial, and other unofficial relations with the people on Taiwan.

On April 10, 1979, President Carter signed into law the Taiwan Relations Act (TRA), which created domestic legal authority for the conduct of unofficial relations with Taiwan. U.S. commercial, cultural, and other interaction with the people on Taiwan is facilitated through the American Institute in Taiwan (AIT), a private nonprofit corporation. The Institute has its headquarters in the Washington, DC area and has offices in Taipei and Kaohsiung. It is authorized to issue visas, accept passport applications, and provide assistance to U.S. citizens in Taiwan. A counterpart organization, the Taipei Economic and Cultural Representative Office in the United States (TECRO), has been established by the Taiwan authorities. It has its headquarters in Taipei, the representative branch office in Washington, DC, and 11 other Taipei Economic and Cultural Offices (TECO) in the continental U.S. and Guam. The Taiwan Relations Act (TRA) continues to provide the legal basis for the unofficial relationship between the U.S. and Taiwan, and enshrines the U.S. commitment to assisting Taiwan maintain its defensive capability.

Following de-recognition, the United States terminated its Mutual Defense Treaty with Taiwan. However, the United States has continued the sale of appropriate defensive military equipment to Taiwan in accordance with the Taiwan Relations Act, which provides for such sales and which declares that peace and stability in the area are in U.S. interests. Sales of defensive military equipment are also consistent with the 1982 U.S.-P.R.C. Joint Communiqué.

The United States position on Taiwan is reflected in the Three Communiqués and the Taiwan Relations Act (TRA). The U.S. insists on the peaceful resolution of cross-Strait differences and encourages dialogue to help advance such an outcome. The U.S. does not support Taiwan independence. President Bush stated on December 9, 2003 that the United States is opposed to any attempt by either side to unilaterally alter the status quo in the Taiwan Strait. While the United States welcomes recent exchanges that enhance channels of communication between leaders in Beijing and Taipei, the United States urges Beijing and Taipei to further advance cross-Strait cooperation and dialogue, including direct discussions between the authorities in Beijing and elected leaders in Taipei.

U.S. commercial ties with Taiwan have been maintained and have expanded since 1979. Taiwan continues to enjoy Export-Import Bank financing, Overseas Private Investment Corporation guarantees, normal trade relations (NTR) status, and ready access to U.S. markets. In recent years, AIT commercial dealings with Taiwan have focused on expanding market access for American goods and services. AIT has been engaged in a series of trade discussions, which have focused on protection of intellectual property rights and market access for U.S. goods and services.

Maintaining diplomatic relations with the P.R.C. has been recognized to be in the long-term interest of the United States by seven consecutive administrations; however, maintaining strong, unofficial relations with Taiwan also a major U.S. goal, in line with our desire to further peace and stability in Asia. In keeping with our one China policy, the U.S. does not support Taiwan independence, but it does support Taiwan's membership in appropriate international organizations, such as the World Trade Organization, Asia-Pacific Economic Cooperation (APEC) forum, and the Asian Development Bank, where statehood is not a requirement for membership. In addition, the U.S. supports appropriate opportunities for Taiwan's voice to be heard in organizations where its membership is not possible.

U.S. Representative Offices
American Institute in Taiwan
Washington Headquarters
Suite 1700, 1700 North Moore Street
Arlington, VA 22209
Tel: 703-525-8474
Fax: 703-841-1385

American Institute in Taiwan
Taipei Office
No. 7, Lane 134, Hsin Yi Road
Section 3, Taipei, Taiwan
Tel: 011-886-2-2162-2000
Fax: 011-886-2-2162-2239

American Institute in Taiwan
Kaohsiung Office
5F, No. 2, Chung Cheng 3rd Road
Kaohsiung, Taiwan 800
Tel: 011-886-7-238-7744
Fax: 011-886-7-238-5237

Taiwan Representative Office
Taipei Economic and Cultural Representative Office (TECRO)
4201 Wisconsin Avenue, NW
Washington, DC 20016-2137
Tel: 202-895-1800
Fax: 202-895-0825

EU - TAIWAN RELATIONS

Taiwan is an important trading partner, and is the EU's third or fourth largest trading partner in Asia, after Japan, the People's Republic of China and sometimes Korea. The EU encourages the healthy flow of trade and investment between Europe and Taiwan, and therefore strongly supported Taiwan's accession to WTO. Taiwan, as the "Separate Customs Territory of Taiwan, Penghu, Kinmen and Matsu" (or "Chinese Taipei"), joined the world trade body on 1 January 2009.

The European Commission holds annual consultations with Taiwan, alternately in Brussels and Taipei, which cover all relevant aspects of the relationship. The last round of Consultations took place in Taipei in June 2011.

On 10 March 2003, the European Commission established a permanent presence on the island, through the opening of its 'European Economic and Trade Office'. The Office, whose establishment had been a Commission priority for some time, will contribute to the strengthening of communications with the Taiwanese authorities and other economic and social interlocutors, and will promote opportunities for collaboration in areas of mutual interest.

The EU pursues a "One China" policy and recognises the Government of the People's Republic of China as the sole legal government of China. However, it recognises Taiwan as an economic and commercial entity, has solid relations with Taiwan in non-political areas and maintains exchanges in various technical fields, such as economic relations, science, education and culture. In line with the EU's "One China" policy, the European Economic and Trade Office will not be engaged in relations of a diplomatic or political nature.

CROSS-STRAITS RELATIONS

The EU supports the peaceful resolution of differences between Taiwan and the People's Republic of China, rejecting the use or threat of force. It urges both sides to resume constructive dialogue, and to eschew dogmatic positions. The EU insists that any arrangement between Beijing and Taipei can only be achieved on a mutually acceptable basis, with reference also to the wishes of the Taiwanese population.

The EU believes that increasing economic integration between the People's Republic of China and Taiwan, to be further strengthened now that both sides have entered into WTO, can make a substantial contribution to creating a more favourable climate for resumption of dialogue and eventual resolution of the question of Taiwan.
You can visit the European Commission's External Relations website at:
http://ec.europa.eu/comm/external_relations/taiwan/intro/index.htm

ANNOUNCEMENT OF THE ESTABLISHMENT OF THE EUROPEAN ECONOMIC AND TRADE OFFICE IN TAIWAN BY THE EUROPEAN COMMISSION - 10 MARCH 2003

The European Commission has opened an office in Taipei, Taiwan. The move will strengthen relations between the EU and Taiwan in areas such as trade, investment, economic co-operation, research and education. Commenting on the event, Commissioner for External Relations Chris Patten said, "The opening of the European Economic and Trade Office in Taipei confirms the steady development of commercial ties between the European Union and Taiwan. The volume of our bilateral trade and investment flows makes Taiwan an important economic partner for the EU. We look forward to the strengthening of this partnership".

With the Office in Taipei, the European Commission will, for the first time, establish a permanent presence on the island. Mr Brian McDonald has been appointed by the European Commission as Head of Office.

The Office will mainly cover economic and trade relations, economic co-operation as well as cultural and information activities. It will contribute to the strengthening of communications with the Taiwanese authorities and other economic and social partners as well as promoting and boosting opportunities for collaboration in areas of mutual interest. In line with the EU's "One China" policy, the Office will not be engaged in relations of a diplomatic or political nature.

The decision to open the Office in Taiwan forms part of the European Union's new strategy for Asia, the core objective of which is to promote the EU's presence in the region, as Enlargement of the Union makes it an ever more significant global player.

The establishment of a local presence in Taiwan has been a Commission priority for some time. This was confirmed in the Commission's Communication of 3 July 2001. It also in line with the objective of reinforcing the EU's presence and raising its profile across Asia, reaffirmed in the Commission's Asia Communication of 4 September 2001.

INTERVIEW WITH CHRIS PATTEN, "EUROPEAN VOICE", 23 JANUARY 2003

'ONE CHINA' POLICY CAN STILL ACCOMMODATE EU RELATIONS WITH TAIWAN

Do you accept criticism that you and the EU have turned your backs on Taiwan in favour of China?

Absolutely not - and I cannot see where European Voice has got this strange idea from. It's not the view of the Taiwanese authorities, by the way. We rightly stick to the principle of 'One China' - but that doesn't mean we are any the less engaged with Taiwan, which is an important economic partner of the EU. On an institutional level, we are about to open a new office in Taiwan: not obviously a sign that we are turning our backs. People have been asking us to do this for years. Next month, the office will open.

What is the EU doing to encourage Taiwan's membership of the international community – for example the United Nations (UN), World Health Organisation (WHO) and so on?

We pushed very strongly for Taiwan's membership of the WTO – an organisation that is important for both Taipei and Beijing.

Our position has long been to support Taiwan's membership in other international organisations, where there is a sufficient added value, economic or otherwise, to justify it, and where the organisation's statutes allow it.

The WHO has its own rules, and is only open to states. But we are happy with others to see whether Taiwan could be more involved in the WHO's work in a different way, because we recognise Taiwan is increasingly active in international aid and health issues.

What will be the goal of the new EU office in Taipei?

It will be an economic and trade office, and it will cover the full range of areas where we have a relationship with Taiwan, including science, technology and education. The office will not, obviously, have diplomatic status, and will not engage in political issues.

Cynics say the presence of Commission officials there is more to help ensure that Taiwan meets the terms of its WTO obligations than anything else. Do you reject this?

Of course, implementation of WTO is an important consideration, but our relations with Taiwan are not limited to ensuring that Taiwan lives up to its WTO commitments.

We are opening an office because Taiwan is our 3rd biggest trading partner in Asia, and, like the 12 EU Member States who also have trade offices in Taiwan, we think it is important to maintain good relations on the ground.

We need to make progress on trade and investment, economic and scientific cooperation and create the conditions for increased regional and global prosperity. WTO membership is an important facet of this. It is crucial to make the new Round of negotiations under the Doha Development Agenda a success. It is not an exaggeration to say that the future of free global trade depends on this. We want to work closely with all like-minded partners to achieve this goal, and Taiwan is definitely a part of this effort.
What could Taiwan itself offer to foster more support from the international community?

Taiwan has impressed the international community, with its successful transition to democracy, and with the impressive economic prosperity it has achieved.

At the same time, of course, the vast majority of countries sensibly follow a 'One China' policy.

Do you believe there is a genuine military threat from the Chinese against Taiwan? How is the EU dealing with this issue?

The situation is indeed of concern to the EU. We are firmly opposed to the use or threat of force across the Taiwan straits, and we have said so consistently. Nobody can be interested in yet another regional arms race. It is up to both sides to refrain from taking steps, or making statements, that increase tensions.

We also think that increasing economic interaction and cooperation between China and Taiwan will help create a more favourable climate between them. Their accession to the WTO should make a positive difference. Both sides should make full use of the channels of communications that the WTO offers.

Overall, how would you evaluate EU-Taiwan relations?

I think our relations are good. There is no reason why this positive trend should not continue. Our office in Taiwan should contribute to this.

Moving forward, in the medium term do you see any further developments beyond the current status quo? Do you think Taiwan will ever get the recognition it yearns for?

The issue of Taiwan's relations with China can only be resolved by the two sides. Economic integration should help to bring them closer, provided that it is seen as an opportunity, not a threat.

But it must be complemented by the resumption of dialogue. I personally believe that both sides should put aside entrenched positions to make this possible.

There are some signs of a growing maturity on both sides in handling this sensitive relationship, and that should be welcome to all friends of Asia.

ROC'S RELATIONS WITH COUNTRIES WITHOUT DIPLOMATIC TIES

In terms of our relations with Southeast Asian nations, Taiwanese investments in this region topped US$40 billion during the past decade. Taiwan has become a major investor in Southeast Asia. Nevertheless, due to Beijing's obstruction we have not been able to join this region's security mechanism. In the future, our government will strengthen its interaction with Southeast Asian nations and take the initiative to establish a dialogue mechanism with them via Track Two or Track Three diplomatic channels so as to step up mutual exchanges and cooperation.

As for our ties with nations of West Asia, we are focusing on setting up more offices in Russia, concluding the ROC-Russia air agreement at the earliest possible date, and maintaining sound interaction with the oil-producing countries of the Middle East.

In recent years, Central and East European nations have conducted political and economic reforms and begun talks to join the EU. Noting that these countries have great potential to become important players in the international arena, we will enhance our efforts to strengthen our relations with Central and East European nations as well as the Baltic states.

In terms of our relations with the third world nations, we will actively promote the Taiwan Experience to assist in the economic development of these nations based on our sincerity to contribute to the international community. We hope to take further steps to develop friendly ties with these countries on the basis of reciprocity and mutual benefit.

3. Active participation in international organizations and related activities

At present, we have official member status in 16 inter-governmental international organizations and 970 international non-governmental organizations. A total of 30 NGOs have set up headquarters or secretariats in Taiwan. From the second half of 2005 to the end of April 2000, we hosted or participated in 951 NGO meetings as well as joined 384 non-governmental international activities. It is our long-term goal to join the United Nations. At present, our goals are to actively participate in other functional and regional international organizations, to assist domestic private organizations in joining NGOs, and to promote our legal rights and status in the international organizations that we have already joined.

Our application to become a member of the United Nations is closely related to our status and rights in the international community. In the past six years, our applications to join the UN failed to be included in the UN's General Assembly's plenary agenda due to Beijing's obstruction. However, in pursuit of our national interests, the new administration will continue to promote our bid to join the UN. Meanwhile, we will seek various channels to join or sponsor the activities of UN special agencies.

With regards to our bid to join the World Health Organization, we have, as of May 2000, applied to become an observer with the WHO for four consecutive years. However, Beijing's obstruction prevented our case from being included in the WHA's plenary agenda. Since this case greatly affects the personal health, public health and national interests of our people, my ministry has mapped out mid and long-term work plans to promote our case in European and North American countries. We will continue to urge the participation of the civilian sector in the WHO bid campaign.

After years of hard work, our application to join the World Trade Organization has reached the final stage. In terms of bilateral procedures, we have completed bilateral negotiations with 26 members that requested talks with us. To date, only Hong Kong has yet to sign an agreement with us. In terms of multilateral procedures, the WTO has called for ten working group meetings and three unofficial working group meetings on our application. We have yet to conclude the last working group meeting before our working group report and accession protocol are adopted. Once the General Council accepts our application, we will proceed to complete the ratification and deposition procedures and then become a full member. However, Beijing has repeatedly stressed that it should enter the WTO ahead of Taipei. Thus the majority of WTO members delayed our case because of Beijing's attitude. After Beijing signed agreements with the US and the EU, it still needs to complete bilateral talks with five members. The US House of Representatives approved granting China Permanent Normal Trade Relations on May 24, and the Senate is expected to vote on this issue in the near future. We expect smoother progress on Beijing's accession to the WTO. My Ministry will keep on watching closely the progress of

Beijing's accession and continue requesting support from WTO members to allow Taiwan to join this organization at the earliest possible date.

As a major trade partner and investor in East Asia, the ROC has always played an active role in various APEC activities. Last September, our proposal entitled "Economic Revitalization through Start-up Companies and Venture Capital" was incorporated in the joint statement of APEC's Ministerial Meeting. Our government then gathered opinions from various sectors to map out relevant working points which were reported and adopted by the first senior officials' meeting this year. In May 2000, my ministry held a seminar on venture capital and representatives from 15 members attended this meeting in Taiwan. We are presently planning another seminar on related issues in October of this year and will report the results of our research to the APEC annual economic leaders' meeting and its annual ministerial meeting in November. Our future goal is to increase our participation in the group's meetings and activities

ECONOMY

Through nearly five decades of hard work and sound economic management, Taiwan has transformed itself from an underdeveloped, agricultural island to an economic power that is a leading producer of high-technology goods. Taiwan is now a creditor economy, holding one of the world's largest foreign exchange reserves of more than $100 billion in 2005. Despite the Asian financial crisis, the economy continues to expand at about 5% per year, with virtually full employment and low inflation. The population also enjoys an annual average income equal to U.S. $13,152 .

In the 1960s, foreign investment in Taiwan helped introduce modern, labor-intensive technology to the island, and Taiwan became a major exporter of labor-intensive products. In the 1980s, focus shifted toward increasingly sophisticated, capital-intensive and technology-intensive products for export and toward developing the service sector. At the same time, the appreciation of the New Taiwan dollar (NT$), rising labor costs, and increasing environmental consciousness in Taiwan caused many labor-intensive industries, such as shoe manufacturing, to move to the Chinese mainland and Southeast Asia.

Taiwan has transformed itself from a recipient of U.S. aid in the 1950s and early 1960s to an aid donor and major foreign investor, especially in Asia. Private Taiwan investment in the P.R.C. is est. to total more than $30 billion, and Taiwan has invested a comparable amount in Southeast Asia.

FOREIGN TRADE

Foreign trade has been the engine of Taiwan's rapid growth during the past 40 years. Taiwan's economy remains export-oriented, so it depends on an open world trade regime and remains vulnerable to downturns in the world economy. The total value of trade increased more than five-fold in the 1960s, nearly 10-fold in the 1970s, and doubled again in the 1980s. The 1990s has seen a more modest, slightly less than two-fold, growth. Export composition has changed from predominantly agricultural commodities to industrial goods (now 98%). The electronics sector is Taiwan's most important industrial export sector and is the largest recipient of U.S. investment.

Taiwan is the world's largest supplier of computer monitors and is a leading PC manufacturer. Textile production, though of declining importance as Taiwan loses its competitive advantage in labor-intensive markets, is another major industrial export sector. Imports are dominated by raw materials and capital goods, which account for more than 90% of the total. Taiwan imports most of its energy needs.

The United States is Taiwan's largest trading partner, taking 25% of Taiwan's exports and supplying 17% of its imports. Taiwan is the U.S.'s seventh-largest trading partner and eigth-largest export market. In 2005, Taiwan's two-way trade with the U.S. amounted to about U.S. $54.3 billion. Imports from the U.S. consist mostly of agricultural and industrial raw materials. Exports to the U.S. are mainly electronics and consumer goods.

The United States, Hong Kong (including indirect trade with the P.R.C.), and Japan account for two-thirds of Taiwan's exports, and the U.S. and Japan provide 45% of Taiwan's imports. As Taiwan's per capita income level has risen, demand for imported, high-quality consumer goods has increased. This trend has driven imports to rise faster than exports and has cut into Taiwan's global trade surplus. Another important factor in the substantial increase in Taiwan's imports has been industrial upgrading, which has pushed up imports of capital goods, raw materials, parts, and components. Taiwan's l999 trade surplus with the United States was $16.1 billion, a significant amount, but a decline from a high of $17 billion in 1987.

The lack of formal diplomatic relations with all but 29 of its trading partners appears not to have seriously hindered Taiwan's rapidly expanding commerce, and Taiwan is currently the world's 14th-largest trading economy. Taiwan maintains trade offices in more than 60 countries with which it does not have official relations. Taiwan is a member of the Asian Development Bank, and it is engaged in negotiations to join the World Trade Organization (WTO) as a special customs territory. In 1991 Taiwan, under the name "Chinese Taipei," became a member of the Asia-Pacific Economic Cooperation (APEC) forum. These developments reflect Taiwan's economic importance and its desire to become further integrated into the global economy.

AGRICULTURE

Although only about one-quarter of Taiwan's land area is arable, virtually all farmland is intensely cultivated, with some areas suitable for two and even three crops a year. However, increases in agricultural production have been much slower than industrial growth. Agriculture only comprises about 269% of Taiwan's GDP. Taiwan's main crops are rice, sugar cane, fruit, and vegatables.

Although self-sufficient in rice production, Taiwan imports large amounts of wheat, mostly from the United States. Meat production and consumption are rising sharply, reflecting a rising standard of living. Taiwan has exported large amounts of frozen pork, although this was affected by an outbreak of hoof and mouth disease in 1997. Other agricultural exports include fish, aquaculture and sea products, canned and frozen vegetables, and grain products. Imports of agriculture products are expected to increase due to the approaching WTO accession, which will open previously protected agricultural markets.

ECONOMIC OUTLOOK

Taiwan now faces many of the same economic issues as other developed economies. With the prospect of continued relocation of labor-intensive industries to countries with cheaper work forces, Taiwan's future development will have to rely on further transformation to a high technology and service-oriented economy. In recent years, Taiwan has successfully diversified its trade markets, cutting its share of exports to the U.S. from 49% in 1984 to 25% in l999. Taiwan's dependence on the U.S. market should continue to decrease as its exports to Southeast Asia and the P.R.C. grow and its efforts to develop European markets produce results. Taiwan's bid to join the WTO and its desire to become an Asia-Pacific "regional operations center" are spurring further economic liberalization.

TRAVEL AND BUSINESS INFORMATION

The U.S. Department of State's Consular Information Program provides Consular Information Sheets, Travel Warnings, and Public Announcements.

Consular Information Sheets exist for all countries and include information on entry requirements, currency regulations, health conditions, areas of instability, crime and security, political disturbances, and the addresses of the U.S. posts in the country.

Travel Warnings are issued when the State Department recommends that Americans avoid travel to a certain country. **Public Announcements** are issued as a means to disseminate information quickly about terrorist threats and other relatively short-term conditions overseas that pose significant risks to the security of American travelers. Free copies of this information are available by calling the Bureau of Consular Affairs at 202-647-5225 or via the fax-on-demand system: 202-647-3000. Consular Information Sheets and Travel Warnings also are available on the Consular Affairs Internet home page: http://travel.state.gov. Consular Affairs Tips for Travelers publication series, which contain information on obtaining passports and planning a safe trip abroad, are available on the Internet and hard copies can be purchased from the Superintendent of Documents, U.S. Government Printing Office, telephone: 202-512-1800; fax 202-512-2250.

Emergency information concerning Americans traveling abroad may be obtained from the Office of Overseas Citizens Services at (202) 647-5225. For after-hours emergencies, Sundays and holidays, call 202-647-4000.

The National Passport Information Center (NPIC) is the U.S. Department of State's single, centralized public contact center for U.S. passport information. Telephone: 1-877-4USA-PPT (1-877-487-2778). Customer service representatives and operators for TDD/TTY are available Monday-Friday, 8:00 a.m. to 8:00 p.m., Eastern Time, excluding federal holidays.

Travelers can check the latest health information with the U.S. Centers for Disease Control and Prevention in Atlanta, Georgia. A hotline at 877-FYI-TRIP (877-394-8747) and a web site at http://www.cdc.gov/travel/index.htm give the most recent health advisories, immunization recommendations or requirements, and advice on food and drinking water safety for regions and countries. A booklet entitled Health Information for International Travel (HHS publication number CDC-95-8280) is available from the U.S. Government Printing Office, Washington, DC 20402, tel. (202) 512-1800.

STRATEGIC INFORMATION FOR CONDUCTING BUSINESS

ECONOMY AND ECONOMIC DEVELOPMENT

Economy of Taiwan	
Currency	New Taiwan dollar (NT$)
Exchange rate (av)	TWD:$ USD = 32.84
Fiscal year	Calendar year (1 Jan to 31 Dec)
Trade organizations	WTO, APEC, and others (as Separate Customs Territory of Taiwan, Penghu, Kinmen and Matsu)
Statistics	
GDP (Nominal)	$383.3 billion (ranked 24th)
GDP (PPP)	$695.4 billion (ranked 19th)
GDP per capita (Nominal)	$16.590 (ranked 40th)
GDP per capita (PPP)	$30,100 (ranked 34th)
GDP growth rate	0.1%
GDP by sector	services (primary) (71.1%) industry (secondary) (27.5%) agriculture (tertiary) (1.4%)
Interest rates (2008-08-27)	Discount rate: 3.625%% Overnight rate:2.161%
Inflation rate (CPI)	1.8%
Household income or consumption by percentage share	lowest 10%: 6.7%, highest 10%: 41.1%
Population below poverty line	0.95%
Gini index	34
Labor force	10.78 million
Labor force by occupation	agriculture (5.3%), industry (36.8%), services (57.9%)
Unemployment rate	4.27%
Industrial production growth rate	7.5%
Main industries	electronics, petroleum refining, armaments, chemicals, textiles, iron and steel, machinery, cement, food processing, vehicles, consumer products, pharmaceuticals
Agricultural products	rice, corn, vegetables, fruit, tea; pigs, poultry, beef, milk; fish
Natural resources	small deposits of coal, natural gas, limestone, marble, and asbestos
Investment (gross fixed)	21.2% of GDP
Stock of direct foreign investment - at home	$92.83 billion

(2006)	
Stock of direct foreign investment - abroad (2006)	$108.9 billion
Market value of publicly traded shares (2006)	$654 billion
Trade	
Current account balance	$31.7 billion (ranked xth)
Exports	$246.7 billion f.o.b.
Principal exports	electronic and electrical products, metals, textiles, plastics, chemicals, auto parts
Main destinations of exports	China 32.3%, US 12.8%, Hong Kong 8.8%, Japan 6.4%, Singapore 5%
Imports	$219.3 billion f.o.b.
Principal imports (2009)	electronic and electrical products, machinery, petroleum, precision instruments, organic chemicals, metals
Main origins of imports (2006)	Japan 22.1%, US 13%, China 10.9%, South Korea 7.3%, Saudi Arabia 4.8%, Singapore 4.5%
Public finances	
Public debt (2006)	27.9% of GDP
External debt	$98.44 billion
Foreign exchange reserves and gold	$274.7 billion
Revenues	$76.2 billion
Expenditures	$75.65 billion
Budget balance	$550 million (surplus)

Taiwan's quick industrialization and rapid growth during the latter half of the twentieth century, has been called the "Taiwan Miracle" (台灣奇蹟) or "Taiwan Economic Miracle". As it has developed alongside Singapore, South Korea, and Hong Kong, Taiwan is one of the industrialized developed countries known as the "Four Asian Tigers".

Japanese rule prior to and during World War II brought forth changes in the public and private sectors of the economy, most notably in the area of public works, which enabled rapid communications and facilitated transport throughout much of the island. The Japanese also improved public education and made the system compulsory for all Taiwanese citizens during this time.

When the KMT government fled to Taiwan it brought the entire gold reserve and the foreign currency reserve of mainland China to the island which stabilized prices and reduced hyperinflation. More importantly, as part of its retreat to Taiwan, KMT brought with them the intellectual and business elites from mainland China. The KMT government instituted many laws and land reforms that it had never effectively enacted on mainland China. The government also implemented a policy of import-substitution, attempting to produce imported goods domestically. Much of this was made possible through US economic aid, subsidizing the higher cost of domestic production.

In 1962, Taiwan had a per capita gross national product (GNP) of $170, placing the island's economy squarely between Zaire and Congo. By 2008 Taiwan's per capita GNP, adjusted for purchasing power parity (PPP), had soared to $33,000 (2008 est.) contributing to a Human Development Index equivalent to that of other developed countries.

Today Taiwan has a dynamic capitalist, export-driven economy with gradually decreasing state involvement in investment and foreign trade. In keeping with this trend, some large government-owned banks and industrial firms are being privatized. Real growth in GDP has averaged about eight percent during the past three decades. Exports have provided the primary impetus for industrialization. The trade surplus is substantial, and foreign reserves are the world's fifth largest as of 31 December 2007.

Agriculture constitutes only two percent of the GDP, down from 35 percent in 1952. Traditional labor-intensive industries are steadily being moved offshore and with more capital and technology-intensive industries replacing them. Taiwan has become a major foreign investor in mainland China, Thailand, Indonesia, the Philippines, Malaysia, and Vietnam. It is est. that some 50,000 Taiwanese businesses and 1,000,000 businesspeople and their dependents are established in the PRC.

Because of its conservative financial approach and its entrepreneurial strengths, Taiwan suffered little compared with many of its neighbors from the 1997 Asian Financial Crisis. Unlike its neighbors South Korea and Japan, the Taiwanese economy is dominated by small and medium sized businesses, rather than the large business groups. The global economic downturn, however, combined with poor policy coordination by the new administration and increasing bad debts in the banking system, pushed Taiwan into recession in 2001, the first whole year of negative growth since 1947. Due to the relocation of many manufacturing and labor intensive industries to mainland China, unemployment also reached a level not seen since the 1973 oil crisis. This became a major issue in the 2004 presidential election. Growth averaged more than 4% in the 2009–2006 period and the unemployment rate fell below 4%. Since the global financial crisis starting with United States in 2007, the unemployment rate has risen to over 5.9% and Economic Growth fallen to -2.9%.

Leading technologies of Taiwan include:

- Bicycle manufacturing, ex: Giant Bicycles, Merida
- Biotechnology
- Semiconductor device fabrication
- Laptops, ex: Acer, Asus, BenQ
- Smartphones, ex: HTC

Taiwan has a dynamic capitalist economy with gradually decreasing guidance of investment and foreign trade by the **Republic of China (ROC)** government which governs Taiwan. In keeping with this trend, most large government-owned banks and industrial firms have been privatized. Real growth in GDP has averaged about 8% during the past three decades. Exports have grown even faster and since World War II, have provided the primary impetus for industrialization. Inflation and unemployment are low; the trade surplus is substantial; and foreign reserves are the world's fourth largest. Agriculture contributes 3% to GDP, down from 35% in 1952, and the service sector makes up 73% of the economy. Traditional labor-intensive industries are steadily being moved off-shore and replaced with more capital- and technology-intensive industries, as well as creative industries.

Taiwanese investors and businesses have become major investors in mainland China, Vietnam, Thailand, Indonesia, the Philippines, and Malaysia. The tightening of labor markets has led to an influx of foreign workers, both legal and illegal. Because of its conservative financial approach and its entrepreneurial strengths, Taiwan suffered little from the Asian financial crisis of 1997-2005 as compared to many of its neighbors. And unlike neighboring Japan and South Korea, small and medium-sized businesses make up a large proportion of businesses in Taiwan, with one in seven people the owner of a business

Taiwan is a member of the Asian Development Bank (ADB), the World Trade Organization (WTO), and the Asia-Pacific Economic Cooperation (APEC) forum. Taiwan is also an observer at the Organisation for Economic Co-operation and Development (OECD). Taiwan's top five trade partners are China, USA, Hong Kong, Japan and Singapore.

FOREIGN TRADE

Foreign trade has been the engine of Taiwan's rapid growth during the past 40 years. Taiwan's economy remains export-oriented, so it depends on an open world trade regime and remains vulnerable to downturns in the world economy. The total value of trade increased more than fivefold in the 1960s, nearly 10-fold in the 1970s, and doubled again in the 1980s. The 1990s saw a more modest, slightly less than twofold, growth. Export composition changed from predominantly agricultural commodities to industrial goods (now 98%). The electronics sector is Taiwan's most important industrial export sector and is the largest recipient of U.S. investment. Taiwan, as an independent economy, became a member of the World Trade Organization (WTO) as Separate Customs Territory of Taiwan, Penghu, Kinmen and Matsu (often shortened to "Chinese Taipei"-both names resulting from PRC interference on the WTO) in January 2009.

Taiwan is the world's largest supplier of contract computer chip manufacturing (foundry services) and is a leading LCD panel manufacturer, DRAM computer memory, networking equipment, and consumer electronics designer and manufacturer. Textile production, though of declining importance as Taiwan loses its competitive advantage in labor-intensive (cheap-labor) markets, is another major industrial export sector. Imports are dominated by raw materials and capital goods, which account for more than 90% of the total. Taiwan imports most of its energy needs. The United States is Taiwan's third largest trading partner, taking 15% of Taiwanese exports and supplying 10.9% of its imports. China has recently become Taiwan's largest import and export partner. In 2006, the PRC accounted for 22.5% and 11.9% of Taiwan's exports and imports respectively (excluding Hong Kong) (According to the CIA World Factbook). This figure is growing rapidly as both economies become ever more interdependent. Imports from China consist mostly of agricultural and industrial raw materials. Exports to the United States are mainly electronics and consumer goods. As Taiwanese per capita income level has risen, demand for imported, high-quality consumer goods has increased. Taiwan's 2009 trade surplus with the United States was $8.7 billion.

The lack of formal diplomatic relations between the Republic of China (Taiwan) with Taiwan's trading partners appears not to have seriously hindered Taiwan's rapidly expanding commerce. The Republic of China maintains cultural and trade offices in more than 60 countries with which it does not have official relations to represent Taiwanese interest. In addition to the WTO, Taiwan is a member of the Asian Development Bank as "Taipei, China" (a name resulting from PRC influence on the bank) and the Asia-Pacific Economic Cooperation (APEC) forum as "Chinese Taipei" (for the same reason as above). These developments reflect Taiwan's economic importance and its desire to become further integrated into the global economy. Taiwan has been negotiating with the U.S. for a Free Trade Agreement (FTA), but this has become difficult due to PRC's diplomatic interference and the expiration of presidential fast track authority.
The prospect of an economic cooperation agreement known as ECFA with the PRC could potentially widen the market for Taiwan's exports. However, the true benefits and impacts brought by ECFA to Taiwan's overall economy are still in dispute.

AGRICULTURE

Although only about one-quarter of Taiwan's land area is suitable for farming, virtually all farmland is intensely cultivated, with some areas suitable for two and even three crops a year. However, increases in agricultural production have been much slower than industrial growth. Today, agriculture only comprises about 2.69% of Taiwan's GDP. Taiwan's main crops are rice, sugar cane, fruits (many of them tropical), and vegetables.

Although self-sufficient in rice production, Taiwan imports large amounts of wheat, mostly from the United States. Meat production and consumption has risen sharply, reflecting a high standard of living. Taiwan has exported large amounts of frozen pork, although this was affected by an outbreak of hoof and mouth disease in 1997. Other agricultural exports include fish, aquaculture and sea products, canned and frozen vegetables, and grain products. Imports of agriculture products are expected to increase due to the WTO accession, which is opening previously protected agricultural markets.

PRINCIPAL GROWTH SECTORS

Taiwan is an export-oriented economy. Exports of goods and services constitute half of its GDP. A steep decline in foreign demand in 2001 led to a double-digit fall in exports and economic recession. In 2009 a sharp increase in exports through Taiwan's production bases on the mainland re-invigorated the island's manufacturing sector, posting growth of 7.5% compared to the 8% decline in 2001.

The relocation of low-end manufacturing bases to the PRC accelerated Taiwan's industrial transformation. Due to this relocation, production of labor-intensive industries declined 1.2% in 2009. Meanwhile, an increase in the export of production inputs to the mainland in 2009 drove up the output of capital- and technology-intensive industries by 10%. The labor-intensive industries' share of manufacturing output shrank from 23% to less than 20% in 2009, compared to an increase from 77% to over 80% for the capital- and technology-intensive industries. Specifically, electronics (including semiconductors and information technology (IT) products) have become the backbone of Taiwan's manufacturing sector. Output of electronics products in 2009 accounted for 40% of total manufacturing production, compared to less than 20% in the early 1990s. Taiwan now ranks first in the world in production of 14 electronic and IT products. It also accounts for over 70% of the global silicon wafer OEM market, and its world market shares for mask ROM, LCD monitors, and IC foundry exceed 55%, 40% and 30%, respectively.

Since the 1980's, liberalization has allowed the service sector to grow faster than the industrial sector, broadening the gap between services and industry/ agriculture. The service sector's share in GDP increased from 50% in the late 1980's to over 67% in 2009. Within the service sector, the share for financial services (including real estate) expanded from 13% to 21% and for wholesale and retail services from 13% to 20%. At the same time agriculture's share of GDP declined from 5% to below 2% and industry's share fell from 38% to 31%.

Accelerated industrial relocation to mainland China prompted approved foreign direct investment (FDI) from Taiwan to the PRC to reverse from a year-to-year (y-to-y) decline of 11% in the first quarter to a y-to-y growth of 34% in the second quarter of 2009. The growth accelerated to 78% in the last quarter of 2009 and 92% in the first quarter of 2003. The flow of approved FDI to the PRC in 2009 totaled US$3.9 billion, bringing the cumulative total as of December 2009 to US$26.6 billion. Over 40% of Taiwan's total outward FDI went to the mainland. The actual investment more than doubled, reaching an est. US$70 billion, as many Taiwan businesses sent their investment funds via other nations. Some of Taiwan's FDI in the PRC also comes from personal accounts overseas.

PUBLIC ROLE IN THE ECONOMY

The public sector's role in the economy of Taiwan has declined steadily. A number of construction projects, including a north-south high-speed railway and a mass rapid transit (MRT) system in Kaohsiung, have been awarded to private firms to execute on a build-operate-transfer (BOT) basis. Private firms also have been permitted to build industrial harbors and power plants. Oil refinery operations and gasoline importation and distribution have been liberalized. Taiwan authorities have reduced public ownership levels to below 50% in 30 state-owned enterprises and shut down 16 inefficient public firms. One-third of the privatized enterprises have been sold and one-quarter of the closures executed since the DPP-controlled government was inaugurated in May 2000. Taiwan authorities have said they will step up the privatization efforts to sell 11 of the other 13 public enterprises in 2003 and 2004, including such giants as Chinese Petroleum Corp., Chunghwa Telecom Corp., and Taiwan Tobacco and Wine Corp.

Taiwan's central budget deficit has increased steadily over the past four years, from 0.6% of GNP in 2005 to an est. 2% for 2009 and 2003. Outstanding debt has expanded from NT$2.1 trillion (US$60 billion) in 2005 to an est. NT$3.1 trillion (US$ 88.6 billion) for 2003; this constitutes an increase from 24% to 30% of GNP. The 2003 ratio in terms of GDP is 31%. Taiwan authorities anticipate debt rollover will push outstanding public debt to 31.5% of GNP by 2006, which is still well below the central government's debt ceiling limit of 48%. The outstanding debt is still manageable and less than the levels of 35% for the United States (in 2000), 64% for Canada, 64% for members of the European Union, and 117% for Japan.

The broadening of the budget deficit and the increase in outstanding public debt can be attributed partially to a series of tax cuts in the past three years and to the economic recession of 2001. Beginning in 2000, the Ministry of Finance (MOF) eliminated double taxation by combining the corporate income tax and the personal income tax. The tax rate for the highest income bracket was lowered from 55% to 40%. The gross business receipt tax (GBRT) was reduced from 5% to 2% to allow financial institutions to use the savings to write off bad debt. In 2001, the land value increment tax was cut by half for two years to stimulate the weak real estate market. Accession to the WTO in January 2009 required Taiwan to reduce import tariffs, harbor service fee, and commodity taxes. To stimulate private investment, the government offered tax incentives for new projects and expansion projects including a five-year tax holiday or tax credit that was made retroactive to the beginning of 2009. Consequently, taxes as a share of central revenue dropped from 75% in 1998 to 67% in 2009. The shares for income tax and import duties declined from 34% to 30% and from 10% to 7%, respectively.

The decline in tax revenue has constituted a constraint for Taiwan authorities. Taiwan's central expenditure has not posted any substantial growth. Total central expenditure in 2009 was NT$1,388 billion (US$40 billion), representing a decline of 2.4% from 2001 and an increase of just 2% over the 2005 level. In the budget for 2003, central expenditure is expected to decrease another 2.5%. Education, science and culture (ESC) and social welfare will dominate the fiscal outlays of Taiwan's central government. For the 2003 central budget, these two categories together account for 37% of spending. Social welfare replaced defense to take the largest portion of central expenditure in 2000, when the share for the former was 18%, compared to 15% for the latter. The defense share of central expenditure declined to 14% in 2009 and 2003, much less than 19% for ESC and 18.5% for social welfare.

BALANCE OF PAYMENTS (BOP)

As in the past four years, Taiwan's BOP in 2009 posted a surplus that nearly doubled from the previous year to reach a record high of US$33,664 million. As a result, Taiwan's foreign exchange (forex) reserves surged 32% in 2009 to a record US$161.6 billion, the third largest in the world after Japan's US$469.7 billion and the PRC's US$286 billion. Taiwan's forex reserves as of December 2009 were equivalent to 57% of GDP, much higher than 11% in Japan and 25%

in China. More significantly, Taiwan's forex reserves were sufficient to meet requirements for 17 months of imports, compared to less than three months for most industrialized nations. In addition, the private sector holds about US$160 billion of foreign assets, far more than Taiwan's foreign debt of US$43 billion.

Taiwan typically runs a current account (C/A) surplus, which in 2009 reached a historical high of US$25.7 billion. The primary contributor was a quick expansion of nearly 30% in exports (mainly production inputs) to Greater China to meet demand from Taiwan manufacturing firms' export bases. As a result, in 2009 Taiwan posted a trade surplus with Greater China of US$31 billion that saved Taiwan from running into a C/A deficit. Taiwan's financial account (F/A) posted a large surplus of US$8.4 billion in 2009 due to an unusual net inflow of short-term capital that far offset net outflow of direct investment (FDI) as well as portfolio investment. In 2009, the strength of the NT dollar (NTD) prompted many Taiwanese residents to switch money from their foreign currency accounts to NTD accounts and banks to recover their short-term call loans from international markets.

Taiwan is likely to achieve huge C/A and BOP surpluses in 2003, as foreign trade continues to expand and Taiwan's public and private investors repatriate earnings. Many in Taiwan believe that the war in Iraq will lead to increased demand for exports from the island and from its production bases in the PRC. However, the outbreak of severe acute respiratory syndrome (SARS) in the PRC and Taiwan this year may disrupt shipments from Taiwan's export bases in mainland China, with the severity of the disruption dependent on the duration of the epidemic.

QUALITY OF INFRASTRUCTURE

Taiwan has a well-developed infrastructure system. There are three international airports, in Taipei (northern Taiwan), Kaohsiung (southern Taiwan) and Hwalien (eastern Taiwan). The airport in Hwalien opened in 2009 to international chartered flights. Fourteen domestic airports connect major cities and key offshore islands. Six international harbors facilitate import and export trade. Toll highways and railways form an extensive inland transport network, including a north-south freeway. The average family has more than one telephone, and the penetration rate of mobile phone services exceeds 100%. Fax machines, personal computers, and Internet communications are common for business firms. Virtually every family has access to electricity and household tap water, except in some remote mountainous areas.

Taiwan's infrastructure construction efforts have improved traffic congestion and power shortage problems, though some difficulties remain. Additional lanes have been added to the first north-south freeway, while many sections of the second north-south freeway have been opened. A business group has started construction of the north-south high-speed railway, scheduled to begin commercial operation in 2011. Construction of a metro system for Kaohsiung is underway. Taiwan authorities recently decided to build a rapid mass-transit system between CKS Airport and downtown Taipei, after the local contractor went out of business. Projects in the planning stage include an international airport in central Taiwan, a round-the-island freeway network, and three light-rail metro systems in the cities of Hsinchu, Taichung, and Tainan. Expansion of harbor facilities, together with privatization of harbor operations, has reduced waiting time for entry into Kaohsiung Harbor, the fifth busiest container port in the world.

Fifteen private firms have been authorized to build power plants, four of which have gone into operation as of March 2003. Two more are scheduled to begin power generation in late 2003 and another two in 2004. Taiwan authorities revoked approvals for seven projects due to the firms' failure to acquire land and/or pass environmental impact assessments. Nevertheless the reserve capacity of the power grid has increased from less than 9% in 2005 to 16% in 2009, and the ratio is expected to reach 17% in 2003 and 22% in 2004. The fourth nuclear power plant now under construction is expected to begin power generation in 2006, although political opposition to the project and delays continue to plague its completion.

ECONOMIC TIES WITH MAINLAND CHINA

The year 1997 marked the tenth anniversary of the beginning of private-sector exchanges between Taiwan and the Chinese mainland. In the past decade, economic relations between the two sides have developed from sporadic trading activities by Taiwanese small and medium-sized enterprises to large-scale investments, involving millions or even billions of US dollars by Taiwanese conglomerates. These Taiwan businesses are eager to invest in the mainland not only to seek cost advantages to maintain a competitive edge, but also to take the lead in gaining access to a market coveted by many advanced nations around the world.

Despite the absence of direct transportation links, economic ties between Taiwan and the Chinese mainland have never been closer than in recent years. In 1992, investment in the mainland by Taiwanese businesses was legalized, quickly pushing the Chinese mainland to the top of the list of major recipients of Taiwan's foreign investment. Cross-strait economic ties have served as an essential link between Taipei and Peking. The two economies are so intertwined now that breaking them off would be next to impossible, as the Chinese mainland has emerged as the primary source of the ROC's trade surplus in recent years. In 1987, Taiwan had a trade surplus of just over US$1 billion with the Chinese mainland, but, by 1998, the surplus had reached US$15.7 billion.

When the ROC first lifted its ban on cross-strait exchanges by the private sector in 1987, the government expected that this would create more favorable conditions for reunification. If interaction between the people on both sides could be gradually increased, then ideological conflicts could eventually be set aside and differences in the ways of thinking and living could be ameliorated. Unfortunately, much to the disappointment of the ROC government, this was not to be the case. As the years went by, Peking authorities voraciously absorbed capital and technology from their Taiwanese compatriots, while, at the same time sparing no effort to suppress Taiwan in the international community.

In light of these strained relations between Taipei and Peking (see also Chapter 7, Mainland Affairs and National Unification Policy), as well as the danger of having Taiwan's economy too dependent on the Chinese mainland, the ROC government decided to put a brake on cross-strait economic ties. In 1996, the government presented a new policy which called for "patience over haste." This policy was opposed by both business and academic circles within the ROC. In the aftermath of the Asian financial crisis, the ROC government reiterated that it will continue the policy in the future as the region's financial situation remains unstable.

According to the ROC's Mainland Affairs Council , the value of two-way trade between Taiwan and the Chinese mainland amounted to US$23.95 billion in 1998. Over 82 percent of the indirect trade was exports from Taiwan, which totaled US$19.84 billion, down 11.67 percent from 1997. Major export items to the mainland included industrial machinery and equipment, electronic parts, plastics, man-made fibers and industrial textiles, etc.

Imports from the Chinese mainland soared 4.85 percent to US$4.11 billion in 1998. The bulk of the imports were agricultural and industrial raw materials.

Taiwan's worry over trade dependence on the mainland is rising. Approximately 11.13 percent of Taiwan's 1998 trade was with the mainland. Export dependency stood at 17.94 percent, and import dependency at 3.93 percent.

INWARD AND OUTWARD INVESTMENT

In recent years, the ROC government has improved the investment climate by removing obstacles, implementing a "one-stop window" policy, and encouraging participation by the private sector in public construction projects. Twenty-six infrastructure projects, including the high-speed rail line in Taiwan's western corridor and 8 private power plants, have been approved. These Build-Operate-Transfer (BOT) projects, with a total investment amount of US$47.9 billion, will help capitalize on private resources and accelerate national development. In 1998, private investment increased by 10.33 percent to reach US$34.2 billion.

During the same year, there were 918 approved inward foreign investments, totaling US$3.2 billion. Compared to the previous year, the total number of approved inward foreign investments increased by 235 and was 34 percent higher than 1997; but the amount of investment fell by US$970 million, representing a decrease of 22.8 percent. Most of Taiwan's inward foreign investments in 1998 came from British territories in Central America (mainly British Virgin Islands and British Cayman Islands), the United States, Japan, Hong Kong and Singapore. The total amount from these areas equaled about 71 percent of the total amount of inward foreign investment in 1998. The top five sectors for foreign investment were electronics and electrical appliances, financial and insurance, international trade, wholesale retailing, and service, accounting for about 75 percent of the total inward foreign investment. Although the amount of investment decreased marginally from 1997, due to the impact of the Asian financial crisis, it was still the second highest in recent years. Obviously, foreigners still consider Taiwan a priority area for investment.

Overseas investments (not including those in the Chinese mainland) by Taiwanese businesses also surged by 13.9 percent to reach US$3.29 billion in 1998. In terms of the area of investment, Taiwan's outward investment focused on the British territories in Central America, the United States, Singapore, Thailand, and Vietnam.

Between 1991 and 1998, the ROC government had approved some US$13.24 billion worth of mainland investments, covering over 21,646 applications. According to statistics released by the mainland authorities, investment agreements through 1998 indicated that Taiwanese entrepreneurs assented to invest in some 41,017 projects worth a total of US$40.4 billion, thereby making Taiwan the fourth-largest mainland investor after Hong Kong, Japan, and U.S. Statistics released by the ROC Ministry of Economic Affairs showed there were 641 approved indirect investments in mainland China in 1998, totaling US$1.5 billion. Compared to 1997, the number of investments decreased by 87 or 11.9 percent, while the amount decreased by US$95 million or 5.9 percent. A large number of Taiwan manufacturers in labor-intensive industries have set up factories on the Chinese mainland to take advantage of the cheap labor and low overhead costs. Many of these manufacturers receive orders in Taiwan, produce their goods in the mainland, and ship the goods from the mainland to their overseas buyers.

As the market on the Chinese mainland becomes more open and lucrative, more of Taiwan's large enterprises, including firms in the information technology, plastics, and food and beverage industries, are beginning to undertake large-scale mainland projects. The majority (nearly 83 percent) of Taiwanese investors like to concentrate their investments on the southeastern coast of the mainland, as transportation facilities in this area are far more developed than in the interior. However, Taiwan investment is spreading beyond the eastern coast of Fujian and Guangdong provinces. Taiwan businessmen are also beginning to invest in activities other than export manufacturing, setting up mainland offices to handle real estate, insurance, banking, and tourism.

On July 15, 1997, the Ministry of Economic Affairs (MOEA) released the revised Review Guidelines for Investment and Technological Cooperation in the Mainland Area. These guidelines went into effect immediately upon release and stipulated that each individual investment case in the Chinese mainland must be reported to the relevant authorities. They further stipulated that such investments cannot exceed US$50 million without first receiving special approval from the appropriate government agencies. The MOEA also widened the scope of prohibited investments, preventing Taiwan businesses from investing in major infrastructure projects on the Chinese mainland, including such projects as railways, highways, harbors, airports, mass transit systems, incineration projects, power plants, and industrial zones. Real estate, insurance, and 17 other manufacturing products are also included in the prohibition. Despite the large number of new restrictions, tourism, leasing, and a number of entertainment businesses have been given investment authorization.

SERVICES

In the Republic of China, the service sector is divided into seven main categories: (1) finance, insurance, and real estate; (2) commerce, which includes wholesale, retail, food and beverage, and international trade; (3) social and individual services; (4) transportation, storage, and telecommunications; (5) commercial services, including legal, accounting, civil engineering, information, advertising, designing, leasing, etc.; (6) governmental services, and (7) others. During the 1960s and 1970s, the rapid growth of industry almost caught up with Taiwan's sluggish service sector in terms of GDP percentage. Roughly two decades ago, however, Taiwan's service sector was revitalized and steadily increased the gap between the service sector and the industrial sector. In 1998, the service sector accounted for 63.2 percent of Taiwan's GDP, a percentage very similar to that of many advanced nations. The total GDP value for the service sector that year reached US$164.7 billion, up 6.09 percent over the preceding year.

Finance, insurance, and real estate continued to comprise the bulk of the service sector, accounting for just over 32 percent.

Commerce rebounded to account for 27 percent of the service sector, with wholesale, retail, and international trade all performing better than the year before. Of these, retail was the strongest sector, recording a 6.8 percent growth rate.

Of the remaining categories, only the social and individual service sectors and the transportation, storage, and telecommunications sectors showed any major changes. The social and individual service sectors registered a moderate 7.84 percent growth, while the transportation, storage, and telecommunications sectors recorded a 9.63 percent growth.

Taiwan's thriving service sector, particularly in the financial and stock market areas, has attracted many young people eager to find careers in recent years. In 1988, the service sector surpassed the industrial sector in attracting more of the total work force. By the end of 1998, over 53 percent of the island's 9.28 million employees were working in the service sector.

INDUSTRY

Industry has long been outpaced by the service sector in terms of GDP percentage. In 1986, industry still accounted for nearly half of Taiwan's GDP. By the end of 1987, it had dropped to slightly over 40 percent of the GDP. This downward trend has continued ever since. In 1998, industry accounted for 34.06 percent of Taiwan's GDP, a further plunge over the same period of last year.

Except for textiles, which rose 1.62 percent, production of processed foods, leather products, and wood and bamboo products, which once dominated exports, continued to decrease in 1998. These labor-intensive industries have gradually been replaced by capital- and technology-intensive industries, such as the production of chemicals, petrochemicals, information technology, electrical equipment, and electronics, all of which experienced moderate to strong growth rates in 1998 despite a general recession in the industrial sector. Electronics and information technology have evolved into the mainstay of industry, accounting for nearly 30 percent of the nation's manufacturing in terms of production values. With respect to production output, manufacturing output constituted over 78 percent of the total industrial production and engaged over 26 percent of the national work force.

In the 1960s, an abundance of well-trained local workers and inexpensive manufacturing sites were the two major factors attracting many foreign companies to set up production branches in Taiwan. By 1987, however, the stock market had become overheated due to excessive savings in the private sector and a lack of investment channels. As a result, a large portion of the population started to play the market, causing a shortage of labor (especially blue-collar workers) in nearly all industrial and business sectors. A steep hike in land prices further aggravated the overall manufacturing environment, forcing many small and medium-sized firms, as well as labor-intensive enterprises, to scale down, shut down, or move their businesses. Those firms that moved often relocated to the Chinese mainland or Southeast Asia, leading to a decline in their relevant sectors.

Fortunately, the establishment of overseas production sites by such technology- and capital-intensive industries as machinery, chemicals, precision equipment, and electronics and information technology products, has not created the aftereffect of reducing the growth of their parent companies in Taiwan. These companies have been able to avoid harmful side effects by streamlining operations and management, thereby increasing international competitiveness and making production more efficient.

INFORMATION TECHNOLOGY INDUSTRY

In 1998, Taiwan's hardware information technology industry (domestic and overseas combined) had a total production value of US$33.8 billion, up 11.9 percent from US$30 billion of the previous year, making it the ROC's most important foreign exchange earner. Taiwan has been the world's third-largest computer hardware supplier since 1995, trailing only the United States and Japan. Taiwan's 900 computer hardware manufacturers provide jobs for approximately 100,000 employees. In 1998, laptop computers, monitors, desktop PCs, and motherboards accounted for about 80 percent of the production value of the information technology industry. Taiwan manufacturers have a large share of the world market because of their competitive prices and high quality. According to statistics released by the Institute for Information Industry ,

Taiwan has already supplanted Singapore to become Japan's second largest supplier of information products, second only to the United States.Amid the generally lackluster performance of the domestic economy, Taiwan's hardware information technology industry still managed to register significant growth. This can be attributed to many factors, including the rapid growth of Internet use around the world, the increased popularity of multimedia computers, and the expansion of production by local PC manufacturers. Taiwan's information technology industry has grown from a minor role in the overall economy to a major contributor to the island's flourishing exports. This is partly a result of governmental inducements and partly because of the extreme flexibility of domestic small and medium-sized enterprises. This flexibility possessed by Taiwan's SMEs allows them to quickly follow and adapt to the latest market trends, and adjust their production accordingly. Nevertheless, the industry still faces problems that are common to all manufacturing sectors: labor shortages and high overhead costs.

The structure of Taiwan's information technology industry is best described as a pyramid. A handful of companies at the top of the pyramid commit themselves to product innovation through costly and time-consuming R&D (see Chapter 18, Science and Technology), while small and medium-sized enterprises at the base of the pyramid form the vast majority (85 percent) of the actual output. The latter comprise a weak and unstable downstream foundation. As in other manufacturing sectors, SMEs generally produce goods on an OEM (original equipment manufacturer) and ODM (original design manufacturer) basis, and therefore spend a negligible percentage of their annual turnover on R&D. This has led to the inability of these companies to make in-depth assessments regarding investment, production, and marketing of new and innovative products. Moreover, heavy reliance upon the imports of key parts and advanced technology from the United States and Japan has tied Taiwan's information technology industry to the economic strength of these countries, thereby offsetting a good portion of Taiwan's trade surplus each year.

AUTOMOBILE INDUSTRY

Taiwan is currently home to 13 automobile manufacturers, the majority of which have contractual joint ventures with foreign makers, mostly from Japan. These companies both produce and import automobiles. The production value of the automotive industry reached US$9.93 billion in 1998, the equivalent to 5.08 percent of Taiwan's aggregate manufacturing production value of that year. Approximately 402,000 automobiles were produced in Taiwan in 1998.

Due to limited parking space and the operation of several mass rapid transit system lines in urban districts, total automobile demand in Taiwan dropped from 542,000 units sold in 1995 to approximately 476,000 in 1998. Sedans for private use continued to dominate the demand, accounting for nearly 80 percent. Whereas the number of domestically made sedans sold in 1998 rose 7 percent to reach 292,000 units, the number of imported units fell 7 percent from the previous year. Domestically-made vans for commercial use accounted for about 94 percent of the market. Over the last couple of years, competition between locally made and imported vehicles has gradually declined and a 4:1 market share ratio has taken shape. In 1998, the domestic automobile industry, threatened by the imports from Japan and the U.S., still managed to capture around 84 percent of the market, proving that the quality of the MIT automobile has been accepted by local consumers.

In 1998, over 70 percent of the 292,000 domestically made sedans were supplied by three companies: Ford Lio Ho Motor Co., Ltd. (20.3 percent), Yulon Motor Co., Ltd. (28.6 percent), and Kuozui Motors Ltd. (22.4 percent). In the commercial vehicle market, China Motor Corporation maintained its traditional top position, producing over 50 percent of the 115,700 commercial vehicles sold.

Although the ROC imposes a quota on autos imported directly from Japan, Japanese vehicles have, like many other commercial products, successfully penetrated the Taiwan market and built a solid customer base. In 1998, nearly a quarter of the imported vans were Japanese brands that had been made in American factories. Toyota alone took 21 percent of the Taiwan market share of imported sedans. Of the top ten best sellers in the Taiwan market, all were either products of Sino-Japanese joint ventures, or they directly carried Japanese brand names. Domestic automobile manufacturers have long worried that once Taiwan's door for imported cars is officially opened with reduced tariffs (from the current 30 percent down to 20 percent), or once

Taiwan is admitted into the WTO, foreign vehicles will flood the market and threaten the survival of domestic manufacturers.

Like many other domestic industries, Taiwan's automobile industry, with decades of government protection, is short on R&D. It needs to develop its own technology in engines, computerized gearing systems, and several other components, and enhance its design capability. For example, Taiwan's reliance on foreign engines has for years hampered its plans to export vehicles. Consequently, in preparation for the impact that the ROC's admission to the WTO will have on the island's automobile industry, the Ministry of Economic Affairs has already begun to allocate budget resources to encourage R&D. Under the joint efforts of the MOEA, the Chungshan Institute of Science and Technology , and the private sector, the government will upgrade local automobile manufacturers' capabilities to produce key parts, such as engines and airbags, that would otherwise have to be imported from Japan.

TEXTILES

In the past five decades, Taiwan has successfully developed from an agricultural backwater to an industrialized nation. During this process, the textile industry has been one of the most important factors in Taiwan's economic growth. Comprised primarily of small, family-run businesses, the textile industry was a key element in the government's export-oriented policy. It occupied an eminent place in exports, earning large amounts of foreign exchange for the nation.

Since the second half of the 1980s, several problems, including the sharp appreciation of the NT dollar, labor shortages, increasing overhead costs, prohibitive land prices, and the environmental protection, forced textile businesses to relocate part or even all of their production to Southeast Asia and the Chinese mainland in order to maintain their competitiveness. Textiles have been dubbed one of Taiwan's labor-intensive "sunset industries." Those textile companies which have stayed in Taiwan have initiated reforms. Small, family-run businesses have been transformed into medium-sized or even large enterprises, with cost-effective measures and innovative management, introduced to raise quality and productivity. Since Taiwan is not blessed with cotton, wool, silk, linen and other natural raw materials, the domestic textile industry has developed man-made fabrics, which have proven to be an excellent alternative to natural products.

Today, Taiwan's man-made fibers have earned a prominent place in the textile industry throughout the world. In 1998, Taiwan produced over 3.2 million tons of man-made fiber, ranking third in the world. Polyester was 80 percent of the total output and placed Taiwan as the world's largest producer of this fiber. In that same year, Taiwan exported and imported over US$17.7 billion worth of textiles, including fiber, yarn, fabric, garments, and accessories. Hong Kong was the primary destination for Taiwan's textile exports, followed by the US and ASEAN. The industry has also been one of Taiwan's prime contributors to its favorable trade balance, accounting for nearly US$11.4 billion of the nation's surplus in 1998.

PETROCHEMICALS

Taiwan's petrochemical industry integrates 45 upper- and middle-stream manufacturers located in Kaohsiung's special chemical zone. In 1998, the industry had a production value of US$11.3 billion (excluding textile and plastics-related industries), of which 82 percent is sold on the domestic market. However, Taiwan's petrochemical production capacity (as measured by ethylene output) could only satisfy about 53 percent of actual domestic demand in 1998; therefore, the Formosa Plastics Group (FPG) , a renowned plastics conglomerate in Taiwan, applied for government approval to build a sixth naphtha cracking plant . The company launched the project several years ago in Yunlin County's Mailiao. The mammoth project was built in an industrial zone that encompasses a total of 39 plants, including an oil refinery, naphtha cracking plant, cogeneration plant, coal-fired power plant, heavy machinery plant, boiler plant, wafer fabrication plant, and petrochemical-related plants. It is noteworthy that this industrial zone of 2,100 hectares of land area is reclaimed land, a great portion of which lies below sea level.

The FPG began its initial operations in the industrial zone at the end of 1998 and is expected to produce 450 thousand tons of ethylene annually. When the US$8.7 billion project is completed, it is est. that Taiwan's ethylene self-sufficiency will jump to 79 percent.

SMES

For decades, Small and Medium-sized Enterprises (SMEs) have been the backbone of the ROC's economic development. Unlike many advanced nations, where conglomerates dominate the economy, Taiwan's manufacturing and foreign trade is built up and fortified by countless SMEs.

SMEs began emerging after World War II, when Japanese conglomerates withdrew from Taiwan and the local market fell into the hands of state-run enterprises and large private companies. The island's SMEs focused on foreign markets to survive. At first, agricultural products and agricultural processed goods made up the bulk of exported items. These were eventually replaced by light industrial products, especially after the government set up several export-processing zones to spur on the economy. An export-oriented policy in the 1960s also created a favorable environment for SMEs to penetrate international markets. SME entrepreneurs are characterized by high adaptability to market trends, hard work, thrift, and a tendency to pass their businesses on to their children. According to the Ministry of Economic Affairs, over 98 percent of Taiwan's 1,024,435 registered enterprises are SMEs. These SMEs employ nearly 80 percent of the total work force and account for half of the island's aggregate export value.

The 1995 revision to the *Small and Medium-sized Enterprise Development Statute* defines small and medium-sized enterprises by sector, paid-in capital/annual turnover, and the number of employees. Industries, including manufacturing, construction, and mining and quarrying, that have a paid-in capital not exceeding NT$60 million (an equivalent of US$1.76 million) or hire less than 200 regular workers, are categorized as SMEs. Companies in the commercial, service, and transportation sectors with an annual turnover not exceeding NT$80 million (an equivalent of US$2.35 million) or that hire less than 50 employees are also considered SMEs. Most SMEs (60 percent) are in the commercial sector, followed by manufacturing (15 percent).

In terms of sales turnover, commercial sector accounted for over 43 percent of SME aggregate turnover, while the manufacturing took up 35 percent in 1997. The two, though distinguished by sector, are complementary in that many SMEs in the commercial sector rely on manufacturers to supply goods. At the same time, a large number of manufacturers also work closely with trading companies to export products.

For decades, Taiwan has been an Asian production outpost for many renowned multinational conglomerates, proof that Taiwan can produce high-quality goods. Today, made-in-Taiwan products, ranging from packaging to toys and from garments to personal computers, are found in shops around the world. A large number of Taiwan's SMEs still rely heavily on OEM and ODM orders, tending to avoid relatively long-term investments and investments in R&D. On average, SMEs spend no more than 3 percent of their annual operating income on R&D, mainly because these companies are reluctant to invest in arduous processes that have no guarantee of successful results. Another factor that influences SME's willingness to invest lies in their difficulty in acquiring bank loans. Although banks generally consider many SMEs financially unstable, they still provide 34 percent of the capital resources for SMEs. Roughly 82 percent of SME funding for

R&D projects comes from the companies themselves, while only 11 percent comes from bank loans.

Nevertheless, SMEs constitute a large portion of Taiwan's investment overseas as the ROC has emerged to become a major investor worldwide. During the pioneering stage, most SMEs tended to invest in the Chinese mainland or in other Southeast Asian nations due to their proximity, with funds that usually did not exceed US$2 million. This has changed in the last couple of years, however, with access to the market and convenient service becoming the two primary factors concerning SMEs in their attempt to consolidate or even expand their post in the world market.

Due to the worldwide economic slump, Taiwan's SMEs have encountered many hardships in exporting goods. A shortage of laborers, increases in wages, and prohibitive prices for land acquisition have also plagued both large-scale firms and SMEs. Fluctuating exchange rates and keen competition from other nations are other major factors that have directly impacted SME operations.

In light of the continuing importance of SMEs in Taiwan's overall economy, the government has made five revisions to the *Small and Medium-sized Enterprise Guidance Regulations* , first stipulated in 1967. The revisions are geared to create a sounder environment for SMEs to increase productivity. Other government measures to assist SMEs include a development fund that provides assistance in case of recession and indemnification for damages caused by natural disasters as well as programs to promote automation and computerization. In addition, seminars to cultivate marketing and managerial expertise have been held, and the functions of the SME service centers located in 22 cities and counties around the island have been strengthened.

ENERGY

Taiwan lacks sufficient energy resources. Its coal reserves amount to only 98 million tons, most of which are distributed throughout the northern part of the island. Oil and natural gas reserves, found mostly in the northern Taiwan counties of Hsinchu and Miaoli, and near the southern city of Kaohsiung, total 0.4 million tons and 2,400 billion cubic feet, respectively. Total hydropower reserves have been est. at 5,047 megawatts, of which 1,973 megawatts have been developed, primarily along several major rivers. Given such limited natural resources, Taiwan must import fossil fuels to meet the bulk of its energy needs.

SUPPLY

The total energy supply in Taiwan increased from 29 million kiloliters of oil equivalent in 1978 to 92 million kiloliters in 1998, with an average annual growth of 6 percent. Over the past two decades, local energy supplies have accounted for a progressively smaller portion of annual usage, dropping from 19 percent in 1978 to 4 percent in 1998; therefore, the imported energy share has had to rise correspondingly. Of the total energy supply, oil accounted for 51 percent and nuclear power accounted for 10 percent.

Expenditures for imported energy totaled US$6.4 billion in 1998, of which imported oil accounted for 66 percent or US$4.2 billion. Imported energy accounted for 6.1 percent of the total value of imports in 1998 and 2.4 percent of GDP, with per capita energy imports at US$293.

CONSUMPTION

Taiwan's annual energy consumption increased from 25 million kiloliters of oil equivalent in 1978 to 81 million kiloliters in 1998, an average growth rate of 6.1 percent per year. By comparison, GDP grew by an average of 7.3 percent during the same period, with an energy demand elasticity of about 0.84. Per capita energy consumption increased from 1,456 liters of oil equivalent in 1978 to 3,725 liters in 1998, an annual growth rate of 4.8 percent.

Over the past 20 years, the industrial sector has been the greatest energy consumer; however, its share of total energy consumption dropped from 65 percent in 1978 to 55 percent in 1998. Energy consumption for transportation increased from 11 percent in 1978 to 17 percent in 1998; for agriculture, it declined from 3 percent to 2 percent; for residential use, it increased from 10 percent to 12 percent; for commercial use, it increased from 2 percent to 6 percent; for other sectors, it dropped from 7 percent to 6 percent. Non-energy use was close to 2 percent in 1998.

Since the second worldwide energy crisis, coal has accounted for a growing percentage of Taiwan's overall energy consumption, rising from 10 percent in 1978 to 12 percent in 1998. By contrast, petroleum products accounted for only 39 percent of overall energy consumption in 1998, down from 49 percent in 1978.

OIL AND NATURAL GAS

Taiwan is heavily dependent on imported oil. In 1998, approximately 62 percent of imported crude oil came from the Middle East. The other 38 percent came from Indonesia, the Congo, and Australia. Consumption of petroleum products totaled 38.8 million kiloliters of oil equivalent in 1998, of which 33 percent was for industrial use, 35 percent for transportation, 18 percent for power generation, 2 percent for agriculture, 4 percent for residential use, and 8 percent for other purposes.

The state-owned Chinese Petroleum Corporation (CPC) is solely responsible for exploring, producing, importing, refining, and marketing petroleum and natural gas in Taiwan. The CPC owns two oil refineries with a total capacity of 770,000 barrels per day and recently has made considerable investment to increase the output of low-sulfur fuel oil to improve air quality.

In 1987, the government began allowing the installation of privately operated gas stations to sell gasoline and diesel oil. At the end of 1998, there were 1,720 gas stations, 1,146 (67 percent) of which were privately owned. In 1998, domestic petroleum production amounted to 38.6 million kiloliters of oil equivalent and 879 million cubic meters of gas, respectively.

To liberalize the oil market, the government authorized the establishment of petroleum refining enterprises and granted them permission to engage in petroleum production, import/export, and marketing in June 1996. The importation of fuel oil, jet fuel, and LPG was opened in January 2005, and the complete opening of petroleum products imports is expected by the end of June 2000.

To diversify the types of energy consumed, the CPC has imported 1.5 million tons of liquefied natural gas (LNG) from Indonesia every year since 1990, and, beginning in 2011, the quantity will increase to 1.84 million tons under a new contract. The CPC also started importing 0.5 million tons of LNG from Malaysia in 1995. This amount is expected to increase to 2.35 million tons at the beginning of the next century. Natural gas consumption in 1998 totaled 5,869 million cubic meters, of which 31 percent was for industrial use, 54 percent for power generation, 12 percent for residential use, and 3 percent for commercial use.

COAL

Coal production continued to decline, dropping from five million tons in 1968 down to 0.08 million tons in 1998. The local coal industry was once the prime source of energy, constituting over 60 percent of industrial energy use in the 1950s, and employing some 65,000 coal miners in over 400 mines around the island. Due to the high costs of coal production under increasingly difficult mining conditions, as well as competition from imported coal, the number of coal mines and miners in Taiwan has decreased dramatically. Today, there are 3 coal mines in Taiwan which employ approximately 300 workers. Tougher times lie ahead for the industry, as the younger generation look for white collar occupations. In addition, once the ROC is admitted into the World Trade Organization, the government must annul rules that protect local coal production. Subsequently, the remaining coal mines will most likely be forced to close within five years.

Coal supply totaled 37 million tons in 1998. Of this, 0.2 percent was domestically produced, while the remaining 99.8 percent was imported from Australia, Indonesia, South Africa, the Chinese mainland, and the United States. In 1998, some 58 percent of the total coal consumption of 21 million tons went to power generation, 5 percent to the cement industry, 15 percent to steelworks, and 22 percent to other industries and users.

ELECTRICITY

In 1998, gross power generation by the Taiwan Power Company(Taipower), totaled 145 billion KWH, a 8.6 percent increase over 1997. Of the total, 7.3 percent was generated by hydropower, 39.8 percent by coal, 18 percent by oil, 9.6 percent by LNG, and the remaining 25.2 percent by nuclear fission. Power cogeneration by auto producers totaled 17.9 billion KWH in 1998. Electricity consumption in 1998 rose to 146.8 billion KWH, up 6.5 percent over the preceding year. At present, nearly all of the population has electricity service.

Taiwan Power Company is the agency responsible for developing, generating, supplying, and marketing electric power for almost the entire Taiwan area. By the end of 1998, the Taiwan area had 16 EHV substations (345/161 KV), with a capacity of 25,500 MVA; 88 primary substations (161/69 KV), with a capacity of 32,724 MVA; and 44 primary distribution substations (161/22-11 KV), with a capacity of 8,464 MVA. A total of 39 hydropower, 18 thermal, and three nuclear plants supply power to these stations. Taipower installed capacity totaled 26,680 megawatts, of which 16.6 percent was hydropower, 30.4 percent coal-fired, 14.7 percent gas-fired, 19.1 percent oil-fired, and 19.3 percent nuclear. By the end of l998, the installed capacity of auto producer cogeneration was 2,865 megawatts, equivalent to 11 percent of Taipower's installed capacity.

With the continuous growth of the domestic economy, the peak load in 1998 reached 23,830 MW, up 7.2 percent over 1997. The average load was 15,904 MW, a 8.7 percent increase compared with the previous year. Facing an increasing requirement for power supplies, the government has already taken several steps to alleviate future potential shortages. In September 1994, the government promulgated the Guidelines for the Opening of the Independent Power Generation Industry to encourage private sector power production. By the end of 1998, eight applications for independent power plants had been approved . Also in 1998, units five, six, seven, and eight of the Taichung Thermal Power Plant , unit five of the New Tienlun Hydro Power Plant , and five units of combined cycle at the Hsinta Power Plant were all put into operation, generating an additional 1,900 megawatts.

In June 2005, Mailiao Power Corp., located in the Yunlin County naphtha cracker complex established by the Formosa Plastics Group, began its initial commercial operations, with a power generating capacity of 1,200 megawatts. The new independent power plant is expected to alleviate the island's power shortage during the summer time. In addition, companies operating at the Hsinchu Science-based Industrial Park (HSBIP) suffered a loss of over US$0.3 billion due to the power outage resulting from the devastating September 21 earthquake in 2005.

Consequently, the government instructed the Science-based Industrial Park Administration to construct a second cogenerator in HSBIP to supply electricity to the park.

NUCLEAR POWER

The six nuclear units in Taiwan provided 17 percent of the total installed capacity (5,144 megawatts out of 29,545 megawatts), but produced 22.4 percent of Taiwan's total electrical output in 1998. The six nuclear units are housed in three nuclear power stations, all of which are owned and operated by Taipower. With increasing demands for electricity, especially for industrial use, the government began plans to construct a fourth nuclear power plant in 1980. Support for the project has been slowly undermined, however, by the general public's environmental concerns and increasingly vehement protests against nuclear power. These protests have generated negative votes against the budget for the power plant, especially by legislators representing constituencies where the plant is slated to be built. In December 1997, the Legislative Yuan approved a proposal by opposition parties to eliminate US$2.12 million from Taipower's budget as a feedback fund for its construction of the fourth nuclear power plant, which is scheduled to be completed in 2004.

RENEWABLE ENERGY SOURCES

Taiwan's subtropical location gives it great potential to develop solar energy resources. A number of solar, thermal, and photovoltaic testing systems are already in service in Taiwan, with the total area of solar collectors reaching 800,000 square meters at the end of 1998. In addition, two 100-kilowatt wind turbines are presently in service on Chimei Island in the Pescadore Islands. Technologies for biogas purification and the assembly of biogas power generators have been investigated over the last decade, and a number of pig farms already have biogas power generators in operation. In 1998, these generators produced 6 megawatts.

ENERGY PRICES

The price structure for electrical power is configured to reflect the cost of supplying energy at different seasons (seasonal rates) and different times of the day (TOU rates). Seasonal rates and TOU rates are designed to encourage peak clipping, valley filling, and/or load shifting. Currently, the electrical service is divided into three categories: lighting, combined lighting and power, and power (metered and flat-rated). Seasonal rates are applied to all customer classes except flat-rated customers. TOU rates are mandatory for those with a contracted capacity of 100 KW and are voluntary for those with a contracted capacity below 100 KW. At present, TOU rates are applied to all customer classes except lighting customers.

Low-tension metered lighting service is applicable to residential as well as small commercial and noncommercial customers. Charges for metered lighting service are calculated solely upon the KWH consumed. Low tension combined lighting and power service is applicable to medium commercial and noncommercial customers. Low tension metered power service is applicable to small and medium-sized industrial/agricultural customers. High or extra-high tension service is applicable to customers with a contracted capacity of around 100 KW. Charges for power service and combined lighting and power service are separated into demand charge and energy charge (a two-part rate). Demand charge is billed on the contracted KW, and energy charge is calculated according to the KWH consumed.

In order to reduce the summer peak load directly, Taipower also offers a menu of interruptible rates (seven options) on a voluntary basis to customers taking high or extra-high tension service. Interruptible rates are designed to reflect capacity cost savings for customers' interruptible loads. The rates require that customers reduce their peak demand to a predetermined level in accordance with the contract in return for demand credits. The latest rate schedules for electrical service came into effect on June 1, 1995.

Domestic oil prices have been allowed to reflect the cost of imported oil as world prices fluctuate. The government also routinely considers the substitutability and heating values of petroleum products and natural gas before setting their prices. In November 2005, the Chinese Petroleum Corporation adjusted its prices for petroleum products in accordance with an oil-price formula. Oil prices were as follows: US$0.57 per liter for most tanked premium gasoline, US$0.56 for 95-octane unleaded gasoline, US$0.53 for 92-octane unleaded gasoline, US$0.41 for premium diesel oil, and US$0.37 for kerosene.

ENERGY CONSERVATION

Energy conservation is a major part of energy policy. The Measures for Energy Conservation and the Energy Management Law mandate a set of incentives for energy customers to conserve energy. So far, energy productivity has risen from US$2.69 per kg of oil equivalent in 1978 to US$3.38 in 1998.

FINANCE AND BANKING

The Asian financial crisis continued to trouble the Republic of China's financial markets during 1998, as an outbreak of defaults among some listed domestic firms dampened domestic economic prospects. The Taiwan Stock Exchange composite index, which rose to 9,300 points in February 1998, took a drastic plunge that pushed it below the 7,000 mark. Meanwhile, the New Taiwan dollar depreciated to an 11-year low against the US dollar, at one point reaching an exchange rate of NT$35:US$1. Imports and exports continued to decrease while overseas orders placed in terms of US dollars also declined in 1998. Beginning in the second half of 1998, several listed corporations defaulted on loans, as a result of highly leveraged stock speculation. All of these developments were strong indicators that the Asian financial crisis had taken its toll on the ROC.

The year 1998 was not without its bright side, however. The ROC government continued its plans to participate in the World Trade Organization and develop Taiwan into a major financial center for the Asia-Pacific region. Agreements were reached with the United States to accelerate the opening of domestic banking, insurance, and securities markets. On July 21, 1998, a new milestone was set in the financial market, when Taiwan International Mercantile Exchange inaugurated stock futures trading, targeted on the weighted index of the spot market. Furthermore, the long-delayed plans to privatize three government-owned commercial banks were finally completed, further liberalizing Taiwan's financial sector.

The average exchange rate used is as follows: US$1:NT$28.7 for the year 1997 and US$1:NT$33.46 for 1998. As for the fiscal year 1997 (from July 1, 1996 to June 30, 1997), an average rate of US$1:NT$25.57 is used. For the fiscal year 1998 (from July 1, 1997 to June 30, 1998), an average rate of US$1:NT$31.56 is used.

PUBLIC FINANCE

GOVERNMENT EXPENDITURES

In FY1998, government expenditures were down 6.9 percent from the FY1997 level of US$74.96 billion to US$69.82 billion. The decrease was mainly due to the devaluation of the NT dollar. In terms of the NT dollar, government expenditures actually increased 6.6 percent from NT$2.067 trillion in FY1997 to NT$2.204 trillion in FY1998. (To avoid confusion resulting from currency fluctuations, the following analysis regarding government expenditures and revenues will be based on the NT dollar as the unit of calculation unless otherwise indicated.)

With the exception of spending on social welfare, the increase in government expenditures occurred across-the-board, with expenditures for economic development registering the second highest growth at 13.2 percent, following miscellaneous expenditures. Current expenditures at all levels of government also rose by 5.6 percent to reach NT$1.545 trillion, while capital expenditures climbed 9.2 percent to NT$658.6 billion.

A breakdown of the FY1998 government expenditures showed that spending on social welfare fell 4.1 percent to NT$282.8 billion compared to the previous year. This decrease reflected a change in policy priorities during the financial crisis. Funding for education, science, and culture--which accounted for 18.7 percent of total government spending in FY1998--rose 9.5 percent from FY1997 to reach NT$411.5 billion. Spending on general administration and national defense also increased 5.1 percent and 7 percent in FY1998 to reach NT$257.3 billion and NT$312.3 billion, respectively. Spending on community development and the environment climbed 9.1 percent in FY1998 to reach NT$74.9 billion; while spending on pension and survivors' benefits increased 4.4 percent to reach NT$187.7 billion. Finally, the figure for debt obligations was up 8 percent from FY1997 to NT$328.0 billion.

GOVERNMENT REVENUES

With increases in revenues from surpluses of public enterprises, profits of public properties, and taxes levied, the total revenue for all levels of government jumped 12.1 percent in FY1998 to reach NT$2.325 trillion. However, revenues from bonds, loans, and monopolies were down. This reflected that governments, as a whole, were somewhat limited in issuing new bonds, given its current debt status.

Revenues from taxes, which accounted for 57.6 percent of government revenues, increased 10.4 percent in FY1998 to reach NT$1.34 trillion. Surpluses from public enterprises and public utilities showed a large increase of 90.5 percent from the previous year to hit NT$361.6 billion, while profits of public properties also rose 114.4 percent to NT$42 billion. Revenues from fees, fines and indemnities, donations and contributions, proceeds from sales of properties, and recalled capital all increased to a lesser extent in FY1998. However, revenues from monopolies declined 1.3 percent from FY1997 to reach NT$57.4 billion. Proceeds from issues of public debts and receipts from loans for economic construction also fell 56 percent and 11.9 percent, reaching NT$59.9 billion and NT$176.3 billion, respectively.

DEBT OBLIGATIONS

In contrast to the deficit that occurred in FY1997, all levels of government actually managed to maintain a surplus of NT$121.7 billion in FY1998--a result of the government's determination to cut the fiscal deficit and the delay of infrastructure projects.

FINANCIAL MARKET ABD BANKING

MONEY SUPPLY

In the first half of 1998, the economy was feeling the impact of the Asian financial crisis as exports started to fall. However, active trading in the Taiwan Stock Exchange saw the growth rate of the widely defined money supply aggregate M2 fall from 9.37 percent in January to 8.13 percent in March, and then rebound to 8.45 percent in May.

Beginning in the second quarter, however, the economy declined further and caused the demand for capital to decline. Trading in stock markets also decreased. In addition, the NT dollar began to depreciate against the US dollar. To mitigate the speed of depreciation, the Central Bank of China (CBC) sold US dollars to defend the NT dollar. As a result, the growth rate of the M2 dropped to 7.76 percent in June, the lowest monthly growth figure of the year.

This decline was amplified by an outflow of capital. The financial account in the Balance of Payments recorded a net outflow of US$1.3 billion in the second quarter and a further net outflow of US$3.7 billion in the third quarter.

The annual growth rate of the M2 probably would have continued to fall had the CBC not intervened. On August 2, the CBC lowered the required reserve ratio for banks, thus injecting NT$46.7 billion into the economy. On September 28, the CBC again lowered the required reserve ratio to release another NT$36.1 billion. The CBC also cut the rediscount rate from 5.25 percent to 5.125 percent and the prime rate for secured loans from 5.625 percent to 5.5 percent.

These relaxed monetary measures produced the desired effect and boosted the growth rate of the M2 to 9.82 percent in October and attained an overall average growth rate of 8.76 percent for 1998. This average was slightly higher than the 8.26 percent of 1997 and was well within the target zone of 6 to 12 percent set up by the CBC for the annual growth rate of the M2. In 2005, the supply of the M2 returned to a steady rate of growth, rising from 7.37 percent in January to 9.32 percent in May.

The growth rate of the narrowly defined money supply aggregate M1b, on the other hand, continued to fall throughout most of 1998--mainly because of the boom-and-bust performance of the stock market, which caused individuals to switch from demand deposits to time deposits. The M1b declined from a peak of 11.52 percent in January to 2.64 percent in August, and then rose again to 2.87 percent in December. The average growth rate of the M1b was 2.58 percent in 1998, well below the 13.82 percent reached in 1997.

Despite lagging trends in 1998, a rejuvenated stock market helped the M1b growth rate to increase sharply in 2005 from 0.33 percent in January to 9.23 percent in May. The 9.23 percent growth rate was above the median of the target zone, and the CBC therefore adjusted its monetary policy stance from expansionary to neutral.

FINANCIAL INSTITUTIONS

By the end of December 1998, the number of financial institutions in Taiwan, including monetary institutions and the Postal Savings System, had decreased by eight from the previous year to reach a total of 499. The reduction of institutions included one new local branch of a foreign bank and three new domestic banks formed either from the combining of credit cooperatives or from the merging of credit cooperatives with existing banks. In addition, the long-delayed plans to privatize three large commercial banks owned by the Taiwan Provincial Government were finally completed in the first half of 1998.

The first half of 1998 witnessed a continuing slowdown in Taiwan's economy. The annual growth rate of loans granted by major financial institutions remained on the decline, dropping from 13.32 percent at the beginning of 1998 to 5.34 percent by the end of 1998. It finally reached 2.9 percent in January 2005--a record low since October 1996--before slowly climbing back up to 5.22 percent in May 2005. On the other hand, the growth rate for portfolio investments increased from 13.13 percent in January 1998 to an annual high of 42.11 percent in September 1998. This was a result of efforts by the Ministry of Finance (MOF) to encourage banks to buy stocks in order to prevent the weighted index from further sliding. After the stock market recovered in March 2005, the monthly growth rate hit 15.85 percent in May 2005.

The non-performing loan ratio for domestic financial institutions rose from 4.16 percent in March 1998 to 5.1 percent in March 2005. This reflected the continued sluggishness of Taiwan's economy and the poor performance of the real estate market. In May 2005, the CBC announced six measures to reduce the non-performing loan ratio for domestic financial institutions; and as stock markets started to recover in the second quarter of 2005, the non-performing loan ratio for domestic financial institutions decreased.

MONEY MARKETS

The money market became an important source of short-term capital for companies. Both transactions in the interbank call-loan market and in short-term bills expanded rapidly. During 1998, transactions worth a total of NT$14.598 trillion were completed in the interbank call-loan market, up 31.8 percent from 1997. Short-term bills valued at NT$13.691 trillion were issued in 1998, representing a 20.6 percent increase over 1997, and the outstanding balance on short-term bills was up 16.8 percent to NT$2.386 trillion. Transactions in short-term bills were 37 percent higher than in 1997, reaching NT$85.071 trillion in 1998. Commercial paper accounted for the majority of those transactions, taking a lion's share of 92.2 percent.

In the first half of 1998, active trading on the Taiwan Stock Exchange and the CBC's moderate stabilization operations kept interest rates stable. This trend continued in the second half of the year, when Taiwan's economy appeared to deteriorate and the CBC moderately relaxed its monetary policy. With the CBC's double reduction of the required reserve ratio and the steady growth of money supply, short-term interest rates declined substantially. The annual average interest rate for the overnight call-loan market was 6.56 percent, down from 6.85 percent in 1997. The weighted average of 31 to 90-day Commercial Paper (CP) rates in the secondary market also declined from 6.83 percent in 1997 to 6.81 percent in 1998.

BOND MARKETS

As a result of decreases in the government deficit and a slowdown of infrastructure projects, the primary bond market saw a sharp decline with the issuance of a mere NT$146 billion worth of bonds (excluding treasury bills) in 1998, down from the NT$174 billion issued in 1997. As a result, the outstanding balance for bonds issued by all levels of government was only NT$1.044 trillion, a slight increase of 0.88 percent from the previous year. On the other hand, corporate bonds issued by private enterprises rose 93.9 percent from 1997 to US$6.45 billion in 1998, due to heavy trading on the Taiwan stock market, the outbreak of the Asian financial crisis, and a drop in short-term interest rates. In December 1998, the outstanding balance for corporate bonds was US$14.11 billion, an increase of 62.1 percent over 1997.

Transactions in the secondary bond market recorded an all-time high in 1998, with US$1.642 trillion worth of securities changing hands to attain a 36.1 percent increase over 1997. The main factors contributing to this development included the sluggish economy, the weak performance of the stock markets, the loose monetary policies implemented by the CBC to keep interest rates low, and an increase in repurchase (repo) and short-term bond transactions. Repo transactions, up 26.6 percent from 1997, made up the largest portion of these factors, accounting for US$1.430 trillion.

INTEREST RATES

The money supply in the first half of 1998 was relatively loose and remained so throughout the second half of the year, primarily because of the weakened economy and the depreciation of the NT dollar against the US dollar. In order to stabilize the foreign exchange market and avoid further slides in the stock market, the CBC lowered the rediscount rate three times from 5.25 percent to 4.75 percent. In addition, the prime lending rate for major commercial banks was lowered from 7.955 percent in the first half of the year to 7.704 percent in December 1998.

FOREIGN EXCHANGE MARKET

The New Taiwan dollar remained stable in the first half of 1998, suffered a moderate devaluation against the US dollar in the middle of the year, and gradually appreciated in the latter half. The average exchange rates were NT$33.04:US$1 and NT$33.63:US$1 in the first two quarters of 1998, dropping to NT$34.54: US$1 in the third quarter. This devaluation was mainly due to a sharp depreciation in the Japanese yen and the CBC's decision to float the NT dollar. On June 10, 1998, the foreign exchange rate fell below the NT$35:US$1 mark to reach an 11-year low. It finally bottomed out following strong defensive actions by the CBC and the stabilization of the Japanese yen. In the fourth quarter, the average exchange rate of the NT dollar rose to NT$32.61:US$1. The annual average exchange rate for the year was NT$33.44: US$1, a depreciation of 16.68 percent compared to 1997.

In order to prevent speculation in the foreign exchange market and alleviate devaluation pressure on the NT dollar, three measures were implemented by the CBC toward the end of May 1998. These measures included bans on nondelivery forward trading (NDF) by domestic firms, margin trading on behalf of clients through joint accounts by authorized foreign exchange banks, and foreign exchange rate swaps among individual investors.

Foreign exchange transactions declined slightly in 1998, with net transactions at authorized foreign exchange banks and local branches of foreign financial institutions at US$1.169 trillion, down 1.5 percent from 1997. Spot transactions were the most popular, accounting for 63.8 percent of total foreign exchange transactions. Following spot transactions were foreign exchange rate swaps at 14.2 percent, margin trading at 9.4 percent, forward contracts at 8.5 percent, and options contracts at 4.1 percent. Compared with 1997, however, options contracts showed the most substantial growth, increasing by 78.7 percent. This was due to the high volatility of the NT dollar against the US dollar caused by the Asian financial crisis and the tumult on Wall Street following the Long-Term Capital Management Company (LTCM) crisis.

STOCK MARKET

The Taiwan Stock Exchange (TSE) started on a brisk note in 1998 before gradually slowing down for the rest of the year. Recovering Asian economies and the subsequent appreciation of their currencies, a booming US stock market, and the high dividend policies announced by Taiwan's listed electronics companies all pushed the TSE composite index from 8,085 points on January 22 to 9,277 points on March 2. The index reached a high of 9,300 in April, but then gradually dropped to below 7,000 in mid-June. This boom-and-bust performance was attributable to many factors: the weaker profits of hi-tech US stocks, disappointing movements in the prices of Taiwan's listed stocks after dividend payments were made to shareholders, a higher number of purchases on margin, continued financial instability in East Asia, growing pressure for further devaluation of the NT dollar, and a deterioration in the external trade sector in the first quarter of 1998. With the exception of a short-term boost in July due to the opening of the Taiwan Stock Index futures market and the record-breaking Dow Jones Industrial Average, the TSE composite index continued to gradually fall for the rest of the year, eventually hitting 6,418 points at the end of 1998.

To stabilize the stock market and restore investors' confidence, the MOF announced five measures on November 13: establishing an ad hoc fund to stabilize the market; encouraging financial institutions to buy stocks when necessary; temporarily halting the trading of stocks owned by troubled firms; investigating rumors unfavorable to the market; and punishing those who engaged in illegal activities that placed firms in financial disorder.

The TSE composite index continued its downward trend in 2005, hitting a low of 5,400 points in February. However, it has since rebounded quite strongly due to the recovery of the global economy, Taiwan's strong export performance, and the continuous inflow of foreign capital. By June, the TSE had increased 60 percent from its low point in February to reach 8,600 points.

The total trading value of the market was US$885.2 billion in 1998, a decrease of 20.5 percent from 1997. Even though the number of listed companies increased from 404 in 1997 to 437 in 1998, the total market value reached only US$250.4 billion, down 13.6 percent from 1997.

FINANCIAL RESTRUCTURING

The ROC economy grew at a phenomenal pace throughout the 1970s and 1980s. The rapid accumulation of assets which accompanied this growth led to a tremendous increase in financial activity and brought about profound structural changes in the local financial market. Increasing labor costs and the appreciation of the NT dollar in the 1980s sped up the globalization of Taiwanese capital by encouraging investment and other financial involvements in overseas financial markets. This trend, in turn, exerted competitive pressure on the domestic financial system and forced the ROC to liberalize itself more to attract foreign investors and financial institutions to Taiwan.

The ROC's financial system has been undergoing restructuring since 1987. Among the many changes which have been made is the relaxation of restrictions on cross-border capital flows. Interest rates have also been gradually liberalized, beginning with discount rates on CDs and bank debentures in 1980 and expanding to include deposit interest rates. In 1989, the revised *Banking Law* was passed, lifting all restrictions on interest rates and bringing an end to Taiwan's long history of interest rate controls. In addition, the island has developed its short-term money market and long-term capital market to help meet the requirements of supply and demand, thereby allowing market mechanisms to play a more active role in the financial system.

When the ROC set up its money market in 1975, it was limited to interbank call loans and other short-term monetary instruments. Since then, it has evolved into the second largest money market in Asia with an annual turnover exceeding US$1.6 trillion. The size of the bond market also expanded drastically after 1989 due to the heavy issuance of government bonds for economic development. As for the stock market, the revised *Securities Transaction Law* of 1989 allowed new entries into the brokerage business and loosened restrictions on inward remittances of foreign capital for portfolio investments, thereby making Taiwan's financial markets much more competitive internationally.

Taiwan has strengthened financial re-regulation and supervision in response to changes in the financial environment. The rapid expansion of financial markets; the deregulation of financial activities, financial innovations, and new entries in the financial sector; and the possible disorder associated with financial realignment have all made re-regulation necessary. In line with the Bank of International Settlements, the ROC has set its capital adequacy ratio at 8 percent of risk assets. The government also established the Central Deposit Insurance Corporation in 1987 to provide a better safety net for depository institutions. The *Banking Law* of 1989, while allowing new entrants into the banking industry, also tightened regulations dealing with problem banks. Regulating some areas while deregulating others has been the most important task of financial restructuring in Taiwan.

After a number of runs on local credit cooperatives in the past few years, the CBC and the MOF decided to form a temporary joint committee to monitor all banking institutions. The MOF also made a proposal to revise the *Statute of Deposit Insurance*, requiring all financial institutions to participate in a system of compulsory deposit insurance.

To promote an active market of corporate bonds and to introduce more positive competition among banking institutions, the first credit rating company began its operation in May 1997. With the passage of the *Statute of Futures Trading*, the local futures exchange was opened in October 1997 and the Taiwan International Mercantile Exchange (TAIMEX) was inaugurated in July 1998. As further trading on indexes of electronic and financial stocks are scheduled to open in the near future, firms and individuals will be able to hedge their risks against the volatility of commodity prices, exchange rates, interest rates, and stock prices. Several new financial instruments, including warrant contracts on approved stocks, exchange rate options, and foreign exchange futures, were also listed on the Taiwan Stock Exchange or allowed to be traded over-the-counter in 1997.

In 1998, a few domestic firms inappropriately engaged in the excessive use of high leveraged funds for speculation. This led to financial disruptions and caused the entire economy to suffer a severe setback. To prevent similar events from happening again, the government has proposed a unified supervisory agency to reinforce financial regulation.

Also, consideration is being given to limit the chairman of the board of directors in financial institutions to only those individuals with financial specialty backgrounds, so as to preclude the chairman from taking personal advantage of funds. To improve the quality of bank assets and to allow an accelerated write-off of nonperforming loans, the Ministry of Finance reduced the business tax rate on financial institutions, including securities firms and insurance companies, from 5 percent to 2 percent.

Other important measures passed include revising the regulations on stock holding by subsidiaries and the encouragement of mergers and acquisitions among financial institutions. In the future, Taiwan will continue its liberalization process and employ the newest technology, such as e-commerce, in the financial system, allowing it to adapt more quickly to the challenging and rapidly changing world of finance.

AGRICULTURE

Brilliant green rice paddies set against a misty backdrop of bamboo and bananas, cicadas droning loudly under the heat of the noontime sun--these are the images of old Taiwan, where once over 90 percent of the island's residents lived in farming villages growing rice, sugar cane, tea, jute, and other crops. This picture has rapidly faded in the wake of industrialization, however, and today Taiwan's farmers make up only 8.9 percent of the workforce and produce less than 3 percent of the island's GDP. Farmers in Taiwan are now confronting falling incomes, rising costs, and increased foreign competition, and they are becoming fewer and older as younger generations abandon farming for city life. As Taiwan gears up for entry into the World Trade Organization (WTO), the predicament of farmers is likely to worsen before getting better.

If the sector is to avoid becoming an anachronism on the margins of Taiwan's modern economy, it must completely reinvent itself. The Century-spanning Agricultural Development Plan implemented in July 1997 is designed to serve this purpose for the next four years. In accordance with this plan, the annual growth rate of the GDP for the agricultural industry will be maintained at 0.5 percent; efficient farming operations will be carried out to increase total agricultural production from US$14.95 billion in 1995 to US$18.36 billion in 2011; and the annual income of each farming household will be raised from US$22,655 in 1995 to US$32,727 in 2011. The plan also calls for agricultural agencies to address environmental problems arising from agricultural development. An est. US$12.7 billion will be needed to carry out this plan through the year 2000.

FARMERS

In 1998, there were nearly 859,000 hectares of farmland worked by more than 782,000 farming households, meaning that each household on average tilled a plot of land only 1.1 hectares (2.7 acres) in size. For the past decade, Taiwan farmers have derived over 60 percent of their annual income from non-farming activities. The rise of part-time farming households, which have accounted for over 80 percent of all farming households since 1980, concerns economic planners, who argue that only full-time farmers are likely to divert the capital and training investment needed to develop large and profitable businesses.

Efficient farming is also being hindered by the rapidly aging agrarian workforce. The number of farmers over the age of 65 has increased annually, and in 1998 they accounted for around 10 percent of the total farming population. Many youths are choosing to leave family farms for the better wages found in cities. Farming incomes have grown, but they have not kept pace with the gains made in other sectors.

To plug the youth drain, the Council of Agriculture (COA) has taken a number of measures to persuade graduates of agricultural institutes and young members of farming families to stay on the farm. Local agricultural authorities encourage potential young farmers to improve farm management and raise farm income after determining that they are capable of farming on their own. Rural development projects are also being developed to make rural life more compatible with the lifestyles and needs of today's youth.

Invariably though, the only long-term solution is to gradually downsize the farming workforce as older farmers retire and raise the efficiency of those that remain. To help farmers displaced by this trend, the COA and the Council of Labor Affairs have been conducting training programs and job counseling over the past several years in accordance with the *Agricultural Development Act*. Recognizing the difficulty of training farmers who are advanced in age and the need to provide alternative forms of assistance to this group, the government promulgated on May 31, 1995, a temporary statute to grant elderly farmers a monthly stipend of US$87. Eligible farmers include those who:

have reached the age of 65;

have been covered by the farmers' health insurance program for more than six months;

are not receiving any old-age pensions from social insurance (such as labor insurance), living allowances, or other types of government;

are solely employed in the agricultural sector;

have lands and houses (private farmlands and farmhouses excluded) whose value does not exceed US$185,185; and

have an individual income that does not exceed the annual basic wage.

In an effort to enhance the welfare of farmers even further, the Legislative Yuan passed several revisions to the temporary statute in October 1998. Items 3, 4, 5, and 6 above were removed, and the act was expanded to include fishermen. These changes made an additional 150,000 people in the farming and fishing industries eligible to receive the stipend. As of June 1998, nearly US$563 million had been granted to nearly 436,000 farmers, and applications for the stipend were still being accepted and reviewed.

LAND

In mountainous Taiwan, farming is largely restricted to the island's arable western slope lands and alluvial plains. Farming plots tend to be small: 75 percent of all farming households have less than one hectare of cultivable land. The small average size of farming plots has created a huge obstacle to Taiwan's agricultural modernization, since advanced methods of farm mechanization and management depend on scale to be cost-efficient. As a result, advances in farming efficiency have not kept pace with other sectors, and in many cases, the land has ceased to be profitable for farming. Roughly 10 percent of Taiwan's total farmland is left fallow because it is no longer profitable to farm it.

To address this situation, the government has been working in cooperation with farmers' organizations and other agencies to convert unprofitable farmland to other uses, consolidate plots into larger areas of land that are easier to farm, and gradually reduce excess farmland. On July 11, 1996, the Executive Yuan passed amendments to the *Agricultural Development Act*, lifting restrictions on the transfer, inheritance, and division of farmland.

FARMLAND REZONING

On August 4, 1995, the Executive Yuan passed the Farmland Release Program to ease restrictions on farmland rezoning. Some 160,000 hectares of farmland have been targeted for release, including 78,000 hectares of coastal subsidence area, 50,000 hectares of polluted area, and 27,000 hectares of low productive farmland. Fish farms in subsidence areas are given priority for release with the goal of reducing the present 50,000 hectares by 40 percent over the next ten years.

The minimum area for plots released for the construction of laborer housing is five hectares; for industrial and commercial use, at least five hectares; and for residential use, at least ten hectares. To ensure safe and efficient land use, all development on rezoned farmland must follow the government's environmental and development policies.

To prevent windfall profits, those who transfer farmland to industrial or commercial use are required to pay a usage fee of up to 12 percent of the current assessed price of the transferred land. Half of this money is donated to government agricultural agencies while the other half is given to local governments. At the same time, 30 percent of the land must be donated to the government for "green belts or infrastructural projects." To encourage businesses to move to eastern Taiwan and to accelerate offshore island development, farmland released in Ilan, Hualien, Taitung, the Penghu Islands, Kinmen, and Matsu is exempt from usage fees. As of December 1998, some 14,392 hectares had been released under the Farmland Release Program, and an additional 4,316 hectares were in the process of being released.

FARMLAND CONSOLIDATION

The farmland consolidation program is designed to combine odd-shaped plots of scattered farmland into one large "pie," which can then be cut into slices that are easier to farm. The reshaped plots of land are then redistributed, giving each farmer a plot of land about the same size as the one he formerly owned but much better proportioned. Under the program, some 380,000 hectares of farmland were consolidated between 1958 and 1998, and an additional 1,454 hectares are slated for consolidation in 2005. Farm roads and irrigation ditches that serve these areas are also being improved, rebuilt, and repaired. This program is helping to overcome a few of the shortcomings of small-scale farming by reducing production and marketing costs and increasing operational efficiency.

FARMLAND UTILIZATION PROJECT

The COA, in cooperation with the now defunct Taiwan Provincial Department of Agriculture and Forestry, enacted a long-term General Farmland Utilization Project in 1992. This project guides county and city governments and grassroots organizations in setting up collective agricultural production districts to meet the needs of farmers based on environmental, economic, and technical requirements. In fiscal 2005, the COA spent US$3.2 million on the project in districts encompassing over 60,000 hectares of farmland.

WATER

Farming is dependent on large quantities of clean water, and although Taiwan seems to be fairly rainy with an annual average precipitation of 2,515 millimeters, its water resources are unevenly distributed. Regional and seasonal water shortages necessitate careful planning and conservation of all water resources. The Water Resources Bureau (WRB) under the Ministry of Economic Affairs est. Taiwan's water usage in 1998 to be 18.03 billion cubic meters (bcm); and of that amount, agriculture accounted for the lion's share, consuming 13.51 bcm or 74.9 percent of the total. In comparison, the residential and industrial sectors consumed 16.16 percent and 8.95 percent, respectively, of the total water used in 1998.

CROPS

Both the types and quantities of crops produced in Taiwan are changing rapidly. The ROC's pending acceptance into the WTO has given farmers impetus to diversify away from traditional crops--which cannot be farmed competitively in an unprotected market--and into horticulture, agritourism, exotic fruits and vegetables, chemical-free organic produce, new cultivars, and other high-value products. These moves have also been made in response to the people's changing dietary habits, with people on Taiwan beginning to eat more wheat-based foods and dairy products and consuming less rice. The island's rising standard of living has also boosted demand for luxury products, such as exotic flowers and processed foods.

Rice ranked as Taiwan's most valuable crop in 1998, followed by betel nuts, corn, sugar cane, mangoes, watermelon, tea, pineapples, pears, and grapes. In terms of harvested area, rice again ranked first, followed by corn, betel nuts, suger cane, peanuts, bamboo shoots, tea, mangoes, watermelon, and sorghum.

RICE

According to the COA, there were 358,000 hectares of ricefields in Taiwan in 1998. Some 1.49 million tons of brown rice were produced during the island's two crop seasons, which exceeded the island's annual demand. This surplus was largely attributed to changes in people's dietary habits, which caused per capita rice consumption to plunge by more than 50 percent between 1974 and 1997, dropping from 134 kilograms to 58 kilograms. As Taiwan opens its doors to rice imports in preparation for entering the WTO, foreign competition will further exacerbate the problem of oversupply and intensify the downward pressure on rice prices.

To help Taiwan rice growers adapt to these trends, the government is working to bring rice supply in line with falling demand through the Rice Production and Ricefield Diversion Program and the initiation of several programs for rice purchasing. In May 1997, a *Grain Control Law* was put into effect to further stabilize the price, upgrade the quality, and regulate the supply and demand of rice.

RICE FIELD DIVERSION PROGRAM

In July 1984, the ROC government implemented the Rice Production and Ricefield Diversion Program to reduce rice production in Taiwan. This program encouraged farmers, through subsidies and incentives, to leave rice paddies fallow, rotate crops, or fully convert their land to other, more profitable uses. The program was concluded at the end of June 1997 and replaced with the Program for Rezoning Paddy Fields and Dry Farmland a month later to further balance the supply and demand of rice. By 1998, these two programs combined had diverted nearly 142,000 hectares of paddies, of which about 84,000 hectares were laid fallow and the remainder was planted with other crops; reduced the total area of rice cultivation from 429,000 hectares in 1991 to about 358,000 hectares in 1998; and dropped rice yields by 156,000 metric tons to 1.49 million metric tons.

RICE PURCHASING PROGRAM

Since April 1974, the government has been buying rice from farmers by means of the Food Stabilization Fund. Altogether, the government has purchased 15.1 million metric tons of rice for US$7.9 billion between 1974 and 1998, increasing growers' income by US$1.3 billion. In 1998 alone, some 398,000 metric tons of rice were purchased in this manner for US$252 million, directly increasing growers' total income by nearly US$33 million. Since the government buys this rice and then sells it at a loss, by fiscal 1998 the Food Stabilization Fund had accumulated a deficit of US$3.1 billion.

RICE QUALITY IMPROVEMENT

The High-quality Rice Production and Marketing Program was enacted in fiscal 1986 and included in the Six-Year National Development Plan of fiscal 1992. In fiscal 2005, 29 farmers' associations participated in this program to improve rice quality, and 73 grain traders contracted with farmers to produce high-quality rice.

VEGETABLE

In 1998, some 178,000 hectares of land were devoted to vegetable cultivation, down from a high of 240,000 hectares in 1986, but still considerably higher than the 1945 figure of 35,000 hectares. The main vegetable producing areas were concentrated in Yunlin, Changhua, Chiayi, and Tainan counties. The leading vegetables grown in 1998 with respect to planted area were bamboo shoots, watermelon, leafy vegetables, vegetable soybeans, cabbage, cantaloupe, garlic, scallions, celery cabbage, Chinese cabbage, and radishes. Due to international trade liberalization, most vegetables produced in Taiwan are now for domestic consumption.

Vegetable production in 1998 was 2,872,571 metric tons. Through technological improvements such as new cultivars, growth regulators, and mechanization, crop yields per hectare of land jumped from 8,600 kilograms in 1945 to 16,384 kilograms in 1998. Taiwan's biggest vegetable crops in 1998 by value were watermelon, bamboo shoots, garlic, cantaloupe, cabbage, scallions, radishes, edible mushrooms, leafy vegetables, and radishes. Currently, more than 100 kinds of vegetables are produced in Taiwan. In northern Taiwan, radishes, Chinese cabbage, leaf-mustard, and garlic thrive in the cooler climate. In southern Taiwan, tomatoes, cauliflower, bamboo shoots, and beans are cultivated. Ginger is grown in central Taiwan.

FRUITS

Around 30 types of fruit are cultivated in Taiwan. Deciduous varieties like apples, pears, and peaches thrive at high elevations, while citrus fruits, bananas, pineapples, lychees, longans, mangoes, papayas, persimmons, loquats, and guavas dot the lower plains and undulating slope lands. The main crops are citrus fruits, mangoes, lychees, bananas, pineapples, wax apples, and Asian pears. In 1998, almost 2.6 million metric tons of fruit were grown in Taiwan on a total planted area of nearly 170,000 hectares. Processed products enjoy stable domestic and international markets: for instance, canned pineapples and lychees are exported, while a wide selection of fruit juices are offered to satisfy local tastes.

Local fruit growers have suffered tremendously from imported foreign produce, which has flooded the domestic market in response to the reduction--and in some cases elimination--of tariffs on imported fruit. To face this growing competition, Taiwan fruit growers have applied advanced horticultural technology to modernize their operations. Through the effective control of diseases, adjustments to fruit maturation periods, the cultivation of improved fruit strains, and the implementation of multiple annual harvests, the fruit sector has witnessed both profitability and growth. Orchards are also diversifying into the lucrative agritourism business (see section on Agritourism below).

SUGAR CANE

Taiwan's sugar industry has lost some of its former vitality due to a stagnation in global sugar prices and the importation of sugar into the domestic market. Both of these signs spell "transition" for the state-run Taiwan Sugar Corporation (TSC), which has expanded its product line and diversified into biotechnology, land development, and overseas investments in order to remain competitive.

Taiwan used to be one of the world's leading sugar exporters. In the 1950s and 1960s, the island boasted some 100,000 hectares of sugar cane fields and produced over one million metric tons of sugar annually. By 1998, however, farm labor shortages and a steady decline in world prices had reduced Taiwan's sugar cane fields down to 48,000 hectares, half of which were owned by the TSC. These decreases in domestic sugar production led to a subsequent increase in sugar imports, and Taiwan now imports almost 190,000 metric tons of sugar annually.

In an effort to bring down sugar prices even further, the Executive Yuan passed the Sugar Industry Management Policy and Sugar Price Adjustment Program in June 1996 to progressively reduce domestic production and increase imports.

TEA

Tea, a product symbolic of China, was once one of the mainstays of Taiwan's early economy. At one time, Taiwan was exporting some 80 percent of its tea production. In 1973, tea exports topped 21,000 metric tons. This situation has reversed since then, however, and the island has been a serious tea importer since 1991. More than 9,000 metric tons of tea were imported in 1998. The transformation of Taiwan from seller to buyer has been driven by local demand.

According to the Council of Agriculture, ever since the government opened Taiwan's market to Southeast Asian tea in 1990, annual tea imports have nearly tripled in weight. In 1998, tea imports increased to 9,034 metric tons while local production dropped to 22,641 metric tons (see chart). Taiwan has transferred tea processing techniques to Vietnam, Indonesia, and Thailand in order to take advantage of these nations' lower labor costs, and the tea produced in these countries is usually exported back to the Taiwan market.

FLOWERS

With a wide variety of fresh, beautiful flowers to choose from, it is no wonder that Taiwan's floriculture industry has been flourishing in recent years. Between 1986 and 1998, output value ballooned from about US$74 million to US$340 million; export value skyrocketed from US$3.7 million to US$41.5 million; and as sales soared, the farmland used for raising flowers expanded from 3,500 hectares to 10,000 hectares. Major markets for export include Japan, Hong Kong, and the US. On most flower farms, half of the planting area is usually devoted to producing cut flowers while the other half is used for nursury production. Annual production for cut flowers stands at 1.4 billion stems, and for potted plants, 25 million.

RECREATIONAL AGRICULTURE

AGRITOURISM

From 1982 to 2005, some 2,005 hectares of land yielding 16 crops were officially converted into tourist farms where visitors could pick their own fruits and vegetables. In 1990, the government began to encourage traditional farm owners to transform their farms into recreational farms. Recreational farms were similar to tourist farms, but also offered visitors picnicking, bird watching, and other low-impact activities aside from the opportunity to harvest their own agricultural products. In the early 1990s, however, it became clear that the agritourism industry was developing to an extent and in a direction that violated a few environmental protection laws and land utilization regulations.

In an effort to bring tourist and recreational farms under the rule of law, the COA drew up a revised set of *Recreational Agriculture Guidance Measures* in April 2005 for review by the Executive Yuan. The purpose of these rules and measures was to protect the environment; utilize land in a wise and appropriate fashion; and promote agricultural, educational, and recreational activities to increase the income of farmers and strengthen farm communities.

FISHING INDUSTRY

Over the past half-century, the island's fishing industry has developed from small-scale coastal fishing to deep-sea commercial fishing. In 1945, only a hundred or so trawlers were tied up at Taiwan's piers to unload an annual catch of about 40,000 metric tons. By 1998, the island's fishing fleet totaled 27,163 ships (of which 25,156 were powered craft) and brought home an annual haul of some 1,090,000 metric tons.

In 1998, Taiwan produced US$2.9 billion worth of fish. Of this, 62 percent came from deep-sea fishing, 20 percent from aquaculture, 15 percent from offshore fishing, and 3 percent from coastal fishing. More than 33 percent of Taiwan's total production was exported, with the biggest export items being skipjack and eel.

The expanding role of deep-sea fishing in Taiwan's fishing industry was largely a product of declining fish stocks close to home caused by overfishing and pollution from industrial and household waste. In 1990, the government began to work on restoring its declining fish stocks. By 1998, a total of US$40 million had been allocated to set up 26 fishery conservation zones, 75 artificial reefs, and 70 reef protection zones along the coasts of Taiwan proper and the Penghu Islands. Sea bream, abalone, and kuruma shrimp were then released into these areas to restore depleted fish stocks.

The COA is also working to reduce the size of Taiwan's fishing fleet through a boat buy-back program. Approximately 2,327 old boats have been bought back since the program's initiation, and displaced fishermen have been retrained to work in other occupations. Furthermore, the ROC government has played an active role in international fishery management organizations and worked to promote international fishery cooperation. As of 1998, the ROC had signed official or private fishery agreements with 27 countries.

AQUACULTURE

The role of aquaculture in Taiwan's overall fishing industry has been growing steadily over the years. Its annual production of 280,000 tons accounts for more than one-fifth of Taiwan's total seafood production. Taiwan's geography and climate are ideal for aquaculture, offering fish farmers tropical, temperate, and frigid conditions to raise a wide variety of fish. Even the North American rainbow trout can be cultivated in some of Taiwan's mountains.

Taiwan's most important farmed fish is eel. Annual production of eel has fluctuated around 17,000 metric tons and is worth more than US$180 million. Taiwan also to be a large producer of grass shrimp, with a peak output of 80,000 metric tons in 1987. Unfortunately, diseases have drastically reduced the grass shrimp population, and in 1998 the aquacultural industry only produced some 4,850 metric tons.

Aquacultural development has not come without environmental cost. Freshwater aquaculture operations draw off huge amounts of groundwater, sometimes causing land to shift or cave in. To tackle this problem, the Ministry of Economic Affairs and the COA have jointly promoted recycling systems that use fresh water more efficiently. Furthermore, they have encouraged aquaculturists to switch to marine ranching.

LIVESTOCK

Starting from backyard farms in poor villages in the 1950s, the livestock industry in Taiwan has grown into a multi-billion dollar business and become a mainstay of the agricultural sector. In 1998, livestock production was valued at more than US$3.6 billion, accounting for 41.56 percent of Taiwan's total agricultural production value. Hog production still ranks first in the livestock industry with respect to value, followed by broiler, chicken eggs, and milk.

In an effort to readjust the structuring of both hog farming and the broiler industry, the Executive Yuan approved a program mapped out by the COA to abandon the livestock business. So far, some 6,751 hog farmers and 974 broiler farmers have applied to join this program.

With the assistance of several animal protection groups, the Animal Protection Law was promulgated in October 1998. In addition, the Animal Husbandry Law went into effect in June 1998 to better balance animal production and consumption, thereby ensuring a steadier income for farmers.

AGRICULTURAL PROSPECTS

Perhaps the single biggest challenge confronting Taiwan farmers today is the increased competition they will face after the ROC is admitted into the World Trade Organization (WTO). To meet WTO requirements, the ROC government has been systematically reducing the trade barriers on its traditionally well-protected agricultural goods market. The current average tariff on Taiwan's agricultural imports is 20 percent; after gaining admittance to the WTO, the ROC will reduce this average to 14.1 percent by the first year and 12 percent by the sixth year. After accession, all area restrictions will be completely eliminated, tariffs will be cut substantially, and products currently subject to import control will be subject to tariff-based conversion measures instead.

Currently, 90 percent of the agricultural products consumed in Taiwan are open to imports. According to the COA, Taiwan's US$4.6 billion trade deficit in agricultural products for 1998 was a direct result of tariff reductions and the Asian financial crisis. That year, agricultural exports declined 21 percent to US$3.2 billion and imports decreased 22 percent to US$7.8 billion. To meet the challenge of liberalization, the government has taken legal steps to soften the impact of imports on local farmers, with the COA promulgating the *Agricultural Producer Import Damage Compensation Guidelines* on January 31, 1996.

TAIWAN MEMBERSHIP IN THE WORLD TRADE ORGANIZATION

BACKGROUND INFORMATION ON TAIWAN WTO ACCESSION

THE ACCESSION PROCESS

- Taiwan applied to become a GATT member on January 1, 1990, as the ¡§Separate Customs Territory of Taiwan, Penghu, Kinmen and Matsu¡¨ (referred to as Chinese Taipei)¡¨. On September 29, 1992, the GATT Council established a Working Party to assess Taiwan¡¦s application.

- On December 15, 1993, while Taiwan¡¦s accession process was underway, the Uruguay Round of GATT negotiations was concluded and the GATT agreements were brought under the institutional framework of the WTO as of January 1, 1995. On December 1st of the same year, Taiwan transferred its accession application to the WTO.

- Since Taiwan¡¦s application for accession was accepted by the GATT to the present, thirty WTO members in all have requested bilateral market access negotiations with Taiwan. The Working Party examining Taiwan¡¦s accession has convened eleven meetings to conduct multilateral negotiations regarding Taiwan¡¦s trade regime. The results of those negotiations are reflected in the draft Protocol of Accession, the Working Party Report, the Schedule of Tariff Concessions and the Schedule of Specific Commitments on Services.

- The eleventh session of the Working Party on Taiwan¡¦s accession was convened on September 18, 2011, and completed the examination of the above-mentioned accession documents.

- Taiwan¡¦s accession was adopted on November 11, 2011, and the Protocol of Accession was signed on the following day during the Fourth WTO Ministerial Conference. Following the formal approval by the Ministerial Conference, Taiwan completed its domestic ratification procedure and formally notified the WTO of the acceptance of the Protocol of Accession on December 2, 2011. Thirty days after the notification reaches the WTO, Taiwan became a WTO member on January 1, 2009.¡@

THE ACCESSION AGREEMENTS

Tariff

AGRICULTURAL AND INDUSTRIAL PRODUCTS

- Before accession, the average levels of tariffs on imports of industrial and agricultural products into Taiwan were 6.03 and 20.02 percent, respectively. Upon accession (2009), the two figures were reduced to 5.78 and 14.01 percent, respectively.

- Following the completion of all the scheduled tariff reductions on the 3,470 industrial and 1,021 agricultural products for which Taiwan has made commitments, the average levels of tariffs applied on industrial and agricultural products will fall further to 4.15 and 12.86 percent, respectively.

THE ZERO-FOR-ZERO PROGRAM

- In accordance with the Zero-for-Zero Program of the Uruguay Round, which forms part of Taiwan¡¦s accession package, tariffs applied on the following products will be phased out based on a pre-determined schedule of annual reductions: selected liquors, pharmaceuticals, medical equipment, furniture, paper products, farm equipment, toys, construction equipment, steel, beer and other products.

CHEMICAL HARMONIZATION

- To facilitate the liberalization of trade in chemical products, WTO members have divided chemical products into three major categories and established fixed tariff rates based on these categories under the Chemical Harmonization program. Taiwan agreed to apply this agreement and bind relevant tariff rates as following:

- Tariff rates on finished chemical products were reduced to 6.5 percent;
- Tariff rates on intermediate chemical products were reduced to 5.5 percent;

- Tariff rates on basic chemical products and those with medicinal applications were reduced to 0 percent.

INFORMATION TECHNOLOGY AGREEMENT (ITA)

- Taiwan became a signatory to the ITA in March 1997. In accordance with this Agreement, tariffs on the vast majority of equipment and products relating to information technology, telecommunications, electronics, semiconductors, and semiconductor manufacturing equipment were reduced to zero in 2000. Tariffs on the few remaining products relating to information technology were reduced to zero in 2009.

ELIMINATING NON-TARIFF BARRIERS TO TRADE

AGRICULTURAL SECTOR

- In accordance with its accession commitments, Taiwan has eliminated area restrictions applied to eighteen types of agricultural products including peaches, lemons, apples, grapes, pears, grapefruit and others. Taiwan has also implemented tariff-rate quotas on the twenty-two agricultural and fisheries products formerly subject to import restrictions. In the case of rice, the rice import quota is now 144,720 metric tons (calculated on a brown rice basis) for the year 2009.

- As part of its accession package, Taiwan committed to employing scientific principles and referring to established international standards when establishing food safety and quarantine standards, and when conducting risk assessments and implementing sanitary and phytosanitary measures. Additionally, the process of drafting, implementing, and issuing sanitary and phytosanitary regulations is now to be conducted according to clearly established procedures in full conformity with the principle of transparency; and Taiwan¡¦s obligations to notify WTO Members.

INDUSTRIAL SECTOR

- As part of its accession commitments, Taiwan has removed area restrictions on the import of automobiles, replacing them with tariff-rate quotas. Additionally, Taiwan has removed local content requirements on the domestic production of automobiles and eliminated export subsidies in this sector.

- Taiwan will eliminate the import ban on motorcycles over 150cc six months after accession to the WTO. In addition, the import ban on passenger cars equipped with diesel engines will also be eliminated two years after accession to the WTO.

LIBERALIZATION OF SERVICES

- In accordance with the results of its bilateral accession negotiations with WTO Members, and in line with the four modes of supply of trade in services (cross-border supply, consumption abroad, commercial presence, and presence of natural persons), Taiwan established a set of horizontal commitments (commitments applicable across sectors) as well as a set of sector-specific commitments. Eleven sectors are covered under these sector-specific commitments, which are: business services; communication services; construction and related engineering services; distribution services; education services; environmental services; financial services; health related and social services; tourism and travel-related services; recreational, cultural and sporting services; and transport services.

HARBOR CONSTRUCTION DUES

- In order to comply with provisions concerning fees and formalities connected with importation and exportation contained in Article VIII of the GATT 1994, Taiwan has abolished the Harbor Construction Dues and implemented instead a system of Harbor Service Fees since 1 January 2009. Unlike the Harbor Construction Dues (which were levied in accordance with the value of the goods), the Harbor Service Fees are levied in accordance with the principle of recovering the cost of the services provided. All trade requiring the use of a harbor, including domestic trade, is subject to the Harbor Service Fees.

TOBACCO AND ALCOHOL PRODUCTS

- In accordance with its accession agreement, Taiwan has dismantled the monopoly on the manufacture and sale of tobacco and alcohol products in Taiwan and replaced it with a market-based system. The Taiwan Tobacco & Wine Monopoly Bureau (TTWMB) reverted to the status of a normal commercial enterprise and no longer holds monopoly rights over the manufacture and domestic distribution of tobacco and alcohol products, nor does it retain any administrative authority over these two products.

- With the removal of the monopoly on alcohol and tobacco products, imported alcohol and tobacco products are now subject to a customs tariff, a tobacco and alcohol tax, and a business tax. Domestically produced tobacco and alcohol products are subject to the tobacco and alcohol tax, and to the business tax.

GOVERNMENT PROCUREMENT

- Taiwan will become a signatory to the WTO Government Procurement Agreement (GPA). In accordance with the GPA, Taiwan will open domestic government procurement contracts, above the certain thresholds, for bidding by contractors from other GPA signatories. Taiwan¡¦s annual government procurement market covered by GPA is est. to be between US$ 6-8 billion.

INTELLECTUAL PROPERTY RIGHTS

- Taiwan¡¦s accession agreement conforms to the requirements of the WTO Agreement on Trade-Related Aspects of Intellectual Property Rights (TRIPs). Since accession, major improvements to Taiwan¡¦s domestic intellectual property protection regime have taken place in the following areas: the protection period for computer software now extends to the same level as that provided for literary works; patents issued prior to January 1994 that are still in effect now have a term of protection of 20 years from the date of filing for invention patents and 12 years from the date of filing for new design patents; efforts to combat counterfeiting is strengthened; and border enforcement is enhanced.

THE IMPLICATIONS OF TAIWAN¡¦S WTO ACCESSION

- To insure conformity between its domestic legal system and the requirements of the various WTO agreements, bilateral accession commitments and the related multilateral obligations, Taiwan amended all non-conforming legislation in its domestic legal system and implemented the new laws as of the time of its accession. Changes to Taiwan¡¦s domestic legal and economic system in relation to its accession will have an inevitable impact on certain sectors of the economy.

BENEFITS TO TAIWAN FROM ITS ACCESSION

- Taiwan enjoys Most Favored Nation and National Treatment status from WTO members, thus ensuring its domestic enterprises an equal opportunity to compete within the international marketplace.

- Taiwan is able to participate directly in the negotiating process of setting future rules for international trade and thus contribute to shaping the international trading system.

- Working through the WTO framework for consultations, negotiations and, as a last resort, having recourse to the WTO Dispute Settlement Mechanism, Taiwan is able to challenge and remove trade barriers existing between other WTO members and itself.

- Taiwan should be able to elevate the level of competitiveness of its domestic industries, facilitate efforts towards job creation, raise the national income, and enhance the ability of its consumers to increase their standard of living.

OPPORTUNITIES CREATED BY ACCESSION

INDUSTRIAL SECTOR

- Following Taiwan¡¦s accession, the cost of imported industrial materials is expected to decrease, thus reducing the cost of production for domestic industries.

- Following Taiwan¡¦s accession, decreases in the price level for imported industrial products should help to enhance domestic consumption and stimulate competition among domestic producers. Efficiency in its national economy should improve, as domestic industries facing direct competition from imported products respond by upgrading their production capabilities.

- Taiwan¡¦s leading export sectors such as the electronics and petrochemicals industries have gained better access to significant markets. Having acceded, Taiwan expects to benefit from agreements such as the Zero-for-Zero Program, the Chemical Harmonization program and others, which should reduce or eliminate tariffs affecting its exports. This will enhance the competitiveness of Taiwan¡¦s export industries.

AGRICULTURAL SECTOR

- Now that Taiwan has acceded to the WTO, we expect to increase exports of those agricultural products where we particularly hold competitive advantage, such as tropical fruits, high quality teas, seedlings, fry, larvae, and embryos of marine species, fish in cages for use in aquaculture, ornamental fish, and processed goods.

- With the MFN treatment that the WTO guarantees our exporters, Taiwan¡¦s most competitive agricultural exports can be traded in the international marketplace under more fair, reasonable and transparent conditions than was the case in the past.

SERVICES SECTOR

- The liberalization of the telecommunication services industry covers telecommunications equipment and switching terminals, large-scale telecommunications information management systems, large-scale telecommunications software systems, advertising, and marketing; thus helping these services operate more efficiently.

- Liberalization of financial services allows the domestic financial services industry to globalize its operations.

GOVERNMENT PROCUREMENT

- By allowing the technology, methods, management and other skills associated with foreign contractors to be eligible in the bidding for and awarding of domestic government contracts, Taiwan will raise domestic technological and engineering standards. This will also strengthen the competitiveness of domestic contractors.

- Taiwan¡¦s accession to the GPA will create new opportunities: for domestic and foreign government contractors to work cooperatively, to expand the government procurement market represented by the GPA, and to create opportunities for domestic contractors to expand their services in foreign markets.¡@

THE RESPONSE TO ACCESSION BY THE DOMESTIC INDUSTRY

AGRICULTURAL SECTOR

- The relaxation of controls on imports of agricultural products, the reduction of tariffs applied to agricultural imports and the reduction of subsidies provided to the domestic agricultural sector is expected to lead to increases in agricultural imports and present a challenge to those producers that are the least efficient.

- Measures available to aid the domestic agricultural sector during the transition to a more liberal agricultural regime include: establishing an agricultural strategic alliance, adjusting the agricultural structure, increasing processing levels and improving the quality of products, improving efficiency in distribution and marketing, applying special safeguard measures and implementing import injury relief measures.

INDUSTRIAL SECTOR

- Taiwan¡¦s accession to the WTO is not expected to have much impact on its industry, because Taiwan has been actively promoting trade liberalization over the past ten years. The old rate of import tariffs for 84% of our industrial products was at or under 10%. The previous average nominal tariff rate was 6.03%, and it will reach 4.15% when the implementation period of tariff reductions is completed. Generally speaking, the range of rate reduction is rather moderate, so the impact on industry of Taiwan¡¦s accession is actually limited. On the contrary, the trade liberalization policy is based on expectations to bring more trade opportunity for our industry. Accession should benefit competitive and primarily export-oriented industries such as the petrochemical raw materials industry, plastics industry and electronic and information industries; while those industries focusing primarily on the domestic-market, such as the home appliances industry, heavy electric machines industry and paper-mills, may have difficulty facing international competition.

- To ensure Taiwan¡¦s industry of sustainable development and competitiveness consistent with WTO rules, the following countermeasures are being implemented: elevating global competitiveness, promoting industry upgrading; enhancing R&D and training of professionals to facilitate industrial structural adjustment; ensuring an environment of fair competition and high efficiency to attract investment and enhance labor productivity; and applying safeguards, anti-dumping duties and countervailing duties as needed.

SERVICES SECTOR

- As an island economy, Taiwan¡¦s continued economic development is heavily dependent upon expanding its participation in international trade. Presently, the domestic services industry is not only a rapidly growing segment of Taiwan¡¦s economy, it is also likely to become a pivotal sector in its future economic growth. Liberalization of the services sector is expected to: attract modern management practices and new technology to the domestic services sector; elevate the quality of Taiwan¡¦s services industry; and provide beneficial spill-over effects for other domestic industries. With a few minor exceptions, the vast majority of the commitments Taiwan made in the services schedule of its WTO accession agreement were already implemented prior to accession. As a result, accession is not expected to bring about any significant effects on the domestic services sector.

- Adjustment measures:

- For the temporary admission of natural persons: Taiwan will create a streamlined visa application procedure for foreign professionals wishing to work there. This process will lead to more effective administration for such measures.
- Regarding capital mobility: Taiwan¡¦s financial markets have historically been very stable, and it is unlikely that accession will negatively affect this trend. With an eye towards the future, the government will continue its policy of ongoing liberalization and promote the expansion of its domestic financial industry.

PUBLIC CAMPAIGN IN TAIWAN REGARDING ITS WTO ACCESSION

- Beginning in 1990, the Ministry of Economic Affairs implemented a public education campaign to inform the public and the private sectors of the expected impact that the accession to the General Agreement on Tariffs and Trade (GATT)/WTO) would have for the domestic economy. Between November 2000 and March 2011, the Board of Foreign Trade, Ministry of Economic Affairs, together with the Council of Agriculture, the Industrial Development Bureau, the Council of Economic Development and Planning and other related government agencies, conducted more than seventy seminars, hearings and meetings about GATT and WTO matters. These sessions were aimed at consolidating domestic support behind Taiwan¡¦s WTO accession, and at encouraging the public and private sectors to take advantage of the opportunities that are created by accession to the WTO.

- Between August 2011 and September 2011, the Council of Agriculture hosted a total of twenty-eight seminars for individual farming groups throughout the island. These helped to increase understanding among farmers, industry groups and local agricultural groups of the potential impact of accession, and of the adjustment measures available to producers following accession. In addition, from December 2011 to January 2009, the Council of Agriculture co-hosted with local governments a series of one hundred and fifty seminars regarding the countermeasures available for the agricultural sector.

- Between June 2005 and July 2011, the Council of Economic Planning and Development hosted twenty-five seminars and informal meetings for each service industry, to discuss the anticipated impact of accession on those respective sectors.

- During December 2005, the Ministry of Transportation and Communications (MOTC) hosted three informational meetings in northern, central and southern Taiwan, to consider the implications of accession for the domestic tourism industry. Between June 2000 and July 2011, the MOTC hosted four informal meetings to discuss the implications of accession for the air- and ocean-transportation sectors.

- Between June 1997 and December 2011, the Public Construction Commission implemented approximately fifty-three courses to provide education and training to procurement officials on the rules of the GPA.

- In addition to the agencies listed above, a number of other agencies participated in the process of implementing WTO-related public education programs and research activities.

- During the course of implementing this comprehensive public education campaign, the government placed great emphasis on sharing information about the various agreements covered under the WTO framework. Efforts were also directed toward encouraging the private sector to implement measures designed to minimize the impact of our WTO accession.

PRACTICAL INFORMATION FOR CONDUCTING BUSINESS IN TAIWAN[2]

STARTING BUSINESS IN TAIWAN - BASIC INFORMATION

MARKET OVERVIEW

With a population of 23 million, Taiwan is a thriving democracy, vibrant market economy, and a highly attractive export market, especially for U.S. firms. Taiwan is our ninth largest trading partner, putting it ahead of Brazil, India, and Italy. It is also our sixth largest agricultural market, and our fifth largest source of foreign students in U.S. higher education. Taiwan is the fourth largest holder in the world of foreign exchange reserves, with over US$ 382 billion in 2010. The Taiwan economy has rebounded sharply from the global financial crisis and enjoyed 10.47% GDP growth last year, low unemployment, and an appreciating currency that makes U.S. goods and services more attractive than ever to Taiwan buyers.

> Taiwan's real GDP increased by 10.47% in 2010, mainly driven by strong export growth and private investment expansion. In 2011, local exports to the emerging markets, especially East Asia, will continue to pick up while the growth of exports to the advanced economies is expected to slow down. The innovation of high-tech products should boost export shipments of locally-made ICT items. In addition, the tariff reductions and exemptions on the early harvest program of the Economic Cooperation Framework Agreement (ECFA), effective on January 1, 2011, will also help Taiwan's exports to China. However, Taiwan's export growth may be significantly impacted by the New Taiwan dollar appreciation against the
>
> U.S. dollar. Local private consumption is expected to continuously expand as a result of the recent economic recovery and low unemployment. Improving ties with China is expected to ease the current cross-Strait and investment restrictions and encourage more foreign investments in Taiwan. With these changing factors, local officials forecast the economic growth for 2011 will be moderate and at an annual rate of about 5.03%.

Total exports increased by 34.8% to $274.64 billion in 2010 and imports rose 44.2% to $251.4 billion. China (including Hong Kong) is Taiwan's largest trading partner, accounting for 29.0% of total trade and 14.95% of Taiwan's imports in 2010. Japan follows, with 13.3% of total trade, including 20.66% of Taiwan's imports. The U.S. is now Taiwan's third-largest trading partner, importing 10.8% of Taiwan's exports and exporting 10.1% of Taiwan's imports.

MARKET CHALLENGES

Taiwan is a sophisticated consumer market, plugged into consumer trends in Japan and Korea, awash in products from China and other lower-cost producers in Asia, and well aware of market developments in America and around the globe. Taiwan is generally a target market for high-quality, differentiated products rather than commodity items.

[2] This section base in part on materials of the US Department of Commerce

At the same time, it is generally a very price-sensitive market, and imported products must conform to certain standards and labeling regulations required for importing products into this market. Generally, a local agent will assist with this regulatory aspect.

A special concern by American firms over the past few decades has been the protection of intellectual property rights (IPR). Right holders continue to express some concern regarding infringement of copyrighted material on the Internet; illegal textbook copying on and around university campus; inadequate protection for the packaging, configuration, and outward appearance of products (trade dress); and the availability of counterfeit pharmaceuticals in Taiwan.

MARKET OPPORTUNITIES

Taiwan's accession to the World Trade Organization (WTO) in 2009 and the WTO Government Procurement Agreement in 2009 led to further dismantling of non-tariff barriers and a general lowering of the remaining tariffs. These actions further enhance U.S. opportunities in this market, including high-value-added components and other inputs for high-tech manufacturing (e.g., petrochemical products and electronic production and test equipment), food and other agricultural products, and "American lifestyle" goods and services sought by Taiwan's affluent population, running the gamut from luxury consumer goods to healthcare products.

Taiwan's imports are dominated by raw materials and capital goods, which account for more than 90% of the total. Taiwan imports a wide variety of electronic, optical and precision instruments, information and communications products, transportation equipment, machinery, and electrical products. With few natural resources, Taiwan also imports coal, oil and gas to meet most of its energy needs. Taiwan's high-tech sector relies heavily on technology licenses and imports of specialty components from the United States.

MARKET ENTRY STRATEGY

Most new-to-market exporters entering Taiwan begin by finding a local partner to serve as an agent, distributor, and/or representative. Agents are the most common partnerships used by foreign firms to gain their initial foothold here. The vast majority of Taiwan firms are small and medium sized enterprises (SMEs). They are quite active in trading and manufacturing, and offer a large pool of prospective trade partners that can capably represent U.S. companies in Taiwan.

Taiwan's banking and international remittance systems are well developed, and there are no foreign exchange regulations that would significantly hamper a U.S. exporter from getting paid. Irrevocable letters of credit are widely used and

"L/Cs" from leading Taiwan financial institutions can generally be confirmed by

SELLING U.S. PRODUCTS AND SERVICES

USING AN AGENT OR DISTRIBUTOR

Most foreign firms gain their initial foothold in the Taiwan market by using a local agent. Many Taiwan firms prefer the partnering aspect of an agent relationship. Although some companies are willing to act only as distributors, there is concern that foreign firms that are merely seeking distributors may not be serious about the market and will not support their distributors. Some U.S. exporters that sell equipment or machinery may find it necessary to locate a partner willing and able to do some assembly, manufacture in Taiwan, or provide after service. Although not necessarily formal joint ventures, these efforts require a higher degree of commitment to the market than simply selling through an agent. If the size of the market warrants, companies may consider setting up a branch office or subsidiary in Taiwan. Taiwan welcomes foreign investment, and although procedures are sometimes bureaucratic, establishing an office in Taiwan is relatively easy.

The U.S. Commercial Service in Taiwan provides a number of services to help U.S. firms, large and small, export their goods and services to Taiwan. Through our office in Taipei (covering northern and central Taiwan) and a branch office in Kaohsiung (covering southern Taiwan), we offer a variety of resources and services (including business matchmaking services, product launches, market research, agent distributor searches, advocacy, trade missions, trade shows, and due diligence) to assist U.S. companies entering the Taiwan market. CS Taiwan contact details are: Tel: 886-22720-1550, Fax: 886-2-2757-7162, Email taipei.office.box@trade.gov Information is also available at: http://www.buyusa.gov/taiwan/en

The first step in using these services is contacting an Export Assistance Center in the United States. A comprehensive list of U.S. Export Assistance Centers (USEAC) can be found at https://emenu.ita.doc.gov/emenu.nsf/ . These offices can help U.S. exporters determine which services are most suited for their export needs as well as which international markets are suitable for their products and services.

Establishing an Office

Establishing a subsidiary, branch, or representative office in Taiwan is generally not particularly burdensome. However, there are a number of structures and issues to consider, and an array of forms and procedures to complete. In addition, a Chinese company name is required. Consultations with reputable local attorneys and accountants are strongly recommended in order to identify the key issues relevant to each business and to complete all the necessary steps for establishing a new entity.

The Ministry of Economic Affairs (MOEA) website has information on investing and setting up a company in Taiwan. Please visit http://www.moea.gov.tw and http://www.moeaic.gov.tw

The U.S. Commercial Service in Taiwan maintains an online listing of local professional service providers, including local attorneys, accountants, consultants, and other professionals. The listing can be found at http://www.buyusa.gov/taiwan/en/businessserviceproviders.htm

Franchising

Franchise operations in Taiwan have been very popular for fast food restaurants, casual restaurants, convenience stores, health and drug stores, spa services, organic products stores, language schools, hair salons, real estate brokerage services, apparel stores, shoe stores and sporting goods. In recent years, Taiwan's investors have become more conservative in adopting new foreign franchises. This is due to the high capital investment required by foreign franchise operators and the increasing competition from local franchises. In order to succeed in the Taiwan market, well-known U.S. franchises should provide considerable support to their local partners, including management best practices, systems integration, personnel and customer service training, and consistency in product quality.

A variety of franchise arrangements exist in Taiwan, ranging from shared joint venture partnerships to a model in which stores are managed and operated by a master franchisee or a regionally based conglomerate. Currently, there is no specific body of laws that regulate franchising in Taiwan. Franchise agreements are generally subject to the Civil Code with some regulated by the Fair Trade Law. The laws, regulations and practices concerning the intellectual property aspects of international franchising are the same as those of Taiwan domestic franchising regardless of whether the transaction involves a foreign entity or is a purely domestic arrangement.

Successful franchisors in Taiwan usually use a reliable professional service provider, such as an attorney and/or accountant, for advice on the structure and implementation of a franchising agreement.

DIRECT MARKETING

Online shopping and TV shopping have become very popular retail sales channels in Taiwan in recent years. Online shopping is expanding robustly, growing by 21.5% from 2009 to $12 billion in 2010, according to the Market Intelligence & Consulting Institute (MIC) under the semi-official Institute for Information Industry (III). B2C accounted for the largest proportion (57.3%) of the direct marketing sales value. Young people aged 20-39 are the main buyers using online shopping. TV shopping in Taiwan reached about US$1.7 billion in revenue sales in 2010.

In addition, multi-level marketing has become a popular second job in Taiwan, which is ranked the ninth in the world in terms of multi-level marketing sales volume. Recent figures indicate that there are approximately 5.6 million people, out of a total Taiwan population of about 23 million, working for multi-level sales businesses in Taiwan, which specialize primarily in healthcare, skin care products, and household items.

JOINT VENTURES/LICENSING

Foreign investors who wish to establish new enterprises in Taiwan through joint venture activities or by furnishing technical know-how, trademarks, patent rights, or other management services to a locally incorporated business enterprise must file an application for approval by the Investment Commission (IC) of the Ministry of Economic Affairs (MOEA). The IC generally issues a decision within two months of receiving a completed application. Capital should not be remitted for joint-venture investment until approvals are first obtained. Information regarding regulations for approval and consideration of foreign investment or technical cooperation is available at IC's website: http://www.moeaic.gov.tw

SELLING TO THE GOVERNMENT

Taiwan acceded to the World Trade Organization's (WTO) Government Procurement Agreement (GPA) in July 2009. According to Taiwan's GPA Agreement, U.S. firms will now compete on equal terms with domestic firms when government tenders for covered entities under the Agreement that meet or exceed the following threshold values:

Federal government contracts valued at over US$194,000 for goods and services and approximately US$7.45 million for construction services.

State-level government contracts valued at over US$296,000 for goods and services and approximately US$22.2 million for construction services during the first year after the Agreement goes into effect. The construction services threshold will drop to US$7.45 million after the third year the Agreement is in effect and will remain at this level.

Government-controlled entities such as utilities and universities/colleges with contracts for goods and services valued at US$593,000 and construction services valued at US$22.2 million for the first year. The construction services threshold will drop to US$7.45 million after the third year the Agreement is in effect and will remain at this level.

The following are statistics on Taiwan's government procurement cases in 2009, which were submitted in a report to WTO. In total,

Taiwan's GPA-covered entities put out to bid 1,016 contracts with a total worth US$5.3 billion.

U.S. firms won 92 contracts worth US$99 million. 46 of the contracts were with federal government entities, 45 with government-controlled entities, and one with state-level government level contract.

U.S. firms' performance was comparable to EU firms who won 81 contracts worth US$136.9 million, and exceeded Japanese firms who won 27 contracts worth US$32.4 million.

Federal Government Entities

The 46 contracts U.S. firms won at the Federal government level were worth US$25.9 million.

Federal government ministries that purchased from U.S. firms included the Office of the President (19 contracts); Ministry of Transport and Communications (7); National Science Council (6); Atomic Energy Council (5); and Department of Health (3).

The types of goods and services that Central Government entities were purchasing from U.S. firms included: aircraft components; refrigeration and air conditioning equipment; electrical components; lab equipment; chemicals; research and development services.

Government-Controlled Entities

The 45 contracts U.S. firms won at Government-controlled entities, such as utilities and universities/colleges, were worth US$72.8 million.

State-Level Entities

The 1 contract a U.S. firm won for the Taipei City Government was worth US$0.3 million.

Among the 45 total contracts won by U.S. firms, 24 included contracts with Taiwan's government-controlled hospitals (Nat'l Taiwan University Hospital; National Cheng Kung University Hospital; Veterans General Hospital-Taipei; Veterans General Hospital-

Kaohsiung); eight contracts with the Taiwan Power Company; seven contracts with Chinese Petroleum Corporation, Taiwan; and six contracts with four separate universities covered under the GPA.

In response to foreign companies' concerns about maintaining fairness in contractual obligations, Taiwan's Public Construction Commission has prepared a model contract template as a reference for government procuring entities. The conditions in this model contract are the same to all bidders - domestic or foreign.

U.S. exporters are encouraged to visit the Commercial Service Taiwan's GPA website http://www.buyusa.gov/taiwan/en/taiwan_gpa.html to find guidance and information on participating in Taiwan's GPA opportunities.

DISTRIBUTION AND SALES CHANNELS

The most common distribution route in Taiwan moves products from suppliers to distributors, from distributors to retailers, and then from retailers to consumers. Some suppliers shorten distribution channels by distributing products directly through retailers. Multi-level marketing is accepted in Taiwan, and some direct-selling organizations are well established here. Foreign firms, especially small- and medium-sized companies, generally rely on agents to sell their merchandise to distributors. For certain products such as apparel, however, the distribution channels tend to be more complex.

Taiwan has four major ports: Kaohsiung, Keelung, Taichung, and Hualien. They also serve as the island's major distribution centers.

SELLING FACTORS/TECHNIQUES

The most important consideration for the majority of Taiwan buyers is price, which is also the most common complaint regarding U.S. goods. American businesses are frequently frustrated that Taiwan firms do not necessarily factor in life-cycle costs when negotiating a purchase. Although attitudes are changing, most Taiwan firms will only pay a higher price for a product if they see a near-term payoff. The second and third most important considerations for Taiwan buyers are quality and after-sales service.

Labeling and instructions and/or sales literature in the Chinese language are required when selling products in the Taiwan market. Detailed information about labeling is available in Chapter 7 of this report.

ELECTRONIC COMMERCE

Taiwan's Internet infrastructure is very well developed and fully capable of supporting the development of electronic commerce, although relevant policies are still evolving. Over 90 percent of Taiwan's companies have corporate networks and a network infrastructure, and 5.8 million (or 76.1% of) households have access to the Internet. According to the Taiwan Institute for Information Industry, Internet sales are expected to increase by 20% from $11.2 billion in 2010 to $13.5 billion in 2011.

In November 2001, the Electronic Signature Law was promulgated, which adopts the principles of the U.N. Commission on International Trade Law's Model Law on Electronic Commerce and recognizes the legal validity of electronic contracts, records, and signatures. To address the issue of identity theft, Taiwan passed the Computer-Processed Personal Data Protection Act in 2011.

Taiwan has not joined the United States in APEC to advocate for a permanent moratorium on taxation of Internet transactions, and the Ministry of Finance imposes business taxes on Internet vendors who sell products for profit and have monthly sales over NT$60,000 (approximately US$1,850).

TRADE PROMOTION AND ADVERTISING

Taiwan businesses are active in the global marketplace. They read trade journals from the U.S., Europe, and Japan, participate in major international trade events, and are well aware of current trends in their industries. There are local trade shows for most major industries and the Taiwan External Trade Development Council (TAITRA) is either the organizer or co-organizer for many of these shows (usually in conjunction with the relevant industry associations).

A local partner can give the best advice on where and how to advertise, but participation in major trade shows and advertisements in relevant Taiwan trade journals and industry newspapers are also important.

Information on trade shows in Taiwan can be obtained from TAITRA's website at http://www.taiwantrade.com.tw. TAITRA also offers several lists, including a frequently updated calendar for international conferences and trade exhibitions held at the Taipei World Trade Center. TAITRA-sponsored trade shows can be found at http://www.taipeitradeshows.com.tw . Most trade exhibitions in Taiwan are export-oriented. Some have a significant number of non-Taiwan exhibitors.

U.S. companies that do not have representatives or agents in Taiwan should target professional journals and magazines. The following are some of Taiwan's major industry/commercial newspapers and business publications with their respective websites:

Commercial Times: http://news.chinatimes.com
Economic Daily News: http://www.udngroup.com/UDNENGLISH/edn.htm
Business Weekly: http://businessweekly.com.tw
Commonwealth: http://www.cw.com.tw
Management Magazine: http://www.managementmagazine.com.tw
Director of Taiwan: http://www.taiwannews.com.tw

Taiwan's advertising sector is comparable to that of other developed economies and covers a wide range of media. The Cable, Radio and Television Act governs TV advertising. All commercials must be pre-approved by the relevant official department. Reference to associated laws and other official department is also necessary to understand the full picture with regard to Do's and Don'ts in the Taiwan market, particularly with regard to the protection of children and women. The duration of advertisements shall not exceed one-sixth of the total transmission time of each program. There are some restrictions to advertising, especially for alcohol and tobacco commercials on television and radio.

The Commercial Service in Taiwan also offers the Featured U.S. Exporters (FUSE), Business Service Provider (BSP), and Single Company Promotion (SCP) services to help U.S. companies promote their products and services in Taiwan. CS Taiwan will be organizing U.S. Pavilions in a variety of industry shows in Taiwan and promoting several conferences in Taiwan recruiting U.S. companies' participation. If a U.S. company would rather exhibit in the U.S. but still meet Taiwan buyers, CS Taiwan regularly recruits and leads Taiwan buyer trade missions to major U.S. trade shows under the auspices of the

U.S. Department of Commerce's International Buyer Program. For further details, please see the CS Taiwan website: http://www.buyusa.gov/taiwan/en

PRICING

Branding is an important factor in developing a pricing strategy, especially in the consumer goods sector. Generally speaking, price margins at the distributor level for international brands are lower than for local or regional brands. Distributor price margins range on average between 15 percent and 40 percent, depending on whether the distributor controls the marketing. Price breaks and discounts for large-volume purchases are commonly offered.

A five percent value-added tax (VAT) of the sales amount is imposed on all products and services sold in Taiwan. Imports are subject to VAT calculated on the landed price, including duties and commodity taxes on certain products. Products including rubber tires, cement, non-alcoholic beverages, oil and gas, certain electrical appliances, flat glass, and motor vehicles are subject to commodity taxes that range from eight percent to 50 percent ad valorem or other specific basis. In addition to customs duties, all imports are assessed a commercial harbor service charge, which is based on cargo weight and net ship tonnage.

SALES SERVICE/CUSTOMER SUPPORT

Taiwan's buyers, especially purchasing commercial and industrial products, consider many factors when making purchase decisions. These factors include technical support, after-sales service, product performance, durability, software availability, and overall commitment. U.S. firms should, however, be aware of the fact that price is often paramount.

PROTECTING YOUR INTELLECTUAL PROPERTY

Taiwan has continued efforts to improve its IPR legal regime and enforcement. The Taiwan Intellectual Property Office (TIPO) under the Ministry of Economic Affairs as well as other relevant agencies have adopted programs to crack down on Internet and physical piracy. In January 2007, the Legislative Yuan passed the Intellectual Property Litigation Law, which stipulates that civil, criminal, and administrative litigation involving intellectual property rights will be tried in a special IPR court. In March 2007, the Legislative Yuan passed the IP Court Organization Law that established a specialized IP court in July 2008.

For more information, please refer to Chapter 6 of this report and the IPR toolkit on the AIT website at http://www.ait.org.tw/en/ipr-Toolkit.html

PROTECTING YOUR INTELLECTUAL PROPERTY IN TAIWAN:

Several general principles are important for the effective management of intellectual property ("IP") rights in Taiwan. First, it is important to have an overall strategy to protect your IP. Second, IP is protected differently in Taiwan than in the U.S. Third, rights must be registered and enforced in Taiwan, under local laws. It is vital that companies understand that intellectual property is primarily a private right and that the US government generally cannot enforce rights for private individuals in Taiwan.

Your U.S. trademark and patent registrations will not protect you in Taiwan. Registration of patents and trademarks is on a first-in-time, first-in-right basis, so you should consider applying for trademark and patent protection even before selling your products or services in the Taiwan market.

Additionally, there is no such thing as an "international copyright" that will automatically protect an author's writings throughout the entire world. Protection against unauthorized use in a particular country depends, basically, on the national laws of that country. However, most countries do offer copyright protection to foreign works under certain conditions, and these conditions have been greatly simplified by international copyright treaties and conventions.

It is the responsibility of the rights' holders to register, protect, and enforce their rights where relevant, retaining their own counsel and advisors. Companies may wish to seek advice from local attorneys or IP consultants who are experts in Taiwan law. The U.S. Commercial Service in Taiwan has an online listing of local lawyers at:
http://www.buyusa.gov/taiwan/en/businessserviceproviders.htm

While the U.S. Government (USG) stands ready to assist, there is little the government can do if the rights holders have not taken these fundamental steps necessary to securing and enforcing their IP in a timely fashion. Moreover, in many countries, rights holders who delay enforcing their rights on a mistaken belief that the USG can provide a political resolution to a legal problem may find that their rights have been eroded or abrogated due to legal doctrines such as statutes of limitations, laches, estoppel, or unreasonable delay in prosecuting a law suit. In no instance should U.S. Government advice be seen as a substitute for the obligation of a rights holder to promptly pursue its case.

It is always advisable to conduct due diligence on potential partners. Negotiate from the position of your partner and give your partner clear incentives to honor the contract. A good partner is an important ally in protecting IP rights. Consider carefully, however, whether to permit your partner to register your IP rights on your behalf. Doing so may create a risk that your partner will list itself as the IP owner and fail to transfer the rights should the partnership end. Keep an eye on your cost structure and reduce the margins (and the incentive) of would-be bad actors. Projects and sales require constant attention. Work with legal counsel familiar with Taiwan laws to create a solid contract that includes non-compete clauses, and confidentiality/non-disclosure provisions.

It is also recommended that small and medium-size companies understand the importance of working together with U.S. trade associations and organizations to support efforts to protect IP and stop counterfeiting. There are a number of these organizations, both Taiwan or U.S.-based. These include:

The U.S. Chamber and local American Chambers of Commerce
National Association of Manufacturers (NAM)
International Intellectual Property Alliance (IIPA)
International Trademark Association (INTA)
The Coalition Against Counterfeiting and Piracy
International Anti-Counterfeiting Coalition (IACC)
Pharmaceutical Research and Manufacturers of America (PhRMA)
Biotechnology Industry Organization (BIO)

IP RESOURCES

A wealth of information on protecting IP is freely available to U.S. rights holders. Some excellent resources for companies regarding intellectual property include the following:

For information about patent, trademark, or copyright issues -- including enforcement issues in the U.S. and other countries -- call the STOP! Hotline:

1-866-999-HALT or register at www.StopFakes.gov

For more information about registering trademarks and patents (both in the U.S. as well as in foreign countries), contact the U.S. Patent and Trademark Office (USPTO) at: 1-800-786-9199.

For more information about registering for copyright protection in the U.S., contact the U.S. Copyright Office at: 1-202-707-5959.

For more information about how to evaluate, protect, and enforce intellectual property rights and how these rights may be important for businesses, a free online training program is available at www.StopFakes.gov

For information on obtaining and enforcing intellectual property rights and market-specific IP Toolkits visit:

www.StopFakes.gov This site is linked to the USPTO website for registering trademarks and patents, both in the U.S. as well as in foreign countries. www.StopFakes.gov is also linked to the U.S. Customs & Border Protection website to record registered trademarks and copyrighted works to assist customs in blocking imports of IP-infringing products and allows you to register for Webinars on protecting IP.

DUE DILIGENCE

Prior to entering into a relationship with an unknown Taiwan company, a U.S. firm would be wise to confirm the reputation of the company. However, Taiwan's privacy laws often make it difficult to collect background information on individuals.

Local attorneys and accountants can be excellent sources of information, as can trade/industry associations.

The Commercial Service offers an International Company Profile (ICP) service to help

U.S. firms with due diligence in Taiwan. For further details, please visit http://www.buyusa.gov/taiwan/en/findbuyers.html#_section2

LOCAL PROFESSIONAL SERVICES

Taiwan has a comprehensive, modern legal system, as well as a respectable number of well-regarded local and international law firms and legal consultants. Many Taiwan attorneys active in international business have studied law in the United States, speak English, and understand the concerns of U.S. businesses. Consultations with a competent local attorney prior to engaging in business in the Taiwan market are highly recommended.

Likewise, the major U.S. and global accounting firms and insurance companies have active offices in Taiwan. Any U.S. firms interested in entering the Taiwan market should make a point of meeting with these professional advisors. Not only can they provide advice on their specific areas of expertise, but also on a range of business and cultural matters.

Up-to-date lists of professional firms may be obtained from the American Chamber of Commerce in Taiwan by e-mail: amcham@amcham.com.tw or from their website http://www.amcham.com.tw

The U.S. Commercial Service in Taiwan maintains an online listing of local professional service providers, including local attorneys, accountants, consultants, and other professionals. The listing can be found at http://www.buyusa.gov/taiwan/en/businessserviceproviders.htm

Web Resources Ministry of Economic Affairs (MOEA): http://www.moea.gov.tw Board of Foreign Trade, MOEA: http://www.trade.gov.tw Investment Commission, MOEA: http://www.moeaic.gov.tw National Information & Communications Initiative, Executive

Yuan: http://www.nici.nat.gov.tw National Tax Administration, MOF: http://www.ntat.gov.tw The Fair Trade Commission, Executive Yuan: http://www.ftc.gov.tw Taiwan Intellectual Property Office, MOEA: http://www.tipo.gov.tw

LEADING SECTORS FOR U.S. EXPORT AND INVESTMENT

1. BOOKS (BOK)

Unit: USD thousands

	2009	2010	2011 (est.)	2014 (est.)
Total Market Size	$1,415,000	$1,383,000	$1,340,000	1,300,000
Total Local Production	1,417,000	1,376,000	1,320,000	1,290,000
Total Exports	151,000	148,000	140,000	134,000
Total Imports	152,000	143,000	136,000	130,000
Imports from the U.S.	40,000	38,000	36,000	35,000
Exchange Rate: 1 USD	33.05	31.85 (f)	31.75 (p)	31.50 (p)

Taiwan's traditional paper-based book market has shrunk 5 percent and 8 percent over the past two years respectively, reaching $1.38 billion in 2010. The increasing availability of e-content viewable on a variety of electronic devices such as iPhones, e-book readers, computers, and smart phones has been readily adopted by local readers. Taiwan's overall book market can be divided into trade books, which accounted for $800 million in sales, and educational and academic books which accounted for $600 million.

In 2010, Taiwan imported $143 million worth of publications, a decrease of 6 percent from the previous year. The U.S. remains as one of the largest suppliers of imported publications in Taiwan with a 30-40 percent market share or $38 million in 2010, of which $34 million was printed books and $2 million was periodicals and journals.

For over a decade, the U.S. has been the leading supplier of licensed titles which comprise about 40 percent of the Taiwan market. Over fifty percent of the translated books in the Taiwan market are English-to-Chinese translations, followed by simplified- to traditional-Chinese (25 percent), and Japanese-to-Chinese (17 percent). The U.S. leads all countries supplying near 1,300 titles per year to be translated accounting for about 40 percent of the translated book market. U.S. publishers should continue focusing on the foreign right sales for bestsellers, award winning titles, business, children's books, novels, self-help, and educational books.

The popularity of U.S. books remains strong in Taiwan, including high demand for translated and imported children's books and educational books for pre-k through 12th grade and higher education. Children's fiction, non-fiction, and learning books are sought after by Taiwan's schools, parents and children Educational books for elementary schools, libraries and higher education continue to make successful sales in Taiwan.

Sub-Sector Best Prospects

Academic/educational books, and examination/reference books

Children's books

Pre-k through12th grade school books

Novels for adults and young readers

Non-fiction books for self-help, business, management, health, and life-style

Opportunities

Taiwan's publishing sector is characterized by a large number of small- to medium-sized enterprises that are very active in publishing as well as in the business of copyrights. With the continued development of trade across the Taiwan Straits, more and more Taiwan publishers, importers and literary agencies have expanded their operations and business into the Mainland China market, which is one of the fastest growing book markets worldwide. Taiwan can act as a pool of prospective book publishers, agencies, distributors or representatives that are able to represent U.S. publishers, authors and dealers in the greater China market. It is easier for Taiwan publishers to penetrate the publishing market in Mainland China than for U.S. publishers to attempt it alone and overcome the linguistic and cultural barriers. U.S. companies interested in selling books to the greater China market may consider Taiwan companies as a potential partner for business expansion in both the lucrative Taiwan and Mainland China markets.

In the past two years, Taiwan's education authorities have implemented more English learning programs in elementary schools in order to improve students' English reading and writing skills. The implementation of English learning programs has generated increased purchases by local public schools for imported English k-12 school books and children's books. U.S. publishers have a great reputation of providing high quality children's and k-12 school books. The lack of locally-developed content in English will increase U.S. publishers' chances for success in the next one to two years.

Every year in February, CS Taiwan hosts a U.S. Pavilion at the Taiwan International Book Exhibition (TIBE), the largest book fair in Asia. During the book fair, CS Taiwan hosts a catalog exhibition within the U.S. Pavilion. CS Taiwan is also pleased to recruit a Taiwan Buyer Delegation to BookExpo America (BEA) that is held in May in New York.

Web Resources

Board of Foreign Trade, MOEA: http://www.trade.gov.tw
Directorate-General of Customs, MOF: http://www.customs.gov.tw
Taipei Book Fair Foundation: www.taipeibookfair.org

U.S. firms wishing to learn more about the book market and expanding U.S. export opportunities to Taiwan at the trade shows mentioned above are encouraged to contact CS Taiwan Commercial Specialist Menny Chen at Menny.Chen@trade.gov or visit http://www.buyusa.gov/taiwan/en

2. COMPUTER SERVICES & SOFTWARE (CSV/CSF)

Unit: USD thousands

	2009	2010	2011 (est.)	2014 (est.)
Total Market Size	$5,155,000	$4,868,000	$5,354,800	$5,890,280
Total Local Production	4,518,000	4,139,000	4,552,900	5,008,190
Total Exports	957,000	909,000	999,900	1,099,890
Total Imports	1,725,000	1,638,000	1,801,800	1,981,980
Imports from the U.S.	1,392,000	1,322,000	1,454,200	1,599,620
Exchange Rate: 1 USD	33.05	31.85 (f)	31.75 (p)	31.50 (p)

Taiwan's computer services and software market relies heavily on imports, and U.S. computer service providers and software vendors have a strong reputation for providing integrated solution capabilities and high-performance products with advanced features that are in high demand. Increasing numbers of U.S. computer service providers are partnering with local IT service providers to better manage time to market and customization issues. Marketplace success depends largely on product localization into traditional Chinese characters which is used in Taiwan, business practice customization, and flexible pricing policies. Despite increased competition from local and third-country suppliers U.S. market dominance is expected to continue in the foreseeable future.

Sub-Sector Best Prospects

Business application software
Information security solutions
Storage solutions (hardware embedded software)
Information systems integration and consolidation solutions
On-line learning/entertainment products and services
Business intelligence-related applications
Services delivered by using cloud computing platform or mobile devices

Opportunities

U.S.software producers have the advanced capability and experience in large-scale and mission-critical software solutions used in high-tech manufacturing and finance. These applications also include data storage requirements and custom-designed business intelligence features. The demand for business applications for small- and medium-sized enterprises is also increasing. The rising popularity of online services such as games, shopping, music, and video has stimulated strong market demand for networking services. U.S. content providers and platform developers have many opportunities to work with domestic service providers. As firms integrate Taiwan into their Mainland China operations, the demand for robust communication links between China and Taiwan is bolstering the expansion of high speed networking hardware, software, and services. The Taiwan authorities have identified cloud computing and mobile computing as the most promising sectors in the Taiwan's computer software and service industries.

U.S.companies specialized in these areas are highly welcomed by Taiwan's market.

Attending trade shows is one of the most effective ways to create international sales opportunities. Computex Taipei is one of the largest computer trade events in Asia and is the second largest in the world. It is the exhibition with largest number of international buyers

(35,000). More than 1,700 exhibitors are participating in the show from across the world to showcase their latest products/services. The show will be held from May 31 to June 4 in Taipei, Taiwan. Detailed information is available at the website: http://www.computextaipei.com.tw/

Web Resources

Institute for Information Industry (III): http://www.iii.org.tw

Industrial Technology Research Institute (ITRI): http://www.itri.org.tw

U.S. firms wishing to learn more about the Computer Services & Software market and expanding U.S. export opportunities to Taiwan at the trade show mentioned above are encouraged to contact CS Taiwan Commercial Specialists Allen Chien at Allen.Chien@trade.gov or visit the website http://www.buyusa.gov/taiwan/en/

3. EDUCATION SERVICES (EDS) OVERVIEW

	2009	2010	2011 (est.)	2014 (est.)
Total Number of U.S. Student Visas Issued to Taiwan Students	10,628	10,740	11,000	11,200
Total Number of Taiwan Students Studying in the U.S.	26,685	27,000	27,100	27,300
Financial Contribution of Taiwan Students to the U.S. Economy (Unit: USD thousands)	$732,000	$740,000	$743,000	$748,000
Exchange Rate: 1 USD	33.05	31.85 (f)	31.75 (p)	31.50 (p)

According to IIE Open Doors data, in 2009, Taiwan was the 5th leading origin of foreign students studying in the U.S., with 26,685 students enrolled in U.S. institutions. The

U.S. remains the top destination for Taiwan students that want to study abroad with 54.8% of the students studying at the graduate level, 24.8% at the undergraduate level, 13.4% Optional Practical Training (OPT), and 7.1% in other non-degree programs. The Consular Section of the American Institute in Taiwan (AIT) issued a total of 10,628 new F1 student visas and 4,966 J1 exchange visas in 2009.

International education remains a high priority for many students and parents in Taiwan. English proficiency or an overseas degree is considered a very important asset in this increasingly competitive job market. Therefore, the international student recruitment market for both long-term and short-term studies will continue to be robust. The U.S. maintains a leading position in this market, but faces strong competition from the U.K., Australia, Canada, and China. Given the highly competitive nature of the market, U.S. schools should allow more flexibility in their programs and admissions requirements. Additionally, marketing in the local language is a key to recruitment success.

The main promotional channels for student recruitment include media advertisements, recruiting agents, education fairs, and student advising centers. Partnering with local schools in joint degree programs or short-term programs has become increasingly popular and local universities actively seek new partnerships. Some main factors that Taiwan schools take into account are the partner schools' ranking and competitiveness in specific areas. The availability of special scholarships or low tuition is also crucial in their decision. Popular areas of study are business management, information management, engineering, computer science and finance.

Short-term for-credit summer programs at partner universities are also very popular with Taiwan students as the cost is normally lower. Exchange programs are popular too as it allow students at partner schools to interact with each other and much of the cost is covered by the host school, which takes the financial burden off of the students. Many Taiwan universities have established Mandarin centers to educate foreign students. U.S. schools should consider increasing cultural and language exchange with Taiwan schools.

Sub-Sector Best Prospects

ESL programs
Work/study programs
MBA or business-related degree programs
TESOL or education degree programs
Engineering degree programs
Healthcare and life sciences degree programs

Opportunities Partnerships with local recruiting agents and local schools. Participating in major education fairs is a good way of marketing directly to prospective students and parents. Some of the major fairs featuring U.S. education include:

OH America Education Fair (Spring/Fall), co-sponsored by CS Taiwan
The Association of Boarding Schools Fair (TABS), co-sponsored by CS Taiwan
American International Education Foundation Fair (AIEF)
Linden Tour
The MBA Tour

• QS Top MBA Fair Web Resources Taiwan Ministry of Education Website: http://www.moe.gov.tw Oh! Study Education Center Website: http://ohstudy.net/expo/ American International Education Foundation (AIEF) Website: http://www.aief-usa.org Top MBA Tour Website: http://www.topmba.com The Association of Boarding Schools Fair (TABS) Website: http://www.schools.com Linden Educational Services (Linden Tour) Website: http://www.lindentours.com MBA Tour Website: http://www.thembatour.com Every year in the Spring and Fall, CS Taiwan co-sponsors the OH! Study Fair, the

largest international education fair in Taiwan. CS Taiwan also co-sponsors the Association of Boarding Schools Fair (TABS) to promote U.S. boarding schools. CS Taiwan is also pleased to recruit an International Buyer Delegation to the National Association of International Conference and Exhibition 2011 (NAFSA 2011) that will be held in Vancouver, Canada this May.

U.S. firms wishing to learn more about the education market and expanding U.S. export opportunities to Taiwan at the trade shows mentioned above are encouraged to contact CS Taiwan Commercial Specialist Grace Tao at Grace.Tao@trade.gov or visit the website www.buyusa.gov/taiwan/en

4. ELECTRICAL POWER EQUIPMENT (ELP)

Unit: USD thousands

Total Market Size	$2,910,066	$1,032,566	$1,135,823	$1,249,405
Total Local Production	4,669,000	4,202,000	4,622,200	5,084,420
Total Exports	5,324,785	8,148,296	8,963,126	9,859,438
Total Imports	3,565,851	4,978,862	5,476,748	6,024,423
Imports from the U.S.	469,064	800,985	881,084	969,192
Exchange Rate: 1 USD	33.05	31.85 (f)	31.75 (p)	31.50 (p)

The Taiwan Power Company (TPC) continues to be the main source of demand for Taiwan's electrical power equipment market. TPC is upgrading its existing facilities and building new fossil-fuel thermal power plants, and it is continuing with its construction of a fourth nuclear power plant. TPC plans to increase its total installed capacity from 33,290 MW to 54,761 MW by the year 2015. TPC awarded design bids to upgrade its two major coal-fired power plants, Shenao and Linkou in 2009 and started to pre-qualify contractors in 2010. Clean coal technology and renewable energy will be the focus for Taiwan's newly installed power capacity.

Sub-Sector Best Prospects

Clean coal technology such as Integrated Gasification Combined Cycle (IGCC)

Emission control products such as CO2 sequestration technology

Renewable energy and energy efficiency products

Digital electric meters

Steam turbines, hydraulic turbines, and gas turbines for power plants

Electrical equipment for switching, protecting, or connecting electrical circuits (for example: switches, relays, fuses, surge suppressors, plugs, sockets, lamp-holders, junction boxes), for voltage not exceeding 1,000 volts

Electrical transformers, static converters (for example, rectifiers), and inductors

Electric (including electrically heated gas) lasers or other light or photon beams; ultrasonic and electron beams; magnetic pulse or plasma arc soldering, brazing or welding machines and equipment (whether or not capable of cutting); electric machines and equipment for hot spraying of metals

Electric motors and generators (excluding generating sets)

Smart Grid technology and products

Opportunities

The Government Procurement Law (GPL) took effect in May 2005, and requires all agencies to publicize any procurement projects worth over NT$1 million (US$30,303) on the Public

Construction Commission's website (http://www.pcc.gov.tw) in order provide easy access to interested bidders. The GPL governs all government procurement for engineering projects, goods, and services -- a massive market, est. at US$30 billion annually.

Taiwan Power Company's current major projects include:

Changgong (2x800MW) Coal-Fired Power Projects

Linkou (Rebuild) Coal-Fired Power Projects (2x800MW)

Shenao (Rebuild) Coal-Fired Power Projects (2x800MW)

Wind Power Project Stage 2

Attending trade shows is one of the most effective ways to create international sales opportunities. Following is a list of U.S. Department of Commerce-certified and Taiwan trade shows:

ELECTRIC POWER 2100, May 10-12, 2011, Chicago, IL (Rosemont), Http://www.electricpowerexpo.com

WINPOWER 2100 Conference & Exhibition, May 22-25, 2011, Anaheim, CA, http://winpowerexpo.org

RETECH 2011 (Renewable Energy Technology Conference & Exhibition), September 20-22, 2011, Washington, DC, http://www.retech2011.com

POWER-GEN International, December 6-8, 2011, Las Vegas, http://www.power gen.com

Taiwan Green Industry Show (TiGIS) 2011, October 26-29, Taipei, Taiwan, http://www.greentaiwan.tw/

Web Resources

Public Construction Commission: http://www.pcc.gov.tw
Ministry of Economic Affairs (MOEA): http://www.moea.gov.tw
Bureau of Foreign Trade (BOFT), MOEA: http://eweb.trade.gov.tw/
Taiwan Power Company (Taipower): http://www.taipower.com.tw

U.S. firms wishing to learn more about the electrical power equipment market and expanding U.S. export opportunities to Taiwan at the trade shows mentioned above are encouraged to contact CS Taiwan Commercial Specialist Allen Chien at Allen.Chien@trade.gov or visit http://www.buyusa.gov/taiwan/en/

5. ELECTRONIC COMPONENTS (ELC)

Unit: USD thousands

	2009	2010	2011 (est.)	2014 (est.)

Total Market Size	$13,008,455	$13,658,940	$14,420,000	$15,060,000
Total Local Production	30,406,415	31,926,840	33,599,400	35,201,300
Total Exports	28,455,147	29,878,000	31,370,000	32,941,500
Total Imports	11,057,187	11,610,100	12,190,600	12,800,200
Imports from the U.S.	281,864	295,960	310,760	326,300
Exchange Rate: 1 USD	33.05	31.85 (f)	31.75 (p)	31.50 (p)

Taiwan's electronics firms, especially information technology product manufacturers, rely on imports of leading edge components (e.g. integrated circuits) to maintain the competitiveness of their assembly operations. Taiwan's push to maintain its international competitiveness will continue to drive the demand for U.S. imports of advanced technologies. The majority, 65%, of local demand for electronic components are for information and communications product applications. U.S.-made semiconductors, especially integrated circuits, are very competitive. U.S. firms face their stiffest competition from Japanese and Korean companies, which lead the passive component and display market sectors. Taiwan-produced components are mainly used in consumer electronic product applications.

Sub-Sector Best Prospects

U.S. products with good sales potential in the Taiwan market are:

- Monolithic digital & hybrid Integrated Circuits (ICs)
- Silicon wafers with dimensions between 8 and12 inches
- Monolithic digital IC chips and wafers
- Transistors and light emitting diodes
- Chips and wafers for light emitting diodes and transistors
- Integrated circuits for central processing units
- Plugs and sockets for co-axial cables and printed circuits
- Dynamic random access memory integrated circuits

Opportunities

Taiwan is increasingly focusing on the production of high value-added electronics, such as notebook computers and handsets, and shifting the manufacture of many low-priced items overseas. This trend has led to continuous demand for the import of cutting edge components, providing American firms with great sales opportunities. The U.S. leads the high-end sector and has been successful in selling to the information and communications industries. U.S. firms are expected to remain as major suppliers of advanced and specialized items due to their excellent performance and reliability.

Participating in major trade shows is one of the most effective ways to generate international sales opportunities. The International Consumer Electronics Show (CES) is the world's largest electronic technologies show, which is held in January every year in Las Vegas, Nevada. International CES is one of the trade shows certified by the U.S. Department of Commerce. CS Taiwan is please to organize an International Buyer Program (IBP) delegation to the show. Taiwan's delegation members consist of a large number of buyers and importers of electronics products. Detailed information about the show is available at the website: http://www.cesweb.org/

In addition, the following electronic products related trade shows will be held in 2011 in Taipei, Taiwan:

Web Resources

Industrial Technology Research Institute (ITRI): http://www.itri.org.tw

Industrial Development Bureau, MOEA: http://www.moeaidb.gov.tw

Taiwan Electrical and Electronics Manufacturers' Association: http://www.teema.org.tw

U.S.firms wishing to learn more about the electronic components market and expanding

U.S.export opportunities to Taiwan at the trade shows mentioned above are encouraged to contact CS Taiwan Commercial Specialist Rita Chen at Rita.Chen@trade.gov or visit http://www.buyusa.gov/taiwan/en/

6. ELECTRONICS INDUSTRY PRODUCTION/TEST EQUIPMENT (EIP)

Unit: USD thousands

	2009	2010	2011 (est.)	2014 (est.)
Total Market Size	$2,073,500	$2,852,940	$3,138,200	$3,373,600
Total Local Production	469,046	683,940	752,300	815,800
Total Exports	158,026	256,000	281,600	309,800
Total Imports	1,762,480	2,425,000	2,667,500	2,867,600
Imports from the U.S.	619,193	679,000	747,000	803,000
Exchange Rate: 1 USD	33.05	31.85 (f)	31.75 (p)	31.50 (p)

Total Market Size = (Total Local Production + Total Imports) – (Total Exports) Data Sources:

Total Local Production: Unofficial estimates Total Exports: Directorate General of Customs, Ministry of Finance (MOF) Total Imports: Directorate General of Customs, MOF Imports from U.S.: Directorate General of Customs, MOF Exchange rates provided by Central Bank of China and The Institute of Economics, Academia Sinica

Taiwan's electronics industry continues to advance towards more sophisticated technologies, such as 12-inch (300-mm) wafer fabrication, 7.5 or higher generation flat panel displays (FPDs), large-sized LCD TVs, and wireless communications. Capital spending for semiconductor and FPD production capacity in 2011 is expected to exceed US$10 billion. Several investment and expansion projects are also ongoing or have been proposed by local photovoltaic (PV) companies. Most of Taiwan's advanced electronics industry production/test (EIP) equipment is imported, and the demand stems mainly from semiconductor and FPD manufacturers. Each of these two industries account for about 40-45 percent of Taiwan's total EIP market, and there are plans to invest approximately US$15-20 billion in more than 10 ongoing and proposed capacity expansion projects for the year 2011. Given these trends, demand for imported EIP equipment, which accounts for over 85 percent of Taiwan's total market, will continue to remain strong. As a major source of specialized EIP equipment, U.S. firms will find excellent sales opportunities given their products' superior performance, high reliability, and durability.

Sub-Sector Best Prospects

U.S. equipment projected to have the best sales potential in the Taiwan market include:

Chemical vapor deposition equipment and parts for semiconductor production
Machine tools for dry-etching on semiconductors
Grinding, polishing and lapping machines and parts for processing of semiconductor wafers
Equipment for wet etching, developing, stripping or cleaning semiconductor wafers and flat panel displays
Physical deposition equipment and parts for semiconductor production
Rapid heating equipment and parts for semiconductor wafer production Ion implanters and parts for doping semiconductor materials
Instruments, equipment, parts and accessories for measuring or checking semiconductor wafers and devices
Optical instruments, appliances, parts, and accessories for inspecting photomasks or semiconductor devices

Opportunities

There are six new 12-inch (300-mm) wafer fabrication investment projects worth approximately $13.3 billion either currently underway or being planned in Taiwan. The island's semiconductor firms are also expanding and upgrading processing technologies of the existing 8- and 12-inch wafer facilities. According to the Industrial Development Bureau (IDB), investment by FPD makers is expected to reach $6.0 billion for upgrading the capacity of flat panel display plants in 2011. Taiwan passed the Renewable Energy Act in 2009 and has plans to allocate a five-year budget of $746 million for the promotion of installation of green energy and $597 million for research and development of green energy technologies. The plans are expected to generate an additional $6.0 billion in private investments in the photovoltaic (PV) industry. In addition, communications and consumer electronics manufacturers are adding new product lines to produce more high value-added items, such as mobile phones and LCD TVs to profit from the increasing worldwide demand.

Participating in major trade shows is one of the most effective ways to generate international sales opportunities. The International Consumer Electronics Show (CES) is the world's largest electronic technologies show, which is held in January every year in Las Vegas, Nevada. International CES is one of the trade shows certified by the U.S. Department of Commerce. CS Taiwan is pleased to organize an International Buyer Program (IBP) delegation to the show. Taiwan's delegation members consist of a large number of buyers and importers of electronics products. Detailed information about the show is available at the website: http://www.cesweb.org/

Web Resources

Industrial Technology Research Institute (ITRI): http://www.itri.org.tw
Industrial Development Bureau, MOEA: http://www.moeaidb.gov.tw
Taiwan Semiconductor Industry Association: http://www.tsia.org.tw
Taiwan Electrical and Electronics Manufacturers' Association: http://www.teema.org.tw

U.S. firms wishing to learn more about the electronics industry production/test equipment market and expanding U.S. export opportunities to Taiwan at the trade shows mentioned above are encouraged to CS Taiwan Commercial Specialist Rita Chen at rita.chen@trade.gov or visit http://www.buyusa.gov/taiwan/en/

7. HOTEL/RESTAURANT EQUIPMENT (HTL) OVERVIEW

Unit: USD thousands

	2009	2010	2011 (est.)	2014 (est.)
Total Market Size	$1,258,936	$1,800,361	$1,860,466	$1,876,795
Total Local Production	997,250	1,362,850	1,389,184	1,396,385
Total Exports	367,777	462,683	508,951	519,846
Total Imports	629,463	900,194	980,233	1,000,256
Imports from the U.S.	32,754	55,682	80,228	93,274
Exchange Rate: 1 USD	33.05	31.85 (f)	31.75 (p)	31.50 (p)

Taiwan has seen a sharp increase in the number of foreign visitors after it lifted restrictions on Mainland Chinese tourists in 2008. In 2010, the number of international visitors to Taiwan is expected to reach 5.4 million, a whopping 23-percent growth from 2009. Among them, mainland Chinese tourists account for about 30 percent, making China the most important source of visitors to Taiwan. Moreover, Taiwan is currently discussing soon allowing individual travel from Mainland China in 2011. This will potentially benefit more hotels across the island, and many local and international hotel operators alike have developed new investment projects in anticipation of this enormous business opportunity. Currently, most mainland Chinese tour groups stay in mid-range hotels. Yet when individual travel is open to mainland Chinese tourists, five-star hotels will enjoy a higher business growth.

International visitors come to Taiwan for a variety of reasons, but gourmet food is one of the most important factors, according to statistics published by the Tourism Bureau in 2009. Indeed, Taiwan has superior "food competitiveness." From luxurious meals using imported white truffles at Michelin restaurants in high-end department stores, to local oyster noodles at street stalls in night markets, Taiwan people love to eat and appreciate good food.

Since good food is widely available and affordable, more and more people dine at restaurants instead of cooking at home. Government statistics show that more than 70 percent of the population eat out on a daily basis, especially those under 35 years old. Moreover, households spend 30 percent of their food expenditure on dining, compared to only 10 percent 20 years ago. Foodservice is a US$10 billion market and still growing. Besides restaurants, food courts, and night markets, convenience stores have become an important foodservice provider in recent years, offering fresh brewed coffee, snacks, and lunch boxes.

Sub-Sector Best Prospects

Industrial Refrigerators
Industrial Fryers
Industrial Roasters
Industrial Ovens
Industrial Beverage Dispensers
Industrial Dishwashers

Opportunities

Thanks to a booming tourism industry and a warming economy, local importers now find business opportunities emerging from new investment projects again after years of stagnation. As the hotel industry is striving to reduce carbon emission and be more environmental friendly, products with a green concept will see a stronger demand.

Taiwan's Executive Yuan adopted the Gourmet Taiwan Action Plan in 2010 to further develop the foodservice sector as one of Taiwan's competitive advantages. The Action Plan, lasting from 2010 to 2014, aims to promote the internationalization of local cuisine as well as the localization of international cuisine. The Action Plan also provides incentives for local foodservice providers to establish central factories, so that they can standardize their products and develop capabilities to expand. U.S. manufacturers of restaurant equipment are strongly encouraged to pursue these opportunities.

Participating in major trade shows is one of the most effective ways to generate international sales opportunities. The National Restaurant Association Restaurant, Hotel-Motel show is one of the trade shows certified by the U.S. Department of Commerce. The show will be held from May 21-24 in Chicago, IL. CS Taiwan is pleased to organize an International Buyer Delegation to the show. Detail information about the show is available at the website: http://show.restaurant.org/NRA11/public/enter.aspx

Web Resources

Taipei Kitchen Commercial Association: www.kitchen.org.tw
Taiwan Tourist Hotel Association: www.ttha.org.tw
Taipei City Hotel Association: www.tphotel.com.tw

U.S. firms wishing to learn more about the hotel/restaurant equipment market and expanding U.S. export opportunities to Taiwan at the trade shows mentioned above are encouraged to contact CS Taiwan Commercial Specialist Cindy Chang at Cindy.Chang@trade.gov or visit the website http://www.buyusa.gov/taiwan/en

8. INDUSTRIAL CHEMICALS (ICH)

Unit: USD thousands

	2009	2010	2011 (est.)	2014 (est.)
Total Market Size	$25,709,000	$37,374,263	$41,111,689	$45,222,858
Total Local Production	26,348,000	36,360,000	39,996,000	43,995,600
Total Exports	9,294,496	12,207,331	13,428,064	14,770,871
Total Imports	9,532,409	13,221,549	14,543,704	15,998,074
Imports from the U.S.	1,095,352	1,399,213	1,539,134	1,693,048
Exchange Rate: 1 USD	33.05	31.85 (f)	31.75 (p)	31.50 (p)

The chemical industry plays a very important role in Taiwan's manufacturing sector, accounting for 25% of the total value of Taiwan's industrial production. Large volumes of up- and mid-stream industrial chemicals are required to produce down-stream products such as fertilizers, pharmaceuticals, cleaning products, paints, dyes, cosmetics, and other products. The following four countries: Japan, United States, South Korea, and Mainland China dominate Taiwan's market for imported industrial chemicals, with more than 60% of the total share of imports. Japan leads the import market, with around 25% market share, followed by the U.S. around 15%, South Korea at 12%, and Mainland China at 12%. Taiwan's demand for imported industrial chemicals will continue to grow due to the strong demand for down-stream chemical products in Mainland China and South East Asia.

Sub-Sector Best Prospects

Cyclic hydrocarbons

Heterocyclic compounds with nitrogen hetero-atom(s) only

Halides and halide oxides of non-metals

Unsaturated acyclic monocarboxylic acids; cyclic monocarboxylic acids and their anhydrides, halides, peroxides, and peroxyacids; halogenated, sulphonated, nitrated, or nitrosated derivatives of cyclic monocarboxylic acids

Acyclic hydrocarbons

Carbonates; peroxocarbonates (percarbonates); commercial ammonium carbonate containing ammonium carbonate

Hydrogen, rare gases, and other non-metals

Hydrides, nitrides, azides, silicides and borides

Epoxides, epoxy alcohols, epoxy phenols, and epoxy ethers with a three-member ring, and their halogenated, sulphonated, nitrated or nitrosated derivatives

Other inorganic acids and inorganic oxygen compounds of non-metals

Opportunities

The Taiwan Chinese Petroleum Corp. (TCPC) is planning to develop a chemical production complex in central Taiwan to further increase Taiwan's manufacturing capacity for mid- and down-stream chemicals. Taiwan's demand for imported industrial chemicals is expected to increase for the foreseeable future.

Attending trade shows is one of the most effective ways to create international sales opportunities. LAGCOE (Louisiana Gulf Coast Oil Exposition) is one of the trade shows certified by the U.S. Department of Commerce. The show will be held from October 2527 in Lafayette, LA. It is the longest-established professional trade show in Louisiana and the second-largest oil and gas show in the United States. Detailed information about the show is available at the website: http://www.lagcoe.com.

Web Resources

Ministry of Economic Affairs (MOEA): http://www.moea.gov.tw

Bureau of Foreign Trade (BOFT), MOEA: http://eweb.trade.gov.tw/

Chinese Petroleum Corporation, Taiwan (CPC, Taiwan): http://www.cpc.com.tw

Formosa Plastics Group: http://www.fpg.com.tw

U.S.firms wishing to learn more about the industrial chemicals market and expanding

U.S.export opportunities to Taiwan at the trade shows mentioned above are encouraged to contact CS Taiwan Commercial Specialist Allen Chien at Allen.Chien@trade.gov or visit http://www.buyusa.gov/taiwan/en/

9. INFORMATION SECURITY SERVICES (SEC)

Unit: USD thousands

	2009	2010	2011 (est.)	2014 (est.)
Total Market Size	$488,000	$527,000	$569,000	$614,000
Total Sales by Local Firms	283,000	316,000	341,000	368,000
Total Sales by Foreign Firms	205,000	211,000	228,000	246,000
Total Sales by U.S. Firms	175,000	185,000	199,000	215,000
Exchange Rate: 1 USD	33.05	31.85 (f)	31.75 (p)	31.50 (p)

According to a recent Ministry of Economic Affairs market analysis, the information security market in Taiwan is expected to grow at a compounded annual growth rate of 8% during 2011 to 2015 reaching a value of approximately US$760 million by the end of 2015. The research further indicated that many enterprises, which rely heavily on information technology, are willing to increase their spending to procure more information security products and services. The basis for an increase of spending dwells on continuous regulatory changes in Taiwan. Technological improvements and new applications also add positive stimulus to the information security services market in Taiwan. And, as the dynamics of the industry continue to shift, US suppliers will find Taiwan a promising market to pursue and should take advantage of the opportunities to gain market share and remain the front runner in the coming years.

Taiwan's information has shown growth in the second half of 2010, as both the private and public sectors resumed their spending. Moreover, as the Personal Data Protection Act is enforced, the Act directly impacts how businesses protect and secure their proprietary information and properties. Companies now not only have to ensure information security is in place for their own operations, they are also required to evaluate the information security capabilities of their suppliers and partners. Since the new Act imposes heavy civil liability and criminal punishment to owners of enterprises that allow any information leakage, enterprises will spend more resources to strengthen their security system and protect their information data. Taiwan is poised to deploy a standard financial reporting system for publicly listed companies in line with international practices by 2014 and expand the deployment to all companies by 2015. This will encourage local businesses to upgrade their information security as well as their financial booking systems.

Sub-Sector Best Prospects

A complete and total security solution has and will remain to be in high demand. For the coming years, the need for Internet-related information security will continue to fuel the demand for product segments such as firewalls, website content filtering, database security, and data loss prevention. US information security products and services providers will find best prospects in the following areas:

Application as a service
Software as a Service
Anti-Virus

Encryption
Content and web filtering
Public Key Infrastructure
Virtual private network
Security assessment
Intrusion prevention and detection
Website content filtering
Data loss prevention

OPPORTUNITIES

Aiming to protect company assets and being compliant with the new regulations, enterprises are driven to continue increasing their investments in information security products and services, pushing the growth of the overall information security market in Taiwan.

The primary end-users of information security in the Taiwan market are enterprises, research institutes, and higher educational institutions. As the emphasis on information security continues, some sectors typically spend more on information security products and services than others because the value of the data that they create and transmit is higher and the cost of security breaches is greater. To name a few, these industries include financial services, healthcare organizations, high-tech industrial manufacturing, government agencies, and the military.

Participating major trade shows is one of the most efficient ways to generate international sales opportunities. The Secutech 2011 will be held from April 20-22 in Taipei, Taiwan. It is the 14th International Exhibition and Conference for electronic security, info security, fire, and safety. Detailed information about the show is available at the website: http://www.secutech.com/11/en/

Web Resources

Board of Foreign Trade, Ministry of Economic Affairs: http://www.trade.gov.tw

Institute for Information Industry (III): http://www.iii.org.tw

Importers and Exporters Association of Taipei: http:// www.ieatpe.org.tw

U.S. firms wishing to learn more about the information security services market and expanding U.S. export opportunities to Taiwan at the trade show mentioned above are encouraged to contact CS Taiwan Commercial Specialist Rita Chen at Rita.Chen@trade.gov or visit http://www.buyusa.gov/taiwan/en

10. MEDICAL DEVICES (MED)

Unit: USD thousands

	2009	2010	2011 (est.)	2014 (est.)
Total Market Size	$1,654,599	$1,873,200	$2,060,100	$2,266,500
Total Local Production	1,222,600	1,435,100	1,578,700	1,736,400
Total Exports	684,654	803,700	884,100	972,400
Total Imports	1,116,653	1,241,800	1,365,500	1,502,500
Imports from the U.S.	345,415	361,100	362,900	364,700

Exchange Rate: 1 USD	33.05	31.85(f)	31.75(p)	31.50(p)

Total Imports: Directorate General of Customs, MOF Imports from U.S.: Directorate General of Customs, MOF Exchange rates provided by Central Bank of China and The Institute of Economics, Academia Sinica

The United States remains the largest medical devices supplier to Taiwan and accounts for over 30 percent of Taiwan imports. Japan and Germany represent 18% and 14% of imports, respectively. Taiwan relies on U.S. medical devices suppliers specifically for technologically sophisticated and innovative equipment. Less sophisticated products, on the other hand, have been gradually replaced by locally made products. U.S. products have faced strong competition from other foreign competitors that are aggressive in their marketing campaigns.

Taiwan's National Health Insurance Program was launched in 1995 as a social insurance program that requires compulsory enrollment of the whole population. The program has in recent years come under tremendous financial stress. In order to control NHI's expenditures, the government has launched a global budget system, which has affected the profit margins of medical devices sales.

As cost considerations have become more crucial than ever, hospitals and clinics generally adopt a stringent procurement policy, which impacts the growth of the market.

Sub-Sector Best Prospects

Cardiovascular equipment
Endoscopy
Computerized tomography
Ultrasonic scanning apparatus
Magnetic Resonance Imaging apparatus
Radiation isotope diagnostic/therapeutic apparatus
Hemodialysis apparatus
Chromatographs and electrophoresis instruments
Shock wave lithotripsy apparatus with X-ray orientor
X-ray apparatus for dental uses
Catheters and cannulae
Enclosseous implants
Artificial joints
Hip prosthesis, plates, bone screws, and bone cement
Prepared diagnostic/laboratory reagents

Opportunities

Taiwan is a rapidly aging society where the elderly accounted for 10.65% of the population in 2009. The Council of Economic Planning and Development (CEPD) estimates by 2028, 22.5% of the population will be above age 65. The demand for quality elderly care and treatment for cancer, cardiovascular diseases, and diabetes will continue to grow accordingly.

Procedures such as plastic surgery/aesthetic and dental implant devices have been gaining popularity. Since many of these elective procedures are not covered by the National Health Insurance and have to be fully paid by patients, they have become a lucrative source of income. This trend will continue to drive the demand for relevant equipment and supplies.

Participating in major trade shows is one of the most efficient ways to generate international sales opportunities. The Annual Meeting and Clinical Laboratory Expo of the American Association for Clinical Chemistry (AACC) is one of the trade shows certified by the U.S. Department of Commerce. The show will be held from July 24-28, 2011 in Atlanta, GA. CS Taiwan is pleased to organize an International Buyer Program (IBP) delegation to the show. Detailed information about the show is available at the website: http://www.aacc.org/events/2011am/pages/default.aspx

In addition, two health care related products trade shows will be held in Taipei, Taiwan. The trade shows attract a large number of local buyers and importers from the health care products sector. The two trade shows are:

SenCARE 2011 Taiwan Int'l Senior Lifestyle and Health Care, June 2326, http://www.sencare.com.tw/

BIO Taiwan 2011 Conference & Exhibition, July 2124, http://www.sencare.com.tw/

Web Resources

Department of Health (DOH): http://www.doh.gov.tw/EN2006/index_EN.aspx

Medical Devices Committee of the American Chamber of Commerce in Taipei:

http://www.amcham.com.tw/content/blogcategory/33/67

Industrial Technology Research Institute (ITRI): http://iek.itri.org.tw/internet/home/home.aspx

U.S. firms wishing to learn more about the medical devices market and expanding U.S. export opportunities to Taiwan at the trade shows mentioned above are encouraged to contact CS Taiwan Commercial Specialist Shirley Wang at shirley.wang@trade.gov or visit http://www.buyusa.gov/taiwan/en.

11. OUTBOUND TRAVEL AND TOURISM (TRM)

	2009	2010 (est.)	2011 (est.)	2014 (est.)
Taiwan Number of Visitors to the U.S.	240,000	275,000	295,000	318,000
Total Spent by Taiwan Visitors to the U.S. (units: USD thousands)	$885,000	$1,102,000	$1,150,000	$1,200,000
Exchange Rate: 1 USD	33.05	31.85 (f)	31.75 (p)	31.50 (p)

The United States continues to be the highest-ranked long-haul destination for the Taiwan travelers and attracted over 232, 400 visitors in the first nine months of 2010, growing an impressive 22.4% compared to the same period in 2009. Taiwan's visitors spent about $1 billion on U.S. travel and tourism related goods and services.

Travel trends are increasingly mirroring the demographic, socio-economic, and behavioral and lifestyle shifts of consumers. Surveys show that Taiwan tourists are opting for more short-haul trips and fewer long-haul trips. Nine of the top ten destinations for Taiwan travelers are all within Asia and the United States rounds out the top ten. Taiwan visitors to the U.S. most often travel for business travel (36%), another 26% travel for leisure/recreational/holiday, 25% visit friends and relatives. Those attending conventions or conferences account for 7% and the remaining 6% of travel are for other purposes. Taiwan visitors to the U.S. took an average of 46 days to decide on their trips. Sixteen percent of these visitors booked a prepaid package, and for 20% of Taiwan visitors, it was their first trip to the U.S. The average length of stay was 21.4 nights, the average number of people traveling together was 1.5 people, and they visited an average of 1.5 states.

Taiwan visitors are strongly motivated by shopping and sampling local cuisines in restaurants. They also place importance on sightseeing, visiting historical places and amusement/theme parks. The most popular U.S. states visited by Taiwan tourists are California, New York, Nevada, Washington and Texas. And the most popular cities are Los Angeles, San Francisco, Manhattan, Las Vegas and Seattle.

Sub-Sector Best Prospects

All-inclusive guided group package tours remain popular with first time visitors and seniors. As Taiwan travelers mature and become more savvy, the trend shifts towards independent travel and a variety of special interest tours. The demand for niche travel experience such as spectator sport travel, adventure tours, health and wellness vacations, gastronomic holidays and short-term study are expected to grow.

The percentage of traveling for business, attending professional conventions or conferences continues to grow steadily. Many Taiwan business travelers also extend their itineraries for leisure travel, which has blurred the line between business and leisure travel. Many companies arrange incentive travel to reward their staff, and the largest users of incentive tours are companies in the financial services and healthcare and pharmaceutical industries.

Opportunities

Taiwan's outbound travel and tourism market offers many opportunities. To effectively promote travel and tourism destinations and services in Taiwan, it is useful to form strategic partnerships or alliances with organizations that are experienced in the local market. Some such organizations include the Discover America Committee in Taiwan, airlines and their key travel agents, major wholesalers or on-line travel agents, and the Taipei offices of U.S. state government travel promotion offices.

To better understand Taiwan's outbound travel market and to network with local travel agencies, CS Taipei encourages U.S. companies to visit the 2011 International Pow Wow in San Francisco on May 21-25, 2011 when CS Taipei will lead a delegation to the event. Another way to promote your destinations in Taiwan is by participating in the 2011 International Taipei Travel Fair (ITF) which is Taiwan's largest annual event for travel and tourism slated for November 11-14. CS Taipei will jointly organize an U.S. Pavilion with the Discover America Taiwan Committee at the ITF.

Web Resources

Discover America Taiwan Committee, http://www.discoveramerica.org.tw

Taiwan Tourism Bureau, http://eng.taiwan.net.tw

Taipei International Travel Fair (ITF) Show Organization, http://www.taipeiitf.org.tw

U.S. firms wishing to learn more about Taiwan's outbound tourism market and expanding U.S. export opportunities to Taiwan at the trade shows mentioned above are encouraged to contact CS Taiwan Commercial Specialist Wendy Tien at Wendy.Tien@trade.gov or visit the website http://www.buyusa.gov/taiwan

12. PET PRODUCTS (PET)

Unit: USD thousands

	2009	2010	2011 (est.)	2014 (est.)
Total Market Size	$630,000	$710,000	$765,000	$810,000
Total Local Production	270,000	295,000	320,000	340,000
Total Exports	50,000	60,000	65,000	70,000
Total Imports	410,000	475,000	510,000	540,000
Imports from the U.S.	225,000	270,000	290,000	310,000
Exchange Rate: 1 USD	33.05	31.85 (f)	31.75 (p)	31.50 (p)

Economics, Academia Sinica In Taiwan, there are about two million dogs and cats owned as pets, and about 12% of households own at least one dog or cat. The number of pet owners has been increasing steadily due to an increase in the number of single households, including young working adults and seniors, and a falling birthrate as young people postpone marriage. Many people treat their pets as family members, keeping them at home as companions, and owners are willing to spend increasing amounts of money on pet products and services. Similar to human trends, owners are investing in preventative health care for their pets, such as vitamins and minerals, rather than merely diagnosis and treatment of existing health problems. Taiwan pet owners demand specialty foods, snacks/treats, toys, and clothing for their pets. Many owners also take their pets to styling salons for haircuts, baths, nail trimming, mouth cleaning, and other beauty treatments. These trends are driving demand for imported, high-quality pet products and supplies, which accounts for 65% of the pet products market in Taiwan.

Shopping for pet products and services is becoming easier than ever with an increasing variety of retail outlets, internet online shopping and animal hospitals/clinics that sell pet products and provide services. Shoppers can also find pet products at local department stores. Large foreign franchise pet stores are being introduced into the Taiwan market. For example, in November 2008, the Japanese Animal HumanBond company introduced Pet Plus into the Taiwan market and opened its first store at the Dream Mall in Kaohsiung, and they currently have opened 6 stores across the island. The company plans to open more than 20 Pet Plus stores in Taiwan in the next three years.

Sub-Sector Best Prospects

Dried and canned pet food

Nutritional supplements, such as vitamins and minerals

Health care products, such as joint care products, digestion assistance, eye care items, and fur and skin care products

Hygiene and beauty products, such as shampoo, mouthwash, and teeth cleaning

Specialty snacks and treats

Toys

Opportunities

Most of the money spent on pet products is spent on dogs, especially health care products and organic food. However, spending on cats and other small animals is increasing. The largest segment of the health care or pet products market will continue to be dogs since they tend to be outdoors for extended periods of time and are more exposed to pests, bacteria, and viruses. The market for pet nutritional supplements is constantly expanding as local pet owners, especially dog owners, are very concerned about the health of their pets.

As more owners treat their pets as children, they are willing to take care of pet's health at high expenses. The numbers of veterinary clinics in Taiwan are increasing as is the demand for medical devices such as anesthesia machines, blood cell count machines, dental scaling and polishing machines, X-ray devices etc.

Due to technological advantages, American firms are expected to enjoy excellent sales in the pet food sector, as well as health care, medical products and nutritional supplements for pets.

In terms of geographical distribution, northern Taiwan accounts for 60% of pet ownership and sales opportunities, Central Taiwan accounts for 25% of the total, and other areas 15%

Participating in major trade shows is one of the most efficient ways to generate international sales. Aqua Pets Taipei is the biggest pet product show in Taiwan. The show will be held from July 15-18, 2011. The show presents the latest popular pet food, products, toys, services, books, educational DVDs etc. CS Taiwan will assist U.S. pet suppliers with a catalogue show booth and provide make match making service for the trade promotion purpose. Detailed information about the show is available at the website: http://www.eventseye.com/fairs/f-aqua-pets-taipei-9070-1.html

Web Resources

Taipei Pets Products Association: http://www.tpfaa.org.tw/E_1.asp

Taipei Commercial Association of Feeds and Animal Health Products: http://www.fahp.org.tw/fahp/index.asp

Importers and Exporters Association of Taipei: http://www.ieatpe.org.tw/

Council of Agriculture: http://www.coa.gov.tw

Taipei Veterinary Association: http://www.tpvma.org.tw

U.S.firms wishing to learn more about the Taiwan pet products market and expanding

U.S.export opportunities to Taiwan at the trade show mentioned above are encouraged to contact CS Taiwan Commercial Specialist Rita Chen at rita.chen@trade.gov or visit http://www.buyusa.gov/taiwan/en/

13. PLEASURE BOATS/ACCESSORIES (PLB)

Unit: USD thousands

	2009	2010	2011 (est.)	2014 (est.)
Total Market Size	$325,000	$250,500	$225,500	$248,000
Total Local Production	160 yachts	124 yachts	112 yachts	123 yachts
Total Exports	158 yachts	99 yachts	89 yachts	98 yachts
Total Imports	$162,500	$125,000	$112,500	$124,000
Imports from the U.S.	$81,000	$62,500	$56,000	$61,500
Exchange Rate: 1 USD	33.05	31.85 (f)	31.75 (p)	31.50 (p)

Taiwan is the largest yacht manufacturer in Asia, with more than 20,000 luxury craft constructed on the island now cruising the world's oceans. In leading trade journals, several of Taiwan's yacht builders consistently rank in the World's Top 20. In 2009, Taiwan ranked 5th globally in terms of mega yacht construction (80-120 feet in length). In Taiwan, there are 30 active yacht manufacturers, 20 of which are located in the Kaohsiung area of southern Taiwan where there is a well-established industry cluster in the vicinity of Kaohsiung Harbor.

Taiwan yacht building revenues more than doubled from 2003 to 2008 while the number of yachts produced decreased slightly during the same period, reflecting Taiwan's recent trend toward building bigger, more expensive yachts. The recent global economic downturn is taking a toll on yacht orders from Taiwan, which fell 20% year-on-year in 2010 and are est. to decline by an additional 10% in 2011.

The United States is the largest market for yachts manufactured in Taiwan (51%) and is also the biggest supplier of components used by Taiwan yacht builders. Interviews with industry executives reveal that imports of these components are down considerably in 2009 to 2011, but demand is expected to rebound as the global economy recovers in in the years ahead.

Sub-Sector Best Prospects

Engines and Generators
Steering Control Systems
Air Conditioning Systems
Vacuum and Marine Toilet Systems
Sprinkler Systems
Stabilizers
Bow and Stern Thrusters
Paint
Water Makers
Hi-Test Chain
PVC Foam
Search Lights
Other Deck Hardware

Opportunities

Energy-saving "green" technology solutions will gain market share as Taiwan continues to focus on new product development and innovative technology. For example, at the 2009 Fort Lauderdale International Boat Show, Taiwan's Horizon Group rolled-out its newly-engineered electric catamaran, dubbed the SunCat 23. The solar-electric 23-foot catamaran is powered by a 2.8 KW electric outboard motor capable of running at 6 knots with 12 people aboard. In 2010, the

Horizon Group advanced its eco-friendly design capabilities with the launch of the SunCat 46, a 46-foot luxury multi-hull yacht powered with 100% solar energy.

Fort Lauderdale, the "Yachting Capital of the World," will host the 52nd Fort Lauderdale International Boat Show on October 27-31, 2011. The world's largest boat show, FLIBS features more than $1.6 billion worth of boats, yachts, super yachts, electronics, engines, and thousands of accessories from every major marine manufacturer and builder worldwide. The show encompasses more than three million square feet of space, both on land and in water, at six sites connected by a transportation network. For more information, please visit the FLIBS website: http://www.showmanagement.com/fort_lauderdale/event/

Web Resources

Taiwan Yacht Industry Association (TYIA): http://www.ship.org.tw/member/tyia

United Ship Design & Development Center: http://www.usddc.org.tw

Taiwan Yacht Net: http://www.taiwanyacht.com

China Business Information Center:
http://www.export.gov/china/marketinsight/TaiwanYachtIndustryInterview.asp

U.S. firms wishing to learn more about the pleasure boats/accessories market and expanding U.S. export opportunities to Taiwan at the trade show mentioned above are encouraged to contact CS Kaohsiung Commercial Assistant Daphne Fan at Daphne.Fan@mail.doc.gov or visit http://www.buyusa.gov/taiwan/en

14. POLLUTION CONTROL EQUIPMENT (POL)

Unit: USD thousands

	2009	2010	2011 (est.)	2014 (est.)
Total Market Size	$665,511	$578,378	$636,216	$699,837
Total Local Production	579,000	405,000	445,500	490,050
Total Exports	349,006	418,119	445,500	505,924
Total Imports	435,517	591,497	650,647	715,711
Imports from the U.S.	105,429	141,690	155,859	171,445
Exchange Rate: 1 USD	33.05	31.85 (f)	31.75 (p)	31.50 (p)

The Taiwan authorities have identified pollution control as an emerging industry, targeting Taiwan to become a major exporter of environmental equipment and services to the Asia Pacific region. In recent years, local manufacturers of pollution control equipment have upgraded their technologies and their exports have become more competitive. Major foreign suppliers include Japan, the United States, Mainland China, Germany and South Korea, comprising more than 75% of the import market. Japan leads the import market, accounting for around 35% of total imports, followed by the United States with around 25%, and Mainland China with around 10%.Local manufacturers supply the majority of the environmental market with low-cost and low- to medium level products, while the market still relies on foreign suppliers for advanced environmental technologies and equipment.

Sub-Sector Best Prospects

Ultra pure water equipment
Process water recycling/reuse equipment
Precious heavy metal extraction and separation technology
Advanced wastewater treatment technologies
Greenhouse gas monitoring and reduction equipment
Polluted soil rehabilitation technology

Opportunities

Taiwan authorities have positively started to address the climate change issue by developing a Greenhouse Gas Reduction Act, which calls for decreasing Taiwan's CO_2 emissions to the level of 2000 by the year 2025. The market demand for greenhouse gas monitoring and reduction will continue to increase for the next few years. As Taiwan retains its major manufacturing base for electronics and electrical equipment, advanced pollution control equipment and technologies for the high-tech manufacturing sector will continue to be in great demand. In addition, the six year national plan to increase household connection rates to public sewage systems will continue to increase the demand for advanced wastewater treatment technologies.

Attending trade shows is one of the most effective ways to create international sales opportunities. Following is a list of U.S. Department of Commerce-certified and Taiwan trade shows:

WasteExpo 2011, May 9-2, 2011, Dallas, Texas,
http://www.wasteexpo.com/wasteexpo2011/public/enter.aspx

American Water Works Association(AWWA) ACE 11, June 12-16, 2011, Washington, DC,
http://www.awwa.org/ace11/index.cfm?showLogin=N

Taiwan Green Industry Show (TiGIS) 2011, October 26-29, Taipei, Taiwan,
http://www.greentaiwan.tw/

Web Resources

Environmental Protection Administration (EPA), Executive Yuan: http://www.epa.gov.tw

U.S. firms wishing to learn more about the pollution control equipment market and expanding U.S. export opportunities to Taiwan at the trade shows mentioned above are encouraged to contact CS Taiwan Commercial Specialist Allen Chien at Allen.Chien@trade.gov or visit http://www.buyusa.gov/taiwan/en/

15. SPORTING GOODS (SPT)

Unit: USD thousands

	2009	2010	2011 (est.)	2014 (est.)
Total Market Size	$1,173,000	$1,200,000	$1,260,000	$1,240,000
Total Local Production	3,550,000	3,200,000	3,050,000	2,900,000
Total Exports	3,127,000	2,780,000	2,640,000	2,560,000
Total Imports	750,000	780,000	850,000	900,000

Imports from the U.S.	150,000	154,000	158,000	162,000
Exchange Rate: 1 USD	33.05	31.85 (f)	31.75 (p)	31.50 (p)

Taiwan public policy strongly advocates fitness. Fueled by the uptick in the construction of sporting venues and the growing number of bike paths in recent years, the popularity of sports among the Taiwan population is rising, thereby increasing consumer demand for sporting goods. In 2009, sporting goods sales reached approximately $1.2 billion, of which about 64% of the market is supplied by imported products. The combined import market share of American brands with direct shipment from the U.S., China, and Southeast Asian countries is est. at 20%. U.S. brands are popular in Taiwan and are sought after for their high-quality. Japan, with a 25% market share, is the primary competitor for U.S. suppliers. Taiwan-produced sporting goods supply about 36% of the domestic market. Serving as the OEM/ODM partner for a number of international brands, Taiwan-manufactured bicycles and parts, fitness equipment, and golf equipment enjoy robust export sales.

Sub-Sector Best Prospects

High-end bicycles
Outdoor equipment and apparel
Water sports equipment and apparel
Commercial fitness equipment for cardio and strength training
Golf equipment and apparel

Opportunities

Taiwan's Cabinet-level Sports Affairs Council (SAC) has drawn an eight-year (20092016) "National Sports Facilities Integration Construction Plan" to enhance Taiwan's sports infrastructure and promote international sports events and plans to construct international-level stadiums and sports centers, establish an integrated bike path network, and support other sports and recreation facilities. The SAC Phase I of this plan (2009-2014), with a budget of $175 million, aims to upgrade two of the island's major athletic training centers located in Kaohsiung and Taoyuan. In Phase II, the SAC plans to allocate $460 million to subsidize the construction of 50 sports centers around the island (2010-2014). To improve the existing bike paths, the SAC is allocating $123 million for an island-wide bike path integration project (2009-2014). As a result of completing the advanced sports infrastructure and integrated bike path network, the popularity of sports in Taiwan is expected to increase 3% annually over the next few years.

Surrounded by the sea and covered by precipitous peaks from north to south, Taiwan is rich in diverse natural landscapes. Taiwan's five longitudinal mountain ranges occupy almost half of the island, including more than two hundred peaks with elevations over 3,000 meters, which provide a playground for a range of open-air activities. Once considered the exclusive domain of extreme athletes, the popularity of outdoor activities in Taiwan, such as trekking, climbing, and river tracing, is increasing. As a result, outdoor gear is now one of the most important sporting goods market segments.

In addition, Taiwan is becoming known for its surfing and attracts wave seekers from the United States, Australia, and New Zealand. The increasing number of surfing clubs being organized is further popularizing the sport in Taiwan and local experts estimate that 25,000 to 30,000 surfers are currently riding the waves throughout Taiwan. Surfing "culture" is quickly becoming embedded in Taiwan's culture and surfing apparel is considered an "in" fashion.

Taiwan is constructing new hotels to cope with the growing demand from Mainland Chinese tourists for more sophisticated accommodation. According to the Taiwan Tourism Bureau, over

40 hotels under construction will be completed in the next two years. These hotels will procure high-end fitness equipment, such as treadmills, cycles, and rowing equipment, to equip their on-site health centers.

Participating in major trade shows is one of the most efficient ways to generate international sales opportunities. Taipei International Sporting Goods Show (TAISPO) will be held from April 27-30, 2011. Detailed information about show is available at the website: http://www.taispo.com.tw/

Web Resources

Sports Affairs Council, Executive Yuan: http://www.ncpfs.gov.tw
Importers and Exporters Association of Taipei: http://www.ieatpe.org.tw
Taiwan Sporting Goods Manufacturers Association: http://www.sports.org.tw
Taiwan Bicycle Exporters' Association: http://www.tbea.org
The Golf Association of Taiwan: http://www.twgolf.org

U.S. firms wishing to learn more about the sporting goods market and expanding U.S. export opportunities to Taiwan at the trade show mentioned above are encouraged to contact CS Taiwan Commercial Specialist Rita Chen at Rita.Chen@trade.gov or visit http://www.buyusa.gov/taiwan/en

16. TELECOMMUNICATIONS EQUIPMENT (TEL)

Unit: USD thousands

	2009	2010	2011 (est.)	2014 (est.)
Total Market Size	$2,751,790	$2,793,750	$2,850,000	$2,907,500
Total Local Production	6,377,303	6,600,750	6,733,000	6,744,500
Total Exports	5,826,944	6,042,000	6,163,000	6,163,000
Total Imports	2,201,431	2,235,000	2,280,000	2,326,000
Imports from the U.S.	185,865	189,950	193,800	197,710
Exchange Rate: 1 USD	33.05	31.85 (f)	31.75 (p)	31.50 (p)

Mobile phones, broadband, and wireless chips are the major trends in Taiwan's telecom industry. Taiwan's fixed-network carriers, mobile operators, and broadcasters (terrestrial TV, radio, and CATV networks) are upgrading their network infrastructure to increase market competitiveness.

Following the recession in 2009, telecommunications equipment sales have rebounded 20% in 2010. Taiwan imports about 80% of its telecommunications equipment and over 50% of Taiwan's imported telecommunications equipment comes from China with most originating in the factories of international OEMs/ODMs. The import market share of direct shipment from the U.S. is about 7%.

Sub-Sector Best Prospects

Audio production equipment
Broadcasting transmission equipment
Cable customer premise equipment (CPE)
Cable television (CATV) digital head end equipment
Digital editing systems
Fixed mobile convergence

Global positioning system (GPS)
Long term evaluation (LTE)
Mobile TV
Smart phone
Voice over Internet protocol (VoIP)
Worldwide interoperability for microwave access (WiMax)

Opportunities

The Taiwan authorities have launched "The Development of Digital Convergence Program" in 2010 and plan to complete it by 2015. The program's objectives are to secure a comprehensive high-speed broadband network to promote the convergence of telecommunications service, to accelerate the process of digital television to construct new video services, and to promote communication and dissemination of industrial upgrading. The goals include 6 million fiber optic subscribers, 2 million wireless broadband subscribers, a digital Cable TV penetration rate of 50% of the national households and a 50% increase in the new video service penetration by 2015.

Originally due to expire in 2014, in December 2010, the Taiwan authorities extended all 2G licenses through to 2017. Chunghwa Telecom, Taiwan Mobile and FarEasTone benefitted from this decision and continue to prepare their bids for one of five 4G licenses, which will be awarded in 2015.

Participating in major trade shows is one of the most efficient ways to generate international sales. The National Association of Broadcasters Show 2011 (NAB) is one of the 10 largest trade shows in North America and provides the world's largest comprehensive gathering of television, radio, film, video, audio and multimedia professionals. The show will be held from April 11-14 in Las Vegas, NV. CS Taiwan will recruit an IBP delegation to attend NAB 2011 for U.S. products purchasing, trade promotion purpose. Detailed information about the show is available at the website: http://www.nabshow.com/2011/index.asp

Web Resources

Ministry of Economic Affairs (MOEA): http://www.moea.gov.tw

Mobile Taiwan Applications Promotion Program, Industrial Development Bureau (IDB), MOEA: http://www.mtaiwan.org.tw/eng/index.php

Industry Technology Research Institute (ITRI): http://www.itri.org.tw

National Communications Commission (NCC): http://www.ncc.gov.tw/english

U.S. firms wishing to learn more about the telecommunications equipment market and expanding U.S. export opportunities to Taiwan at the trade show mentioned above are encouraged to contact CS Taiwan Commercial Specialist Rita Chen at Rita.Chen@trade.gov or visit http://www.buyusa.gov/taiwan/en

AGRICULTURAL SECTORS EXPORT IMPORT OPPORTUNITIES

1. BEEF

Unit: metric tons

	2009	2010*	2011 (est.)	2014 (est.)
Total Market Size	114,789	131,828	139,050	144,120
Total Local Production	6,099	5,100	4,400	4,500
Total Exports	443	341	350	380
Total Imports	109,133	127,069	135,000	140,000
Imports from the U.S.	32,378	46,843	46,000	47,500
Exchange Rate: 1 USD	33.05	31.85 (f)	31.75 (p)	31.50 (p)

*Annual totals est. based on available trade data Note: Figures are for bovine meat in metric tons (carcass weight equivalent). The conversion ratio from trade data into beef carcass weight equivalent is 1:1.36. Source: Council on Agriculture, Global Trade Atlas

Domestic beef production generally accounts for less than five percent of beef consumed in Taiwan. The top-three suppliers, the United States, Australia and New Zealand, have maintained their dominance of Taiwan's beef market since the 1990s.

In 2010, the United States surpassed Australia as Taiwan's largest beef supplier on both volume and value basis. With the reopening of the Taiwan market for U.S. bone-in beef, imports of U.S. boneless and bone-in beef surged by nearly 60% for the year to US$218 million and a 47% market share, followed by Australia and New Zealand at 29% and 20% respectively.

NOTE: Est. imports of U.S. beef for 2011 and 2014, as reflected in the table above, depend to a great extend on the prompt resolution of an ongoing dispute over Taiwan's enforcement of a ban on ractopamine in beef as of January 2011 (see following sections for more information)

Sub-Sector Best Prospects

The U.S. beef industry is able to supply large volumes of "Asian cuts" at prices competitive with New Zealand and Australia. These cuts include boneless ribs, chuck, and short plate for ethnic Japanese and Korean cuisines, and middle meat items for Western restaurants. The quality of U.S. chilled beef has been recognized by Taiwan consumers and dominates sales and retail space.

Unfortunately, in January 2011, several shipments of U.S. beef tested positive for ractopamine, a feed ingredient that is approved for use in the United States but not approved in Taiwan. Following the initial detections, Taiwan increased testing for ractopamine and ordered some U.S. beef products removed from local supermarkets. This has created uncertainty among Taiwan importers and U.S. exporters, causing imports of U.S. beef to fall sharply.

All major export markets for U.S. beef except Taiwan and the EU have set maximum residue levels (MRLs) for ractopamine. Taiwan also previously reviewed the use of ractopamine, determined it to be safe and in 2007 notified the WTO of Taiwan's intent to adopt MRLs for ractopamine. However, Taiwan subsequently suspended plans to implement the MRLs in response to pressure from domestic swine producers. AIT and Taiwan authorities are working to resolve this issue and hope to see trade resume quickly.

Opportunities

Taiwan's per capita beef consumption (about 10 pounds) now nearly equals consumption in Japan (12 pounds) but is still well below South Korea (18 pounds). Family eating habits and life style choices combine to constrain the growth of consumption in Taiwan. However younger people are showing a growing preference for beef, so consumption is expected to grow.

The U.S. beef industry is able to supply large volumes of "Asian cuts" at prices competitive with major competitors New Zealand and Australia. These cuts include boneless rib, chuck, and short plate for ethnic Japanese and Korean cuisines, and middle meat items for Western restaurants. The quality of U.S. chilled beef has been recognized by Taiwan consumers and dominates sales and retail space. If the issue with ractopamine can be resolved, U.S. exports to Taiwan should continue to grow.

Web Resources

For current information on export requirements for Taiwan:
http://www.fsis.usda.gov/regulations_&_policies/Taiwan_Requirements/index.asp
For general information on U.S. food and agricultural exports and USDA's export market development programs:
Foreign Agricultural Service: http://www.fas.usda.gov
U.S. Food Taiwan: http://www.usfoodtaiwan.org
For more information on the Taiwan market for food and agricultural products, please contact the AIT Agricultural Trade Office at ATOTaipei@fas.usda.gov

2. CHEESE

Unit: USD thousands

	2009	2010*	2011 (est.)	2014 (est.)
Total Exports	176	153	115	115

Total Imports	67,818	92,041	107,688	125,995
Imports from the U.S.	9,612	14,777	17,289	20,230
Exchange Rate: 1 USD	33.05	31.85(f)	31.75(p)	31.50(p)

* Annual totals est. based on available trade data Source: Global Trade Atlas (HS code: 0406)

Sub-Sector Best Prospects

The use of cheese in the Taiwan food service sector has strong growth potential as chefs learn the versatility of mozzarella and cheddar, particularly in western style dishes.

Sliced cheese accounts for 65% of consumption in the retail sector. Frequent retail promotions in up-scale retail stores will improve consumer awareness of U.S. cheese and help consumers understand possible applications of cheese with other foods.

Opportunities

On a per capita basis, cheese consumption in Taiwan (0.7 kg in 2008) is still very small compared to most Western countries and Japan. However, Taiwan consumers have developed more sophisticated tastes for cheese products in recent years. In the past, consumers tended to associate cheese only with pizza or sandwiches. However, consumers now eat cheese in a variety of foods and meals. Cheese is also being applied as a topping to baked potatoes or as an ingredient in Chinese buns.

Web Resources

For further information, please see the following Foreign Agricultural Service (FAS) report:

Taiwan Dairy Annual 2010 (TW10023):

http://gain.fas.usda.gov/Recent%20GAIN%20Publications/Dairy%20and%20Products%20Annual_Taipei_Taiwan_10-20-2010.pdf

For other information on U.S. dairy exports: US Dairy Export Council: http://www.usdec.org For general information on U.S. food and agricultural exports and USDA's export market development programs: Foreign Agricultural Service: http://www.fas.usda.gov

U.S. Food Taiwan: http://www.usfoodtaiwan.org

For more information on the Taiwan market for food and agricultural products, please contact the AIT Agricultural Trade Office at ATOTaipei@fas.usda.gov

3. CHOCOLATE & OTHER CANDIES (EXCLUDING CHEWING GUM)

Unit: USD thousands

	2009	2010*	2011 (est.)	2014 (est.)
Total Market Size	153,135	158,000	157,000	155,800
Total Local Production	91,273	96,000	96,500	97,000
Total Exports	17,868	20,000	22,000	24,200
Total Imports	79,730	82,000	82,500	83,000
Imports from the U.S.	8,019	8,100	8,200	8,300
Exchange Rate: 1 USD	$33.05	$31.85 (f)	$31.75 (p)	$31.50 (p)

* Annual totals est. based on available trade data Source: Global Trade Atlas

Taiwan imported nearly $80 million worth of chocolate and candy (excluding chewing gum) products in 2009, a 0.41% decrease compared with the previous year. Chocolate candy products accounted for nearly 64% of the candy import market. In 2009, Japan was the largest supplier with a 20% market share, followed by Italy (18%), the United States (10%), Malaysia (6%), France (6%), Germany (5%), and Switzerland (4%). Italy and other EU countries mainly supplied chocolate products.

Sub-Sector Best Prospects

Part of the success of imported candy products from the EU and the United States is that they compare favorably to domestic products in both price and quality. The United States previously held a slightly larger market share. However, the entry of major European chocolate product manufacturers as well as lower-priced candies from Southeast Asia has shifted some market share away from U.S. suppliers. Industry sources estimate slight growth in production and an approximately 10% growth for exports over the next few years due to increasing demand from China and Southeast Asia. Local consumption is anticipated to remain flat due to a greater emphasis on healthy eating.

Opportunities

U.S. candy products are considered competitive in terms of both quality and cost. The Taiwan candy market has become more mature and consumers are beginning to demand a wider variety of candies. With an increasing focus on healthy eating, candies that provide a health benefit or at least do not contribute to weight gain and cavities have the best prospects. The key to success in the Taiwan market is providing unique flavors and creative packaging.

Web Resources

For further information, please see the following Foreign Agricultural Service (FAS) reports:

Taiwan Candy, Gum, and Chocolate (TW9040)
http://gain.fas.usda.gov/Recent%20GAIN%20Publications/Candy%20and%20Gum%20a nd%20Chocolate_Taipei%20ATO_Taiwan_7-28-2009.pdf

For general information on U.S. food and agricultural exports and USDA's export market development programs: Foreign Agricultural Service: http://www.fas.usda.gov

U.S. Food Taiwan: http://www.usfoodtaiwan.org

For more information on the Taiwan market for food and agricultural products, please contact the AIT Agricultural Trade Office at ATOTaipei@fas.usda.gov

4. DRIED AND FROZEN FRUIT

Unit: USD thousands

	2009	2010*	2011 (est.)t)	2014 (est.)
Total Market Size	N/A	N/A	N/A	N/A
Total Local Production	N/A	N/A	N/A	N/A
Total Exports	3,463	2,496	2,600	2,700
Total Imports	5,938	6,500	6,600	6,800
Imports from the U.S.	1,760	1,900	2,000	2,100
Exchange Rate: 1 USD	$33.05	$31.85 (f)	$31.75 (p)	31.50 (p)

* Annual totals est. based on available trade data Source: Taiwan Directorate General of Customs, Ministry of Finance

Sub-Sector Best Prospects

Fruit and berry flavors lead market trends toward new and innovative tastes. Taiwan consumers generally like the taste of dried and frozen fruit and welcome new products. In addition, natural fruit ingredients offer processed food manufacturers new opportunities to promote associated nutrition and health (functional) benefits. Raisins and prunes continue to dominate the dried fruit category, although U.S. exporters are facing growing competition from competitors such as China (prunes) and Argentina (raisin).

Opportunities

U.S. exports of snack fruits such as dried cranberries, mixed dried fruits, and ingredient-ready dried and frozen berries (e.g., blueberries, raspberries, and cranberries) continue to enjoy a steadily increasing share of the overall segment. These products promise to maintain bullish growth as new flavors work their way into the mainstream prepared food market.

Web Resources

For further information, please see the following Foreign Agricultural Service (FAS) reports:

Taiwan Stone Fruit Annual (TW10020)
http://gain.fas.usda.gov/Recent%20GAIN%20Publications/Stone%20Fruit%20Annual_Taipei_Taiwan_8-23-2010.pdf

Taiwan Fresh Deciduous Fruit Annual (TW10026):

http://gain.fas.usda.gov/Recent%20GAIN%20Publications/Fresh%20Deciduous%20Fruit%20Annual_Taipei_Taiwan_11-1-2010.pdf

For general information on U.S. food and agricultural exports and USDA's export market development programs: Foreign Agricultural Service: http://www.fas.usda.gov

U.S. Food Taiwan: http://www.usfoodtaiwan.org

For more information on the Taiwan market for food and agricultural products, please contact the AIT Agricultural Trade Office at ATOTaipei@fas.usda.gov

5. FISH AND SEAFOOD PRODUCTS

Unit: USD thousands

	2009	2010*	2011 (est.)	2014 (est.)
Total Market Size	2,146,814	2,841,901	2,930,000	3,015,000
Total Local Production	2,606,000	3,461,000	3,565,000	3,670,000
Total Exports	1,030,267	1,246,640	1,280,000	1,320,000
Total Imports	571,081	627,541	645,000	665,000
Imports from the U.S.	15,094	17,638	18,200	18,700
Exchange Rate: 1 USD	$33.05	$31.85 (f)	$31.75 (p)	$31.50 (p)

*Annual totals est. based on available trade data Source: Global Trade Atlas; Fishery Agency, Council on Agriculture

Sub-Sector Best Prospects

Taiwan's domestic fish production fell to just over US$2.6 billion in 2009, an 18% decrease from the previous year. Taiwan's top seafood suppliers in 2009 were China, Vietnam, Norway, Thailand and India.

The value of fishery products imported from the United States to Taiwan is est. at $17 million. The major U.S. export items to Taiwan are: rock lobsters and other shellfish; dried/smoked fish liver and roe; and oysters.

The seafood market is highly competitive in Taiwan. China has been the leading supplier to Taiwan since 2006. Continuing trade liberalization between China and Taiwan will strengthen China's market position further with reduction in tariffs slated for imports of live, chilled and frozen fish from mainland China.

Opportunities

U.S. fish and seafood products are perceived by Taiwanese consumers to be of high quality and cutting edge. Prospects for U.S. fish and seafood exports to Taiwan are promising. Seafood is an important part of the Taiwan diet, and imported seafood items occupy a unique and growing niche in Taiwan's domestic seafood market. The demand for quality seafood is growing due to increasing incomes and new dietary trends.

Most U.S. seafood is consumed in restaurants, rather than purchased in supermarkets or traditional wet markets. There is a niche market for seafood imports as demand for quality seafood is growing. Consumers are not always aware if the seafood they purchase is imported or domestically produced. Promotion or taste testing would help make consumers aware that their purchases are from the United States. Importers and wholesalers however have an awareness and appreciation for the quality of U.S. seafood.

Web Resources

For general information on U.S. food and agricultural exports and USDA's export market development programs:

Foreign Agricultural Service: http://www.fas.usda.gov

U.S. Food Taiwan: http://www.usfoodtaiwan.org

For more information on the Taiwan market for food and agricultural products, please contact the AIT Agricultural Trade Office at ATOTaipei@fas.usda.gov

6. FRESH FRUITS

Unit: USD thousands

	2009	2010*	2011 (est.)	2014 (est.)
Total Market Size	2,308,403	2,404,000	2,518,000	2,577,000
Total Local Production	1,988,119	2,100,000	2,200,000	2,250,000

Total Exports	39,725	46,000	42,000	43,000
Total Imports	360,009	350,000	360,000	370,000
Imports from the U.S.	154,282	155,000	160,000	170,000
Exchange Rate: 1 USD	$33.05	$31.85 (f)	$31.75 (p)	31.50 (p)

*Annual totals est. based on available trade data Source: Global Trade Atlas; Taiwan Council of Agriculture

Taiwan has the world's highest per capita consumption of fresh fruit at 135 kilograms. In 2009, Taiwan imported approximately US$360 million worth of fresh fruit, a 8% decrease from the previous year. The United States remained the largest supplier, accounting for 43% of Taiwan's total fresh fruit imports, followed by Chile (15%), New Zealand (13%), Japan (10%), and Korea (6%).

Sub-Sector Best Prospects

The major U.S. export items to Taiwan in 2009 were: apples (US$43 million); peaches & nectarines ($35 million); cherries (US$39 million); grapes (US$18 million), plums & sloes (US$8 million), and oranges (US$4 million).

Opportunities

U.S. exporters have been successful in introducing new fruit types and varieties to the Taiwan market. The best growth opportunities for U.S. suppliers include relatively newto-market temperate fruits like cherries, strawberries, and blueberries. Other fresh fruits not previously sold in significant quantities in Taiwan, such as raspberries, blackberries, and pomegranate, also have significant growth potential, both in consumer/retail and food service channels. As these products become more widely available, they will increasingly enter mainstream consumption and become more attractively priced for the mass market. There is also the potential for more "new" niche fruits to win high-value beachheads in Taiwan as well.

Web Resources

For further information, please see the following Foreign Agricultural Service (FAS) reports:

Taiwan Stone Fruit Annual (TW10020)

http://gain.fas.usda.gov/Recent%20GAIN%20Publications/Stone%20Fruit%20Annual_Taipei_Taiwan_8-23-2010.pdf

Taiwan Fresh Deciduous Fruit Annual (TW10026):

http://gain.fas.usda.gov/Recent%20GAIN%20Publications/Fresh%20Deciduous%20Fruit%20Annual_Taipei_Taiwan_11-1-2010.pdf

For general information on U.S. food and agricultural exports and USDA's export market development programs: Foreign Agricultural Service: http://www.fas.usda.gov

U.S. Food Taiwan: http://www.usfoodtaiwan.org

For more information on the Taiwan market for food and agricultural products, please contact AIT Agricultural Trade Office at ATOTaipei@fas.usda.gov

7. PET FOOD

Overview Unit: USD thousands

	2009	2010*	2011 (est.)	2014 (est.)
Total Market Size	92,929	102,607	106,900	109,900
Total Local Production**	16,000	16,500	16,500	16,500
Total Exports	875	1,559	1,600	1,600
Total Imports	77,804	87,666	92,000	95,000
Imports from the U.S.	31,183	33,046	34,000	35,000
Exchange Rate: 1 USD	$33.05	$31.85 (f)	$31.75 (p)	$31.50 (p)

* Annual totals est. based on available trade data ** Estimates - No official data for local pet food production Source: Taiwan Council of Agriculture

Taiwan's imports of pet food (dog & cat food put up for retail sale) have nearly tripled in 10 years, growing from $31 million in 2001 to US$88 million in 2010. The United States continues to be the leading supplier with a 38% market share followed by Thailand (21%), Australia (18%), France (12%), and Canada (4%).

Official data on local production of pet food is not available. It is est. that domestic production accounts for less than 20% of the total pet food market even though retail prices for imported pet food are higher than locally produced pet food products. Currently, the est. ratio of dog to cat food is 70:30. The ratio of dried to canned pet food is 80:20.

Sub-Sector Best Prospects The growth in the Taiwan pet food market can be attributed to a change in attitude toward animals as pets and a subsequent shift from feeding table scrapes to stray animals to serving pet food to well cared for pets. With rising incomes and strong western influences, dogs are now a symbol of affluence in Taiwan. Taiwan pet food imports are expected to continue to grow moderately over the next few years.

In Taiwan, pet food is sold in pet specialty stores, pet clinics, supermarkets, hypermarkets, and convenience stores. Larger pet food importers with significant market share employ duel channels of distribution. The first channel is to sell to a distributor, who in turn sells directly to the various retail outlets, breeders, and veterinarians. The second channel is for the importer to sell directly to larger retail outlets and breeders. Currently, large retail stores are increasingly importing directly to avoid the higher cost of products purchased from importers or local manufacturers.

Opportunities

The long-term trend for U.S. pet food exports to Taiwan points to more competitive but still favorable market conditions, with U.S. imports expected to maintain a nearly 40% market share. U.S. pet food brands are commonly viewed as being significantly higher in quality, which is the primary reason that Taiwan pet owners are willing to pay higher prices. However, the recent entry of pet food in significantly large volumes with low prices from Thailand and other Southeast Asian countries is anticipated to impact U.S. pet food exports to Taiwan in the near future. These pet foods, generally with local private labels, are mainly marketed through supermarket/hypermarket stores.

Web Resources

For further information, please see the following Foreign Agricultural Service (FAS) report:

Taiwan Pet Food Report (TW8041):

http://www.fas.usda.gov/gainfiles/200807/146295236.pdf

For general information on U.S. food and agricultural exports and USDA's export market development programs:

Foreign Agricultural Service: http://www.fas.usda.gov

U.S. Food Taiwan: http://www.usfoodtaiwan.org

For more information on the Taiwan market for food and agricultural products, please contact the AIT Agricultural Trade Office at ATOTaipei@fas.usda.gov

8. PORK

Unit: METRIC TONS

	2009	2010*	2011 (est.)	2014 (est.)
Total Market Size	931,783	909,962	917,600	922,550
Total Local Production	857,155	850,000	850,000	850,000
Total Exports	2,696	2,408	2,400	2,450
Total Imports	77,324	62,370	70,000	75,000
Imports from the U.S.	32,763	23,793	28,000	30,000
Exchange Rate: 1 USD	$33.05	$31.85 (f)	$31.75 (p)	$31.50 (p)

*Annual totals est. based on available trade data Note: Figures are for porcine meat in metric tons (carcass weight equivalent). The conversion ratio from trade data into pork carcass weight equivalent is 1:1.43. Source: Council on Agriculture, Global Trade Atlas

Taiwan's pork consumption is relatively stable, and local producers supply most of the market (92%). Historically, significant imports have occurred only in response to occasional short supplies and high local pork prices. During the past decade, however,

U.S. pork has gained acceptance by Taiwan food processors. As a result, there is now a steady demand for imports of pork for further processing, although imports declined in 2010 due to high prices in North America.

Sub-Sector Best Prospects

Imports of pork were disrupted in 2007 due to the detection of ractopamine, a feed ingredient that is approved for use in the United States but not approved in Taiwan, in some samples of U.S. pork. Total pork Imports in 2008 recovered, due mainly to high prices of locally produced pork resulting from lower production. However, during this period of heightened scrutiny of U.S. pork, Canada replaced the United States as the leading exporter of pork to Taiwan.

Ractopamine is approved for use with pigs in the United States and many other countries. Taiwan also previously reviewed the use of ractopamine, determined it to be safe and in 2007 notified the WTO of Taiwan's intent to adopt MRLs for ractopamine. However, Taiwan subsequently suspended plans to implement the MRLs in response to pressure from domestic swine producers. As a result, Taiwan importers are still cautious about bringing in certain cuts of U.S. pork until the issue with ractopamine can be resolved.

Opportunities

Although the Taiwan pork market is dominated by local production, certain variety meats are in high demand and are undersupplied. By exporting these niche market pork muscle meats and variety meat products to Taiwan, U.S. exporters may find room for market growth.

U.S. valued-added products such as natural pork and processed pork products are recognized and accepted in retail and foodservice operations. Several U.S. pork and processed meat products have recently entered the Taiwan market and found strong demand in niche food and retail sectors.

Web Resources

For current information on export requirements for Taiwan:

http://www.fsis.usda.gov/regulations_&_policies/Taiwan_Requirements/index.asp

For general information on U.S. food and agricultural exports and USDA's export market development programs: Foreign Agricultural Service: http://www.fas.usda.gov

U.S. Food Taiwan: http://www.usfoodtaiwan.org

For more information on the Taiwan market for food and agricultural products, please contact the AIT Agricultural Trade Office at ATOTaipei@fas.usda.gov

9. POULTRY MEAT

Unit: METRIC TONS

	2009	2010*	2011 (est.)	2014 (est.)
Total Market Size	701,492	758,200	760,200	763,200
Total Local Production	625,369	635,000	630,000	630,000
Total Exports	6,351	4,800	4,800	4,800
Total Imports	82,474	128,000	135,000	138,000

Imports from the U.S.	70,522	115,000	120,000	122,000
Exchange Rate: 1 USD	$33.05	$31.85 (f)	$31.75 (p)	$31.50 (p)

* Annual totals est. based on available trade data Source: Council of Agriculture, Global Trade Atlas

Generally, Taiwan's rate of self-sufficiency for poultry products is over 80%. The U.S. and Canada are the only two poultry product suppliers eligible to ship to Taiwan. Due to the price competitiveness of U.S. chicken, Taiwan's imports of U.S. poultry meat rose two-thirds by volume to reach 96,614 metric tons during the first ten months of 2010.

The WTO special safeguard (SSG) for chicken wings and legs was triggered on July 10, 2010 when total imports of the product reached 73,827 metric tons. The trigger volume for other chicken cuts in 2010 was 3,104 MT, and the import volume of this category was only 300 MT below the trigger volume as of Dec. 31, 2010. The strong increase in imports of poultry wings and legs will not reflect on the SSG levels until 2014, so the 2011 SSG trigger volume for chicken wings and legs will remain at 2010 level of 73,827 metric tons.

Sub-Sector Best Prospects

Taiwan consumers prefer dark meat over breast meat, so the top import items are poultry legs, thighs and wings. Imports of U.S. poultry meat are expected to continue to grow as the market adjusts to increasing competition. Significant opportunities exist, in particular for those producers who are able to address importer concerns regarding cut and packaging specifications. Imported poultry has gained market acceptance in processed food and food service channels, while the situation in retail market has also been changing due to better defrost technology and consumer acceptance of frozen chicken. Consumer preference for home use is still for locally raised "fresh/chilled" product or live chickens selected and slaughtered at neighborhood wet markets.

Opportunities

At present, the United States is the only major exporter permitted to export to Taiwan. Imports from Canada, however, are becoming a threat because Canadian poultry products are considered to have less water added after slaughter. While the U.S. currently has a virtual monopoly on poultry imports, the strong potential for real competition in the next few years should encourage U.S. suppliers to increase their service and responsiveness to Taiwan importers in order to maintain solid relationships that will be less subject to price-based switching when suppliers from other countries gain access.

Web Resources

For current information on export requirements for Taiwan:

http://www.fsis.usda.gov/regulations_&_policies/Taiwan_Requirements/index.asp

For general information on U.S. food and agricultural exports and USDA's export market development programs:

Foreign Agricultural Service: http://www.fas.usda.gov

U.S. Food Taiwan: http://www.usfoodtaiwan.org

For more information on the Taiwan market for food and agricultural products, please contact the AIT Agricultural Trade Office at ATOTaipei@fas.usda.gov

10. READY-TO-USE PROCESSED FOODS/INGREDIENTS

Overview Ready-to-use processed foods are scattered among various HS Codes. Sauces/condiment preparations and coffee are just two of the more promising categories: HS Code 2103: Sauces/Condiment Unit: USD thousands

	2009	2010*	2011 (est.)	2014 (est.)
Total Market Size	NA	NA	NA	NA
Total Local Production	NA	NA	NA	NA
Total Exports	32,520	36,000	35,000	36,000
Total Imports	64,025	68,000	69,000	70,000
Imports from the U.S.	11,879	11,900	12,000	12,500
Exchange Rate: 1 USD	$33.05	$31.85 (f)	$31.75 (p)	$31.50 (p)

* Annual totals est. based on available trade data Source: Global Trade Atlas

HS CODE 0901: COFFEE UNIT: USD THOUSANDS

	2009	2010*	2011 (Est.)	2014 (Est.)
Total Market Size	N/A	N/A	N/A	N/A
Total Local Production	N/A	N/A	N/A	N/A
Total Exports	1,039	1,800	1,890	1,900
Total Imports	49,056	64.500	69,000	72,000
Imports from the U.S.	8,433	9,000	9,500	10,000
Exchange Rate: 1 USD	$33.05	$31.85 (f)	$31.75 (p)	31.50 (p)

* Annual totals est. based on available trade data Source: Global Trade Atlas

Sub-Sector Best Prospects

Increasingly vigorous competition for consumer attention continues to drive many food processors to innovate their mainstream and traditional food product lines. Importer education and technical/application support will help introduce new products and encourage increased sales.

Other examples of ready-to-use products are sauces/condiment preparations, especially tomato ketchup/paste/sauces and mustard flour/meal which are used in the local food service sector. In 2009, Japan led the overall market with a 53% market share followed by the United States (19%), China (7%), Thailand (4%), Hong Kong (4%), Malaysia (2%), and Italy (2%).

Taiwan's insatiable demand for coffee continues to grow at a rapid pace. Taiwan's coffee consumption grew an est. 10% in 2009. Local coffee production is also on the rise. Much of the domestic coffee output is consumed locally by tourists visiting coffee farms, but official data shows that Taiwan coffee exports are also growing. In 2009, Indonesia was the leading supplier of coffee to Taiwan with 26% market share, followed by the United States (17%), Brazil (12%), Italy (6%) and Columbia (6%).

Opportunities

Trends that bode well for this category include: 1) the increasing numbers of people dinning out on a regular basis; 2) the strong uptick in the number of retail coffee outlets. The growth in Western-style restaurants and coffee shops is contributing to the growing demand for processed foods and food ingredients. In addition, U.S. suppliers of flavorings, nutritional additives, product performance enhancers, and labor saving (preprocessed) ingredients can also expect to find high demand for their products in Taiwan.

Web Resources

For further information, please see the following Foreign Agricultural Service (FAS) reports:

Taiwan Retail Food Sector (TW6015)

http://www.fas.usda.gov/gainfiles/200604/146187588.pdf

HRI Food Service Sector (TW6008)

http://www.fas.usda.gov/gainfiles/200603/146187161.pdf

For general information on U.S. food and agricultural exports and USDA's export market development programs:

Foreign Agricultural Service: http://www.fas.usda.gov

U.S. Food Taiwan: http://www.usfoodtaiwan.org

For more information on the Taiwan market for food and agricultural products, please contact the AIT Agricultural Trade Office at ATOTaipei@fas.usda.gov

11. SOFT WOOD AND TREATED LUMBER OVERVIEW UNIT: CUBIC METERS

	2009	2010*	2011 (est.)	2014 (est.)
Total Market Size	596,473	727,000	746,000	756,000
Total Local Production	18,947	17,000	16,000	16,000
Total Exports	10,896	10,000	10,000	10,000
Total Imports	588,422	720,000	740,000	750,000
Imports from the U.S.	112,166	120,200	124,000	126,000
Exchange Rate: 1 USD	$33.05	$31.85 (f)	$31.75 (p)	$31.50 (p)

*Annual totals est. based on available trade data Source: Council on Agriculture, Global Trade Atlas

The U.S. is Taiwan's second largest softwood and treated lumber supplier. Total softwood and treated lumber exports to Taiwan in 2010 are est. to be worth more worth more than $30 million. Of the products in this category, Southern Yellow Pine accounts for most of the export volume and value, totaling 60,592 cubic meters during the first 10 months of 2010 with a total value of $18 million. In fact, trade data shows that U.S. pine products, treated and non-treated, jumped 28% and 3% in 2009 and 2010 respectively in volume over the previous years' levels. U.S. Southern Yellow Pine products are well accepted and are used in many applications in Taiwan such as flooring, decks, fences, marinas, patio and mountain trails.

Sub-Sector Best Prospects

A number of efforts are being undertaken by the Taiwan authorities to demonstrate the benefits of green building technologies, increase the practice of green building, and to make information on green building more readily available. With the Ministry of Interior's announcement on increasing the use of green building materials used in both public and commercial buildings from 5% to 30%, the utilization of sustainable energy resources has become a major focus of the construction industry.

In addition, after many years of negotiations and consultations, the Taiwan Construction and Planning Agency of the Interior Ministry (CPAMI) announced on October 31, 2008, a working set of fire code regulations which should result in a significant increase in the use of U.S. wood products in Taiwan construction/housing projects in the future.

With several U.S. wood industry associations' collaborative efforts, Taiwan authorities recently accepted a request to modify the Chinese National Standards for wood and wood products that was submitted by American Institute in Taiwan. The proposal is with the Wood Codes Committee for review. If these modifications are accepted, there should be more opportunities for U.S. wood exports.

Opportunities

The bulk of the engineered wood market consists of low-end plywood and fiber/particle board. Changes in construction regulations, government procurement priorities, and consumer attitudes promise to spur interest in high-end engineered wood products such as structural glulam and special-application laminated wood -- categories in which U.S. suppliers have particular expertise and competitive advantages.

With the recent U.S. economic downturn, U.S. wood exporters have been offering more attractive prices to buyers with certain specifications for export to Taiwan.

In order to reflect the central government agencies' green building policies, the forestry, and building and construction authorities also hope to revise the building regulations in National parks, limiting buildings and construction to adopt only wood structure designs.

The 2010 Taipei International Flora Expo, which opened for the first time in Taiwan on November 5, 2010 and will continue through April 25, 2011, also brings many opportunities to the U.S. wood industry. Major exhibition sites at the Expo, including several other country pavilions, are designed with treated wood lumber from the United States.

Major importers in Taiwan also discovered a new opportunity for U.S. engineered wood products -- moldboard used in construction sites, traditionally made of tropical hardwood, can be produced by U.S. laminated Veneer Lumber (LVL) with better persistence and elasticity performance.

Web Resources

For further information, please see the following Foreign Agricultural Service (FAS) reports:

Announcement of Taiwan Fire Codes for Wood Frame Construction (TW8066):

http://www.fas.usda.gov/gainfiles/200811/146306360.pdf

Quarantine Requirements for Wood Packaging Material used in Imported Commodity (TW9023)

http://gain.fas.usda.gov/Recent%20GAIN%20Publications/Quarantine%20Requirements%20for%20Wood%20Packaging%20Material%20used%20in%20Imported%20Commodity%20_Taipei%20ATO_Taiwan_4-10-2009.pdf

For general information on U.S. food and agricultural exports and USDA's export market development programs: Foreign Agricultural Service: http://www.fas.usda.gov

U.S. Food Taiwan: http://www.usfoodtaiwan.org

For more information on the Taiwan market for food and agricultural products, please contact the AIT Agricultural Trade Office at ATOTaipei@fas.usda.gov

12. WINE & SPIRITS

Wine

Unit: USD thousands

	2009	2010*	2011 (est.)	2014 (est.)
Total Market Size	NA	NA	NA	NA
Total Local Production	NA	NA	NA	NA
Total Exports	280	400	320	340
Total Imports	68,471	88,037	101,250	116,500
Imports from the U.S.	6,356	8,113	9,350	10,700
Exchange Rate: 1 USD	$33.05	31.85(f)	$31.75(p)	$31.50(p)

*Annual totals est. based on available trade data Source: Global Trade Atlas (HS code: 2204)

SPIRITS & OTHERS

Unit: USD thousands

	2009	2010*	2011 (est.)	2014 (est.)
Total Market Size	NA	NA	NA	NA
Total Local Production	NA	NA	NA	NA
Total Exports	12,541	16,011	19,213	23,055
Total Imports	268,783	306,329	337,000	370,000

Imports from the U.S.	1,394	1,708	1,600	1,700
Exchange Rate: 1 USD	$33.05	$31.85(f)	$31.75(p)	$31.50(p)

Sub-Sector Best Prospects

Taiwan imports of wine and spirits in 2010 are projected to increase by 17% compared to 2009 due to the recovery of the economy and the strong demand from on-premise channels. The demand for wine and spirits is expected to remain strong in 2011.

In terms of product mix, whisky accounts for the largest share with an est. 56% share by volume and 98% share by value for the 2010 calendar year. Taiwan imports of whisky have increased by 15% in 2010 compared to the same period in 2009. The growth is attributed to the rebounding economy, especially the resumption of companies holding year-end appreciation parties for their employees and clients.

The grape wine import market is anticipated to increase in volume by 30% in 2010 compared to 2009 because of the growing economy that supports increasing bar and restaurant patronage. Grape wine accounts for 22% of wine and spirits import value. Over past two years, the consumer profile of wine has extended to young professionals. The entry-level wine that consumers prefer is dark-color and round-tannin wine while off-dry wine remains popular among female drinkers. The proposed health tax on alcoholic beverages is anticipated to have more of an impact on the sales volume of low-priced wines but is anticipated to have little impact on premium-priced wine and spirits.

The image of U.S. wine is commonly associated with California, which is well recognized by Taiwan consumers and the media. In recent years, there has been more diversity in sourcing from other American states and grape varieties, such as wine from Washington State being sold in Costco retail stores, and Pinot Noir from Oregon being promoted by the industry.

Opportunities

American Bourbon has great potential in this market but requires an aggressive marketing push to make impact on the single malt scotch market. Suppliers from the UK have held a 95% market share for five consecutive years. After many years of educating Taiwan consumers by local UK whisky experts through various media outlines have translated into preferences by consumers for single malt scotch and as a symbol of status and are willing to pay higher prices to give premium scotch as a gift. According to domestic retailers, the market for single malt scotch is expected to continue to grow. American spirit producers should take advantage of demand and appreciation in Taiwan for premium quality products by launching consumer education programs.

U.S. wine has the potential to grow if the players can create more promotions by taking advantage of important festival occasions at the retail and VIP sectors. The shopping pattern is more and more concentrated before major festival occasions, such as Moon Festival, company year-end parties and Chinese New Year. Long-term consumer education will cultivate future consumers and brand awareness while "right-timing" promotions may result in immediate purchases.

Web Resources

For further information, please see the following Foreign Agricultural Service (FAS) reports:

Wine and Spirits Market Update (TW7027)

http://www.fas.usda.gov/gainfiles/200706/146291374.pdf

Grape Wine Market Update (TW9039)

http://gain.fas.usda.gov/Recent%20GAIN%20Publications/Wine_Taipei%20ATO_Taiwa n_7-28-2009.pdf

For general information on U.S. food and agricultural exports and USDA's export market development programs:

Foreign Agricultural Service: http://www.fas.usda.gov

U.S. Food Taiwan: http://www.usfoodtaiwan.org

For more information on the Taiwan market for food and agricultural products, please contact the AIT Agricultural Trade Office at ATOTaipei@fas.usda.gov

TRADE REGULATIONS, CUSTOMS AND STANDARDS

IMPORT TARIFFS

Taiwan's tariff schedule is based on the Harmonized Commodity Description and Coding System (HS) of the Customs Cooperation Council. On July 1, 2006, Taiwan promulgated a comprehensive revised tariff schedule in compliance with Taiwan's Free Trade Agreement with Guatemala. This revised tariff schedule applies to all of Taiwan's trade partners. In order to meet the requirements for the 2007 version of the World Customs Organization's Harmonized System (HS), starting on January 1, 2009, Taiwan put into effect a new version of its tariff schedule and reclassified 297 items of the tariff lines of the ten-digit level in 2010.

Taiwan continues to make unilateral improvements to its tariff structure on finished goods and raw materials. In 2010, the average nominal tariff rate for industrial products was 4.18% and 13.88% for agricultural products. The overall average nominal tariff rate for imported goods was 5.85% in 2010. U.S. industry continues to request that Taiwan lower tariffs on imports of many products, including large motorcycles, wine, canned soups, cookies, savory snack foods, vegetable juices, potatoes and potato products, table grapes, apples, fresh vegetables, and citrus products.

When Taiwan became a WTO member in January 2009, Taiwan implemented tariff-rate quotas (TRQs) on small passenger cars and chassis, three categories of fish and fish products, as well as a number of agricultural products. On January 1, 2007, in accordance with its WTO commitments, Taiwan made additional tariff cuts and increased TRQ amounts on these products. In addition, Taiwan has committed to fully eliminate TRQs on small passenger cars by 2011.

TRADE BARRIERS

Although authorities have taken steps to improve the business and investment climate,

U.S. firms report that impediments remain in some sectors, especially services. Rules on local licensing of professionals are cited as a barrier to foreign providers of some services. Some foreign investors complain of lengthy and non-transparent approval processes. Taiwan's science-based industrial parks and export processing zones, by contrast, offer streamlined procedures.

IMPORT REQUIREMENTS AND DOCUMENTATION

Under the terms of the Foreign Trade Act, most commodities can be imported freely. In general terms, no import permit or licensing is required and importers can apply for customs clearance directly. However, there are some exceptions. Import permits or documents are required for commodities under the Negative List, which are subject to import restrictions. Commodities under the Negative List include those under certain international treaties or trade agreements and items subject to national defense, society security, cultural protection, hygiene, and environmental and ecological concerns, as well as those subject to policy demands. Products subject to import bans can be imported only with a special import permit from the Board of Foreign Trade, while documents, such as a letter of consent from the relevant authorities, are required for those commodities that are subject to certain importation conditions.

A foreign supplier's pro forma invoice (quotation) is required for application of an import permit and the establishment of a letter of credit. Documents required for shipments to or from Taiwan include a commercial invoice, bill of lading or airway bill, and packing list. A certificate of origin is also required for designated commodities such as sedans, other small passenger cars and chassis, tobacco and alcohol products, and some agricultural products. Shipments of agricultural products, plants, and animals to Taiwan may require certificates of inspection or quarantine issued in the country of origin and are subject to inspection and quarantine upon importation into Taiwan.

The commercial invoices are required for all shipments and must show the import license number; FOB, C&F, or CIF value; insurance; freight; and discounts or commissions, if any. The commodity description and value shown on the commercial invoices must agree with those on the import license, if any. No requirements exist as to the form of a commercial invoice or a bill of lading. A packing list is required for all shipments if the number of cartons in the shipment exceeds two. In addition to the information generally included in a standard bill of lading, all marks and case numbers appearing on packages must be shown. Customs does not permit the grouping of marks or numbers on a shipment of mixed commodities. Most documents presented for use in customs clearance processing must be prepared in Chinese to avoid delays and expedite clearance processing.

U.S. EXPORT CONTROLS

The U.S. Department of Commerce's Bureau of Industry and Security (BIS) is responsible for implementing and enforcing the Export Administration Regulations (EAR), which regulate the export and re-export of designated "dual-use" commercial items. Dual-use items are defined as those having both commercial and potential military applications.

The majority of exports do not need an export license. Only a relatively small percentage of total U.S. exports and re-exports require an application to BIS for a license. Licensing requirements are dependent upon an item's technical characteristics, the destination, the end-user, and the end-use. It is the responsibility of the U.S. exporter to comply with all BIS licensing requirements.

If an item requires an export license, the exporter must file an application with BIS. If the application is approved, a license number and expiration date will be provided for use on the export documentation.

A good starting point for U.S. exporters to obtain hands-on information about licensing requirements and regulations is to attend a U.S. Department of Commerce export control seminar on complying with U.S. Export Controls. For counseling assistance, please contact one of the following Department of Commerce offices:

U.S.

Department of Commerce Washington D.C. Trade Information Center Tel: 1-800-USA-TRADE Fax: 202-482-4473

U.S.

Department of Commerce Washington D.C. BIS – Office of Exporter Services Tel. 202-482-4811 Fax: 202-482-2927

BIS Western Regional Office Newport Beach, California Tel: 949-660-0144 Fax: 949-660-9347

Northern California Branch San Jose, California Tel: 408-998-8806 Fax: 408-998-7470

Further information is available from BIS at http://www.bis.doc.gov

TEMPORARY ENTRY

Taiwan is not a member of the Admission Temporaire/Temporary Admission (ATA) Carnet system. However, Taiwan has signed bilateral agreements with 42 nations, including the United States, to implement provisions of the ATA Carnet. These agreements grant temporary customs exemptions for commercial samples, professional instruments and equipment, as well as exhibition goods that are brought into Taiwan for sales promotion and exhibition purposes. They facilitate international business by avoiding extensive customs procedures, eliminating payment of import duties and value-added taxes, and replacing the purchase of temporary import bonds. Items must be shipped out of Taiwan within one year of the event's conclusion to avoid imposition of import tariffs and other taxes.

The agreement with the United States to implement the TECRO/AIT Carnets was signed in December 2005. Like the ATA Carnet, TECRO/AIT Carnets are valid for up to one year and allow U.S. exporters to avoid duties and taxes for commercial samples and professional equipment when entering Taiwan. The TECRO/AIT Carnets issued exclusively for Taiwan are very similar to the traditional ATA Carnets, but must be applied for separately (due to the U.S.'s lack of diplomatic recognition of Taiwan). For example, if traveling to both Taiwan and an ATA Carnet country, one would have to apply for a TECRO/AIT Carnet and an ATA Carnet. Questions regarding the process of the TECRO/AIT Carnets should be directed to:

U.S. Council for International Business ATA Carnet Department 1212 Avenue of the Americas New York, N.Y. 10036 Tel: 212-703-5078 Fax: 212-944-0012 Email: atacarnet@uscib.org Website: http://www.uscib.org

In the case of imported goods on which only a rental is incurred, without a transfer of ownership, the duty shall be determined on the basis of the rental amount plus the transportation and insurance fees. Duty for goods entering Taiwan for repair or assembly will be based on the costs of repair or assembly (excluding freight and insurance).

LABELING AND MARKING REQUIREMENTS

Taiwan labeling regulations require that the net contents of packaged goods shall be shown in metric units. Dual labeling in metric and non-metric units is permitted. Measuring instruments calibrated in non-metric units must show metric equivalents. Taiwan's Consumer Protection Law requires that all imported goods have Chinese language labels and instructions, which shall be at least as comprehensive as the language-of-origin labels and accompanying instructions.

All imported cargo must bear a mark of distinctive design, a set of three or more letters, or a combination of design and letters indelibly stenciled, stamped, or burned on the packing or on the cargo itself. For cargo packed in cases, boxes, crates, casks, drums, or cylinders, each container should bear a separate number that cannot be repeated for two years. Bags or bales also must bear a nonrecurring number, date, or set of three or more letters. In addition, each package of a consignment must be numbered consecutively. Numbering is not essential for large lots of cargo except when packaged in cases, boxes, or crates, provided that each package of the consignment contains cargo of identical weight.

Food Product Labeling: As required by the March 1995 amendment to Taiwan's "Law Governing Food Sanitation," Taiwan requires Chinese language labeling for food items sold at retail (with some exemptions for selected food-service items) and requires that the labels be affixed before customs clearance. Required information includes product name; weight; volume or quantity of the contents (if a mixture of two or more components, they must be listed separately); name of food additives; name, address, and telephone number, of importer (mandatory) and manufacturer (not mandatory); country of origin; and expiry date. For imported foreign foods, the following information is also required in Chinese on the label: type of frozen foods; method and conditions of storage; and cooking instructions if the products require cooking or are not ready-to-eat. In addition, all food products containing five percent or more bioengineered soybean or corn ingredients by weight must be labeled as "Genetically Modified (GM)" or "Containing Genetically Modified." Highly processed food items (items with no proteins or DNA) do not require GM labels. If you have questions on labeling requirements for food products, please contact the AIT Agricultural Trade office at ATOTaipei@usda.gov

Organic Labeling: The Council of Agriculture (COA) implemented new regulations for organic products on January 29, 2009 and announced certification recognition of USDA's National Organic Program (NOP) on March 18, 2009. Under the new regulations, once a foreign country's organic standards have been recognized by the COA, importers will be responsible for 1) notifying the COA for each shipment on a batch basis, and 2) coordinating with their foreign suppliers and certification agencies to apply for approval from the COA to mark "organic" on the labels. The increased paperwork and coordination of shipments has raised costs. However, some importers replace the listing of "organic" on the label with similar but more ambiguous language such as "natural". More information is available at COA's website: http://www.coa@mail.gov.tw

PROHIBITED AND RESTRICTED IMPORTS

In order to comply with its WTO commitments, Taiwan has eliminated more than 99 percent of its import controls on 10,892 official import categories. Currently, there are 101 product categories facing import restrictions. Of those categories, 15 require import permits from the Board of Foreign Trade (BOFT) and 86 are prohibited. Most of the permit-required categories are related to public sanitation and national defense concerns, and include some agricultural products and ammunition. In addition, Taiwan maintains a lengthy list of products that are banned if made in China, including chocolate confectionary and meters for medical equipment. In April 2006, the Ministry of Economic Affairs (MOEA) lifted the ban on certain unfilled chocolate from China.

Presently, Taiwan can import from and export directly to China. Taiwan is significantly liberalizing imports of products from China as both have joined the WTO. As of January 1, 2010, 8,643 categories or 79.4 percent of all import categories in the Taiwan tariff schedule can be imported from China. Taiwan continues to review imports from China and considers further relaxation once every six months or as requested by the business sector.

The Economic Cooperation Framework Agreement (ECFA), which was signed by Taiwan and China in June 2010, includes a list of 267 goods permitted to enter Taiwan from China with tariff reductions and exemptions. The list will be phased in over three years starting on January 1, 2011, with the goal of eliminating tariffs on all of the 267 items at the end of the three-year period. Taiwan still retains import bans on more than 2,000 products from China. U.S. industry reports that these bans inhibit their regional supply chains, and prevent certain categories of goods produced in their China-based facilities from entering Taiwan's market.

Starting May 19, 1998, Taiwan extended to all banned China imports the same rules and regulations it applies to all other imports with regard to country of origin and value-added processing. In other words, banned goods from China can be imported if it can be shown that they were primarily made elsewhere, and did not undergo substantial transformation in China. The definition of "substantial transformation" is value added exceeding 35 percent of the final export value of the goods. In addition, companies working in bonded facilities, enterprises located in export processing zones, and science-based industrial parks which produce wholly for export are permitted to import banned manufacturing components and raw materials from China.

CUSTOMS REGULATIONS AND CONTACT INFORMATION

Although Taiwan's trade rules and regulations are at times quite complicated, it is becoming easier and more convenient for foreign businesspeople and manufacturers to do business with Taiwan. Rules and regulations have been simplified, infrastructure facilities improved, and trade services enhanced.

All goods shipped to Taiwan must have a value and description for the goods shipped. Duties assessed are based on the Cost, Insurance, and Freight (CIF) value. The duties payable on imported goods are essentially defined on an ad valorem, specific, or selective basis, depending on the items involved. If, for some reason, accurate values cannot be determined, the wholesale domestic market value at the port of importation is used instead.

The contact information for Taiwan's customs office is provided below:

Department of Customs Administration Ministry of Finance (MOF) No. 2, Aiguo W. Rd., Taipei
Tel: 886-2-2322-8000 Fax: 886-2-2356-8774 Website: http://doca.mof.gov.tw

Standards

Overview

Standards Organizations

Conformity Assessment

Product Certification

Accreditation

Publication of Technical Regulations

Labeling and Marking

Contacts

Overview

The Bureau of Standards, Metrology and Inspection (BSMI) under the Ministry of Economic Affairs (MOEA) is the authority responsible for the development, compilation, and publication of "Chinese National Standards" (CNS) as well as for conformity assessment. BSMI also implements commodity inspection measures as stipulated in Taiwan's Commodity Inspection Law.

Taiwan's national standards are based primarily on international standards such as those set up by the International Standards Organization (ISO), International Electrotechnical Commission (IEC), and International Telecommunications Union (ITU).

Taiwan acceded to the WTO on January 1, 2009. The preparation, adoption and application of national standards comply with the requirements of the Agreement on Technical Barriers to Trade (TBT) of the WTO.

National standards are classified under 26 categories. As of 2010, the BSMI has 14,462 national standards. Of these standards, 3,244 correspond with international standards, and the harmonization for 2,813 of them has been completed. The harmonization of Taiwan's national standards with international standards increased from 46 % in 2001 to 86.7% in 2010. The BSMI administers the CNS Market Certification System whereby products meeting standards are allowed to carry the CNS mark.

As of January 1, 2011, the Taiwan Food and Drug Administration has taken over from BSMI all necessary food safety inspection measures while the Bureau of Animal and Plant Health Inspection & Quarantine (BAPHIQ) continues to be responsible for inspection and quarantine for purpose of safeguarding animal and plant health. Taiwan's sanitary and phytosanitary (SPS) standards are generally different from U.S. standards or those established by international regulatory bodies such as the Office f International Epizootic (OIE) or the Codex Alimentarius. In some cases, these differences – more specifically, the absence of maximum residue level (MRL) standards for many agricultural chemicals in common use internationally – have resulted in mark disruptions and created uncertainty among U.S. exporters and Taiwan importers.

STANDARDS ORGANIZATIONS

The Standards Division (First Division) of the Bureau of Standards, Metrology and Inspection (BSMI) is responsible for drafting standards policies and regulations. This division consists of four sections, with the First Section responsible for general standardization activities including the drafting of regulations, guidance, harmonization planning, administration of the CNS mark, compilation of the standards gazette, and promotion of national standards. The remaining three sections are each responsible for standards in specific industry sectors.

In addition, there are four standards-related institutions under BSMI involved in the development and promotion of Chinese National Standards. These are the National Standards Review Council, the Information & Communication National Standard Promotion Committee, the National Standards Technology Committees, and the Electronic Information Exchange Committee.

BSMI issues plans for standards development semi-annually. These plans are published in the National Gazette and filed with the WTO Secretariat in accordance with the TBT agreement.

BSMI has established an on-line system for the public to obtain Chinese National Standards information (http://www.bsmi.gov.tw). The website also provides access to updated standards gazettes.

NIST NOTIFY U.S. SERVICE

Member countries of the World Trade Organization (WTO) are required under the Agreement on Technical Barriers to Trade (TBT Agreement) to report to the WTO all proposed technical regulations that could affect trade with other Member countries. Notify U.S. is a free, web-based e-mail subscription service that offers an opportunity to review and comment on proposed foreign technical regulations that can affect your access to international markets. Register online at Internet URL: http://www.nist.gov/notifyus/

CONFORMITY ASSESSMENT

The Sixth Division of BSMI is in charge of testing and inspection methods. This division currently conducts testing in areas including electromagnetic compatibility (EMC), biochemistry, chemistry, polymers, materials, electrical engineering, and mechanical engineering. Nearly 600 industrial goods including chemical, mechanical and electronics products, and more than 1,800 agricultural, food and fishery products are subject to inspection. Testing of commodities can only be done by BSMI or testing laboratories recognized by the BSMI.

Taiwan's testing system is called the "Registration of Product Certification" (RPC). Under the testing system, products are subject to the appropriate conformity assessment modules as determined by the authorities. The conformity assessment modules cover both the design and production phases of product manufacture. The Declaration of Conformity (DoC) is the least trade restrictive conformity assessment procedure, and is currently applied only to low-risk products with stable manufacturing technology and few concerns of risk or danger. Under the DoC scheme, manufacturers may have testing done by BSMI designated laboratories, prepare their own technical documents, and draft the declaration of conformity themselves.

Currently, a total of 67 commodities are covered by the DoC system. These products are digital cameras, digital video cameras, typewriters, cash registers, electronic calculators, card punching machines, optical disc devices, data storage units, class B main boards of computers, add-on cards with I/O devices, and vulcanized rubber tubes. A complete list of national testing organizations or conformity assessment bodies is available on BSMI's website at http://www.bsmi.gov.tw

PRODUCT CERTIFICATION

Products specified by the Ministry of Economic Affairs (MOEA) must comply with inspection requirements before they are shipped from the manufacturing premises or imported and placed on the market. Manufacturers or importers of these products must apply to BSMI for inspection before shipment or importation. Beginning on January 1, 2004, BSMI adopted a dual-track approach to allow manufacturers or importers to choose the "Registration of Product Certification" (RPC) scheme or a Batch-by-Batch inspection (BBI) with Type Approval.

The RPC scheme encompasses requirements for the product design stage (type testing) and manufacturing stage (quality management system). In other words, while applying for the RPC, both product design and manufacturing processes must conform to the requirements specified by BSMI. With the RPC certificate, domestic manufacturers may ship their products, and importers may proceed directly with customs clearance.

Importers or firms having small numbers of products for sale in the domestic market may find the BBI with Type Approval approach easier. According to BSMI, upon approval of the sample product, the random inspection rate is about 10 percent.

Taiwan's safety regulations follow IEC and CNS standards. All safety testing for end products must be done in Taiwan by Taiwan-accredited laboratories. The UL safety certification alone is not considered sufficient to meet Taiwan requirements for end product safety certification. Home appliances, certain fire fighting products, electrical power distribution devices (including cables and switches), lighting products for in-door use and motors require safety testing or inspection in Taiwan.

To enhance the protection of consumers from hazards posed by telecommunications and electrical and electronics products, and to meet international requirements for electromagnetic compatibility (EMC), BSMI has promulgated "Regulations Governing Electromagnetic Compatibility of Commodities." Manufacturers or importers must obtain type approval of their products from BSMI and all products must apply for inspection based on the EMC type approval certificate. Currently, 266 products are subject to EMC inspection, of which 11 are mechanical products, 146 electrical items, and 109 electronic products.

There is currently an Electromagnetic Compatibility (EMC) Mutual Recognition Agreement (MRA) between the U.S. and Taiwan covering information technology products. In accordance with the terms of this MRA, BSMI accepts EMC testing by any laboratory located in the United States and accredited by the National Institute of Standards and Technology (NIST) under the National Voluntary Laboratory Accreditation Program (NAVLAP). NIST accredited labs outside the U.S. are not accepted by BSMI.

As a result of discussion with NIST in 2009, BSMI now recognized 99 U.S. Conformity Assessment Bodies (CABs) to conduct product testing as described in the Asia-Pacific Economic Cooperation (APEC) Mutual Recognition Agreement. However, except for EMC, all the other safety related testing required by BSMI must be conducted in Taiwan.

U.S. industry and importers of toys, sunglasses, lighting, handbags, and other consumer products seek cooperative resolutions with Taiwan officials to reduce cost and eliminate redundant testing through an establishment of mutual recognition programs to recognize tests done overseas.

ACCREDITATION

Taiwan Accreditation Foundation (TAF) is the island's sole national body recognized by the Taiwan authorities for the accreditation of conformity assessment against international standards. Under the TAF, the Department of Certification Body Accreditation is responsible for executing and managing the assessment and accreditation of domestic certification bodies for quality management, product and personnel. As for the Department of Laboratory Accreditation, its main mission is to execute and manage the assessment and accreditation of laboratory inspection bodies and proficiency test providers.

Accreditation for labs is conducted on a voluntary basis. At present, TAF provides laboratory accreditation in four major categories -- calibration, testing, civil engineering, and medical – with a total of 32 fields. So far, TAF has accredited 1,347 laboratories in Taiwan. There are 38 accredited bodies under TAF engaged in the accreditation of management systems -- which include quality, environmental, occupational health and safety, information security, food safety, and green products management systems -- and 39 handling accreditation for commodities.

Detailed information about accreditation in Taiwan and a list of accreditation bodies are available on TAF's website: http://www.cnla.org.tw/tafweb/indexEng.aspx

PUBLICATION OF TECHNICAL REGULATIONS

Proposed and final technical regulations are submitted to the MOEA by the BSMI for publication. This information is then published in the National Standards Gazette. In addition to the Gazette, BSMI also publishes several pamphlets to propagate information on standards. These pamphlets include the Catalogue of National Standards Categories, List of CNS Mark Product Items and Directory of CNS Mark Companies, Compilation of Laws & Regulations of Applying for CNS Mark, Q&A on Standards and CNS Mark, and Q&A on Technical Barriers to Trade. BSMI's website (http://www.bsmi.gov.tw) also provides updated information from standards gazettes and on standards regulations.

U.S. entities can provide their comments about local technical regulations or other related issues by contacting the BSMI directly or through the National Enquiry Point under the WTO TBT Agreement in the U.S. The BSMI Information Center performs the functions of National Enquiry Point under the WTO TBT Agreement for other countries.

LABELING AND MARKING

Taiwan's Commodity Labeling Act, amended on June 25, 2004, stipulates that all labeling shall be made in Chinese and may be supplemented by English or other foreign languages. When an imported commodity is introduced for sale in the domestic market, labeling, instructions, and sales literature written in Chinese must be added to the commodity by the importer. The contents provided in the Chinese language must not be simpler or more condensed than those from the place of origin of the commodity. The name/title and the address of the foreign manufacturer of an imported commodity to be labeled may not be written in the Chinese language.

Where a commodity is introduced for sale in the Taiwan market, the following particulars shall be labeled:

Name of the commodity;

Name, telephone number and address of the producer or manufacturer, the place of origin of the commodity, and the name, telephone number, and address of the importer for imported commodity;

Contents or composition of the commodity;

-Major components/ingredients or materials.

-Net weight, volume or quantity, or measurements shall be labeled in statutory measuring units and other measurements may be added when it is deemed necessary.

Date of manufacture in the Chinese calendar or Gregorian calendar; the expiration date or the term of validity if the commodity has a limited duration of storage; and other particulars as required by the Central Taiwan authorities.

If any of the following conditions apply, the scope of application, date of expiration, methods of use and storage of the commodity, and other points requiring attention must be indicated:

Hazardous or dangerous in nature;

Related to health and safety; and

Having special characteristics or requiring special handling.

Contacts

For more information about standards related issues, please contact the following relevant organizations:

Bureau of Standards, Metrology and Inspection, Ministry of Economic Affairs No. 4 JiNan Rd., Sec. 1, Taipei 100, Taiwan Tel: 886-2-2343-1700 Fax: 886-2-2356-0998 Website: http://www.bsmi.gov.tw

Taiwan Accreditation Foundation 8F, No. 20 Nan-Hai Road, Taipei 10074, Taiwan Tel: 886-2-2391-4626 Fax: 886-2-2397-1744 Website: http://www.taftw.org.tw

Ministry of Economic Affairs No. 15 Fuzhou St., Taipei 10015, Taiwan Tel: 886-2-2341-4986 Fax: 886-2-2391-9973 Website: http://gcis.nat.gov.tw

TRADE AGREEMENTS

Taiwan joined the WTO on January 1, 2009. Taiwan became a member of the Asia Pacific Economic Cooperation (APEC) in November 1991, and joined the Central American Bank for Economic Integration in 1992. Taiwan is also a member of the Asian Development Bank (ADB), the Pacific Economic Cooperation Council (PECC), and the Pacific Basin Economic Council (PBEC). Further information about Taiwan's bilateral and multilateral trade agreements is available on the Board of Foreign Trade's (BOFT) website: http://www.trade.gov.tw

Web Resources Board of Foreign Trade, Ministry of Economic Affairs (MOEA): http://www.trade.gov.tw Department of Customs Administration, Ministry of Finance

(MOF): http://doca.mof.gov.tw Directorate General of Customs, MOF: http://www.customs.gov.tw

Bureau of Standards, Metrology and Inspection, MOEA: http://www.bsmi.gov.tw Department of Commerce, MOEA: http://gcis.nat.gov.tw Taiwan Accreditation Foundation: http://www.taftw.org.tw

INVESTMENT AND BUSINESS CLIMATE - STRATEGIC INFORMATION AND CONTACTS FOR STARTING BUSINESS

Contact for More Information

-Michael Pignatello
-Deputy Chief, Economic Section, American Institute in Taiwan
-No. 7, Lane 134, Sec. 3, Xinyi Road, Taipei 110659 Taiwan
-+886-2-2162-2000
-pignatellomx@state.gov

Strategically located between Northeast and Southeast Asia, Taiwan is an important hub for regional and global trade and investment, especially in the high-technology industry. Indicative of its developed and open investment environment, Taiwan ranks in the upper 15th percentile of major global indices measuring ease of doing business, economic freedom, and competitiveness. To promote Taiwan's regional economic integration and as part of seeking participation in multilateral free trade arrangements, regulatory agencies have initiated reforms across many sectors of the economy, including enhancements to protection of intellectual property rights and other investment-related regulations.

As a relatively open and liberal economy, Taiwan benefits from substantial foreign direct investment, with a total cumulative stock of USD 137 billion in approved investment as of December 2015. Taiwan's GDP growth slowed to 0.65 percent in 2015, largely as a result of declining exports due to slow regional and global economic growth. Taiwan attracts a wide range of U.S. investors, including in high-tech, traditional manufacturing, and services. The United States is Taiwan's largest single source of foreign investment, with the stock of committed U.S. foreign direct investment reaching USD 17.1 billion in 2014. U.S. private commercial services exports to Taiwan totaled over USD 12.8 billion in 2014.

Structural impediments in Taiwan's investment environment include stalled progress on the privatization of Taiwan's state-owned enterprises (SOEs), which exert influence in the utilities, aerospace, energy, postal, transportation, financial, and real estate sectors. Foreign ownership limits remain in place for wireless and fixed-line telecommunications, television broadcast, and transportation. Restrictions on investments from mainland China in some sectors have been relaxed as cross-Strait ties have improved. The Taiwan Central Bank retains a currency convertibility policy in which it reserves the right to require large transactions that could impact the foreign exchange market to be scheduled over several days. Foreign private equity firms have noted a lack of transparency and predictability in the investment approvals process.

Aiming to promote Taiwan as a regional financial hub, Taiwan's Financial Supervisory Commission (FSC) adopted a series of liberalization measures in 2014, including liberalization of financial firms' overseas investments and expansion of overseas business units. Amendments passed by the Legislative Yuan in June 2015 to investment-related statutes clarified review criteria for mergers and acquisitions. Other regulatory revisions and amendments to existing statutes proposed in 2015 aim to clarify review criteria for foreign investment in Taiwan, but these were not implemented or passed by the legislature.

Table 1

Measure	Year	Index or Rank	Website Address

TI Corruption Perceptions index	2015	30 of 167	http://www.transparency.org/cpi2015#results-table
World Bank's Doing Business Report "Ease of Doing Business"	2015	11 of 189	doingbusiness.org/rankings
Global Innovation Index	N/A	N/A	https://www.globalinnovationindex.org/content/page/data-analysis/ Taiwan data are not provided
U.S. FDI in partner country ($M USD, stock positions)	2015	23,631	Taiwan Ministry of Economic Affairs http://www.moeaic.gov.tw/system_external/ctlr?PRO=DownloadFile&t=4&id=807
World Bank GNI per capita	N/A	N/A	N/A

1. OPENNESS TO, AND RESTRICTIONS UPON, FOREIGN INVESTMENT

Attitude toward Foreign Direct Investment

Promoting inward FDI has been an important policy goal for the Taiwan authorities because of Taiwan's self-imposed public debt ceiling that limits public spending and Taiwan's low levels of domestic private investment, which on average grew only 2.8 percent per year over the last five years. Taiwan has pursued various measures to attract FDI from both foreign companies and Taiwan firms operating overseas. A network of science and industrial parks, export processing zones, and free trade zones aims to expand trade and investment opportunities by granting tax incentives, tariff exemptions, low-interest loans, and other favorable terms.

Taiwan maintains a negative list of industries closed to foreign investment for reasons the authorities assert relate to national security and environmental protection, including public utilities, power distribution, natural gas, postal service, telecommunications, mass media, and air and sea transportation. These sectors constitute less than one percent of the production value of Taiwan's manufacturing sector and less than five percent of the services sector. Railway transport, freight transport by small trucks, pesticide manufactures, real estate development, brokerage, leasing, and trading are open to foreign investment. The negative list of industries is available at http://www.moeaic.gov.tw/system_external/ctlr?PRO=LawsLoad&lang=1&id=32.

At the end of 2015, accumulated FDI stock in Taiwan totaled approximately USD 137 billion, according to Taiwan's Ministry of Economic Affairs (MOEA) foreign investment approval data. However, discrepancies exist between Taiwan official data and the 2015 World Investment Report of the United Nations Conference of Trade and Development (UNCTAD), which calculated Taiwan's net FDI stock at a much lower USD 68 billion as of 2014. The Taiwan authorities assert that the difference was due to UNCTAD's deduction of outward remittances of profits by foreign investors, in addition to foreign investors' ability to easily obtain low-cost financing directly from within Taiwan.

Other Investment Policy Reviews

Taiwan has been a member of the WTO since 2002. In September 2014, the WTO conducted the third review of the trade policies and practices of Taiwan. Related reports and documents are available at: https://www.wto.org/english/tratop_e/tpr_e/tp402_e.htm

The OECD and UNCTAD have not conducted investment policy reviews of Taiwan.

Laws/Regulations on Foreign Direct Investment

Regulations governing FDI principally derive from the *Statute for Investment by Foreign Nationals* and the *Statue for Investment by Overseas Chinese*. These two laws permit foreign investors to transact either in foreign currency or the New Taiwan Dollar (NTD). The laws specify that foreign-invested enterprises must receive the same regulatory treatment accorded local firms. Foreign companies may invest in state-owned firms undergoing privatization and are eligible to participate in publicly financed research and development programs.

Amendments the Legislative Yuan passed in June 2015 to investment-related statutes clarified investment review criteria for mergers and acquisition transactions. Other amendments were proposed in 2015 but were not passed, including one that would replace a pre-investment approval requirement with a post-investment reporting system for investments under a USD 1 million threshold. Ex ante approval would still be required for investments in restricted industries and those exceeding the threshold. In 2015, Taiwan authorities ceased consideration of a private equity investment's impact on capital markets and resulting thin capitalization as review criteria. Other criteria remain listed on the Ministry of Economic Affairs (MOEA) Investment Commission's Frequently Asked Questions website (located in Chinese only at http://www.moeaic.gov.tw/system_external/ctlr?PRO=FAQLoad&id=464).

In recent years, the Taiwan authorities revised rules to improve the business climate for startups. With the goal of developing Taiwan into a startup hub in Asia, Taiwan launched an entrepreneur visa program allowing young foreign entrepreneurs to remain in Taiwan if they raise minimum funding of NTD 2 million (USD 66,000). Taiwan has initiated rules to enable intellectual property (IP) rights holders to use IP as collateral in obtaining bank loans, and this and other rules would apply to foreign investors.

Please refer to the "Doing Business" section of the MOEA's Invest in Taiwan Center website, which provides useful information for foreign investors:

http://investtaiwan.nat.gov.tw/eng/show.jsp?LV=1&ID=18&MID=3

The Investment Commission website lists the rules, regulations, and required forms for seeking foreign investment approval: http://www.moeaic.gov.tw/

Business Registration

The MOEA operates a business registration website that describes the process: https://onestop.nat.gov.tw/oss/web/Show/engWorkFlow.do

Approval from the Investment Commission is required before proceeding with business registration. After receiving an approval letter from the Investment Commission, an investor can apply for capital verification and may then file an application for a corporate name and proceed with business registration. The new company must register with the Bureau of Labor Insurance and the Bureau of National Health Insurance before it can start recruiting and hiring employees.

The MOEA Department of Investment Services' (DOIS) Invest in Taiwan Center serves as Taiwan's investment promotion agency and provides streamlined procedures for foreign investors. DOIS services are available to all foreign investors.

For the manufacturing, construction, and mining industries, the MOEA defines small and medium-sized enterprises (SMEs) as companies with less than NTD 80 million (USD 2.5 million) of paid-in capital and fewer than 200 employees. For all other industries, SMEs are defined as having less than NTD 100 million (USD 3.1 million) of paid-in capital and fewer than 100 employees. Taiwan runs a Small and Medium Enterprise Credit Guarantee Fund to help SMEs obtain financing from local banks. Foreign firms may pay a fee to obtain a guarantee from the Fund. Taiwan's National Development Fund has set aside NTD 10 billion (USD 330 million) to invest in SMEs.

Industrial Promotion

MOEA's Invest in Taiwan Center website provides information about government programs to attract foreign investment. The *Statute for Industrial Innovation*provides the legal basis for offering tax credits for companies' research and development (R&D) expenditures. MOEA also runs several research and development subsidy programs. MOEA's current target industries for investment are offshore wind energy, logistics, electric passenger and cargo vehicles, information services, mobile broadband services, digital content, semiconductor equipment, biotechnology, and electronic materials.

Limits on Foreign Control and Right to Private Ownership and Establishment

Foreign entities are entitled to establish and own business enterprises and engage in all forms of remunerative activity as local firms unless otherwise specified in relevant regulations. Taiwan sets foreign ownership limits in certain industries, such as a 60 percent limit on direct foreign ownership of wireless and fixed line telecommunications firms, and a 49 percent limit on direct foreign investment in that sector. State-owned Chunghwa Telecom Co., which controls 97 percent of the fixed line telecom market, maintains a 55 percent limit on indirect foreign investment and a 49 percent limit on direct foreign investment. There is a 20 percent limit on foreign direct investment in cable television broadcasting services, but foreign ownership of up to 60 percent is allowed through indirect investment via a Taiwan entity. In addition, there is a foreign ownership limit of 49.99 percent for satellite television broadcasting services and piped distribution of natural gas, and a 49 percent limit for high-speed rail services. The foreign ownership cap on airport ground services firms, air-catering companies, aviation transportation businesses (airlines), and general aviation businesses (commercial helicopters and business jet planes) is less than 50 percent, with a separate limit of 25 percent for any single foreign investor. For Taiwan-flagged merchant ships, foreign investment is limited to 50 percent for Taiwan shipping companies operating international routes.

Since 2009, Taiwan has gradually been relaxing restrictions on investments from the People's Republic of China (PRC) in some sectors as cross-Strait relations have improved. Taiwan has opened more than two-thirds of its aggregate industrial categories to PRC investors, with 97 percent of manufacturing sub-sectors and 51 percent of construction and services sub-sectors open to PRC capital. PRC investors, however, continue to be prohibited from serving as a Taiwan company's Chief Executive Officer, although a PRC board member may retain management control rights of a Taiwan company. In June 2013, Taiwan and the PRC signed the cross-Strait Agreement on Trade in Services under the Economic Cooperation Framework Agreement (ECFA), but legislative review of the services agreement has stalled due to public opposition in Taiwan. As of early 2016, regulators were assessing whether to relax rules regarding PRC investment in portions of Taiwan's integrated circuits sector, and separately the Legislative Yuan was reviewing legislation that would create an oversight mechanism for cross-Strait agreements.

Privatization Program

There are currently no privatization program is in progress. Taiwan's most recent privatization, of the Aerospace Industrial Development Corporation (AIDC) in 2014, included institution of a foreign ownership ceiling of 10 percent due to the sensitive nature of the defense sector.

Screening of FDI

The Investment Commission screens applications for FDI, mergers, and acquisitions. Taiwan authorities claim that 95 percent of investments not subject to the negative list and with capital less than NTD 500 million (USD 18 million) obtain approval at the Investment Commission staff-level between two and four days. Investments between NTD 500 million and NTD 1.5 billion (USD 50 million) in capital take three to five days to screen and the approval authority rests with the Investment Commission's Executive Secretary. For investment in restricted industries, in cases where the investment amount or capital increase exceeds NTD 1.5 billion (USD 50 million), or for mergers, acquisitions, and spin-offs, screening takes 10 to 20 days and includes review by relevant supervisory ministries and final approval from the Investment Commission's Executive Secretary. Screening for foreign investments involving cross-border mergers and acquisitions or other special situations takes 20-30 days, as these transactions require interagency review and deliberation at the Investment Commission's monthly meeting.

The screening process has provided Taiwan's regulatory agencies opportunities to attach conditions to investments in order to mitigate concerns about ownership, structure, or other factors. Screening also may include an assessment of the impact of proposed investments on a sector's competitive landscape and protection of the rights of local shareholders and employees. Screening is also used to detect investments with unclear funding sources, including PRC-source capital. To ensure monitoring of PRC-source investment in line with Taiwan law and public sentiment, Taiwan's National Security Bureau has participated in every investment review meeting since April 2014 regardless of the size of the investment.

Foreign investors must submit an application form containing the funding plan, business operation plan, entity registration, and documents certifying the inward remittance of investment funds. Applicants and their agents must provide a signed declaration certifying that any PRC investors in a proposed transaction do not hold more than a 30 percent ownership stake and do not retain managerial control of the company. When an investment fails review, an investor may re-apply when the reason for the denial no longer exists. Foreign investors may also petition the regulatory agency that denied approval, or may appeal to the Administrative Court.

U.S. investors have expressed concerns about a lack of transparency, consistency, and predictability in the investment review process, particularly with regard to transactions involving private equity investment. Current guidelines on foreign investment state that private equity investors seeking to acquire companies in "important industries" must provide, for example, a detailed description of the investor's long term operational commitment and the investment's impact on sector competition. Investors have experienced lengthy review periods for private equity transactions.

Competition Law

Taiwan's Fair Trade Act was enacted in 1992. Taiwan's Fair Trade Commission examines business practices that might impede fair competition.

2. CONVERSION AND TRANSFER POLICIES

Foreign Exchange

There are few restrictions in place in Taiwan on converting or transferring direct investment funds. Foreign investors with approved investments can readily obtain foreign exchange from designated banks. The remittance of capital invested in Taiwan must be reported in advance to the Investment Commission, but the Commission's approval is not required. Declared earnings, capital gains, dividends, royalties, management fees, and other returns on investment may be repatriated at any time.

For large transactions requiring the exchange of NTD into foreign currency that could potentially disrupt Taiwan's foreign exchange market, the Taiwan Central Bank may require the transaction to be scheduled over several days. There is no written guideline on the size of such transactions, but according to law firms servicing foreign investors amounts in excess of USD 100 million may be affected. Capital movements arising from trade in merchandise and services, as well as from debt servicing, are not restricted. No prior approval is required for movement of foreign currency funds not involving conversion between NTD and foreign currency. The exchange rate is based on the market rate offered by each bank. The NTD fluctuates under a managed float system.

Remittance Policies

There are no restrictions on remittances deriving from approved direct investment and portfolio investment. No prior approval is required if the cumulative amount of inward or outward remittances does not exceed the annual limit of USD 5 million for an individual or USD 50 million for a corporate entity. There is no legal parallel currency market in Taiwan.

Taiwan is not a member of Financial Action Task Force (FATF) but is a member of the Asia-Pacific Group on Money Laundering, a FATF-style regional body. In January 2016, a new draft *Terrorist Financing Prevention Act* was forwarded to the Legislative Yuan for review.

3. EXPROPRIATION AND COMPENSATION

According to Taiwan law, the authorities may expropriate property whenever such a course is determined to be necessary for the public interest, such as for national defense, public works, and urban renewal projects. The U.S. government is not aware of any previous or recent cases of nationalization or expropriation of foreign-invested assets in Taiwan. There are no reports of indirect expropriation or any official actions tantamount to expropriation. Under Taiwan law, no venture with 45 percent or more foreign investment may be nationalized, as long as the 45 percent capital contribution ratio remains unchanged for a period of 20 years after the establishment of the foreign business. Taiwan law requires fair compensation be paid within a reasonable period when the authorities expropriate constitutionally-protected private property for public use.

4. DISPUTE SETTLEMENT

Legal System, Specialized Courts, Judicial Independence, Judgments of Foreign Courts

Taiwan has a codified system of law. In addition to the specialized courts, Taiwan has a three-tiered court system composed of the District Courts, the High Courts, and the Supreme Court. The *Compulsory Enforcement Act* provides a legal basis for enforcing the ownership of property. Taiwan does not have discrete commercial or contract laws. A variety of different laws regulate businesses and specific industries, such as the *Company Law*, *Commercial Registration*

Law,Business Registration Law, and *Commercial Accounting Law*. Taiwan's Civil Code provides the basis for enforcing contracts.

Taiwan's court system is generally viewed as independent and free from overt interference by other branches of government. The U.S. Department of State's 2015 Human Rights Report stated that although Taiwan authorities made efforts to eliminate corruption and diminish political influence in the judiciary, some residual problems remained. Judicial reform advocates pressed for greater public accountability, reforms of the personnel system, and other procedural reforms. Some political commentators and academics publicly questioned the impartiality of judges and prosecutors involved in high-profile and politically sensitive cases.

Taiwan established its Intellectual Property Court in July 2008, in response to the need for a more centralized and professional litigation system for disputes relating to intellectual property rights. There are also specialized divisions in the District Courts and High Courts to deal with labor disputes. Foreign courts' judgments are final and binding, and enforced on a reciprocal basis.

Bankruptcy

Taiwan has a bankruptcy law that guarantees creditors the right to share the assets of a bankrupt debtor on a proportional basis. Secured interests in property are recognized and enforced through a registration system. Bankruptcy is not criminalized in Taiwan. Corporate bankruptcy was generally governed by the*Company Act* and the *Bankruptcy Act*. In 2014, there were 132 rulings on bankruptcy petitions.

Investment Disputes

Foreign investment disputes with the Taiwan authorities are rare. Taiwan resolves disputes according to its domestic laws and based on national treatment or investment guarantee agreements.

International Arbitration

Taiwan is not a signatory of any international investment treaties, but it has entered into bilateral investment treaties with countries including Singapore, Thailand, Malaysia, and India. Taiwan does not have an investment treaty with the United States. Taiwan's bilateral investment treaties serve to promote and protect foreign investments.

A court order on recognition and enforcement must be obtained before a foreign arbitral award can be enforced in Taiwan. Any foreign arbitral award may be enforceable in Taiwan, provided that it meets the requirements of Taiwan's *Arbitration Act*. In November 2015, the Legislative Yuan amended the *Arbitration Act*to stipulate that a foreign arbitral award, after an application for recognition has been granted by a court, shall be binding on the parties and have the same force as a final judgment of a court, and is enforceable. Taiwan referred to the UNCITRAL model law when the *Arbitration Act* was revised in 1998.

Parties to a dispute may pursue mediation by a court, a mediation committee of a town or city, and/or the Public Procurement Commission. Mediation is generally non-binding unless parties agree otherwise. Civil mediation approved by a court has the same power as a binding ruling under civil litigation.

Arbitration associations in Taiwan include the Chinese Arbitration Association, Taiwan Construction Arbitration Association, Labor Dispute Arbitration Association, and the Chinese Construction Industry Arbitration Association in Taiwan.

ICSID Convention and New York Convention

In part due to its unique political status, Taiwan is not a member of the International Centre for the Settlement of Investment Disputes (ICSID Conventions), and is not a signatory to the 1958 New York Convention on the Recognition and Enforcement of Foreign Arbitral Awards.

Duration of Dispute Resolution – Local Courts

There is no time limit for court rulings on disputes.

5. PERFORMANCE REQUIREMENTS AND INVESTMENT INCENTIVES

WTO/TRIMS

Taiwan has not notified the WTO of any measures that are inconsistent with the Trade Related Investment Measures (TRIMs) obligations. Taiwan does not require foreign firms to transfer technology, locate in specified areas, or hire a minimum number of local employees as a prerequisite to investment.

Investment Incentives

Taiwan has instituted investment incentives as stipulated in the *Statute for Industrial Innovation* and the *Act for the Establishment and Management of Free Trade Zones*. Domestic and foreign investors can receive tax incentives for investing in free trade zones, in public construction, and in biotechnology/pharmaceuticals. Investment support from the central authorities may be available for priority projects. Industrial zones, export processing zones, science parks, and local governments offer various types of subsidies, financing, and tax deductions. For a detailed list of investment incentives programs, please refer to the Invest-in-Taiwan website at: http://investtaiwan.nat.gov.tw/eng/show.jsp?ID=10&MID=3

Research and Development

Investors may receive low-interest loans or subsidies for participating in industrial R&D and industry revitalization programs. Research and development tax credits, equivalent to 15 percent of total R&D expenditures, are available only to companies who file corporate income taxes in Taiwan. Government procurement tenders are open to the public, including foreign firms. Under the *Government Procurement Act*, government procurement includes construction work, purchase or lease of property, and retention or employment of services.

Performance Requirements

Taiwan does not mandate any performance requirements.

Data Storage

Taiwan does not have forced localization policies related to data storage.

6. PROTECTION OF PROPERTY RIGHTS

Real Property

Interests in property are enforced in Taiwan. Taiwan maintains a reliable recording system for mortgages and liens. Taiwan law protects the land use rights of indigenous peoples. Taiwan's *Land Act* stipulated that forests, fisheries, hunting grounds, salt fields, mineral deposits, sources of water, and lands lying within fortified and military areas and those adjacent to the national frontiers may not be transferred or leased to foreigners. As in other investment categories, Taiwan has specific regulations governing property acquisition by PRC investors.

Intellectual Property Rights

Taiwan is not a member of the World Intellectual Property Organization (WIPO) but adheres to key international agreements such as the Berne Convention and the Agreement on Trade-related Aspects of Intellectual Property Rights (TRIPS). Reflecting progress in Taiwan's IPR legal regime and enforcement, the Office of the U.S. Trade Representative (USTR) removed Taiwan from the Special 301 Watch List in 2009. The United States continues to monitor a number of IPR issues in Taiwan, including online piracy of copyrighted materials, illegal textbook copying on university campuses, end-user piracy of software, satellite signal theft, corporate trade secret theft, and weak pharmaceutical patent protections. The importation and transshipment of counterfeit products, mainly from mainland China, is also a problem. The United States is actively working with the Taiwan authorities to address these issues.

Taiwan authorities have announced their intent to revise IP-related laws to meet criteria stipulated in the Trans-Pacific Partnership text, such as extending copyright protection from life plus 50 years to life plus 70 years, adopting a patent linkage system, extending market protection on biologics, and imposing criminal liability on persons importing counterfeit products. Amendments to the *Pharmaceutical Affairs Act* in 2015 increased penalties for the production, distribution, and sale of counterfeit medicines. The law authorizes pharmaceutical regulatory data protection for five years, the same period as in the United States, for chemical compound drugs. Amendments extending regulatory data protection to new indications were submitted to the Executive Yuan in December 2015 and are currently pending submission to the legislature.

Taiwan's Intellectual Property Police reported that the value of trademark and copyright seizures in 2015 totaled NTD 14.4 billion (USD 432 million). Taiwan Customs reported that the number of cases involving seizures of imported counterfeit branded goods increased by 34 percent from 149 cases in 2014 to 199 cases in 2015. Customs officials attribute the rise in seizures to increased detection of small parcel air freight shipments of counterfeit goods purchased from mainland Chinese e-commerce sites.

A trademark or patent applicant must file an application with Taiwan's Intellectual Property Office (TIPO). TIPO normally renders a decision within six months after it receives all supporting documents. If the application is approved, the mark/patent will be published and registered after the applicant pays registration fees within two months upon receiving the approval notice. Taiwan's patent application review period was expected to shorten from an average of 41 months in 2013 to less than 22 months in 2016, following the implementation of Patent Prosecution Highway (PPH) agreements with the United States, Japan, Spain, and the Republic of Korea in 2011, 2012, 2013, and 2015 respectively.

Taiwan has no patent linkage system, and there have been several cases of approvals and reimbursements for generic drugs despite of the existence of valid patents. As of April 2016, Taiwan was conducting final public hearings on *Pharmaceutical Affairs Act* amendments that would establish a patent linkage system, prior to their submission for Executive Yuan and legislative approval.

Patent holders may request the Taiwan Customs authorities suspend clearance and detain goods suspected of infringing their patent rights. An affected rights holder must submit a written statement detailing the infringement allegation and a security deposit equivalent to the import value. If final judgment confirms that the detained goods have infringed the patentee's rights, the owner of the detained goods will be responsible for all relevant expenses incurred.

Resources for Rights Holders

Contact at AIT:
-Kris Kvols
-Economic Officer
-+886-2-2162-2000
-kvolsdk@state.gov
American Chamber of Commerce in Taipei (http://amcham.com.tw/)

7. TRANSPARENCY OF THE REGULATORY SYSTEM

Taiwan has transparent policies and effective laws that foster competition and establish clear rules. Accounting, legal, and regulatory procedures are mostly transparent and consistent with international standards. All publicly listed companies were required to prepare financial reports using International Financial Reporting Standards (IFRS) as of 2013. Unlisted public companies, credit cooperatives, credit card companies, and insurance intermediaries were required to prepare financial reports using IFRS starting in 2015.

In November 2015, the Executive Yuan extended the public comment period for the amendment, promulgation, and abolishment of legislation from seven days to no less than 14 days, a step toward greater regulatory transparency. To help foreign investors obtain updated information regarding regulatory changes, the Executive Yuan Gazette in September 2015 launched an online platform and email subscription service to release draft bills and regulations for public comment. In February 2016, the Gazette dedicated a section to providing information concerning technical barriers to trade (TBT) and sanitary and phytosanitary measures (SPS), which require a public comment period of at least 60 days under WTO rules. Taiwan's National Development Council (NDC) operates the Regulatory Reform Platform (http://law.ndc.gov.tw) with the goal of enhancing policy communication with the general public. Through the platform, the public can submit comments on specific legislation, offer policy suggestions, and obtain information on newly promulgated or amended regulations.

8. EFFICIENT CAPITAL MARKETS AND PORTFOLIO INVESTMENT

Taiwan authorities welcome foreign portfolio investment in the Taiwan Stock Exchange (TWSE), with foreign investment now accounting for 37 percent of TWSE capitalization. In recent years, in addition to the offshore banking units that have been in operation since 1983, Taiwan launched offshore securities and offshore insurance units, aiming to attract a broader investor base. The Financial Supervisory Commission (FSC) has switched to a negative list approach toward local banks' overseas business not involving the conversion of the NTD.

Taiwan's capital market is mature and active. As of the end of 2015, there were 874 companies listed on the TWSE, with total market trading volume of USD 703 billion (including transactions of stocks, Taiwan Depository Receipts, exchange traded funds, and warrants). Foreign portfolio investors are not subject to a foreign ownership ceiling except in certain restricted companies, and are not subject to any ceiling on portfolio investment. Payments and transfers resulting from international trade activities are fully liberalized in Taiwan. A wide range of credit instruments, all allocated on market terms, are available to both domestic- and foreign-invested firms.

Money and Banking System, Hostile Takeovers

Taiwan's banking sector is healthy and banks are tightly regulated. The sector's non-performing loan (NPL) ratio has remained below one percent since 2010, with a sector average of 0.23 in December 2015. Capital-adequacy ratios (CAR) are generally high, and several of Taiwan's leading commercial lenders are government-controlled, enjoying implicit state guarantees. The sector as a whole had a CAR of 12.67 percent as of September 2015, far above the Basel III regulatory minimum of 10.5 percent required by 2019. Taiwan banks' liquidity coverage ratio, which was required by Basel III to reach 100 percent by 2019, already averages about 119 percent. Taiwan's banking system is mostly deposit-funded and has little exposure to global financial wholesale markets. Regulators have encouraged local banks to expand to overseas markets, especially to Southeast Asia, and to minimize exposure to mainland China. Taiwan Central Bank statistics show that Taiwan banks' exposure to mainland China on an ultimate risk basis declined for five consecutive quarters to USD 65 billion in 2015, after peaking at USD 94 billion in the third quarter of 2014. Taiwan's largest banks in term of assets are the state-owned Bank of Taiwan, which has USD 157 billion in assets, followed by the state-controlled Mega Bank, with USD 100 billion in assets.

The Taiwan Central Bank operates as an independent agency under the Executive Yuan free from political interference. The Central Bank's mandates are to maintain financial stability, develop Taiwan's banking business, guard the stability of the New Taiwan Dollar's external and internal value, and promote economic growth within the scope of the three aforementioned goals.

To promote the asset management business in Taiwan, starting May 2015 foreigners holding a valid visa entering Taiwan have been allowed to open an NTD account with local banks, replacing the previous dual-identification (passport and resident card) requirements.

Mergers and acquisitions are governed by a variety of laws and regulations (see Section 1). Hostile takeovers are rare in Taiwan.

9. COMPETITION FROM STATE-OWNED ENTERPRISES

Taiwan launched privatization programs in 1989 transforming many state-owned enterprises (SOEs) into private industries. In March 2016, the Executive Yuan instructed the NDC to compile a consolidated list of all SOEs in Taiwan managed by different ministries, but the list had not been published as of April 2016. As of December 2015, the authorities owned 19 SOEs, including official agencies such as the Taiwan Central Bank. Some existing SOEs are large in scale and exert significant influence in their industries, especially monopolies such as Taiwan Power Co. (Taipower) and Taiwan Water Co. MOEA plans to amend the*Electricity Industry Act* to liberalize the power generation and distribution businesses. Other SOEs such as the CPC Corporation (petroleum) and Taiwan Tobacco and Liquor Co. remained industry giants after their sectors were opened to competition. CPC controls over 70 percent of Taiwan's gasoline retail market. In August 2014, the Aerospace Industrial Development Corp. (AIDC) was successfully privatized through a public listing in the TWSE. MOEA holds a 45.7 percent stake in AIDC and intends to lower its stake to 34 percent by 2017.

The Taiwan authorities retain control over some SOEs that were privatized, including through managing appointments to boards of directors. These enterprises include Chunghwa Telecom,

China Steel, Taiwan Fertilizer Co., Taiwan Salt, China Shipbuilding Co., Yang Ming Marine Transportation Co., as well as eight public banks. Taking the banking sector as an example, as of 2015, Taiwan's four largest banks were either wholly owned or controlled by the authorities and accounted for 30 percent of Taiwan domestic banks' total assets.

In 2014, the 19 SOEs contributed NTD 210 billion (USD 7 billion) to Taiwan's treasury, with the Taiwan Central Bank contributing NTD 180 billion (USD 6 billion) of that total. The number of employees working in SOEs was 118,000 in 2014 after several years of gradual decline. R&D spending among SOEs in 2014 totaled NTD 5.7 billion (USD 190 million), concentrated in oil field exploration, drilling technology, and development of alternative energy.

Taiwan acceded to the WTO's Agreement on Government Procurement (GPA) in 2009. Taiwan's central and local government entities, as well as SOEs, are now all covered by the GPA. Except for the state monopolies, SOEs compete directly with private companies. SOEs' purchases of goods or services are regulated by the *Government Procurement Act* and are open to private and foreign companies via public tender. Private companies in Taiwan have the same access to financing as SOEs. Taiwan banks are generally willing to extend loans to enterprises meeting credit requirements. SOEs are subject to the same tax obligations as private enterprises and are regulated by the *Fair Trade Act* as private enterprises. The Legislative Yuan reviews SOEs' budget each year.

OECD Guidelines on Corporate Governance of SOEs

Taiwan has not adopted the OECD Guidelines on Corporate Governance for SOEs. In Taiwan, SOEs are defined as public enterprises in which the government owns more than 50 percent of the shares. Public enterprises with less than a 50 percent government stake are not subject to Legislative Yuan supervision but the authorities may retain managerial control through senior management appointments, which may change with each administration. Each SOE operates under the authority of the supervising ministry, and government-appointed directors should hold more than one-fifth of an SOE's board seats. The Executive Yuan, the Ministry of Finance, and MOEA have criteria in place for selecting individuals for senior management positions. Each SOE has a board of directors, and some SOEs have independent directors sitting on the board.

Sovereign Wealth Funds

Taiwan does not have a sovereign wealth fund. Members of the incoming administration that will take office in May 2016 have publicly stated they may consider setting up a quasi-sovereign wealth fund to promote economic development.

10. RESPONSIBLE BUSINESS CONDUCT

The Taiwan public has high expectations for and is sensitive to responsible business conduct (RBC), in part due to concerns about such issues as food safety and environmental pollution. The Taiwan authorities actively promote responsible business conduct. MOEA and the FSC have issued guidelines on ethical standards and internal control mechanisms to urge businesses to take responsibility for the impact of their activities on the environment, consumers, employees, and communities. MOEA maintains an online newsletter to publicize best practices and raise awareness of about latest RBC-related developments in Taiwan and abroad.

Companies with more than NTD 10 billion (USD 330 million) in capital and firms with direct impact on consumers such as food processing, restaurants, chemicals, and financial services were mandated to prepare annual social responsibility reports as of 2015. According to the TWSE, 77 percent of Taiwan's top 100 companies have published social responsibility reports, and 30 percent (or 255) of all total listed companies have issued reports. In August 2014, the TWSE launched the Taiwan Top Salary 100 Index, a government effort to promote corporate social responsibility and expand the use of profit-sharing for the benefit of employees.

In response to a series of food safety and environmental protection scandals in recent years, the authorities have imposed stricter monetary penalties on violators and launched a registration platform for food industry suppliers to track food ingredients used in the industry's production chain. Taiwan authorities encourage Taiwan firms to adhere to the OECD Due Diligence Guidance for Responsible Supply Chains of Minerals from Conflict-Afflicted and High-Risk Areas. Taiwan does not participate in the Extractive Industries Transparency Initiative.

11. POLITICAL VIOLENCE

Taiwan is a relatively young and vibrant multi-party democracy. The January 2016 presidential and legislative elections were peaceful and orderly, as was the transition of power between administrations. There are no recent examples of politically motivated damage to foreign investment.

12. CORRUPTION

Taiwan has implemented laws, regulations, and penalties to combat corruption, including in public procurement. The *Corruption Punishment Statute and Criminal Code* contain specific penalties for corrupt activities, including maximum jail sentences of life in prison and a maximum fine of up to NTD 100 million (USD 3.3 million). Laws provide for increased penalties for public officials who fail to explain the origins of suspicious assets or property. The U.S. government is not aware of cases where bribes have been solicited for foreign investment approval.

UN Anticorruption Convention, OECD Convention on Combatting Bribery

Taiwan is not a party to the OECD Convention on Combatting Bribery.

Resources to Report Corruption

-Agency Against Corruption (AAC), Ministry of Justice
- Overall Planning Division
- No. 318, 2nd floor, Song-jiang Road, Taipei
- aac2043@mail.moj.gov.tw

Transparency International Chinese Taipei http://www.tict.org.tw/front/bin/home.phtml

13. BILATERAL INVESTMENT AGREEMENTS

Bilateral Taxation Treaties

Taiwan does not have a bilateral taxation treaty with the United States. Taiwan has 29 bilateral tax agreements entered into force (available athttp://investtaiwan.nat.gov.tw/cht/show.jsp?ID=58) and has concluded similar agreements with Japan and Canada that are pending approval by those governments.

Taiwan has concluded economic cooperation (free trade) agreements with El Salvador, Guatemala, Honduras, Nicaragua, Panama, Singapore, and New Zealand, and has concluded 29 bilateral investment or related agreements (available at http://www.dois.moea.gov.tw/asp/relation1_1_3.asp).

Under the Taiwan Relations Act, the terms of the 1948 Friendship, Commerce, and Navigation Treaty between the Republic of China and the United States remain in force. U.S. investors are guaranteed national treatment and are provided a number of protections, including protection against expropriation. Representatives of the United States and Taiwan signed a Trade and Investment Framework Agreement (TIFA) in 1994 to serve as the basis for consultation on trade and investment issues. TIFA discussions were suspended in 2007 in response to Taiwan policies affecting U.S. beef imports, but resumed in 2013.

14. OPIC AND OTHER INVESTMENT INSURANCE PROGRAMS

Taiwan and the United States have an Overseas Private Investment Corporation (OPIC) agreement. The agreement, signed in 1952, is called the Agreement Dealing with Guaranty of American Investment of Private Capital in Taiwan. There are no active OPIC projects in Taiwan.

15. LABOR

Taiwan's unemployment rate declined to 3.78 percent in 2015 from 3.96 percent in the previous year. The unemployment rate for people aged between 15 and 24 years was 15.4 percent in 2015. Taiwan's labor force is decreasing as the society ages, with residents over 65 years of age expected to account for 20 percent of the total population by 2025. In the industrial sector, the number of blue-collar foreign workers increased from 331,585 in 2014 to 363,584 in 2015. Industry groups claim that a lack of blue-collar workers is one of the major issues facing manufacturers operating in Taiwan and have urged the authorities to increase the ceiling on foreign workers. Skilled white-collar labor, especially in the information technology sector, remains a strength of Taiwan's talent pool. However, Taiwan's low wage growth compared with neighboring economies poses a challenge for talent recruitment and retention. The authorities sponsor training and certificate programs for college graduates to increase the talent pool for the manufacturing industry.

Private companies are not subject to rules requiring the hiring of nationals. Local workers have expressed concern about displacement by lower-cost foreign workers. Employers may institute unpaid leave with employees' consent but must notify the labor authorities and continue to make health insurance, labor insurance, and pension contributions. Taiwan provides unemployment relief based on the *Employment Insurance Law*, vocational training allowances for jobless persons, and employment subsidies to encourage hiring.

Labor flexibility is the main reason Taiwan firms hire temporary workers. Financial and logistics industries hire temporary workers for entry-level administrative positions such as customer services representatives, administrative clerks, security guards, and janitors. SOEs also hire contract workers. Companies in specific hardship (labor-intensive) industries are entitled to a higher foreign labor quota. The authorities are considering relaxing rules for the hiring of foreign white-collar professionals in designated foreign trade zones.

Labor unions have become more active in Taiwan over the past decade, and the *Collective Agreement Act* outlines the negotiation mechanism for collective bargaining in order to protect labor's interests in the negotiations. If a proposal is refused, a union may submit an application for arbitration to the Committee for Dispute Resolution for Unfair Labor Practices under the Ministry of Labor Affairs (MOL). Taiwan has labor dispute resolution mechanisms in operation at all levels of labor, and the authorities accept about 20,000 cases per year. Starting in 2011, an arbitration mechanism was introduced to preempt disputes through a professional and neutral mediation system, which resolves about 60 percent of all cases.

Labor relations in Taiwan are generally harmonious. Although Taiwan is not a member of the International Labor Organization (ILO), it adheres to ILO conventions on the protection of workers' rights. Taiwan law, including related regulations and statutory instruments, protects the right to join independent unions, conduct legal strikes, and bargain collectively. Taiwan's labor authorities have sought to increase the frequency and coverage of labor inspections. MOL has proposed a law that would allow temporary workers to receive the same pay as full-time employees in equal positions.

Link to the U.S. Department of State Human Rights Report on Taiwan: http://www.state.gov/j/drl/rls/hrrpt/humanrightsreport/index.htm#wrapper

16. FOREIGN TRADE ZONES/FREE PORTS/TRADE FACILITATION

The first free trade/free port zone began operation in 2004 at Keelung, Taiwan's northern port. Another four were established in 2005 at Taoyuan International Airport and the international harbors in Kaohsiung, Taichung, and Taipei. In May 2010 and August 2013, the Executive Yuan approved free trade zones at Suao and Anping ports, respectively, bringing total free trade zones in Taiwan to seven. Taiwan authorities have relaxed restrictions on the movement of merchandise, capital, and personnel into and out of these zones. As part of a broader restructuring and to increase the competitiveness of Taiwan's ports, the Ministry of Transportation and Communication established the Taiwan International Ports Corp. (TIPC) in 2012 to manage commercial activities of Taiwan's ports and free trade zones. TIPC facilitates cooperation with foreign shipping operations and related businesses.

Taiwan seeks to promote the unique advantages its ports offer as hubs for the Asian regional market. In June 2013, the London Metal Exchange (LME) board approved Kaohsiung Port as an LME delivery port of primary aluminum, aluminum alloy, copper, lead, nickel, tin, and zinc.

17. FOREIGN DIRECT INVESTMENT AND FOREIGN PORTFOLIO INVESTMENT STATISTICS

Table 2: Key Macroeconomic Data, U.S. FDI in Host Country/Economy

		Host Country Statistical source*	USG or international statistical source	USG or International Source of Data: BEA; IMF; Eurostat; UNCTAD, Other	
Economic Data	Year	Amount	Year	Amount	
Host Country Gross Domestic Product (GDP) ($M USD)	2015	523,567	2015	518,816	https://research.stlouisfed.org/fred2/series/TWNNGDPDUSD
Foreign Direct Investment		Host Country Statistical source*	USG or international statistical source	USG or international Source of data: BEA; IMF; Eurostat; UNCTAD, Other	
U.S. FDI in partner country ($M USD, stock	2015	23,631	2014	17,073	BEA

positions)					
Host country's FDI in the United States ($M USD, stock positions)	2015	14,209	2014	5,676	BEA
Total inbound stock of FDI as % host GDP	2015	26.2	2014	13.0	UNCTAD

* Local GDP data source: Directorate General of Budget, Accounting, and Statistics (DGBAS). * Local FDI data source: Ministry of Economic Affairs (MOEA). Taiwan FDI data reflect approved investments and do not take into account disinvestment.

American Institute in Taiwan

LIST OF ATTORNEYS

American Institute in Taiwan
美國在台協會

American Institute in Taiwan
No. 7, Lane 134, Xin Yi Road, Sec. 3, Taipei, Taiwan
台北市信義路三段 134 巷 7 號
Tel: 886-2-2162-2000 Fax: 886-2-2162-2239
E-mail: Amcit-ait-t@state.gov

The attorneys listed below have expressed an interest in representing American citizens in Taiwan. The American Institute in Taiwan assumes no responsibility or liability for the professional ability reputation of, or the quality of services provided by, the following persons or firms. Inclusion on this list is in no way an endorsement by the Department of State or AIT. Firms practicing in the Taipei area are listed first, followed by a list of firms practicing in Northern Taiwan and Central Taiwan. Names are listed alphabetically, and the order in which they appear has no other significance. The information in the list on professional credentials, areas of expertise and language ability are provided directly by the lawyers. You may receive additional information about the individuals by contacting the local bar association or the local licensing authorities.

No. 7, Lane 134, Xin Yi Road, Sec. 3, Taipei, Taiwan 台北市信義路三段134巷7號
Tel: 886-2-2162-2000 Fax: 886-2-2162-2239
E-mail: Amcit-ait-t@state.gov

Attorneys listed as Resident Foreign Attorneys are not licensed to practice before courts in Taiwan. However, in many cases such attorneys are either associated with a Taiwan law firm or have lawyers in their offices who can appear before the court.

The Republic of China Bar Association can be reached by telephone at (02) 2331-2865, by fax at (02) 2375-5594, or by email at bartw@ms27.hinet.net . However, please note that English is not spoken. The address of the Association is 5F, No. 130, Chungking South Road, Section 1, Taipei.

To call Taipei from the United States, dial 011-886-2 plus the eight-digit number. To call Hsinchu and Taoyuan from the United States, dial 011-886-3 plus the seven-digit number. To call or Taichung from the United States, dial 011-886-4 plus the eight-digit number.

Registered mail may be sent through the Taiwan postal system and return receipts obtained. International reply coupons should be used when a prepaid reply is desired.

AIT's Kaohsiung branch office maintains a separate list of attorneys practicing in southern Taiwan. A copy of that list may be obtained by contacting AIT-Kaohsiung through AIT's website, by telephone at 07-238-7744, or by fax at 07-238-5237. To call Kaohsiung from the United States, dial 011-886-7 plus the seven-digit number.

ATTORNEYS IN THE TAIPEI AREA

Ace Tax, Patent & Law Office/ Yale & Yale Law Office

Address: 7F, No. 132, Section 3, Xinyi Road, Taipei, Taiwan
Tel: (886-2) 2705-8077; 2705-6999 Fax: (886-2) 2705-8099
Email: acelaw72@gmail.com ; yaleandyale@hotmail.com
Website: www.yaleyale.com
Areas of practice: Anti-dumping, countervailing, safeguard, WTO, arbitration, aviation, banking and financial law, BOT, child custody (divorce), construction, contracts, corporations, criminal, customs, estates, foreign investment, governmental relations, high tech, immigration, information technology, insurance, international, labor relations, licensing, litigation (civil, criminal, and administrative), maritime, marketing, patent/trademark/copying law, real estate, security, taxes, telecommunications.

Asia Law International Attorneys

Address: 17F, Suite B, No. 167, Dunhua North Road, Taipei, Taiwan
Tel: (886-2) 2717-1999
Email: info@asialaw.biz
Website: www.asialaw.biz
Areas of practice: Diverse legal matters for companies doing business in Asia, particularly commercial and corporate transactions and disputes, with an emphasis on technology and intellectual property rights.

Baker & McKenzie, Taipei

Address: 15F, Hung Tai Center, No. 168, Dunhua North Road, Taipei, Taiwan
Tel: (886-2) 2712-6151 Fax: (886-2) 2712-8292
Email: taipei@bakerandmckenzie.com
Website: http://www.bakermckenzie.com/Taiwan/Taipei/
Areas of practice: Banking and financial law, collections, contracts, corporations, marketing agreements, foreign investment, labor relations, insurance, real estate, patent/trademark/copyright law, maritime, aviation, taxes, and government relations.

CHEN CHANG & ASSOCIATES

Address: 3F-7, Taipei Entrepreneur Building, No. 2, Fuxing North Road, Taipei, Taiwan
Tel: (886-2) 2741-5091 Fax: (886-2) 2741-5090
Email: chenclaw@ms22.hinet.net
Areas of Practice: Banking and financial law, contracts, corporations, marketing agreements, foreign investment, labor relations, insurance, patent/trademark/copyright law, maritime, aviation, criminal law.

CHIEN YEH LAW OFFICES, TAIPEI

Address: 62F, Taipei 101 Tower, No. 7, Section 5, Xinyi Road, Taipei, Taiwan

Tel: (886-2) 8101-1973 Fax: (886-2) 8101-1972
Email: eleanorchin@chienyeh.com.tw
Website: http://www.chienyeh.com.tw
Contact: Eleanor Chin, Managing Partner
Areas of practice: Mergers and acquisitions, intellectual property, institutional investment, international investment, IPO and OTC listing, corporate governance, commercial investment, corporate reorganization, liquidation, bankruptcy, securities finance dispute resolution, government procurement and construction bids, public construction arbitration, private investment in infrastructure (BOT, BOO, BT), business, consumer protection, labor, employment and fair trading, insurance, real estate, technology and science, land law and administrative litigation, criminal law, medical and health law.

DEEP & FAR, ATTORNEYS-AT-LAW

Address: 13F, No. 27, Section 3, Zhongshan North Road, Taipei, Taiwan
Tel: (886-2) 2585-6688 Fax: (886-2) 2598-9900
Email: email@deepnfar.com.tw
Website: http://www.deepnfar.com.tw
Areas of practice: Child custody, marriage/divorce, estates, contracts, corporations, marketing agreements, foreign investment, labor relations, insurance, real estate, patent/trademark/copyright law, personal injury, maritime, immigration, criminal law, and government relations.

DING & DING LAW OFFICES

Address: 10F, No. 458, Section 4, Xinyi Road, Taipei, Taiwan
Tel: (886-2) 2762-5659 Fax: (886-2) 2761-7682
Email: ddinglaw@ms12.hinet.net
Areas of practice: Banking and financial law, contracts, corporations, marketing agreements, foreign investment, labor relations, insurance, patent/trademark/copyright law, maritime, aviation, taxes, and government relations.

Eiger Law, Taipei

Address: 12F, Building A, No. 25, Section 4, Ren'ai Road, Taipei, Taiwan
Tel: (886-2) 2771-0086 Fax: (886-2) 2771-0186
Website: www.eigerlaw.com
Contacts: Nathan Kaiser & John Eastwood
Email: nathan.kaiser@eigerlaw.com ; john.eastwood@eigerlaw.com
Areas of practice: Corporate law, fair trade and competition, mergers and acquisitions, foreign investment, commercial contracts, international trade, construction and infrastructure, labor and employment law, real estate, intellectual-property, licensing and technical cooperation, telecommunications, litigation and arbitration.

First International Law & Intellectual Property Offices

Address: 3F, No. 43, Section 1, Minsheng East Road, Taipei, Taiwan
Tel: (886-2) 2521-5900 Fax: (886-2) 2521-5311
Email: office@firstlaw.com.tw
Website: http://www.firstlaw.com.tw
Areas of practice: Trademark, patent, copyright, establishment of company or its branch office, labor relationship, stock's ownership dispute, construction dispute, real estate, etc.

Formosa Transnational, Attorneys-at-Law

Address: 13F, No. 136, Section 3, Ren'ai Road, Taipei, Taiwan
Tel: (886-2) 2755-7366 Fax: (886-2) 2755-6486

Email: ftlaw@taiwanlaw.com
Website: http://www.taiwanlaw.com
Areas of practice: Adoptions, child custody, marriage/divorce, estates, banking and financial law, collections, contracts, corporations, marketing agreements, foreign investment, labor relations, insurance, real estate, patent/trademark/copyright law, personal injury, maritime, aviation, immigration, criminal law, and taxes.

Formosan Brothers, Attorneys-at-Law

Address: 8F, No. 376, Section 4, Ren'ai Road, Taipei, Taiwan
Tel: (886-2) 2705-8086 Fax: (886-2) 2701-4705
Email: fblaw@mail.fblaw.com.tw
Website: http://www.fblaw.com.tw
Areas of practice: Adoptions, child custody, marriage/divorce, estates, banking and financial law, collections, contracts, corporations, marketing agreements, foreign investment, labor relations, insurance, real estate, patent/trademark/copyright law, personal injury, maritime, immigration, criminal law, and taxes.

Jones Day, Taipei

Address: 8F, No. 2, Section 2, Dunhua South Road, Taipei, Taiwan
Tel: (886-2) 7712-3399 Fax: (886-2) 2704-6791
Contact: Jack Huang
Email: jhuang@jonesday.com
Website: http://www.jonesday.com/taipei
Areas of practice: Banking and financial law, collections, contracts, corporations, marketing agreements, foreign investment, patent/trademark/copyright law, personal injury, maritime, criminal law, and taxes.

Kew & Lord, Attorneys-at-Law

Address: 9F, No. 17, Section 3, Ren'ai Road, Taipei, Taiwan
Tel: (886-2) 2771-3393 Fax: (886-2) 2772-5911
Email: kewnlord@ms19.hinet.net
Areas of practice: Criminal law, human rights law, general commercial law.

Lee & Li, Attorneys-at-Law

Address: 7F, No. 201, Dunhua North Road, Taipei, Taiwan
Tel: (886-2) 2715-3300 Fax: (886-2) 2713-3966
Email: attorneys@leeandli.com
Webpage: www.leeandli.com
Areas of practice: Estates, banking and financial law, collections, contracts, corporations, marketing agreements, foreign investment, labor relations, insurance, real estate, patent/trademark/copyright law, maritime, aviation, immigration, taxes, and government relations.

Lin & Partners, Attorneys-at-Law

Address: 27F, No. 99, Section 2, Dunhua South Road, Taipei, Taiwan
Tel: (886-2) 2705-5929 Fax: (886-2) 2731-2896
Email: attorneys@linandpartners.com.tw
Website: www.linandpartners.com.tw
Areas of Specialization: Banking and finance, commercial and personal insolvency, mergers and acquisitions, securities, general corporate law, contracts, construction law, international business transactions, foreign investment, antitrust, China-related matters, electronic commerce, privacy and data protection, intellectual property, computer law, technology law, administrative, taxation,

maritime, aviation, labor law, commercial, civil and criminal litigation, and alternative dispute resolution.

Thomas Liu Law Offices

Address: 4F-2, No. 1, Fuzhou Street, Taipei, Taiwan
Tel: (886-2) 2396-8519 Fax: (886-2) 2356-7056
Email: liulawo@yahoo.com.tw
Areas of practice: Adoptions, child custody, marriage/divorce, estates, contracts, corporations, marketing agreements, labor relations, insurance, real estate, patent/trademark/copyright law, personal injury, immigration, and criminal law.

OmniService Law Offices

Address: 8F, No. 27-5, Section 2, Zhongzheng East Road, New Taipei City, Taiwan
Tel: (886-2) 8809-1122 Fax: (886-2) 8809-7890
Email: wchern@omniservice.com.tw
Website: http://www.omniservice.com.tw
Areas of practice: International and domestic business transactions, intellectual property, banking, construction, real estate, labor and general legal matters.

Pamir Law Group

Address: 7F, No. 214, Dunhua North Road, Taipei, Taiwan
Tel: (886-2) 5588-1799 Fax: (886-2) 5588-1790
Email: info@pamirlaw.com
Website: www.pamirlaw.com
Areas of practice: General corporate and commercial matters including contract (outsourcing, distribution, OEM), employment, estate planning, finance, intellectual property, litigation/arbitration, mergers and acquisitions, venture capital/high-tech matters, China-related and cross-border matters, family law, government procurement and criminal law matters.

Taiwan Commercial Law Offices

Address: Suite 501, No. 131, Section 3, Minsheng East Road, Taipei, Taiwan
Tel: (886-2) 2717-6658 Fax: (886-2) 2717-7429
Email: info@tclo.com.tw
Website: http://www.tclo.com.tw/
Areas of practice: Banking and financial law, collections, contracts, corporations, marketing agreements, foreign investment, labor relations, insurance, real estate, patent/trademark/copyright law, aviation, and immigration law.

Saint Island International Patent & Law Offices

Address: 7F, No. 248, Section 3, Nanjing East Road, Taipei, Taiwan
Tel: (886-2) 2775-1823 Fax: (886-2) 2731-6377
Email: siiplo@mail.saint-island.com.tw
Website: http://www.saint-island.com.tw
Areas of practice: Contracts, marketing agreements, patent/trademark/copyright law, aviation.

Tai E International Patent & Law Office

Address: 9F, No. 112, Section 2, Chang'an East Road, Taipei, Taiwan
Tel: (886-2) 2506-1023 Fax: (886-2) 2501-1666
Email: lawoffice@taie.com.tw
Website: http://www.taie.com.tw

Areas of practice: Child custody, marriage/divorce, estates, collections, contracts, corporations, marketing agreements, foreign investment, labor relations, insurance, real estate, patent/trademark/copyright law, personal injury, immigration, and criminal law.

Tsar & Tsai Law Firm, Taipei

Address: 8F, No. 245, Section 1, Dunhua South Road, Taipei, Taiwan
Tel: (886-2) 2781-4111 Fax: (886-2) 2731-5581
Email: law@tsartsai.com.tw
Website: www.tsartsai.com.tw
Areas of practice: Banking and financial law, contracts, corporations, marketing agreements, foreign investment, labor relations, insurance, patent/trademark/copyright law, taxes, and government relations.

Wang & Wang

Address: 4F-2, No. 146, Songjiang Road, Taipei, Taiwan
Tel: (886-2) 2537-2694 Fax: (886-2) 2541-9662
Email: tpo@wangandwang.com
Website: http://www.wangandwang.com
Areas of practice: Estates, contracts, corporations, marketing agreements, foreign investment, labor relations, patent/trademark/copyright law, and government relations.

Winkler Partners

12F, No. 86, Section 1, Chongqing South Road, Taipei, Taiwan Tel: (886-2) 2311-2345 Fax: (886-2) 2311-2688 Email: info@winklerpartners.com
Website: www.winklerpartners.com
Areas of practice: Banking and financial law, contracts, corporations, marketing agreements, foreign investment, patent/trademark/copyright law, government relations.

Wong & Company Law Offices

Address: 9F, No. 39, Section 1, Zhongxiao West Road, Taipei, Taiwan
Tel: (886-2) 2382-0255 Fax: (886-2) 2382-0244
Email: attorney@wongandcompany.com.tw
Areas of practice: Adoptions, child custody, marriage/divorce, estates, banking and financial law, collections, contracts, marketing agreements, foreign investment, labor relations, insurance, real estate, patent/trademark/copyright law, personal injury, maritime, aviation, immigration, criminal law, taxes, and government relations.

World Law Offices

Address: 9F-1, No. 72, Section 2, Nanjing East Road, Taipei, Taiwan
Tel: (886-2) 2561-0361 Fax: (886-2) 2561-0363
Email: worldlaw@ms6.hinet.net
Areas of practice: Adoptions, child custody, marriage/divorce, estates, collections, contracts, corporations, marketing agreements, foreign investment, labor relations, real estate, patent/trademark/copyright law, personal injury, aviation, criminal law, and government relations.

WTW Taipei Commercial Law Firm

Address: 7F, No. 149, Section 2, Minsheng East Road, Taipei, Taiwan
Tel: (886-2) 2516-9577 Fax: (886-2) 2516-9715
Contacts: David Enterline & Dennis Tsai
Email: david@wtwct.com.tw ; dennis@wtwct.com.tw
Website: www.wtwct.com.tw

Areas of practice: Telecommunication and information technology, investment, e-commence, child custody, marriage/divorce, estate, banking and financial law, collections, contracts, corporations, mergers and acquisitions, capital markets and securities, commercial agreements, foreign investment, insurance, real estate, intellectual property-patent/trademark/copyright law, personal injury, labor relations, aviation, immigration, criminal law, taxes, dispute resolution mediation, arbitration and litigation, administrative law, fair trade and consumer rights, government relations and procurement..

Yangming Partners

Address: 10F, No. 89, Songren Road, Taipei, Taiwan
Tel: (886-2) 8725-6677 Fax: (886-2) 2729-5577
Email: yangming@yangminglaw.com
Website: www.yangminglaw.com
Areas of practice: Banking and financial law, contracts, corporations, marketing agreements, foreign investment, patent/trademark/copyright law, government relations.

ATTORNEYS PRACTICING IN NORTHERN AND CENTRAL TAIWAN

TAOYUAN

Rong-Teh Tsai, Attorney-at-Law

Address: No. 93, Datong Road, Taoyuan City, Taiwan
Tel: (886-3) 334-6223 Fax: (886-3) 333-4671
Email: h0367@ms17.hinet.net
Areas of practice: Adoptions, marriage/divorce, labor relations, insurance, personal injury, criminal law, taxes, and government relations.

HSINCHU

Lee & Li, Attorneys-at-Law

Address: 5F, No. 1, Science Park Life Hub, Industry East Second Road, Hsinchu Science Park, Hsinchu, Taiwan
Tel: (886-3) 579-9911 Fax: (886-3) 579-7880
Email: attorneys@leeandli.com
Website: www.leeandli.com
Areas of practice: Estates, banking and financial law, collections, contracts, corporations, marketing agreements, foreign investment, labor relations, insurance, real estate, patent/trademark/copyright law, maritime, aviation, immigration, taxes, and government relations.

Tsar & Tsai Law Firm, Hsinchu

Address: A6, 3F, No. 1, Lixin First Road, Hsinchu Science Park, Hsinchu, Taiwan
Tel: (886-3) 563-3999 Fax: (886-3) 577-9965
Email: law@tsartsai.com.tw
Website: www.tsartsai.com.tw
Area of practice: Patent/trademark/copyright law, foreign investment, commercial agreements, corporations, labor relations, tax, insurance, banking and financial law, and government relations.

TAICHUNG

Clayton P. Yang, Attorney-at-Law
Address: 9F-2, No. 308, Section 2, Wenxin Road, Taichung, Taiwan
Tel: (886-4) 2313-8662 Fax: (886-4) 2314-4779

Email: claylaw@ms26.hinet.net
Areas of practice: General law.

LIST OF ATTORNEYS PRACTICING CRIMINAL LAW

The attorneys listed below practice criminal law and have expressed an interest in representing American citizens in Taiwan. All of the law firms have English-speaking staff, and all are willing to take cases outside Taipei.

The American Institute in Taiwan assumes no responsibility for the professional ability or integrity of the persons or firms whose names appear on the list below. Firms practicing in the Taipei area are listed first, followed by a list of firms practicing in northern Taiwan outside Taipei. The names listed are arranged alphabetically by firm, and the order in which they appear has no other significance.

Attorneys listed as Resident Foreign Attorneys are not licensed to practice before courts in Taiwan. However, in many cases such attorneys are either associated with a Taiwan law firm or have lawyers in their offices who can appear before the court.

The Republic of China Bar Association can be reached by telephone at (02) 2331-2865, by fax at (02) 2375-5594, or by e-mail at bartw@ms27.hinet.net . However, please note that English is not spoken. The address of the Association is 5F, No. 130, Chungking South Road, Section 1, Taipei.

To call Taipei from the United States, dial 011-886-2 plus the eight-digit number. To call Hsinchu and Taoyuan from the United States, dial 011-886-3 plus the seven-digit number. To call or Taichung from the United States, dial 011-886-4 plus the seven-digit number.

Registered mail may be sent through the Taiwan postal system and return receipts obtained. International reply coupons should be used when a prepaid reply is desired.

AIT's Kaohsiung branch office maintains a separate list of attorneys practicing in southern Taiwan. A copy of that list may be obtained by contacting AIT-Kaohsiung through AIT's website, by telephone at 07-224-0154, ext. 15, or by fax at 07-223-8237. To call Kaohsiung from the United States, dial 011-886-7 plus the seven-digit number.

ATTORNEYS IN THE TAIPEI AREA

Ace Tax, Patent & Law Office/ Yale & Yale Law Office
Address: 7F, No. 132, Section 3, Xinyi Road, Taipei, Taiwan
Tel: (886-2) 2705-8077; 2705-6999 Fax: (886-2) 2705-8099
Email: acelaw72@gmail.com ; yaleandyale@hotmail.com
Website: www.yaleyale.com

Chen Chang & Associates

Address: 3F-7, Taipei Entrepreneur Building, No. 2, Fuxing North Road, Taipei, Taiwan
Tel: (886-2) 2741-5091 Fax: (886-2) 2741-5090
Email: chenclaw@ms22.hinet.net

Chien Yeh Law Offices, Taipei

Address: 62F, Taipei 101 Tower, No. 7, Section 5, Xinyi Road, Taipei, Taiwan
Tel: (886-2) 8101-1973 Fax: (886-2) 8101-1972
Email: eleanorchin@chienyeh.com.tw

Website: http://www.chienyeh.com.tw

Deep & Far, Attorneys-at-Law

Address: 13F, No. 27, Section 3, Zhongshan North Road, Taipei, Taiwan
Tel: (886-2) 2585-6688 Fax: (886-2) 2598-9900
Email: email@deepnfar.com.tw
Website: http://www.deepnfar.com.tw

Eiger Law

Address: 12F, Building A, No. 25, Section 4, Ren'ai Road, Taipei, Taiwan
Tel: (886-2) 2771-0086 Fax: (886-2) 2771-0186
Email: nathan.kaiser@eigerlaw.com ; john.eastwood@eigerlaw.com
Website: www.eigerlaw.com

Formosa Transnational, Attorneys-at-Law

Address: 13F, No. 136, Section 3, Ren'ai Road, Taipei, Taiwan
Tel: (886-2) 2755-7366 Fax: (886-2) 2755-6486
Email: ftlaw@taiwanlaw.com
Website: http://www.taiwanlaw.com

Formosan Brothers, Attorneys-at-Law

Address: 8F, No. 376, Section 4, Ren'ai Road, Taipei, Taiwan
Tel: (886-2) 2705-8086 Fax: (886-2) 2701-4705
Email: fblaw@mail.fblaw.com.tw
Website: http://www.fblaw.com.tw

Jones Day, Taipei

Address: 8F, No. 2, Section 2, Dunhua South Road, Taipei, Taiwan
Tel: (886-2) 7712-3399 Fax: (886-2) 2704-6791
Email: jhuang@jonesday.com
Website: http://www.jonesday.com/taipei
Kew & Lord, Attorneys-at-Law
Address: 9F, No. 17, Section 3, Ren'ai Road, Taipei, Taiwan
Tel: (886-2) 2771-3393 Fax: (886-2) 2772-5911
Email: kewnlord@ms19.hinet.net

Thomas Liu Law Offices

Address: 4F-2, No. 1, Fuzhou Street, Taipei, Taiwan
Tel: (886-2) 2396-8519 Fax: (886-2) 2356-7056
Email: liulawo@yahoo.com.tw

Tai E International Patent & Law Office

Address: 9F, No. 112, Section 2, Chang'an East Road, Taipei, Taiwan
Tel: (886-2) 2506-1023 Fax: (886-2) 2501-1666
Email: lawoffice@taie.com.tw
Website: http://www.taie.com.tw

Wong & Company Law Offices

Address: 9F, No. 39, Section 1, Zhongxiao West Road, Taipei, Taiwan
Tel: (886-2) 2382-0255 Fax: (886-2) 2382-0244

Email: attorney@wongandcompany.com.tw

World Law Offices

Address: 9F-1, No. 72, Section 2, Nanjing East Road, Taipei, Taiwan
Tel: (886-2) 2561-0361 Fax: (886-2) 2561-0363
Email: worldlaw@ms6.hinet.net

WTW Taipei Commercial Law Firm

Address: 7F, No. 149, Section 2, Minsheng East Road, Taipei, Taiwan
Tel: (886-2) 2516-9577 Fax: (886-2) 2516-9715
Email: david@wtwct.com.tw ; dennis@wtwct.com.tw
Website: www.wtwct.com.tw

ATTORNEYS PRACTICING IN NORTHERN TAIWAN OUTSIDE TAIPEI

TAICHUNG

Chien Yeh Law Offices, Taichung

21F-1, No.201, Section 2, Wenxin Road, Taichung, Taiwan
Tel: (886-4) 2251-1973 Fax: (886-4) 2252-1974
Email: alanli@chienyeh.com.tw
Website: http://www.chienyeh.com.tw/

Clayton P. Yang, Attorney-at-Law

Address: 9F-2, No. 308, Section 2, Wenxin Road, Taichung, Taiwan
Tel: (886-4) 2313-8662 Fax: (886-4) 2314-4779
Email: claylaw@ms26.hinet.net

TAOYUAN

Rong-Teh Tsai, Attorney-at-Law

Address: No. 93, Datong Road, Taoyuan City, Taiwan
Tel: (886-3) 334-6223 Fax: (886-3) 333-4671
Email: h0367@ms17.hinet.net

TRADE AND PROJECT FINANCING

How Do I Get Paid (Methods of Payment)

METHODS OF PAYMENT

There are four common methods of international payment: cash in advance, letters of credit (L/C), documentary collections, such as documents against payment (D/P) and documents against acceptance (D/A), and open account (O/A). Cash in advance terms are generally used in new relationships where transactions are small and the buyer has no choice but to pre-pay. Bank-to-bank letters of credit (L/C) are the most common form of international payment because they provide a high degree of protection for both the seller and the buyer. D/P and D/A terms are commonly used in ongoing relationships and provide a measure of protection for both the seller and the buyer. Open account (O/A) is used only when the seller has significant trust and faith in the buyer's ability and willingness to pay once the goods have been shipped. O/A terms give maximum security to the buyer and greatest risk to the seller.

The Commercial Section of the American Institute in Taiwan (AIT) recommends that

U.S. exporters minimize financial risk by requiring their Taiwan trading partners to finance their imports through L/Cs. A large majority of Taiwan's importers utilize L/Cs with validity of up to 180 days. On the whole, U.S. companies find Taiwan's trade finance system to be efficient and report no widespread pattern of deferred payment.

Banks authorized to handle foreign exchange may issue L/Cs. This includes all 37 local banks (and their branch offices), six U.S. banks and their branches, and 23 third-country banks. All banks in Taiwan that are authorized to handle foreign exchange have correspondent relations with one or more U.S. banks. This relationship includes test-key exchanges.

HOW DOES THE BANKING SYSTEM OPERATE

As of 2010, Taiwan has a Central Bank, 37 domestic banks (with 3,326 branch offices), and 29 foreign banks (with 98 branch offices). In addition, there are 26 credit cooperatives, 276 farmers' credit unions, and 25 fishermen's credit unions. These banks, cooperatives, and credit unions have traditionally played a dominant role in finance on the island.

The Central Bank performs all of the functions normally associated with central banks in other countries. It issues currency, manages foreign-exchange reserves, handles treasury receipts and disbursements, sets interest-rate policy, oversees the operations of local financial institutions, and serves as a lender of last resort.

Taiwan's domestic banks offer a wide range of services – receiving deposits, making loans, handling trade financing and providing guarantees, and discounting bills and notes. Most are also involved in the securities business, in underwriting and trading securities and managing bond and debenture issues, as well as in providing savings-account facilities. The Mega International Commercial Bank assists with long-term financing for industries and projects, while the Export-Import Bank of the Republic of China and the Farmers Bank focus on trade financing and agricultural development, respectively.

Foreign banking institutions have played an important role on the financial scene. Foreign banks are essentially treated like domestic commercial banks; they are permitted to engage in trade financing, foreign-exchange dealings, private and corporate lending, and various kinds of trust businesses. In order to build a greater overall market presence, many foreign banking institutions also concentrate on the development of consumer loan and credit card services.

FOREIGN-EXCHANGE CONTROLS

There are no foreign exchange (FX) limitations for trade, insurance, and authorized investment transactions. Similarly, there are no FX limitations on repatriating capital and profits related to direct and portfolio investment, provided that such investment has been permitted or approved by Taiwan authorities. There are no limitations on inward and outward remittances not involving any exchange between the NT dollar and the foreign currency. All other inward or outward remittances for business firms are subject to a US$50 million annual ceiling per account if such remittances involve exchange between the NT dollar and the foreign currency. Individuals are allowed to remit a maximum of US$5 million yearly to or from overseas if such remittance involves exchange between the NT dollar and the foreign currency.

U.S.BANKS AND LOCAL CORRESPONDENT BANKS

U.S.Commercial Banks Operating in Taiwan

Citibank N.A. Taipei, Taiwan Branch Manager: Audrey Chen Tel: 886-2-2725-9800 15F, No. 1, Song Zhi Road Fax: 886-2-2725-2988 Taipei, Taiwan http://www.jpmorganchase.com Tel: 886-2-8726-9821 Fax: 886-2-8786-7980 State Street Bank & Trust Company http://www.citibank.com.tw VP & General Manager: Jane Huang

19F, No. 207 DunHua S. Rd., Sec. 2, JPMorgan Chase Bank, N.A. Taipei, Taiwan Senior Country Officer: Carl K. Chien Tel: 886-2-2735-1200 8F, No. 108 XinYi Rd., Sec. 5 Fax: 886-2-2735-1012 http://www.statestreet.com

Wells Fargo Bank, N.A.
General Manager: Michael Lin
17F, No. 44 Chung Shan N. Rd., Sec. 2
Taipei, Taiwan
Tel: 886-2-8175-8688
Fax: 886-2-2567-8516
http://www.wellsfargo.com

Bank of America
CEO: Eric Liu
43 and 48F, No. 7 Xin Yi Rd., Sec. 5
Taipei, Taiwan
Tel: 886-2-8101-1288
Fax: 886-2-8101-1130
http://www.bankofamerica.com

The Bank of New York Mellon General Manager: James Liu 4F, No. 245 Dun Hwa S. Rd., Sec. 1 Taipei, Taiwan Tel: 886-2-2771-6612 Fax: 886-2-2771-2640 http://www.bankofny.com

Major Local Correspondent Banks

Bank of Taiwan Chang Hwa Commercial Bank The First Commercial Bank Hua Nan Commercial Bank, Ltd. Mega Int'l Commercial Bank Co., Ltd. Citibank Taiwan Limited China Trust Commercial Bank Land Bank of Taiwan Taishin International Bank Taiwan Cooperative Bank Shanghai Commercial & Savings Bank Cathay United Bank

PROJECT FINANCING

Taiwan does not rely on money from multilateral institutions to facilitate investment projects. In the public sector, the Taiwan authorities rely heavily on bond issuance to cover the huge outlays connected with construction of major public works. Beginning in 1997, some major public projects were opened to private investment on a build-operatetransfer (BOT) basis. Private investment projects can easily be financed through banks on the island. Moreover, many Taiwan investors, especially large-sized companies, employ financial instruments (including corporate bonds) to raise funds in capital markets, both at home and abroad.

Web Resources Export-Import Bank of the United States: http://www.exim.gov Country Limitation Schedule: http://www.exim.gov/tools/country/country_limits.html OPIC: http://www.opic.gov Trade and Development Agency: http://www.tda.gov/ SBA's Office of International Trade: http://www.sba.gov/oit/ USDA Commodity Credit Corporation: http://www.fsa.usda.gov/ccc/default.htm

U.S. Agency for International Development: http://www.usaid.gov Central Bank (Taiwan): http://www.cbc.gov.tw/mp1.html

Financial Supervisory Commission, Executive Yuan: http://www.fscey.gov.tw

IMPORTANT CONTACTS

AMERICAN INSTITUTE IN TAIWAN (AIT)

Commercial Section Chief: Helen Hwang Suite 3207, No. 333 Keelung Rd., Sec. 1, Taipei, Taiwan Tel: 886-2-2720-1550 ext. 382 Fax: 886-2-2757-7162 Website: http://www.buyusa.gov/taiwan

Agriculture Trade Office Director: Valerie Brown-Jones Suite 704, No. 136 Jen Ai Rd., Sec. 3, Taipei, Taiwan Tel: 886-2-2705-6536 ext. 287 Fax: 886-2-2706-4885 Website: http://www.ait.org.tw

Agriculture Section Chief: Jeffrey Hesse No. 7, Lane 134, Hsin Yi Rd., Sec. 3, Taipei, Taiwan Tel: 886-2-2162-2000 ext. 2317 Fax: 886-2-2162-2238 Website: http://www.ait.org.tw

Economic Section Chief: Alan R. Tousignant No. 7, Lane 134, Hsin Yi Rd., Sec. 3, Taipei, Taiwan Tel: 886-2-2162-2000 ext. 2374 Fax: 886-2-2162-2240 Website: http://www.ait.org.tw

WASHINGTON, D.C.-BASED COUNTRY CONTACTS

U.S. Department of Commerce Trade Information Center 1401 Constitution Ave., NW, Washington, D.C. 20230 Tel: 1-800-USA-TRADE

Fax: 202-482-4473 Website: http://www.export.gov

AIT/Washington Trade and Commercial Programs Director: Rick Ruzicka Suite 1700, 1700 N. Moore Street Arlington, VA 22209 Tel: 703-525-8474; Fax: 703-841-1385 Website: http://www.ait.org.tw/en/ait washington.html

U.S.Department of Commerce US & Foreign Commercial Service, East/Asia Pacific Regional Director: Patrick Santillo Room 3122, 14th and Constitution Ave. NW, Washington, D.C. 20230 Tel: 202-482-0423; Fax: 202-501-6165 Website: http://www.export.gov

U.S.Department of Agriculture Foreign Agricultural Service (FAS) Office of Trade Program South Building, 1400 Independence Ave. SW, Washington, D.C. 20250 Tel: 202-690-3576 Website: http://www.usda.gov

TRADE OR INDUSTRY ASSOCIATIONS

American Chamber of Commerce in Taipei President: Andrea Wu Suite 706, No. 129 Minsheng E. Road, Sec. 3, Taipei, Taiwan Tel: 886-2-2718-8226 Fax: 886-2-2718-8182 Website: http://www.amcham.com.tw

Importers and Exporters Association of Taipei Chairman: Kuo Chao Liu No. 350 Sungchiang Rd.,Taipei, Taiwan Tel: 886-2-2581-3521 Fax: 886-2-2523-8782 Website: http://www.ieatpe.org.tw

Chinese National Association of Industry & Commerce Chairman: Kenneth C.M. Lo 13F, No. 390 FuXing S. Rd., Sec. 1, Taipei, Taiwan Tel: 886-2-2707-0111 Fax: 886-2-2707-0977 Website: http://www.cnaic.org

US-Taiwan Business Council President: Paul D. Wolfowitz Suite 1703, 1700 North Moore Street Arlington, Virginia 22209 Tel: 703-465-2930; Fax: 703-465-2937 Website: http://www.us-taiwan.org

Taiwan External Trade Development Council (TAITRA) President and CEO: Yuen-Chuan Chao 5-7F, No. 333 Keelung Rd., Sec. 1, Taipei, Taiwan Tel: 886-2-2725-5200 Fax: 886-2-2757-6652 Website: http://www.taitra.org.tw

Chinese National Federation of Industries Chairman: Preston W. Chen 12F, No. 390 FuXing S. Rd., Sec. 1, Taipei, Taiwan Tel: 886-2-2703-3500 Fax: 886-2-2705-8317 Website: http://www.cnfi.org.tw

TAIWAN AGENCIES

Ministry of Economic Affairs (MOEA) Minister: Shih, Yen-shiang No. 15 FuZhou St., Taipei, Taiwan Tel: 886-2-2321-2200 Fax: 886-2-2391-9398 Website: http://www.moea.gov.tw

Ministry of Finance (MOF) Minister: Lee, Sush-Der No. 2 AiGuo W. Rd., Taipei, Taiwan Tel: 886-2-2322-8000 Fax: 886-2-2356-8774 Website: http://www.mof.gov.tw

Board of Foreign Trade (BOFT), MOEA Director General: Chih-Peng Huang No. 1 HuKou St., Taipei, Taiwan Tel: 886-2-2321-0271 Fax: 886-2-2351-7080 Website: http://www.trade.gov.tw

Financial Supervisory Commission (FSC) Chairman: Sean C. Chen 18F, No. 7 SianMin Blvd., Sec. 2, Banciao City, Taipei County, Taiwan Tel: 886-2-8968-0899 Fax: 886-2-8968-1215 Website: http://www.fscey.gov.tw

Ministry of Transportation and Communications (MOTC) Minister: Mao, Chi-Kuo No. 50, Ren-Ai Rd., Sec. 1, Taipei, Taiwan Tel: 886-2-2349-2900 Fax: 886-2-2349-2491 Website: http://www.motc.gov.tw

Council of Agriculture (COA) Minister: Chen, Wu-Hsiung No. 37 NanHai Rd., Taipei, Taiwan Tel: 886-2-2381-2991 Fax: 886-2-2331-0341 Website: http://www.coa.gov.tw

Department of Health (DOH) Minister: Chih-Liang Yaung No. 36 Tacheng St., Taipei, Taiwan Tel: 886-2-8590-6666 Fax: 886-2-8590-6051 Website: http://www.doh.gov.tw

Environmental Protection Administration (EPA) Minister: Shen, Shih-Hung No. 83 ZhongHua Rd., Sec. 1, Taipei, Taiwan Tel: 886-2-2311-7722 Fax: 886-2-2311-6071 Website: http://www.epa.gov.tw

Bureau of Standards, Metrology and Inspection (BSMI), MOEA Director General: Chen Jay-San No. 4 Jinan Rd., Sec. 1, Taipei, Taiwan Tel: 886-2-2343-1700 Fax: 886-2-2356-0998 Website: http://www.bsmi.gov.tw Small & Medium Enterprise Administration, MOEA Director General: Dr. Robert Sun-Quae Lai 3F, No 95 Roosevelt Rd., Sec. 2, Taipei Taiwan Tel: 886-2-2366-2200 Fax: 886-2-2367-3896 Website: http://www.moeasmea.gov.tw

OTHER U.S. GOVERNMENT CONTACTS

U.S. Department of State Bureau of Economic and Business Affairs Office of Commercial and Business Affairs 2201 C Street NW Washington, D.C. 20520 Tel: 202-647-4000 Fax: 202-647-3953 Website: http://www.state.gov

Export-Import Bank of the United States 811 Vermont Avenue, N.W. Washington, D.C. 20571 Tel: 202-565-3910 Fax: 202-565-3930 Website: www.exim.gov

Overseas Private Investment Corporation 1100 New York Avenue, NW Washington, D.C. 20527 Tel: 202-336-8400 Fax: 202-336-7949 Website: http://www.opic.gov

PROMISING MARKETS AND PRODUCTS FOR BUSINESS AND INVESTMENTS[3]

COAL AND ELECTRIC POWER

Coal plays an important role in Taiwan's power generation structure because it is not as costly as other fuels such as oil or Liquefied Natural Gas (LNG); furthermore, the party currently in power has been promoting a "Non-Nuclear Homeland" policy. However, Taiwan seeks to follow the worldwide movement to reduce the use of coal to decrease emissions, mainly sulfur dioxide (SO2) and nitrogen oxides (NOx), and the greenhouse effect caused by carbon dioxide (CO2) emissions. This means that new and advanced clean coal technologies (CCTs) should play a significant role in Taiwan's future energy market. Taiwan faces the challenge of obtaining investment in these clean coal technologies and equipment. Signs of economic recovery following very weak performance in 2011 and plans to build more coal-fired plants will bring export opportunities for U. S. companies.

In 2011, Taiwan imported 48.8 million metric tons of coal, valued at NT$56 billion or US$1.66 billion. Although the U.S. is one of the world's leading coal producers, U.S. coal exports to Taiwan have fallen precipitously over the past few years due to international price competition. U.S. firms that can meet the price competition and integrate market strategies to promote CCTs will be most successful.

State-run Taiwan Power Company (Taipower) and privately owned power generation companies have started to explore CCTs and related advanced technologies, e.g., Integrated Gasification Combined Cycle (IGCC) introduced by Western countries. The petrochemical and oil industries have also begun to utilize IGCC in order to recycle their residual oil to maximize returns.

MARKET HIGHLIGHTS & BEST PROSPECTS

1. Market Profile

In 2011, coal accounted for 32 percent of Taiwan's total energy capacity (all purposes, including electric power), surpassed only by oil at 49 percent and followed by nuclear at eleven percent, natural gas at six percent, and hydroelectric power at three percent. In 2011 alone, coal produced 39 percent of Taiwan's total electricity generated. The Energy Commission (EC) of the Ministry of Economic Affairs had targeted a reduction in the use of coal as a percentage of total installed capacity from 33.4 percent in 2000 to 30.5 percent in 2014. However, as installed capacity increases from 30,136 MW to 43,467 MW between 2011 to 2014, projected electric power generation from coal will grow from 39 percent in 2011 to 41.6 percent in 2014. Annual growth in coal consumption averaged 10.97 percent from 1981 to 2011. Coal's share of Taiwan's total energy market increased from 16 percent to 32 percent during the same period.

Since Taiwan is a densely populated island with limited natural resources, 97 percent of the total energy supply was imported in 2011. In that year,
imported energy expenditures amounted to US$11.32 billion, accounting for 10.6 percent of total imports and 3.8 percent of gross domestic product (GDP).
Energy consumption has been growing by 6.1 percent per year from 1981 to 2011; this corresponds with an average GDP growth rate of 6.7 percent per year for the past twenty years. A soft global economy and steep decline in Taiwan's GDP in 2011 did not slow electricity consumption and average peak load increases.

[3] This section based in part on materials of the US Department of Commerce

In early 2009, signs of economic recovery appeared. Production in high tech industries headed for a year-on-year growth of 7.5 percent in the first quarter and reached 16.5 percent for April 2009. A number of construction projects, including a north-south high-speed railway, a mass rapid transit (MRT) system in Kaohsiung, and another MRT system between Taipei and CKS International Airport, along with the expansion of semiconductor fab plants are expected to spur the use of electricity. Now the island's GDP is projected to grow at a stable three to four percent over the next two years, and the average annual growth rate of the electric power load is expected to grow at a similar rate. This optimistic forecast warrants continuous building of more power plants.

CURRENT INSTALLED CAPACITY AND FUTURE OUTLOOK

Taiwan's total installed capacity was 30,136 MW at the end of 2011, a 1.7 percent increase over the previous year. Of this capacity, 14.7 percent came from hydro, 68.2 percent from thermal, and 17.1 percent from nuclear power. For thermal-installed capacity, coal-fueled power plants contribute 32.9 percent alone. However, actual coal-fired power production peaked at 42.6 percent of electricity generated in 2011.

At the end of 2011, there were ten major thermal power plants that were fired either by oil, coal, LNG, or diesel. Six of these thermal power plants used coal and are listed below.

Station (Taipower's except Mailiao) Fuel Type/Years Established Capacity
Taichung Coal/Oil 1991-1997 8x550 MW= 4400 MW
Hsinta Coal/Oil 1982-1986 2x500 MW +2x550 MW = 2100 MW
Linkou Coal/Oil 1968-1972 2x300 MW = 600 MW
Talin Coal/Oil 1969-1970 2x300 MW = 600 MW
Shenao Coal/Oil 1960-1966 75 +125+200 = 400 MW
Mailiao (IPP) Coal 2005-2000 3x600 MW = 1800 MW
Total =9,900 MW
Source: Taiwan Power Company, Power Development Department, February 2009

LNG is a preferred alternative fuel to coal; the current government favors its cleanliness and efficiency. The recent granting of licenses to four LNG-fired Independent Power Producers (IPPs) has shown Taiwan's determination in promoting the LNG. However, Taiwan imports 88 percent of its LNG, a more expensive fuel. Taiwan's effort to promote LNG use is further challenged by the fact that Taiwan has only one receiving terminal, located in the south and lacks sufficient capacity.

Oil is a cheaper fuel than LNG, but is not favored due to environmental concerns stemming from CO_2 emissions.

Taiwan has three nuclear power plants with installed capacity of 5,144 MW. A Fourth Nuclear Power Plant is under construction. Its completion date was delayed to July 2007 as a result of a four-month suspension in 2011. The "Non-Nuclear Homeland" policy of the new Democratic Progressive Party administration has prompted fresh debate over Taiwan's nuclear needs, and was the main factor leading to the four-month suspension. This policy also led Taiwan's Energy Commission to call for early decommissioning of existing nuclear power plants in 2011, 2014 and 2017, respectively. Taipower plans to replace the lost capacity with coal-fired and/or LNG-fired plants.

Taipower est. costs of producing one-kilowatt hour from each fuel are below:

Type of fuel In NT$ In US$
Nuclear Power NT$0.85 US$0.026 (using US$:NT$=1:33)

Coal 0.89 0.027
Oil 1.34 0.041
LNG 2.14 0.065

LONG RANGE POWER DEVELOPMENT PROGRAM

In late 2011, Taipower announced that their long-range power development program for the period 2009 to 2014 is designed to install 16,322 MW of capacity. The breakdown of additional installation will be:

76.8 percent: thermal power, 12,536 MW
16.6 percent: nuclear, 2700 MW
4.6 percent: renewable energy,756 MW
2 percent: hydro, 331 MW

Of the 12,536 MW of thermal power to be installed, 4,000 MW will come from the LNG-fired Tatan Power Plant. This is supposed to compensate for lost power from the decommissioning of the First Nuclear Power Plant and address the growing demand for energy. By 2014, Taiwan's installed capacity is forecast to reach 43,467 MW, with coal-fired plants accounting for 30.5 percent of the total. Planned coal-fired unit projects are as follows:

Year Coal-fired Projects Capacity
2009 Hoping (IPP) 2x648.5 MW= 1297 MW
2004 Taichung #9 (Taipower) 1x550 MW = 550 MW
2011 Taichung #10 (Taipower) 1x550 MW = 550 MW
2014 Shenao#4 (Taipower) 1x600 MW = 600 MW
2014 Changbin#1 (Taipower) 1 x750 MW = 750 MW
2014 New addition (Taipower) 1x600 MW = 600 MW

Total: 9,900 MW + 4,347 MW (addition) -1,000 MW (Decommissioning) = 13,247 MW (2014)
Source: Taiwan Power Company, Power Development Department, February 2009

Last Year's Import Market Share (Percent for US and Major Competitors):

US: 0.38 percent; Australia: 33.9 percent; China: 30 percent; Indonesia: 25 percent

SOURCES: Statistics on local imports and exports, Statistics Department, Directorate General of Customs. Other information is based on interviews with personnel related to the coal power generation.

BEST SALES PROSPECTS

The development and future direction of Taiwan energy markets must be analyzed to determine best sales prospects. Taiwan shares international concern to reduce coal emissions. Coal-fired power plants face increasing pressures to further reduce particulate discharge and emissions of SOx, NOx, and CO2. The objective of the Kyoto Protocol (and United Nations Framework Convention on Climate Change, UNFCCC) is to stabilize the level of greenhouse gas (GHG) concentrations in the atmosphere to prevent human interference with the climate system. Reduction of GHG emissions is assessed in terms of efficiency and cost of new technology. There is a wide range of options to reduce emissions that can also increase efficiency of fossil fuels. Taiwan will evaluate least-cost solutions that comply with UNFCCC guidelines. Even though Taiwan does not have representation in the UN, the island's authorities adhere to many UN environmental resolutions, including the Kyoto Protocol. In line with Taiwan's desire to stay in step with international norms, the island promulgated an Environmental Impact Assessment Act in 1994.

For existing fossil power plants, Taipower has adopted various measures to reduce emissions beginning in 1989. It reduced emissions by adapting its facilities to use low-sulfur oil and coal, Fluid Gas Desulfization (FGD) for DeSOx, Selective Catalytic Reduction (SCR) technology for DeNox and Electrostatic Precipitators (EP) for fly ash. In 1995, Taipower began a DeSOx and DeNox retrofitting project at an est. cost of NT$23.2 billion (US$703 million) over a ten-year period. Given the long-term availability of coal as a fuel, coal-fired power plants will doubtless remain one of the preferred choices as technology is increasingly used to overcome environmental concerns.

Clean Coal Technologies (CCTs) make coal burn more efficiently and reduce emissions of sulfur and nitrogen oxides, enhancing the environmental acceptability of coal extraction, preparation, and use. Taiwan's Energy Commission has been instrumental in introducing CCTs to the island. Furthermore, research has been undertaken to increase the efficiency of coal-fired plants and reduce pollution. Back in 1988, the EC appointed the Energy and Resources Laboratory (ERL) of the Industrial Technology Research

Institute (ITRI) to undertake clean coal studies on different combustion methods, e.g., LN NOx Burner technology. In 2005 further studies were done on CCTs and IGCC from Europe and America. The ERL conducted feasibility studies by comparing plants using CCTs in Asian countries, including Japan, South Korea and mainland China. They also provide CCT demonstration projects for small to medium enterprises. Taipower has done feasibility studies since 1992 in an array of disciplines, from gasification technologies to utilizing supercritical steam to increase coal-fired power plant efficiency. However, Taiwan's industries have not yet scaled up manufacturing using advanced CCT, apparently cautious about the reliability of CCT.

The study of CCTs has a long history in the U.S. and Europe. Commercial viability was established with the successful operation of the Cool Water Demonstration Plant in 1984 in California. CCTs operate on various technological platforms, including pre-combustion, advanced combustion, post-combustion and conversion technologies. Pre-combustion technologies use physical, chemical, and biological cleaning to improve general coal quality and to remove sulfur, ash, and other contaminants from the feed coal. Taiwan's existing coal-fired power plants that use conventional burners have adapted pre-combustion technologies. However, the benefits of emissions reduction are enhanced with other advanced combustion or post-combustion technologies. These advanced technologies are not necessarily more expensive.

More advanced combustion technologies involve atmospheric and pressurized fluidized bed combustion (AFBC and PFBC) and supercritical and ultra-supercritical steam to achieve higher efficiency. Research suggests efficiency levels could increase 10 percent from the current 35 percent for conventional pulverized coal (PC) plants, and carbon dioxide emissions will fall by adopting the advanced combustion methods. AFBC and PFBC technologies can also be applied to recycle residual oil or petrochemical coke for oil refinery companies. Chinese Petroleum Corporation (CPC) and Formosa Petrochemical Corporation (FPC) have shown interest in AFBC and PFBC to turn waste into commercial products. Taipower has already started a feasibility study to build a supercritical power plant in central Taiwan.

Using pulverized coal to heat the boiler, the most widely used CCTs are post-combustion technologies. Flue Gas Desulfization (FGD) methods can remove 90 to 97 percent of the SOx from flue gases. Selective Catalytic Reduction (SCR) and Low-NOx burners are also effective techniques to reduce emission of NOx up to 70 percent. Electrostatic

Precipitators (EP) and/or fabric filters can remove more than 99 percent of fly ash from flue gases. However, flue gas scrubbing adds cost and hinders industrial and utility steam power performance by one to two percent. Furthermore, issues on dealing with greenhouse gases and solid waste remain unresolved, further aggravating concerns over coal-fired plants owned by Taipower and local IPPs.

More advanced CCTs are being developed, including conversion technologies that convert coal into clean gas or liquid fuel prior to combustion in order to bypass or eliminate direct coal combustion altogether. Integrated Gasification Combined Cycle (IGCC) is one of the most advanced technologies. IGCC replaces existing boilers with gasifiers that supply coal gas to a combustor after passing through a gas cleanup system. The combustor drives a gas turbine, creating additional electric power capacity. Residual heat can be used to produce high quality steam for a steam cycle (combined cycle). During the gasification process in IGCC operation, sulfur is converted almost entirely into hydrogen sulfide, which is then recovered.

Generating efficiencies can reach fifty percent. SO_2 and NO_x emissions are reduced by over 95 percent. Taipower is very interested in using IGCC for a coal-fired plant in the Changpin Industrial Park. However, commercial feasibility studies looking at deployment and at the relatively high capital investment are ongoing to address the costs of building an IGCC installation, which remains relatively high compared to the combination of PC and FGD technologies. The payoff for adopting IGCC will be the ability to use lower grade coal, thus lowering costs, in the future.

COMPETITIVE SITUATION

Taiwan will continue to increase coal imports for power and industrial usages. Increasing competition from low international prices and high transportation costs have hindered U.S. coal exports to Taiwan. Taiwan can source from the nearby Asian countries such as China and Australia. High production costs will be the key issue for the U.S. coal industry if it wants to increase exports to Taiwan.

The most well known companies for IGCC or gasification processing are Shell (Dutch), Global Energy (U.S.) and Texaco (U.S.). For CCTs or related processes or technologies, Texaco outpaces competitors in world market share due to long term research and successful demo plants all over the world. Both Shell and Texaco claim that CCTs have matured and are commercially viable. However, because the processes involve complicated chemical reactions and result in volatile products, potential users in Taiwan are still skeptical of commercial application. Taipower, concerned with stability of supply to its end users, is even more cautious than other potential end users.

While researchers claim that the efficiency rate of power plants using CCTs could increase from 35 percent to 45 percent compared with traditional coal-fired power plants, the real attraction for Taiwan is the reduction of emissions. However, the est. initial investment in building power plants using gasification technologies is about 50 percent more than for traditional operations. Potential Taiwan users are waiting for the costs to come down.

END-USER ANALYSES

State-owned Taipower is still the largest user of coal and largest potential user of CCTs. State-run Chinese Petroleum Corporation (CPC) has adopted gasification technology from Texaco to produce CO and Nitrogen by gasification of coke, at zero cost. Recently, other petrochemical companies such as Formosa Petrochemical Corporation as well as the paper industry have expressed interest in the technologies, but they have not yet adopted them for large-scale use.

Taiwan Power Company (Taipower)

Taipower imported 22.5 million tons of coal in 2011 and expects to import 27.5 million tons in 2014. Coal will continue to be the dominant fuel for Taipower.

Taipower has plans for the construction of a clean-coal technology thermal power 300 MW demo plant in the Changpin Industrial Park. The Industrial Park is located in a coastal area of Changhwa County in Central Taiwan. Gibsin Engineers, Ltd., a U. S. -Taiwan joint venture firm, with help from Foster Wheeler Italy, are handling architectural engineering and design. Construction of this power plant is expected to be delayed due to slowing economic growth and weak electricity demand. In addition, the high initial investment of the project is difficult to justify when there is no successful reference plant in Taiwan. Taipower is watching the progressof other IGCC projects in the region as a reference.

Taipower also plans to construct an additional thermal coal-fired plant with supercritical technology in the Changpin Industrial Park. This project is to accommodate six large coal-fired units on the site, starting with two 750 MW units in the first stage. These two units are scheduled to start commercial operations in 2014 and 2014, respectively. Pacific Engineers & Constructors, Ltd., a Bechtel subsidiary, is the A/E contractor for the project.

Taipower uses nuclear and coal-fired power to provide base loads due their relatively low cost. A non-nuclear policy could jeopardize plans for further nuclear power projects. Proposals for early-decommissioning of nuclear power plants and the retirement of the 1,000 MW Hsiehho and Linkou units could lead to higher costs to produce energy should they be replaced by LNG-fired plants.

According to Taiwan's Energy Commission, Taipower plans to replace the Hsiehho and Linkou units with more advanced higher efficiency coal-fired units to avoid a power shortage from 2014 to 2014. In addition, Taipower is also planning to build another 6,000 MW coal-fired power plant at the planned new Taipei port facility in order to reduce transportation costs and to meet future power demand. This plant is slated for completion by 2014.

For the existing ten major coal-fired plants, major post-combustion CCT methods have been adopted to meet all EPA standards.

Formosa Plastics Group (FPG)

Besides Taipower, FPG supplies power from their 1,800 MW coal-fired plant:
Mailiao Power Corporation (Mailiao). Mailiao is located in Yunlin County in southern Taiwan with three 600 MW (conventional) units, and started commercial operation in 06/2005, 09/2005, and 09/2000, respectively. Formosa Plastics Corporation, Nan Ya Plastics Corporation, Formosa Chemicals & Fiber Corporation, and Formosa Petrochemical Company of the Formosa Plastics Group (FPG) each hold a 25 percent stake in the Mailiao Power Corporation joint venture. The Formosa Plastics Group is the largest industrial conglomerate in Taiwan. FPG is Taiwan's largest supplier of plastics, synthetic textiles, petrochemicals and plywood. FPG's businesses also include electronics, machinery, transportation, medical care and education. FPG's total sales were NT$504.7 billion (US$14.8 billion) in 2000 with 71,939 employees worldwide. The Mailiao Thermal Power Project is built on the site of FPG's petrochemical complex, which includes Taiwan's sixth naphtha cracker, an oil refinery, and several downstream petrochemical plants.

The Mailiao plants have installed conventional EP, FGD and SCR devices for reduction of emissions. Interest in IGCC applications stem from a desire to dispose of waste product from its oil refinery business. FPG is also interested in the gasification process for converting

petrochemical waste into
acetic acids for petrochemical raw materials.

AMERICAN INSTITUTE IN TAIWAN

The American Institute in Taiwan is a private non-profit corporation established to carry out relations between the people of the United States and people of Taiwan. AIT's Commercial Section is charged with the mission of helping U.S. firms export their goods and services to Taiwan. To accomplish this mission, we conduct a number of services on behalf of the U. S. Department of Commerce. AIT's Commercial Sections offers a variety of resources and services (including market research, agent distributor searches, advocacy, trade missions and trade shows) to assist U. S. Companies entering the Taiwan market.

AIT's Commercial Section can be contacted at:

Address: Suite 3207, 32nd Floor, No. 333
Keelung Road, Section 1
Taipei, 110 Taiwan
Tel: 886-2-2720-1550, Fax: 886-2-2757-7162

Contact: Becky Yu, Commercial Specialist
E-Mail: becky.yu@mail.doc.gov
Contact: Mark Lewis, Commercial Officer
E-Mail: mark.lewis@mail.doc.gov

SNACK FOOD

With the rapid increase in the number and scale of convenience stores, hypermarkets, warehouse stores, and shopping malls, the market for snack foods in Taiwan has been expanding in recent years. Growing at a rate of approximately 10-15 percent in the past two years, the market for snack foods in Taiwan was US$174 million in 2011 and is expected to reach US$188 million and US$221 million in 2009 and 2003, respectively (all figures are approximate and based on the exchange rate of NT$33 : US$1).

The major categories of snack foods featured in this report include candies, chips, cookies, and processed fruits and nuts. In 2011, candies dominated the snack foods market with 52 percent of the overall market share, followed by cookies (22 percent), processed fruits and nuts (17 percent), and chips (9 percent).

In Taiwan, youth are the primary consumers of snack foods, favoring chewing gum, chips, chocolate, candy, and cookies. Small and pocket-sized packages of such items are extremely popular in the market. Generally, local consumers of snack foods have diversified and varied preferences, and are eager to try new products and tastes. In recent years, the concept of healthy snack foods has also been welcomed in Taiwan.

In 2011, snack foods imported from the U.S., est. at 13 percent of the total market, totaled US$22 million, a value projected to increase 23 percent to US$27 million in 2009. U.S. snack food items popular in Taiwan include chewing gum, popcorn, potato chips, corn flakes, chocolate, sweet biscuits, and processed fruits and nuts. Japan, China, Hong Kong, Korea, Thailand and Italy comprise the bulk of the remainder of the Taiwanese snack foods market.

Taiwan's entry into the World Trade Organization (WTO) has allowed greater access to the market. With many food import barriers to be eliminated and specific tariffs to be reduced gradually, the market for imported snack foods in Taiwan will be particularly promising over the next 2-3 years. U.S. products, especially chips, raisins, processed almonds, and chewing gum, are expected to continue to dominate the market.

The Harmonized System (HS) codes for the snack foods covered in this report are as follows:

H.S. Code Product Description
Chips and other crisp snacks
20112000 potato chips and sticks, prepared or preserved
18069070 corn flakes

Cookies and crackers
19051000 crisp bread
19052000 gingerbread and other similar products
19053010 sweet biscuits
19053020 waffles and wafers
19054000 toasted bread
19059050 rice crackers
19059060 ships' biscuits
19059070 doughnuts, pancakes, or other mixtures
19059090 other articles beginning with No. 1905

Candy
17041000 chewing gum
17049000 other sugar confectioneries
18063100 other chocolate preparations, filled
18063200 other chocolate preparations, not filled

Dried fruits and nuts
08062020 raisins, boxed
20060090 fruits, nuts, fruit-peels, and other parts of plants preserved by sugar
20081190 ground nuts, in shell or shelled, prepared or preserved
20081910 almonds, prepared or preserved
20081920 pistachios, prepared or preserved
20081930 pecans or macadamia nuts, prepared or preserved
20081990 watermelon seeds and other nuts and seeds including mixtures, prepared or preserved
20082000 pineapple, prepared or preserved
20083000 citrus fruit, prepared or preserved
20084000 pears, prepared or preserved
20085000 apricots, prepared or preserved
20086000 cherries, prepared or preserved
20087000 peaches, prepared or preserved
20088000 strawberries, prepared or preserved
20089910 litchis, prepared or preserved
20089920 longans, prepared or preserved
20089930 mangoes, prepared or preserved
20089991 fruits with or without added sugars or other sweetening materials, prepared or preserved

MARKET HIGHLIGHTS & BEST PROSPECTS

For years, imports have met the local demand for chips, candies, and processed and prepared fruits and nuts. Despite the 1.9 percent contraction of Taiwan's economy in 2011, the consumption of snack foods, especially by the island's youth, has continued to increase. Moreover, the expansion of retail outlets has stimulated demand in the snack foods market.

In 2011, candies dominated the snack foods market with a total value of US$91.9 million, followed by cookies (US$38.2 million), processed and prepared nuts and fruits (US$28.8 million), and chips (US$15.2 million). The import market for snack food was valued at US$118 million, supplying approximately 68 percent of the total market. U.S. firms enjoy a significant share of this market, supplying primarily processed nuts, chips, and other crisp snacks. Cookies and rice crackers are mainly imported from Japan and Korea while chocolates from Italy and Belgium are popular among domestic consumers.

Convenience store chains, hypermarkets, supermarkets, health/beauty-aid stores, snack foods chains, and mom and pop retail stores are the major sales channels for snack foods. In addition, domestic consumers welcome vendors located in shopping malls, department stores, theaters, and transportation centers. In line with the continuous expansion of the retailing sector, the snack foods market looks promising for the next 2-3 years. Local consumption of snack foods through retail channels is expected to grow approximately 12 percent annually.

BEST SALES PROSPECTS

The following snack foods are considered to have the greatest sales potential in the Taiwan market:

H.S. Code	Product Item
17041000	chewing gum
17049000	sugar confectioneries
18069070	corn chips
18063100	chocolate preparations, filled
19053010	sweet biscuits
19053020	waffles and wafers
20112000	potato chips and sticks, prepared or preserved
20060090	fruits, nuts, fruit-peels, and other parts of plants preserved by sugar
20086000	cherries, prepared or preserved
20087000	peaches, prepared or preserved

COMPETITIVE ANALYSIS

Domestic Production

Seeking lower production costs, most domestic manufacturers of food-related products have moved off the island to mainland China over the past decade. Mainland China's domestic market has been an additional important factor in drawing the transfer of production from Taiwan to China. High labor and land costs in Taiwan as well as the lack of research and development (R&D) and shortage of raw materials limit the development of local snack foods production.

Nevertheless, there are several well-known domestic manufacturers of snack foods in Taiwan, including President Enterprise, Chu Shui Chen Foods, and I Mei Foods which continue production in Taiwan mainly to supply traditional cookies. For the past two years, local production accounted for approximately 32 percent ofthe total snack foods market, and amounted to US$56 million

U.S. Market Position

U.S. imports totaled US$22 million in 2011, comprising about 13 percent of the total market. Major products imported from the U.S. include chips, raisins, processed mixed nuts, chewing gum, and chocolate. U.S. chip imports totaled US$6.7 million. As Taiwan's largest supplier of snack chips, with an overall market share of 44 percent, the U.S. has dominated that market for years. Pringles, with a significant share of the market, is the most popular brand of chips in the Taiwan market. Other well-known U.S. brands are Doritos and Lay's. Processed and prepared nuts and fruits from the U.S. accounted for 18 percent of the market, amounting to US$5.2 million. Taiwan's import market for processed fruits and nuts is forecasted to grow at an average annual rate of 7-15 percent over the next several years. Raisins packed in boxes or small packages are popular, and totaled US$2.2 million in 2011. In Taiwan, Sunsweet is the brand of choice for raisins. U.S. suppliers are expected to continue to lead the market for processed and prepared nuts and fruits over the next two years. Western style cookies and crackers from the U.S. comprised 7 percent of the market, with an import value of US$2.6 million in 2011. Oreo brand cookies and Ritz brand crackers are well received in the Taiwan market. U.S. jellybeans and chocolates are the most important component of U.S. candy imports. Candies from the U.S. made up 8 percent of the candy market in 2011, amounting to US$7.6 million. U.S. competition comes mainly from Japan, Australia, Italy, Korea, Hong Kong, and Mainland China.

3rd-Country Imports

Japan supplied 16 percent of the snack food market in Taiwan, amounting US$28 million in 2011. Major snack food items from Japan include sweet biscuits and rice crackers. Import value of sweet confectionery from Japan amounted to US$18 million in 2011. Japan comprised over 50 percent of the import market for rice crackers and sweet biscuits, valued at US$8 million and US$1.1 million respectively in 2011. While Korean fever in Taiwan has recently stimulated demand for Korean tastes in snack foods, Italy has dominated the market for chocolates for years. Imported chocolates from Italy totaled US$9.4 million in 2011, making up about 10 percent of the total.

Almonds mixed with dried fish are primarily imported from Japan. Other major suppliers of processed and prepared nuts and fruits include Thailand, Iran, and Mainland China. Thailand provides mainly preserved and dried fruits while Iran is Taiwan's largest supplier of pistachios. Supplying preserved fruits, Mainland China holds approximately 90 percent of the market for dried black dates and a significant share of the market for preserved specialty fruits such as Wu Mei plums.

Yogurt-covered raisins have been popular in the Taiwan market in recent years. In addition, almonds, cashew nuts, and walnuts with honey and sugar coatings are among the snacks favored by local consumers. Garlic-flavored snacks are also well received. Low-fat, low-calorie, and non-GMO products are popular with the growing health-conscious portion of the population.

Providing products that accord with the taste preferences of local consumers is the most important factor for successful sales in the snack foods market in Taiwan. Additionally, price and brand recognition will influence consumer purchasing decision, while promotional events through retail channels are generally effective in stimulating sales. Appropriately sized (small) packaging makes it easy for snack foods to be sold in convenience stores and products packaged in this manner are very popular. Family-sized snack foods are generally sold through hypermarkets, supermarkets, warehouse markets, and traditional markets.

MARKET ACCESS

Import Climate

The current Taiwan tariff rate system is based on the Harmonized CommodityDescription and Coding System. The dutiable value of an import is defined as its cost, insurance, and freight (CIF) value. Import duties for snack foods range from 3.5-40 percent. A Harbor Construction Fee, amounting to 0.3 percent of declared value, is levied on all goods arriving by ocean carrier. In addition, there is a five-percent value-added tax (VAT) levied on all products.

Customs information may be obtained from:

Board of Foreign Trade, Ministry of Economic Affairs
No. 1, Hu Kou Street, Taipei, Taiwan
Phone: 886-2-2397-7210
Fax: 886-2-2351-3603
Website: www.trade.gov.tw

Department of Customs Administration, Ministry of Finance
No. 2, Ai Kuo West Road, Taipei, Taiwan
Phone: 886-2-2322-8217
Fax: 886-2-2394-1479
Website: www.mof.gov.tw

Directorate General of Customs, Ministry of Finance
No. 13, Ta Cheng Street, Taipei, Taiwan
Phone: 886-2-2550-5500
Fax: 886-2-2550-8124
Website: www.dgoc.gov.tw

Import Regulations

Imported food products are required to list the following items in Chinese on the outer packaging materials:

- Product name
- Name of manufacturer with address
- Name of importer with address
- Content volume, weight, and quantity
- Date of manufacture in order of 'year/month/day' and expiration date
- Food ingredients and additives

Any ingredients or additives not already approved for consumption in Taiwan require import approval from the Department of Health (DOH). The application process usually takes four to six months. The following information should be prepared and submitted to the DOH as part of the application process:

- Animal safety test data (relevant to meat products)- International status of food ingredients in question- Statement certifying that the ingredient is necessary in the production of the food product
- Analysis method used- Production specifications

Distribution/Business Practices

Metropolitan areas such as Taipei, Taichung, and Kaohsiung will continue to have the highest sales potential for snack foods in Taiwan due to their higher standards of living and greater disposable incomes. Advertising and promotional events are important methods for marketing, increasing sales, and enhancing brand recognition. Advertising via television and radio is the most effective method for promoting snack foods.

Snack foods are mainly sold through the retail channels of convenience chain stores, hypermarkets, supermarkets, department stores, shopping malls, health/beauty-aid stores, snack food chains, and mom and pop retail shops. There are about 5,200 chain convenience stores and over 55 department stores on the island. Over 65 percent of retail stores are located in metropolitan areas. To promote snack foods through different retail channels in Taiwan, U.S. firms should consider using local agents or distributors with experience in handling import procedures and performing promotional tasks and sales.

Price and brand recognition are important additional influences on consumer purchasing decisions. In addition to building brand recognition, promotional events at retail outlets achieve sales by stimulating immediate consumption.

In addition to purchases by individual consumers, major commercial users of snack foods include hotels and airlines. Pubs, theaters, KTV houses and transportation centers (airports, train stations, bus depots, highway rest area operators, etc.) are additional important points of sale.

Financing

Bank-to-bank Letters of Credit (L/C) constitute Taiwan's most important import payment process. On a lesser scale, company-to-company payments are made via Open Account (O/A), Documents against Payment (D/P), and Documents against Acceptance (D/A). The AIT Commercial Section recommends that U.S. exporters minimize their financial risk by requiring their Taiwan trading partners to finance their imports through L/C's. A large majority of Taiwan's importers utilize L/C's with validity of up to 180 days.

Upcoming TradeShows

The Taipei International Food Show (Food Taipei) is an annual trade show held in Taiwan. Food Taipei is the largest show highlighting food products and food-processing technologies in Asia. Presenting a wide range of product categories and featuring 11 national pavilions, Food Taipei 2009 attracted approximately 52,000 visitors and recruited 687 exhibitors, including 171 foreign exhibitors. Food Taipei 2003 will be held from June 11-14, 2003 in the Taipei World Trade Center Exhibition Hall, a 26,800 square meter venue. For more information on upcoming event, please contact the show organizer:

China External Trade Development Council
No.5, Hsin Yi Road, Sec. 5, Taipei, Taiwan
Phone: 886-2-2725-1111 Fax: 886-2-2725-1959
E-mail: foodshow@cetra.org.tw
Website: www.taipeitradeshows.com.tw/food
Contact: Richard Chen, Show Manager
Phone: 886-2-2725-1111, ext. 618
E-mail: jtchen@cetra.org.tw

Taiwan is a major market for U.S. food products. U.S. firms interested in the processed food market in Taiwan are welcomed to contact the Commercial Section of American Institute in Taiwan (AIT) for further information or services.

Commercial Section
American Institute in Taiwan
Room 3207, 32 Fl., 333 Keelung Road, Sec. 1, Taipei, Taiwan
Phone: 886-2-2720-1550
Fax: 886-2-2757-7162
E-mail: Taipei.Office.Box@mail.doc.gov

Attention:

Ireas Cook, Commercial Officer
E-mail: ireas.cook@mail.doc.gov, or
Menny Chen, Commercial Assistant
E-mail: menny.chen@mail.doc.gov

In addition, individual shows and promotional activities are helpful in penetrating the local market and building up brand awareness. Many Taiwan importers of snack food are interested in visiting food shows in the U.S. The International Supermarket Industry Convention & Educational Exposition (FMI) and the Institute of Food Technologists Annual Meeting & Food Expo are two shows in the U.S. that attract Taiwanese visitors.

The American Institute in Taiwan is a private non-profit corporation established to carry out relations between the people of the United States and the people on Taiwan. AIT Commercial Section places primary emphasis on the promotion of exports of goods and services from the United States, particularly by small businesses and medium-sized businesses, and on the protection of United States business interests in Taiwan. To accomplish this mission, we conduct a number of services on behalf of the U.S. Department of Commerce. AIT Commercial Section offers a variety of resources and services (including market research, agent distributor searches, advocacy, trade missions and trade shows) to assist U.S. companies to compete in the Taiwan marketplace.

AIT Commercial Section can be contacted at phone: 886-2-2720-1550, fax: 886-2-2757-7162. AIT Commercial Section is also on the World Wide Web at the following address: www.ait.org.tw. If this report has alerted you to a commercial opportunity in Taiwan and you subsequently pursue it with successful results, please let us know. We track U.S. successes and want to know how our market reports and services are being used.

For additional information regarding market research specific to your products and services, ask about our Flexible Market Research and Customized Market Analysis programs by contacting us at 1-800-USA-TRAD(E) or www.usatrade.gov. Both reports provide timely, customized, reliable answers to your inquiries about a market and its receptivity to your products and services.

ELECTRICAL TEST & MEASURING INSTRUMENTS

Rapid and sustained economic development over the past forty years has elevated Taiwan from a developing to a newly developed economy. Due to global economic recession and reduced capital spending of the private sector, Taiwan's economy declined 2.12 percent in 2011 and is expected to expand by 2.7 percent in 2009. Taiwan currently holds foreign exchange reserves of about USD 148 billion. The continuing export expansion is one of the driving forces behind Taiwan's economic growth. Technological advances have been made with research and development assistance from Taiwan public and private sectors. With a number of on-going and proposed high-tech investment projects and increasing production of semiconductors, optoelectronics products, electronic products and components as well as wireless communication equipment and components, the demand for quality electrical test and measuring instruments will be further stimulated.

The total market for electrical test and measuring instruments in Taiwan registered an impressive growth of 18.28 percent between 2005 and 2011 from USD 1,039.8 million to USD 1229.9 million. This represented an average annual growth of about 9 percent. Imports of electrical test and measuring instruments grew 17.8 percent from USD 1,011.9 million in 2005 to USD 1,192.5 million in 2011. Taiwan imported its electrical test and measuring instruments mostly from the United States, Japan, and Germany. Sales of electrical test and measuring instruments have risen in the computer, semiconductor, optoelectronics, and communications sectors. Growth of personal computers, semiconductors, optoelectronics products, and cellular phones has boosted the need for electrical test and measuring instruments in the Taiwan market. With the authorities' emphasis on increased R&D, and the resulting demand for quality and sophistication, the Taiwan market for electrical test and measuring instruments should continue to grow an annual rate of 15 percent over the next few years.

There is little competition from local manufacturers, which are small, and whose growth potential is limited by their research and development (R&D) expenditures which are insignificant compared to those of large multinational electrical test and measuring instrument manufacturers.

The electrical test and measuring instruments covered in this report include:

H.S. Code Product Item

8543.2000 Signal generators
9030.1000 Instruments & apparatus for measuring and detecting ionizing radiations
9030.2000 Cathode-ray oscilloscopes & cathode-ray oscillographs
9030.3100 Multimeters
9030.3910 Wattmeters, integrating
9030.3920 Voltmeter
9030.3930 Ammeters
9030.3940 Ohmmeters
9030.3990 Other instruments & apparatus for measuring or checking voltage, current, resistance or power without a recording device
9030.4000 Other instruments & apparatus specially designed for telecommunications
9030.8200 Instruments and apparatus for measuring and checking semiconductor wafers or devices
9030.8300 Other instruments and apparatus with a recording device
9030.8910 Exposure meters, photoelectric
9030.8990 Other articles of heading No. 9030 without a recording device such as resistivity circuits testers analyzers, automatic integrated circuits testers
9030.9010 Parts & accessories of semiconductor wafers measuring and checking semiconductor wafers or devices
9030.9090 Other parts & accessories of articles of heading No. 9030

The primary end-users of electrical test and measuring instruments in the Taiwanmarket are public and private research institutes, educational research institutes, state-run enterprises and the manufacturers of electronics, information, semiconductors, optoelectronics, communications and electrical products.

MARKET HIGHLIGHTS & BEST PROSPECTS

Market Profile

Recognizing science and technology are a major driving force behind economic growth, the Taiwan authorities have committed to develop high-technology industries in Taiwan. The plan to develop a knowledge-based economy in Taiwan was approved by the Executive Yuan (Cabinet) in August 2000. Its basic goal is to build the sound macroeconomic environment for investment in and operation of knowledge-intensive enterprises.

The authorities have selected the electronic, semiconductor, optoelectronics, and communication industries as target high-tech industries for special development and innovation. Over a dozen of Taiwan and foreign enterprises have worked out plans to set up innovation and research and development centers in Taiwan in accordance with Taiwan's six-year national development program. Consequently, sales of electrical test and measuring instruments will increse in the computer, semiconductors, optoelectronics, communications and electrical product sectors in the next several years. Taiwan's industrial structure has changed tremendously with capital- and technology-intensive endeavors replacing labor-intensive industries. Technological advances have been made with research and development assistance from Taiwan public and private sectors. With a number of on-going and proposed high-tech investment projects and increasing production of semiconductors, optoelectronics and electronic products as well as wireless communication equipment and components, the demand for quality electrical test and measuring instruments will be further stimulated.

Electrical test and measuring instruments are widely used in Taiwan in the public and private research institutes, educational research institutes, state-run enterprises, and the electronics industry for research & development, as well as in the production, checking and testing of consumer electronics products, computers & peripheral equipment, semiconductors and other electronic components, electrical products, optoelectronics and communication equipment.

The size of the Taiwan market for electrical test and measuring instruments in Taiwan registered an impressive growth of 18.28 percent between 2005 and 2011 from USD 1,039.8 million to USD 1,229.9 million. This represented an average annual growth of about 9 percent. Imports of electrical test and measuring instruments grew 17.8 percent from USD 1,011.9 million in 2005 to USD 1192.5 million in 2011. Taiwan imported its electrical test and measuring instruments mostly from the United States, Japan, and Germany. U.S. suppliers led this market with 47.7 percent of the import market. Japanese firms were the second biggest suppliers with 29.8 percent of the market, while German had a 9.6 percent share of imports. As the information technology industry is export oriented and fast growing, the Taiwan market for electrical test and measuring instruments is forecasted to grow at an average annual rate of 15 percent over the next three years.

As research and development are a major driving force behind economic growth, the authorities will manage to maintain a 10 percent annual growth rate in the science-technology research and development budget in the coming decade, in order for Taiwan's R&D spending to reach 3 percent of Taiwan's gross domestic product by 2010. Taiwan spent NT$ 190.5 billion (approx. US$5.95 billion) on research and development in 2005 (the most recent available), up 7.73 percent from 1998's NT$177 billion (approx. US$5.53 billion). The percentages of R&D expenditures on basic research, applied research and technological development were 10.6, 31.6 and 57.8 respectively. By area, the greatest research expenditure was on the engineering and applied sciences, at 77.9 percent of total R&D expenditures, followed by 7.2 percent on agricultural science, 6.1 percent on the natural sciences, 5.4 percent on the medical science, and 3.4 percent on the humanities and social sciences. Taiwan's research intensity (R&D expenditure as a percentage of GDP) in 2005 was 2.05 percent, which was lower than other industrialized countries. The public and private sectors accounted for 37.9 percent and 62.1 percent, respectively, of total R&D spending in 2005. Within private industry, the manufacturing sector had the highest R&D expenditure. 88,708 research personnel were engaged in scientific and technical research in 2005, up 6.6 percent from a year earlier. The number of researchers per 10,000 population rose from 38 in 1998 to 40.3 in 2005.

The Taiwan market for imported electrical test and measuring instruments will grow as the Taiwan authorities continue to actively promote industrial upgrading and emphasize the need for increased research and development over the next five years. The authorities plan to inject NTD 23.17 billion (about USD 665.8 million) in the development of the nanotechnology, and NTD 26 billion (about USD 742.8 million) in the information technology to spur faster industrial development during the next five years. A NTD 10 billion national silicon IC design plan jointly endorsed by the public and private sectors has officially launched. The plan calls for the establishment of three IC design platforms during 2009-2004 to develop Taiwan into a world-class stronghold of IC design and innovation, and a global center for silicon-related sectors. Additionally,

The Executive Yuan (Cabinet) will earmark NTD 50 billion in the form of low-interest loans of just 1 percent per annum to companies that plan to increase their R&D spending and cultivation of researchers. The fund put in by the government is expected to help induce an additional NTD 62.5 billion R&D fund from the private sector. In the private sector, Hon Hai Precision Industry Co., Taiwan's largest computer component maker, plans to invest between NTD 20 billion and NTD 30 billion to establish a global R&D headquarter in Taiwan. The chipmakers will increase investment spending this year by 53 percent to USD 6.4 billion from USD 4.2 billion last year.

The organic light-emitting diode (OLED) display has become the hottest investment target for Taiwanese firms. The OLED display manufacturers plan to invest at least USD 860 million within the next few years. The wireless communication industry will serve as an engine industry to drive the development of local semiconductor, information technology, and relevant industries.

The Taiwan authorities will also help with the establishment of a wireless communication application and innovation center, thus promoting R&D and the relevant development of local communication, computer, consumer electronics, relevant components, and other value added products. The island's wireless communication industry had a production value of NTD 140 billion and is expected to reach NTD 300 billion in 2011. Chunghwa Telecom Co., Ltd. plans to invest NTD 24.88 billion to expand its fixed line network telecommunication project. The firm also plans to invest NTD 17.2 billion to expand data telecommunication system. Supported by a continuing and growing need for R&D and export expansion, the market is promising for imported electrical test and measuring instruments over the next several years.

The United States remains the technological leader in the test and measuring instrument industry. U.S. test and measuring equipment enjoys an excellent reputation in Taiwan for the quality, reliability, and advanced technology. Many of the engineers in public and private sectors were educated in the United States and are very receptive to U.S. electrical test and measuring instruments.

Statistical Data

The following appraisal of the market size of electrical test and measuring instruments in Taiwan is based on customs' import and export statistics and industry estimates.

BEST SALES PROSPECTS

The following types of U.S. electrical test and measuring instruments are considered to have the best sales potential in the Taiwan market:

H.S. Code Product Item

9030.8200 Instruments and apparatus for measuring and checking
semiconductor wafers or devices
9030.9021 Parts of instruments and appliances for measuring and checking
semiconductor wafers or devices
9030.8990 Other articles of heading No. 9030 without a recording device
such as resistivity circuits testers, analyzers, automatic integrated circuits testers
9030.8301 Other instruments and apparatus with a recording device
9030.2000 Cathode-ray oscilloscopes & cathode-ray oscillographs
9030.3990 Other instruments & apparatus for measuring or checking voltage,
current, resistance or power
9030.4000 Other instruments & apparatus specially designed for

telecommunications
8543.2000 Signal generators
9030.9090 Other parts & accessories of articles of heading No. 9030
9030.3910 Wattmeters, integrating
9030.1001 Instruments & apparatus for measuring and detecting ionizing radiations
9030.3100 Multimeters

COMPETITIVE ANALYSIS

Business competition is keen in the test and measuring instrument market in Taiwan. Although U.S. test and measuring equipment is well known and highly regarded for its good quality and reliability, competition from Japanese suppliers is strong. It is important for U.S. suppliers to have a long-term strategy for marketing and expanding in the Taiwan market. The following factors, in order of importance, influence purchasing decisions by local end-users: reliability, precision, low down-time rate, price, durability, reputation, ease of operation and maintenance, delivery time, and after-sales service. Aggressive promotion efforts will help U.S. suppliers boost sales in Taiwan. Local end-users are concerned about the availability of spare parts for repair. Particular emphasis should be given to selecting Taiwan agents or distributors who can expand sales and provide after-sales service. Timely delivery is also a critical factor in the purchaser's decision making.

Domestic production

Taiwan depends mainly on imports of advanced electrical test and measuring instruments. The lack of state-of-the art technology and insufficient research and development investment have limited local manufacturers to producing low to medium quality test and measuring instruments. There are about 15 major electrical test and measuring instrument manufacturers in Taiwan. They are: Chy Firemate, Microtest, Good Will Instrument, Chroma ATE, Topward Electric Instruments, Motech Industries, Extech Electronics, Sink Testing, Precision International, Pintek Electronics, Utron Technologies, Sysgration, Brymen Technology, Appa Technology, and Lutron Electronic Enterprise.

Chy Firemate Co., Ltd., with paid-up capital of NTD 100 million, was established in Taiwan in 1984. The firm, with 120 employees, is a medium-sized manufacturer and exporter of digital multimeters, Frequency counters, light meters, insulation tester, Component testers, capacitance meters, and digital temperature meters.

Microtest Corporation, with paid-up capital of NTD 202 million, was established in Taiwan in 1993. The firm, with 80 employees is a medium-sized manufacturer and exporter of electrical test and measuring instruments, leakage current testers, PCB and cable testers and other automated test instruments.

Good Will Instrument Co., Ltd., with paid-up capital of NTD 595 million, was established in Taiwan in 1975. The firm, with 266 employees, is a manufacturer and exporter of electrical test and measuring instruments, digital multimeters, oscilloscopes, Function and pulse generators, audio and video systems, automatic distortion meters, cable and digital IC testers, and power supplies.

Lutron Electronic Enterprise Co., Ltd., with 200 employees, was established in Taiwan in 1976. The firm is a medium-sized manufacturer and exporter of electrical test and measuring instruments, digital ammeters, digital voltmeters, digital ohmmeters, digital multimeters, digital panel meters, leakage current testers, watt meters, vibration testers, automotive testing systems, PH meters, torque meters and other test instruments.

Chroma ATE Inc., with paid-up capital of NTD 1 billion, was established in 1987. The firm, with 522 employees, is a large manufacturer and exporter of electrical test and measuring instruments, function generators, memory IC Testers, power supply automatic test systems, monitor automatic alignment systems, color analyzers, power sources, and frequency converters.

Topward Electric Instruments Co., Ltd., with paid-up capital of NTD 26.5 million, was established in 1978. The firm, with 90 employees, is a manufacturer and exporter of electrical test and measuring instruments, digital multimeters, Function and pulse generators, distortion meters, frequency counters, power suppliers and oscilloscopes.

Motech Industries Inc., with paid-up capital of NTD 171 million, was established in 1981. The firm, with 80 employees, is a manufacturer and exporter of digital clamp meters, digital multimeters, frequency counters, function generators, RF signal generators, power meters, transmission line testers, power suppliers and photovoltaic cells and modules.

Appa Technology Corporation, with 110 employees, is a medium-sized manufacturer and exporter of capacitance testers, digital multimeters, and measuring instruments for voltage, current or power and other test instruments.

Precision International Corp.., with paid-up capital of NTD 60 million, was established in Taiwan in 1983. The firm is a manufacturer and exporter of electrical test and measuring instruments, digital meters, Function and RF signal generators, sweep and pulse generators distortion meters, frequency synthesizers, power meters, IC testers, and oscilloscopes

3rd-Country Imports

In 2011, Taiwan imported approximately USD 1.192.5 million or about 96 percent of its total electrical test and measuring instrument demand. The Taiwan market for electrical test and measuring instruments should grow at an average annual rate of 15 percent over the next three years. In 2011, American suppliers led this market with 47.7 percent of the import market. Japanese firms were the second biggest suppliers with 29.8 percent of the market, while German, Israelitic, and British suppliers had a 9.6 percent, 3.2 percent, and 1.9 percent share of imports respectively. U.S. suppliers of electrical test and measuring instruments should continue to lead this market over the next several years. Most of the major foreign suppliers of electrical test and measuring instruments are represented in the Taiwan market. Major Japanese suppliers include Anritsu, Advantest, Jeol, Tokyo Seimitsu, Shimadzu, Fujitsu, Kyoritsu, Hitachi, Hioki, and Yokogawa, while major European suppliers are Marconi, Rohde & Schwarz, Schlumberger, and Siemens.

U.S. market position

Taiwan imports most of its electrical test and measuring instruments from the United States, Japan, and Germany. Imports of electrical test and measuring instruments from the United States in 2011 were USD 569.2 million. U.S. suppliers active in this market include Agilent Technologies (Hewlett-Packard), Tektronic, Acterna (Wavetek), Fluke, Keithley Instruments, Teradyne, QuadTech (GenRad), Credence Systems and National Instruments. There is little competition from local suppliers, but competition from third country suppliers of electrical test and measuring instruments is strong. Japanese firms are the major competitors in this market, while Germany pose moderate competition to U.S. suppliers. As the market grows increasingly sophisticated, prospect for sales of U.S. electrical test and measuring instruments should remain promising due to their excellent precision, reliability, and durability. American suppliers of electrical test and measuring instruments will continue to maintain the lion's share of the market over the next several years.

END-USER ANALYSIS

End-user profile
The primary end-users of electrical test and measuring instruments in the Taiwan market are public and private research institutes, educational research institutes, state-run enterprises and the manufacturers of electronics, information, semiconductors, optoelectronics, communications and electrical products.

The main public sector end-users are:
Chung Shan Institute of Science and Technology (CSIST),
Industrial Technology Research Institute (ITRI),
Electronic Research & Service Organization (ERSO),a unit of ITRI,
Chunghwa Telecom Co., Ltd. (CTC)
Telecommunication Laboratories (TL), a unit of Chunghwa Telecom
Hsinchu Science-Based Industrial Park.
Tainan Science-Based Industrial Park

The Chung Shan Institute of Science and Technology (CSIST), established in 1968, is Taiwan's leading military R&D organization. The institute, with over 6,300 scientists and about 8,000 technicians, has four major research divisions: aeronautics, missiles and rockets, electronics, and chemistry. The CSIST has six centers for systems development, system maintenance, quality assurance, materials research and development, aeronautic development and missile manufacturing. CSIST is highly capable in the following fields: space and aviation, rocket and missile, radar, artillery fire control, electronics warfare, propellant, high-performance explosives, composite material, optoelectronics, and automated examination.

The CSIST also assists local industries in upgrading their technological levels, capacity building, the commercialization of defense technology. Since 1998, CSIST has completed 31 projects under the Ministry of Economic Affairs and the Ministry of Transportation and Communications, with a total budget of NT$2.9 billion. It has accepted 3,708 contracts from other ministries and private enterprises worth a total of NT$1.253 billion. CSIST continues to strengthen market-oriented research and provides materials testing and analytical services to local electronic, computer, metal fabrication, and transportation industries.

The Industrial Technology Research Institute (ITRI), established in 1973, has a staff of about 6,100. As a national research institute, ITRI undertakes R&D programs in electronics and information technology, Structural composite materials, biomedicaland materials, automation and machinery, energy and resources, industrial pollution control, industrial health and safety, and aerospace technology. ITRI provides assistance to small and medium-size enterprises, carries out short-term research with cooperation and support from the industrial sector, and transfers the results of its applied research to local industries. In addition, ITRI's research supports the development, production and maintenance of military weaponry systems. ITRI also provides testing and analytical services for private companies to do quality certification on a fee for service basis.

The Electronic Research and Service Organization (ERSO) is an important user of test instruments. Established in 1974, ERSO promotes the electronics industry in Taiwan. It engages in R&D on flat-panel display, advanced packaging technology and microwave technologies. ERSO also provides technical services to the domestic electronics industry for product quality certification and improvement. ERSO is the largest and most developed electronics research organization in Taiwan. It researches, develops, and transfers electronic technologies to the local electronics industry.

Chunghwa Telecom is Taiwan's largest telecom operator and is a major end-user of test and measurement instruments. Chunghwa Telecom was legalized to inherit the business operation of the former Directorate General of Telecommunications (DGT) on July 1, 1996. Chunghwa

Telecom operates both domestic and international telecom business and also invests in related businesses and other ventures approved by the Ministry of Transportation and Communications (MOTC). Chunghwa Telecom a business enterprise providing basic (Type 1) services and value-added network (Type 2) services. Chunghwa Telecom is a major end-user of test and measurement instruments.

Telecommunication Laboratories (TL) under Chunghwa Telecom, is an important end-user of test and measurement instruments. TL provides Chunghwa Telecom with technical support such as the Integrated Customer Service System (ICSS) and the Telecom Order Processing System (TOPS). TL participates in national telecom technology R&D projects, and it also provides testing service of terminal equipment products. With its existing resources and R&D accomplishments, TL will continue to develop new generation telecom network technology.

The Hsinchu Science-Based Industrial Park (HSIP), opened in 1980, is also a major end-user of test instruments, as most of the semiconductor and computer companies in Taiwan are located in the park. The park is in essence a high technology industrial zone devoted to the research and manufacture of computers, semiconductors, telecommunications, electro-optical and automation equipment. HSIP is under the direction and supervision of the National Science Council. There are 312 local and foreign invested firms in this park as of the end of 2011. HSIP firms purchase most of their imported test instruments from
U.S. suppliers.

Companies in the communications industry are the major industrial users of electrical test and measuring instruments in Taiwan. In 2000, Taiwan's 400 communications equipment manufacturers had a production value of USD 4.63 billion, an increase of 32.8 percent over the previous year. Primary products included telephone sets, cordless phones, hubs, LAN cards, LAN switches, automatic telephones, private branch exchanges, fax machines, beepers, modems, cable modems, network access equipment and other customer premise equipment (CPE). The current growth and future planned development of this industry have stimulated a demand for advanced electrical test and measuring instruments. Leading communications equipment manufacturers in Taiwan include:

Lucent Technologies Taiwan Telecommunications Co., Ltd.
Motorola Electronics Taiwan, Ltd.
Tatung Co.
Sampo Corporation
Proton Electronic Industrial Co., Ltd.
General Instrument of Taiwan Ltd.
Microelectronics Technology, Inc.
Siemens Telecommunication System Ltd.
Taiwan Telecommunication Industry Co., Ltd.
Tecom Co., Ltd.
TAISIL Electronics Materials Corp.
Tailyn Communication Co., Ltd.
Vidar-SMS Co., Ltd.

The IT hardware industry is another major industrial user of electrical test and measuring instruments in Taiwan. Taiwan's hardware manufacturers had a production value of USD 47 billion In 2000. The production value of IT hardware industry is expected to grow 9.4 percent to USD 46.7 billion in 2009, after posting a 9.2 percent contraction in 2011 to USD 42.7 billion. Primary products included notebook PCs, monitors, desktop PCs, motherboards, CD/DVD devices, cases, keyboard, UPS, scanners, graphics cards, and sound & vides cards. With the increased R&D spending and future planned development of this industry, the demand for advanced electrical test and measuring instruments is increasing. Leading IT hardware

manufacturers in Taiwan include:
Acer Inc.
Inventec Corp.
Hon Hai Precision Industry Co., Ltd.
Quanta Computer Inc.
Compal Electronics Inc.
Asustek Computer Inc.
Arima Computer Corp.
Acer Perpherals Inc.
First International Computer Inc.
Shamrock Technology Co., Ltd.
Giga-Byte Technology Co., Ltd.
Lite-On Technology Corp.
Micro-Star International Co., Ltd.
Ritek Corp.
Mitac International Corp.
Universal Scientific Industrial Co., Ltd.
Delite Group.
Mitac Technology Corp.

Consumer electronics manufacturers are also major users of electrical test and measuring instruments. In 2000, there were 230 manufacturers of consumer electronics products in Taiwan with a production value of USD 2.47 billion. Primary products included audio and video equipment, digital cameras and other consumer electronics products. The rising labor costs have hurt the local consumer electronics industry, inducing local manufacturers to invest overseas. Leading manufacturers of consumer electronics products in Taiwan

include:
Tatung Co., Ltd.
Taiwan Kolin Co., Ltd.
Matsushita Electric (Taiwan) Co., Ltd.
Sanyo Electric (Taiwan) Co., Ltd.
Taiwan Teac Corporation
TDK Taiwan Corp.
Action Electronics Co., Ltd.
Pioneer Electronic (Taiwan) Corp.

Other important industrial users of electrical test and measuring instruments are the manufacturers of electronic components, electrical products, precision instruments, and electrical machinery. Major producers in Taiwan are:

Philips Electronics Industries (Taiwan) Ltd.,
Philips Electronic Building Elements Inc.
Taiwan Hitachi Co., Ltd.
Nan Ya Plastics Corp.
Taiwan Futaba Electronics Corp.
Taiwan Semiconductor Mfg. Co., Ltd.
United Microelectronics Corp.
China Electric Mfg. Corp.
OMPEG Manufacturing Co., Ltd.
Primax Electronics Ltd.
Universal Scientific Industrial Co., Ltd.
Ritek Corp.
Mitac International Corp.

Universal Scientific Industrial Co., Ltd.
Delite Group.
Mitac Technology Corp.

MARKET ACCESS

Import Climate

The Taiwan authorities have recognized that science and technology is a major aid to continued economic growth and industrial upgrading. Therefore, the information technology, semiconductors and communications industries have been selected as target high-tech industries for special development. Sales of electrical test and measuring instruments have risen in the computer, optoelectronics, semiconductors and communications sectors. Growth in the information technology products, semiconductors, optoelectronics products and cellular mobile phones has boosted the need for electrical test and measuring instruments in the Taiwan market.

The authorities are providing major tax and R&D incentives to private investment projects to accelerate industrial transformation and promote industrial upgrading. These efforts will create a favorable import climate for U.S. electrical test and measuring instruments in Taiwan.

There are no known non-tariff barriers imposed on imports of electrical test and measuring instruments in Taiwan. Nor are there any Impediments that threaten market access. Currently, there are no forthcoming regulations and no legislation that might prove to be an impediment to imports. The Taiwan tariff rates for electrical test and measuring instruments range from 1.3 to 7.5 percent. Import duties are levied on a CIF basis. In addition to the tariff, importers must also pay a five percent value-added tax.

There are no special technical standards to which imported electrical test and measuring instruments must conform. U.S. standards are generally accepted in Taiwan. The metric system of weights and measurements is the official system and in wide use. Taiwan's electricity standard is alternating current (a.c.) 60 cycles, single and three phase 110-220 volts.

Distribution/Business Practices

Electrical test and measuring instruments are marketed in Taiwan through locally established branch offices as well as through local sales agents or distributors. Some well-known U.S. manufacturers are marketing their electrical test instruments in Taiwan through their Taiwan branch offices. Japanese and European suppliers are using local sales agents or distributors to market their equipment in the Taiwan market. Hewlett-Packard and Tektronix have established their Taiwan branch offices to market their electronic test equipment and provide technical support and after-sales services to their Taiwan customers.

Purchases of electrical test and measuring instruments by public research organizations, academic research institutes, and military organizations are usually made by domestic and/or international open tenders. International open tenders for the purchases of test and measurement instruments are usually handled by the Central Trust of China, the public purchasing agency. In the private sector, imported test instruments are usually procured through local agents, distributors and/or Taiwan branch offices of foreign suppliers.

Although U.S. test and measuring instruments are well known and highly regarded in Taiwan, there is strong competition from third countries. U.S. suppliers could increase their exports to Taiwan through more competitive pricing, increased advertising, and good technical support and after-sales services. American suppliers must be able to address the problems and concerns of the Taiwan users in an expeditious manner.

Financing

Taiwan's private firms source their capital through domestic and foreign commercial banks and supplier credits. Most payments for imported test and measurement instruments are made by letter of credit in a foreign currency. Banks require deposits of 10 percent when opening a letter of credit; the balance is paid upon the arrival of the goods. After developing a satisfactory working relationship with local firms, foreign suppliers also accept the following methods of payment: Documents against payment, or Documents against acceptance. Settlement will be made in foreign currency by the importer at maturity, or at the time of receipt of goods or the relevant shipping documents.

Trade Promotion Opportunities

The following 2004 exhibition in Taiwan is recommended as suitable promotional vehicle for U.S. suppliers of electrical test and measuring instruments interested in selling to the Taiwan market. Taipei World Trade Center (TWTC) shows attract both foreign and domestic suppliers. There is no suitable exhibition in 2009 or 2003 in Taiwan to be recommended as a promotional vehicle for U.S. suppliers of electrical test and measuring instruments.

Event Date Location

9th Taipei Int'l Instruments Show
Mid-2004 TWTC
Sponsor: The Taipei Instruments Commercial Association
3/F, 73 Chang Sha Street, Sec. 2, Taipei, Taiwan
Tel: 886-2-23703177 Fax: 886-2-23703170

For further information, please contact:
Peter Yen, Commercial Specialist
AIT Commercial Section
Tel: 886-2-2720-1550 ext. 315
Fax: 886-2-2757-7162
E-mail: Peter.Yen@mail.doc.gov

ENTERPRISE APPLICATION SOFTWARE

The total Taiwan software and information services market was valued at US$ 3.5 billion (NT$ 119 billion) in 2011, with software accounting for US$ 1.4 billion of that total, up seven percent from 2000 (all figures approximate and based on exchange rate of NT$ 33.5/US$ 1) . Within the packaged software market, US$ 439.4 million of enterprise application software (EAS) was sold, 30.5 percent of the total. The utilization of and market demand for EAS are most significant in the packaged software sub-sector. The EAS market grew only 4 percent from 2000 to 2011 due to the global economic downturn. Domestic industry experts estimate that demand within this market will reach US$ 491.2 million in 2009 and increase approximately 20 percent annually for the next two years. The market's impressive performance is directly related to the growing importance of e-commerce within industry, the Taiwan government's e-commerce plans and strategies, and the global logistic and supply chain management system requirements from foreign business partners of Taiwan's high-tech manufacturers. Taiwan's and Mainland China's entry into the WTO, as well as the need for information systems to manage migration of Taiwan industry to Mainland China, will also be contributing factors.

As a newly developed market, Taiwan offers excellent growth potential. With the emergence of integrated global logistics strategies, Taiwan firms continue to follow major foreign companies in deploying software dealing with: automated Enterprise Resource Planning (ERP), Supply Chain

Management (SCM), Customer Relationship Management (CRM), Sales Force Automation (SFA), e-procurement, data mining and warehousing, Human Resource Planning (HRP), Product Lifecycle Management (PLM), Enterprise Application Integration (EAI), and business intelligence management.

U.S. firms are Taiwan's primary EAS suppliers, with total U.S. imports reaching US$ 249.6 million in 2011. In 2009, U.S. imports are expected to increase 8 percent to US$ 270.4 million. Taiwan users recognize U.S. vendors as world leaders with a solid reputation in computer software and hardware technology. U.S. market domination is expected to continue in the foreseeable future, despite increased competition from local and third-country suppliers.

The most important factors for successful software product entry into the Taiwan market are language localization and business practice customization, continuous upgrading and development of new software versions, tailored promotional activities and flexible pricing policies. U.S. companies should also work to cultivate a reputation for reliable service and aggressive representation in the local market.

Enterprise Resource Planning (ERP), Customer Relationship Management (CRM), Supply Chain Management (SCM), e-procurement, Enterprise Application Integration (EAI), Product Lifecycle Management (PLM), various vertical industrial software, document management software, Computer Aided Designing and Manufacturing (CAD/CAM), and office productivity software are all considered Enterprise Application Software (EAS). The core EAS products featured in this report include ERP, CRM, SCM, EAI and e-Procurement.

MARKET TRENDS AND HIGHLIGHTS

Market Profile

The growing importance of e-commerce has increased the use of enterprise-related application software in Taiwan and around the world. To meet the global logistic requirements of major U.S. IT marketers such as Compaq, IBM, Dell and HP, many Taiwan IT firms have conducted management information system (MIS) re-engineering overhauls and upgraded their computer systems for e-commerce applications. Taiwan's manufacturing-based economy relies heavily on online purchasing and marketing channels to remain globally competitive.

In response to the global 2011economic downturn, many Taiwan manufacturers have moved (or are considering moving) to Mainland China. Furthermore, the anticipated future impact and competition resulting from Taiwan's WTO accession are forcing Taiwan companies to re-evaluate their business strategies. In the past, demand for EAS products resulted from the desire to improve operating efficiency and revenue growth. Post-2011 demand has focused on improving customer service and response time as well as operational efficiency. Enterprise integration software plays a critical role by facilitating the communication of software packages and products across a series of digital and geographical barriers.

The Market Intelligence Center (MIC) of the Institute for Industry Information (III) reports that in Taiwan, business users accounted for 85 percent of the software and information services market. By 2011, 47 percent of Taiwan's enterprises were using network applications, such as on-line cataloging, on-line ordering, inventory and order checking, and on-line quotation. However, only 22 percent of enterprises had on-line transaction capability, up 4 percent from the 2000. Taiwan's enterprise development platforms are largely Java (21 percent) and Visual Basic (31 percent) based. The DotNet platform is not yet popular in Taiwan. The value of Taiwan's EAS market has grown in recent years, increasing from US$ 422.6 million (NT$ 13.1 billion) in 2000 to US$ 439.4 million (NT$ 14.72 billion) in 2011. The market is est. to reach US$ 491.2 million (NT$ 16.95 billion) in 2009.

Despite Taiwan's 2011 economic recession, the annual growth rate for the next three years in the EAS market is predicted to remain stable at 20 percent. The core driving forces include various Taiwan governmental Cash, Distribution, Engine Collaboration (Industrial Automation and E-Commercialization Projects; also know as CDE projects) projects, the growing recognition of e-commerce, and the necessity of appropriate information systems to manage the migration of industries to the PRC.

The authorities have adopted a variety of strategies to promote Taiwan industry automation and e-business integration. The ultimate goal is to encourage IT manufacturers to foster the development of e-commerce practices among small- to medium-sized businesses, and to establish electronic supply chains.

To assist local traditional manufacturing industries employ the Internet to enhance their competitiveness, the MOEA announced a host of CDE projects. The Ministry of Economic Affairs (MOEA) selected 12 traditional local industries for financial support and promotion of e-commerce business methods. Sectors include the petrochemical, textile, transportation-related (such as automobile, motorcycle and bicycle), metalworking, mold making, machine tool and precision instrument industries. The MOEA will assist manufacturers and their satellite facilities in Taiwan to develop an integrated series of B2B electronic commerce methods. Such efforts will serve to strengthen supply chain systems, reduce overall operating costs, shorten delivery times, improve competitiveness and expand business opportunities. These initiatives should generate substantial business prospects for U.S. software developers and systems integrators.

Within the enterprise application sector, EAS demand was est. at US$ 439.4 million in 2011 and demand is projected to increase approximately 12 percent through 2009.

Breakdown of EAS: Percent
Office Productivity Software (dominated by Microsoft Office) 19.1
ERP 18.8
SCM 5.0
CRM 11.1
E-Procurement Software 8.5
Engineering Software 17.7
Other (Document management, vertical industries software, etc.) 19.8

Taiwan market growth can be attributed to several factors:
1) The popularity of the Internet and increased use of related applications;
2) The aggressive deployment of global logistical support systems by Taiwan firms;
3) The growing importance and awareness of e-commerce;
4) The heightened use of information technology, particularly in the areas of web-based applications and electronic commerce;
5) Recognition of the attributes of the B2B EC business model and its capabilities;
6) The Taiwan government's promotional plans and strategies;
7) The global logistics and supply chain management system requirements of foreign business partners of Taiwan high-tech manufacturers;
8) WTO accession for both Taiwan and Mainland China; and
9) The necessity of appropriate information systems to manage migration of various industries to Mainland China.

Reasons for the high receptivity include:
- Taiwan has a long established commercial relationship with the U.S.
- The U.S. is the primary manufacturer/developer of computers and related technologies.

- U.S. information technology equipment and software have a reputation for better performance and more advanced functions with integrated solution capability.
- Many Taiwan scholars, engineers and industrial experts received advanced education and training in the U.S. and are familiar with American IT products and software solutions.

BEST SALES PROSPECTS

As the Taiwan e-business market develops, several EAS applications are particularly promising. Major EAS demands range from back-office support operation products to front-end applications and analytical tools. The best prospective enterprise software applications for the Taiwan market are ERP, SCM, CRM, E-procurement Software, data mining and warehousing, vertical industries applications (with various industrial domain know-how), Product Lifecycle Management (PLM), Business Intelligence Tools (BIS), Advanced Planning Systems (APS) and Enterprise Application Integration (EAI) systems.

COMPETITIVE ANALYSIS

Market Position of Locally Owned Enterprises

Although Taiwan is the world's third largest producer of computer hardware, the local software industry is still in its infancy. Taiwan's software industry faces market limitations due to a small local market and limited economies of scale. The majority of Taiwanese software companies are small- and medium-sized businesses and lack the necessary financial resources to conduct large-scale market research and long-term R&D. Moreover, local software firms have only recently initiated development of EAS products. At present, only a few locally owned firms are producing ERP and CRM for the Taiwan market. The mainstream domestic EAS vendors are mostly ERP vendors. Taiwan firms involved in CRM, SCM and e-procurement businesses are acting as distributors for various international products. Locally made ERP products were valued at US$40.9 million in 2011, while domestically produced CRM reached US$ 12.2 million in 2011.

Many domestic firms have gained EAS experience by assisting foreign vendors enter the Taiwan market. Small- and medium-sized enterprises are major clients fordomestic developers. Local firms enjoy a strong familiarity with the domestic market environments and business practices, can be flexible with their pricing policies, and are willing to assist with clients' specialized inquiries. The production value of locally developed EAS products totaled US$ 182.4 million in 2011 - a 9 percent increase from 2000. Top local developers include Trilogy Technologies, Data Systems Consulting, Proyoung Business Information systems, Trade-Van Information Service, and Jade Pacific.

Taiwan's 2011 EAS exports reached US$ 5.7 million, a 3.6 percent increase over 2000, the majority of which goes to the PRC.

Foreign Imports

Taiwan imports most of its EAS products from American companies (95%), with the rest from the Netherlands and Germany (5%). According to figures released by the MIC, foreign-made (including U.S.) EAS in Taiwan totaled US$ 262.7 million in 2011, an amount expected to increase 8 percent to US$ 284.6 million in 2009. Germany, the second largest foreign vendor with approximately 4 percent of the import market, supplies Taiwan with ERP, SCM and CRM software. The sole German vendor is SAP. Other suppliers include the Netherlands-based Origin Company, which supplies enterprise resource planning solutions.

U.S. Market Position

U.S. providers dominate Taiwan's software market for both large- and medium-sized enterprises.

These products are often integrated with consulting services, systems integration, installation and/or implementation applications. Business mergers, capital investment and strategic alliances with local firms are also common methods of product implementation. American EAS products have enjoyed a distinct advantage over Taiwan EAS products. This has been especially true in the fields of ERP, CRM, EAI and e-procurement. Further, Taiwan consumers are very brand conscious.

American name brands are recognized in Taiwan and associated with quality support services. Taiwan customers believe that with buying an American brand they reduce their implementation challenges, thereby making U.S. vendors more appealing. Still, disadvantages of U.S.-origin EAS packages exist in their higher price levels and suitability for larger enterprises. U.S. software providers continue to invest in domestic EAS providers and establish strategic alliances and license arrangements.

Annual market growth for imported software is expected to reach 15-20 percent through 2004. Leading U.S. EAS firms, such as Oracle, PeopleSoft, Broad Vision, Computer Associate, I2, JD Edward, Ariba, Manugistics, Siebel, Adexa, Genesys, Onyx, and Davox, operate in Taiwan through agents or branch offices.

END-USER ANALYSIS

Manufacturing and service sector companies are the most important end-users of EAS products. ERP products were first used by high-tech manufacturing companies, and later spread to traditional manufacturing industries. The logistic, trading and distribution sectors comprise the second largest user base for ERP. The majority of users for SCM and e-procurement software are still in the high-tech manufacturing industries. CRM software is utilized in banking, financing, securities and telecommunication services. Traditional manufacturing industries should increase their demand of EAS in coming years as competitive forces and incentive programs take effect.

Ratio of EAS software use
Manufacturing: Service industries (Based on sales) Ratio
ERP 8:2
SCM 9:1
CRM 1:9
E-procurement 10 :0

MARKET ACCESS

Import climate

Taiwan's tariff system is based on C.I.F.(Cost, Insurance and Freight) prices. There are no non-tariff barriers on U.S. products. There are no import duties for software products. Taiwan does not impose a harbor construction tax.

There are no import restrictions on software except for those classified under HS codes 8525.10, 8525.20 and 8526, which must comply with Taiwan Import Regulation 602. [Note: Regulation 602 states that: (1) Imports of controlled radio frequency-devices as classified by the Ministry of Transportation and Communications (MOTC) shall be released by Customs against an import license issued by the Taiwan Directorate General of Telecommunications (DGT) under the MOTC, but that imports for military use shall be released by Customs against an import license issued by the Taiwan Ministry of National Defense; (2) Imports of non-controlled radio frequency-devices as classified by the MOTC may be released by Customs without the above-referenced import licenses, whether for military use or not.] There are no specific restrictions against software downloaded from the Internet.

Taiwan's five percent VAT is levied on CIF prices (landed price), plus import tariffs and taxes (commodity tax, harbor tax, etc.). The VAT can be deferred until the products are sold.

Distribution/Business Practices

The majority of imported EAS products are sold through the Taiwan branch offices of U.S. companies, the Big Five consulting firms, major international full-service IT companies in Taiwan, or major domestic system integrators. Branch offices of U.S. suppliers work closely with domestic partners to expedite product localization and help educate local potential users. Strategic alliances are also a practical method to capture market share. To reduce manpower costs, most foreign EAS vendors separate their business into licensing (software authorization) and professional services. Foreign EAS suppliers concentrate on software licensing and their local partners take care of professional services.

The most important requirements for successful EAS entry into the Taiwan market are: language localization, business practice customization, scalable capability, continuous upgrading and development of new software versions, flexible pricing packages, reputation for reliable service and aggressively marketing a company's presence.

It should be noted, however, that foreign vendors face some obstacles when entering Taiwan's EAS market. The main barrier is localization. Unestablished American EAS firms in Taiwan have few local connections. Although the brand name may already be well known, local support for customers is often limited. The support networks that rely on overseas correspondence, e-mails or telephony are often inconvenient. Taiwanese consumers value local support, and they like to have someone on hand who is familiar with the product and is able to offer assistance in Chinese. Furthermore, domestic vendors working with American branch offices in Taiwan often lack the practical experience and technical knowledge necessary to effectively address local problems. American suppliers need to allow their local partners to accumulate experience and knowledge.

Flying-in foreign specialists to Taiwan is very time consuming and expensive. In essence, small American branch offices do not have the ability to solve local problems, and resellers or partners do not have total knowledge of, or familiarity with the product.

In addition to a weak support network, many Taiwan EAS customers find the product to be very costly, and the scale of the EAS solutions offered by foreign firms is often too large for them. Together with the language barrier and cultural differences, adaptation to the local market may be difficult for foreign firms. Being the 4th or 5th largest software and information service market in Asia, Taiwan is also a showcase for marketing to the greater China area. Even given such disadvantages, U.S. companies should take special care to present an adaptable Chinese version to Taiwan. The local support network should also prioritize after-sale service.

Trade Journals

Taiwan information technology-related trade journals promote and facilitate foreign sourcing of locally manufactured products. Selected professional journals are suitable for advertising or sourcing local agents and distributors and arelisted below:

Info.Com (Information and Computer, Monthly, in Chinese)
Information and Computer Magazine Co.
Tel: 886-2-2325-5750
Fax: 886-2-2531-0760
Web site: http://www.digi-age.com.tw

eBusiness Executive Report (Monthly, in Chinese)
ARC Consultants, Ltd.
Tel: 886-2-8770-7777
Fax: 886-2-2718-9702
Web site: http://www.arcknows.com

Computerworld/InfoWorld Taiwan (Weekly, in Chinese)
IDG communications, Taiwan
Tel: 886-2-2547-0604
Fax: 886-2-2547-5742
Web site: http://cw.infopro.com

Asia IT Report (Monthly, in English)
Institute of Information Industry
Tel: 886-2-2735-6070
Fax: 886-2-2732-1353
Web site: http://mic.iii.org.tw

DigiTimes (Weekdays, in Chinese)
The Infopro Group
Tel: 886-2-2715-7700
Fax: 886-2-8791-9369
Web site: http://www.digitimes.com.tw

TRADE PROMOTION OPPORTUNITIES

Computex is the third largest computer hardware trade show in the world and the largest in Asia. This exhibition is an excellent means for U.S. software and peripherals suppliers to enter and/or increase their presence in the Taiwan market. The American Institute in Taiwan (AIT) sponsors a U.S. pavilion every year. Other trade shows in Taiwan for software and information services are more domestic in nature. For information on Computex or other related trade events in Taiwan, interested firms should contact AIT directly.

CONTACTS

U.S. firms wishing to learn more about Taiwan's software and information services market are encouraged to contact the following individuals for additional information:

Jacy Huang, Commercial Specialist
American Institute in Taiwan
32F, 333, Keelung Rd., Sec. 1, Taipei, Taiwan
Tel: 886-2-2720-1550, Ext. 323
Fax: 886-2-2757-7162
E-mail: jacy.huang@mail.doc.gov

VOICE SIMPLE RESALE SERVICE

Telecommunication liberalization and continued expansion of Taiwan's e-commerce industry stand to greatly benefit International VSR service providers wanting to enter the Taiwan market. Growth of the Voice Simple Resale (VSR) market as well as reduced rates for international service will continue to drive sector expansion. Value-added services using the VSR network such as Unified Messaging Services (UMS), integrating voice mail, fax, short message, e-mail, etc.) and Web-based call centers are also an area of strong potential.

Taiwan's telecommunications service market is expected to grow by 10 percent in 2009, providing numerous opportunities for U.S. companies, especially those with international broadband and Voice Over Internet Protocol (VoIP) experience. The value of the Taiwan telecommunications services market is expected to reach USD10.5 billion in 2009, up 10 percent from 2011. Liberalized in July 2011, the VSR service market is expected to grow over 60 percent in 2009 to an est. USD 115 million.

For purposes of this study, VSR service refers to international voice services provided over private lines connected to the public telephone network, and cellular telephone networks utilizing the Internet to transfer voice and data information. In other countries and markets, VSR services are known by the name "International Simple Resale" (ISR). ISR and VSR are synonymous throughout this report. VSR service enables carriers to route international traffic outside traditional systems, thereby allowing telecommunications companies to provide international service at lower rates. As experienced in other VSR-authorized countries, the VSR market accounts for 20-30% of the total international service market.

MARKET OVERVIEW

Taiwan's commitment to fully liberalize and open its telecom market is a product of its bilateral World Trade Organization (WTO) accession negotiations with the U.S. Taiwan's 1996 Telecom Act established the legal framework for liberalization. The Directorate General of Telecommunications (DGT) under the Ministry of Transportation and Communications (MOTC) was the former regulator/operator before the Act removed its operation responsibilities. Operations were shifted to a newly formed state-run company, Chunghwa Telecom (Chunghwa).

The Telecom Act further divided services into Types I and II. Type I facility-based services include fixed-line, satellite communications and wireless services. Type II (also called value-added network services, or VANS) includes those services using the Type I network while also providing additional value-added services. A 2005 amendment authorized direct foreign ownership up to 20%, and 40% indirect foreign ownership in a local Type I telecom service. Type II service providers are allowed up to 100 percent foreign ownership.

General and Special Type II Services

The 1997 Type II Services Administrative Rules were amended to include VSR service in mid-2011 to coincide with Taiwan's WTO accession commitments. Type II service is categorized into General and Special services. VSR is a Special Type II service. An English translation of the rules and application documentation can be accessed through DGT's web site (http://www.dgt.gov.tw). The Special Type II license requires an inspection process that is not required for General Type II licenses. The Special Type II license is similar to an Individual License. A General Type II license is similar to the Class License offered by many other countries.

Taiwan is a dominant force in global technology development, especially in the areas of semiconductor production, and notebook and peripheral assembly design. Consequently, demand for international telecommunications through conventional telephone and Internet networks has increased significantly. According to Chunghwa Telecom, outbound international communication traffic reached 1.5 billion minutes in 2011, and grew an average of 15% per annum between 1995 and 2011. VSR service, which offers international telephone calls at greatly reduced rates, is expected to reach a market size of USD 200 million

MARKET TRENDS

IP-based VSR service promises to have the most potential in Taiwan's market due to improved IP integration/compatibility technology and voice quality over IP networks, and the demand for a synchronized voice/data infrastructure to support e-commerce development. VSR service suppliers have targeted various niche markets in Taiwan instead of engaging in an all-out price war. In facing fierce competition from VSR service providers, fixed network carriers have reduced fees for international calls by an average of 20-30%.

COMPETITION

Taiwan officially opened its VSR service market in mid-2011. Approximately 16 VSR licenses have been awarded to date: 14 to Taiwan-owned companies and two to foreign firms.

Local Competition

The vast majority of local VSR licensees also hold other types of telecom licenses including Type I cellular and paging, General Type II Internet Service Provider (ISP), and data service licenses. Only a handful of local VSR licensees -- such as Mackay, Infoserve and SeedNet -- have established their own domestic and international infrastructure. Mackay, the first private company to obtain a Type II license, targets enterprise users and provides turnkey solutions to other VSR providers. SeedNet, Taiwan's second largest ISP with substantial VoIP execution capability, provides a voice/data integrated product to their enterprise users.

Local VSR licensees are looking for business alliances with fixed network carriers in order to expand their international connectivity. Currently, most local VSR licensees target customers requiring Taiwan-China coverage. These VSR providers have also been in the Taiwan area telecom market for years, and have a well-established client base and system of distribution channels.

Major local VSR service providers are:
-- SeedNet (Seed.net.tw)
-- Mackay Telecommunications (mky.com)
-- Infoserve (infoserver-group.com)
-- SaveCom (savecom.net.tw)
-- FarEasTone (fet.net.tw)
-- Chief Telecommunications (unigate.net.tw)
-- Vopier Communications (vopier.com)

Third Country

Presently there is only one major foreign company with a strong presence in the Taiwan market, SingTel. Singapore's SingTel, with investments in Taiwan's fixed network carrier New Century Infocomm, targets its VSR service to customers requiring Hong Kong-Taiwan-China coverage.

U.S. Market Position

As the recognized leaders in the international broadband market, U.S. companies are in a strong position to provide products and services to Taiwan VSR service providers instead of directly to Taiwan consumers. WorldCom is one U.S. company that has already received permission to enter the Taiwan VSR service market.

END USERS

Taiwan is an export-oriented economy with well-developed international communication and Internet networks. Ninety-five percent of Taiwan's enterprises are small-to-medium-sized firms (with capital less than USD 1.5 million). These 950,000 small-to-medium commercial users, as well as home office users, comprise the most significant market for VSR service.

SALES PROSPECTS

IP-based VSR service is a promising telecommunications sector due to the growing demand by both commercial and household users. Value-added services in addition to VSR such as Unified Messaging Services (UMS), integrating voice mail, fax, short message, e-mail, etc.) and Web-based call centers are also an area of great potential.

MARKET ACCESS

Licensing

A Special Type II ten-year license is required to provide VSR service in Taiwan. A permit fee of one percent of a company's annual sales will be levied on VSR service providers. Taiwan DGT's Public Telecommunications Department, First Division, is responsible for issuance of all telecommunications service licenses. Technical information regarding VSR service is available from DGT's System Technical Division under its Public Telecommunications Department.

Two-part Dialing Access

In theory VSR service providers and Type I fixed network carriers should share an equal dialing access mechanism (equal length and complexity of access codes). This is not the case in Taiwan. Due to limited numbering allocation possibilities and the insufficient capacity of Chunghwa Telecom's master public switch system, VSR services are given a five-digit access code. End users will be required to dial the five-digital VSR access code, the international prefix, and then the area code and telephone number.

Distribution

VSR service licensees are required to establish an office in Taiwan. VSR services are currently marketed through the traditional methods of branch offices and sales agents. New means of conducting online sales and advertising are rapidly being developed.

Establishing an Office

Establishing a subsidiary or representative office is not especially challenging or risky in Taiwan. However, there are a number of different corporate structures to choose from and a series of forms and procedures to complete. Among other details, a Chinese name is required. Consultations with a reputable local attorney and/or accountant are highly recommended to complete all necessary steps required in establishing a legal Taiwan business presence.

CONTACTS

U.S. firms wishing to learn more about Taiwan's VSR market and related opportunities are encouraged to contact the following individual for additional information:

Frances Li, Commercial Specialist
Commercial Section
American Institute in Taiwan
Room 3207, 333 Keelung Road, Sec. 1
Taipei 110, Taiwan
Tel: 886-2-2720-1550, Ext. 329
Fax: 886-2-2757-7162
E-mail: frances.li@mail.doc.gov

SPECIALTY STEEL

SPECIFIC MARKET OPPORTUNITIES

Moderate yet steady growth in steel demand, as well as a host of infrastructure projects in Taiwan, offer potential for US specialty steel exporters targeting East Asia. In addition to a thriving domestic specialty steel industry, Taiwan imports approximately 30% of its total specialty steel for product manufacturing and construction. Taiwan produces large quantities of stainless steel. However, many manufacturers rely heavily on imports for flat-rolled stainless steel bars and rods, hot-rolled stainless steel, and stainless steel wire.

According to the Taiwan Steel Association, Taiwan's demand for specialty steel is est. to grow by 5% annually from 2009 to 2011. Stainless steel bars and rods are expected to enjoy the largest rate of sales growth at 5.9%. Demand for hot and cold-rolled stainless steel products, as well as other specialty alloys, will grow by nearly 5%. As a result, there should be opportunities for American companies producing specialty steel. Despite the economic downturn affecting Taiwan's economy in 2011-2, long-term construction projects will continue to increase specialty steel market expansion. Major infrastructure and construction work includes the North-South High Speed Rail System, the Kaohsiung Mass Rapid Transit System, and new power plants and industrial complexes demanding significant quantities of various steel products.

MARKET DESCRIPTION

According to its applications or characteristics, specialty steel is divided herein into stainless steel, various alloys, and hollow and free-cutting steel. Taiwan's total demand for specialty steel reached 1.98 million metric tons in 2000, a 17.6% increase over 2005. Imports increased by 8.87% from 2005's 564,000 metric tons, still 93,000 metric tons short of 1998's record of 707,000 metric tons. Almost 50% of the specialty steel imports are from Japan, followed by South Korea and other European countries. Taiwan has 12 manufacturers of specialty steel, which produce a total of 2.2 million metric tons annually. Yieh United Steel Corporation has the largest production capacity and facility in both Taiwan and Southeast Asia, and ranks as the fifth largest in the world. The company's output of hot and cold-rolled stainless steel coils reached 1 million metric tons after continuous casting machines were modified for billets in early 2000. The vast majority of specialty steel manufacturers are located in the Southern Taiwan cities of Tainan and Kaohsiung, and they include China Steel Corp., Tang Eng, Gloria Heavy, Walsin Lihwa, Chang Mien, Feng Hsing, and Yieh Hsing.

ECONOMIC SITUATION IN TAIWAN

Taiwan's gross domestic product (GDP) contracted 4.21% in the third quarter of 2011, the largest quarterly decline since 1975. Taiwan had three straight quarters of negative economic growth in 2011 indicating that the island is in recession. The gross domestic product (GDP) forecast also dropped 2.12% for the year.

Taiwan's economic expansion is predicted to resume in 2009, with forecasted GDP growth put at 2.23%. Private consumption in 2009 is predicted to grow at just 1.28%, the lowest est. growth rate in 45 years. Private consumption is also expected to rise slightly in 2009, reaching 2.43%. Exports for 2011 are est. to fall 16.9%, while imports should have a sharper decline of 22%. However, both exports and imports should rise 3.26% and 5%, respectively, in 2009.

MARKET OVERVIEW

Industry Development

The 1960s witnessed major growth and development in Taiwan's overall steel industry. During this period of expansion, Taiwan authorities prioritized construction work on the "Ten Major Development Projects." These development projects promoted the integration of Taiwan's steel production and facilities. During the 1960s, China Steel Corporation completed two major expansions of its production facilities, and other local hot and cold-rolled stainless steel companies invested in these expansions. The booming demand for steel by downstream market sectors such as the metal working, vehicles, high-tech, hand tools and construction industries provided Taiwan's steel companies with the capital and market demand necessary for rapid expansion.

Specialty steel is classified according its applications or characteristics. Product categories include stainless steel, various alloys, hollow steel and free-cutting steel. Taiwan has 12 manufacturers of specialty steel, which produce a total of 2.2 million metric tons annually. Stainless steel plates and bars constitute the largest amount of any one metal type sold. Taiwan's 12 manufacturers producing specialty steel employ an average of 1,315 persons per company. The specialty steel industry can be classified as capital-intensive industry in Taiwan, with an average initial required investment of US$ 30.8 million per facility.

In further examining market trends, Taiwan's domestic specialty steel industry emphasizes the development of ultra pure steel, dual phase stainless steel, and free-cutting steel. In terms of refining techniques, the emphasis will remain on top oxygen blowing, stainless steel dephosphorizing methods, electromagnetic stirring, and slag splashing techniques. For casting technologies the priority will remain on increasing high continuous casting rates and thin strip continuous casting.

Specialty steel products covered in this report are categorized within the 4-digit Schedule B/Harmonized System (HS) codes. Product-specific listings include:

7219 Flat-rolled products of stainless steel, of a width of 600mm or more
7220 Flat-rolled products of stainless steel, of a width of less than 600mm
7221 Bars and rods, hot-rolled, in irregularly wound coils of stainless steel
7222 Other bars and rods of stainless steel; angles, shapes and sections of stainless steel
7223 Wire of stainless steel
7225 Flat-rolled products of other alloy steel, of a width of 600mm or more
7226 Flat-rolled products of other alloy steel, plated, coated or clad, of a width of 600mm or more
7227 Bars and rods, hot-rolled, in irregularly wound coils, of other alloy steel
7228 Other bars and rods of other alloy steel; angles, shapes and sections, of other alloy steel; hollow drill bars and rods, of alloy or non-alloy steel
7229 Wire of other alloy steel
7304 Tubes, pipes and hollow profiles, seamless, of iron or steel
7306 Other tubes, pipes and hollow profiles of iron or steel

Industry Profile

In addition to a thriving domestic specialty steel industry, Taiwan imports a significant amountof the total specialty steel used for product manufacturing and construction. In 2000, total imports reached 614,835 metric tons, accounting for approximately 31% of the total market demand. Approximately fifty percent of the imports were from Japan, followed by South Korea and numerous European countries. The bulk of Taiwan specialty steel exports went to Hong Kong (850,754 metric tons representing 38.4% of total exports).

Final 2011 specialty steel market figures will not be released until early 2009. However, the demand volume for specialty steel was forecast to reach 2.35 million metric tons in 2011, with demand for stainless steel expected to increase 4.5% to a total of 2.15 million metric tons. For 2009, the hot-rolled stainless steel market will be especially promising, while the supply of cold-rolled stainless steel should exceed market demand driving down prices. However, new production lines of cold-rolled stainless steel are being planned potentially limiting the chance for future price hikes.

Est. Demand and Growth Rates
Of Taiwan's Specialty Steel Market in 2011
(Unit: thousand metric tons) *

Demand Volume 2011 Growth Rate (est.)*
Stainless Steel 2,152 4.5%
Alloy Steel 0.144 2.9%
Other Special Steel 0.054 1.9%

Environmental Concerns

Solid waste and factory emissions treatment remain critical environmental issues for Taiwan's overall steel industry. Based on industry estimates, annual solid waste produced by the domestic steel industry is 0.5 million metric tons. Additionally, the industry emitted 26 million tons of CO2 in 2000, accounting for 13.5% of Taiwan's total emissions (190 million metric tons). Increasingly strict environmental air pollution control legislation over the last two decades has served to drastically reduce Taiwan's green house gas emissions. Such legal and regulatory progress, however, has caused some Taiwan steel producers to investigate moving operations overseas, especially to Mainland China.

SALES PROSPECTS

Product Types

Taiwan is capable of producing large quantities of stainless steel. However, many manufacturers rely heavily on imports for flat-rolled stainless steel bars and rods, hot-rolled stainless steel, and stainless steel wire. Stainless steel remains both a vital import and export specialty steel commodity for Taiwan.

U.S. manufacturers will find sales prospects in the following items:

(1) Flat-rolled products of stainless steel, of a width of 600mm or more
(2) Flat-rolled products of stainless steel, of a width of less than 600mm
(3) Bars and rods, hot-rolled of stainless steel
(4) Wire of stainless steel

COMPETITION

Domestic

There are 12 specialty steel manufacturers in Taiwan, and their product lines focus primarily on stainless steel plates and bars. In 2000, these companies generated combined annual sales of US$5.2 billion. Among the 12 companies, two major players are introduced below:

Yieh United Steel Corporation (YUSCO): Founded in December 1988, YUSCO's facilities are located in Southern Taiwan's Kaohsiung County. The company employs approximately 1,500 employees, and their total investments exceed US$1.3 billion. YUSCO's factory is the largest integrated stainless steel mill in Southeast Asia. The steel melting operation has an annual capacity of 1 million metric tons, most of which is sold as stainless steel slabs and billets. The hot rolling mill can produce 900,000 metric tons of hot-rolled stainless steel coils and plates per year.

The cold-rolling plant has the capacity to produce 250,000 metric tons of cold-rolled No. 1 coils, 340,000 metric tons of 2D and 2B stainless steel coils, and 60,000 metric tons of Bright Annealed stainless steel coils. YUSCO has a skilled work force and continues to improve its production by adopting state-of-the-art technology and equipment. Each process and product is monitored by a computerized system for strict quality control. Certified by ISO 9002 and 14001, YUSCO is committed to environmental protection and stewardship.

China Steel Corporation (CSC): CSC, the largest domestic steel manufacturer listed on Taiwan's Stock Exchange (the TAIEX), was established in December 1971. CSC is currently the sole integrated steel producer in Taiwan with an annual production that reached 8.054 million tons in 2000. Roughly 80% of its production is sold to the domestic market, with the remaining 20% exported. CSC's reputation for product quality is solid domestically and internationally. The company has also earned the National Quality Award from Taiwan's government, the highest such honor awarded. For the first quarter of 2009, CSC kept its export prices at their 2011 levels for all steel products exported to Japan. For the export markets in Mainland China, Southeast Asia, the U.S. and Europe, CSC raised its export prices per metric ton of hot-rolled steel and electromagnetic steel sheets by US$10 each. CSC also adjusted down the price of steel wire rods, galvanized steel, and hot-dip galvanized steel by US$5-US$15, thereby maintaining the price of cold-rolled steel and steel plates.

International Competitors

According to Industry Technology Information Services, major Japanese specialty steel companies active in Taiwan include Daido Corporation, Hitachi-Metals, Aichi-steel, Sanyo steel, Koshuha, NYK, NSC and Sumikin. Allegheny Ludlum, ARMCO and Carpenter Technology are the American specialty steel manufacturers present. European manufacturers include Thyssen Krupp and Krupp Thyssen Nirosta from Germany, Unisor and Ugine from France, and Avesta Sheffield from Sweden.

MARKET TRENDS

WTO entry

Taiwan's import tariffs on steel products closely resemble those of other nations. The impact of WTO entry on Taiwan's steel industry will therefore be relatively minor. However, the relocation of downstream industries will significantly influence the steel industry in the mid to long-term. The volume of steel trade across the Taiwan Strait has increased in the last five years, especially the demand for electro galvanized, tinplate, hot galvanized, steel rod and cold-rolled stainless steel products.

Dumping and Anti-dumping

Dumping and anti-dumping activities are motivated by the desire to protect domestic production interests amidst a production glut. During the past four to five years, over 30 countries have set import limits on steel products, with the U.S. filing the largest number of formal international anti-dumping grievances.

In November 2011, The U.S. International Trade Commission (ITC) judged that imports of low-price hot-rolled steel from two Taiwanese manufacturers -- China Steel Corp. and Yieh Loong Co., Ltd. -- harmed the U.S.'s steel manufacturing industry. Nine steel manufacturers, the United Steelworkers of America, and another U.S. steel workers union jointly filed dumping charges with the ITC in 2000 against manufacturers of hot-rolled steel in 11 countries, including Taiwan. The ITC's ruling stated that imported steel products have hurt the American manufacturers of 12 steel products covering steel plates, hot-rolled steel, and cold-rolled steel. The import volume of the 12 steel products occupies 79% of the total U.S. import volume of all steel products. The ITC's judgment of dumping means the U.S. Department of Commerce will impose anti-dumping tariffs on foreign manufacturers deemed guilty.

In response to the ITC's judgment, CSC and Yieh Loong believe they will not be substantially affected because their export volumes to the U.S. are small. CSC exported only 318 metric tons of hot-rolled steel to the U.S. during the first three quarters of 2011, while Yieh Loong's main export markets are in Europe, Southeast Asia, and Mainland China. The dumping charge concerns fair trade, and therefore the two companies will appeal upon receiving formal documentation of the ITC's ruling.

The Online Steel Business

Key developments related to the emergence of E-commerce can be summarized as accelerated competition, technological advancements in IT, the increased popularity of networking, and the maturation of the global supply chain. In
April 2000, World Steel Dynamics published a report entitled "E-commerce in Steel," which included an estimate that B2B steel transactions reached 5 million tons in 2000, and 24 million tons in 2011. Another significant increase is expected by 2009 with the total amount of product sold exceeding 44 million metric tons. Furthermore, Arthur Anderson and Co. estimates that 40% - 60% of the global metal transactions will be conducted via the Internet by 2011.

In Taiwan, China Steel Corporation (CPC) announced in October 2011 that it would construct new platforms integrating metal, cement, petrochemical, and automobile and electronics industries. The new platform will be called the Universal Exchange Inc., and total sales volume is expected to reach US$17.1 billion within a year.

A further consideration is whether B2B platforms selling production capacity instead of product will result in additional dumping allegations. Whether local steel websites will be able to compete with other large multinational B2B platforms remains uncertain. In Taiwan, steel trading is based on personal relationships, and visits between buyers and sellers are vital to doing business. Consequently, acceptance of such a new and different means of sales is uncertain.

Government Procurement

The market for government procurement in Taiwan can be attractive. Taiwan fundamentally reformed the procurement regime when it enacted the Government Procurement Law (GPL) in 2005. Information relating to the GPL can be obtained through the World Wide Web (http://www.pcc.gov.tw).

Administrative Structure of Procurement - Procurements are usually administered by the government entity undertaking the project and controlling the budget. However, the procurement entity may authorize the Central Trust of China, a state-owned enterprise, to make purchases on its behalf. Taiwan authorities have not adopted a centralized procurement system, except for procurements by central government entities of foreign goods with a value over NT$50 million (approximately US$1.51 million at NT$33/US$1). In the case of such procurements, the Central Trust of China solicits foreign tenders. (The Ministry of National Defense, educational institutes established by Taiwan and state-owned companies may at times conduct their own procurements). The acquisition process by a sub-central government procurement entity is similar to but independent from that of a central procurement entity.

Scope of Procurement - Government procurement covers the public purchase of construction project goods and services. Article 2 of the GPL stipulates that the term "procurement" as used in this law shall refer to the contracting of construction work, the purchase or lease of property, and/or the retention of employment or services.

Classification of Tendering Procedures - Tendering procedures are categorized into open tendering, selective tendering, and single tendering. Details are described in several documents available from the Central Trust of China, including Statute for Inspection Procedures Governing Construction Works, Procurement of Products, and Disposal of Properties by Government Agencies. Open tendering is used when the est. value at or exceeding NT$50 million (approximately US$1.51 million), or NT$5 million (approximately US$151,515) depending on the project. In the instance of selective tendering, the procuring entity selects two or more responsible suppliers for quotations. Single tendering may be used in cases where the value of a proposed procurement is below NT$5 million (approximately US$151,515).

Procurement Information - For procurements worth NT$50 million (approximately US$1.51 million) or more involving the purchase of goods, services and construction works, tender notices are published in local newspapers for a minimum of two days, and posted in the building of the procuring entity for a minimum of five days. The procuring entity is also encouraged but not mandated to enter the tender notice into the online database operated by the Public Construction Commission (PCC). The PCC will then put the data in the Government Procurement Gazette, which has been officially published since November 1, 1996. Unless otherwise specified, the time limit for receipt of tenders should be no less than 14 days, and no less than 28 days for special or complex procurements. The time limit for a procurement that is open to foreign tenders shall be no less than 40 days.

Award Criteria - Contracts will, in principle, be awarded upon consideration of two criteria: the lowest price and the government estimate. The tender with the lowest price, which is not higher than the government estimate, will be awarded the contract. If the tender price is higher than the government estimate, the tenderer may be given a one-time opportunity to reduce the price. If the reduced tender prices are still higher than the government estimate, all acceptable tenders may be given the opportunity to re-tender. If the lowest tender price is higher than the government estimate by 20 percent or is higher than the budget amount, all tenders will be rejected. A government entity may specify in the tender documentation that a contract be awarded based on the most advantageous, not necessarily the lowest price, tender. In judging the most advantageous tender, criteria such as technology, quality, function, commercial terms and/or price of products and services may be used for evaluation.

MARKET ACCESS

Direct Sales

Direct Export - Foreign companies typically attempt to sell construction equipment or engineering services directly to a purchaser in Taiwan. The foreign company is not required to have a base in Taiwan to export directly. Direct export sales usually result from unsolicited inquiries, or from advertisements distributed internationally or in Taiwan.

Sales Agent - One alternative to direct export is hiring a sales agent that can actively solicit sales. A sales agent in Taiwan is usually a private citizen or entity that receives a commission based upon sales achieved. Approval from the Investment Commission (IC) of the Ministry of Economic Affairs (MoEA) is not necessary to enter into a relationship with a sales agent. The main advantage of hiring a foreign sales agent, as opposed to selling directly, is that a representative who knows the market, language and culture will be able to support the product locally.

Sales Branch - A sales branch is a direct legal presence in Taiwan. The use of a foreign branch may be desirable because it is often easier to shut down than a Taiwan company.

Company - Creating a company in Taiwan is the most expensive and most complex way of establishing a presence in Taiwan. However, establishing a local company gives the foreign company more prestige and conveys a longer-term commitment to the domestic market. Moreover, it allows the foreign firm to engage in manufacturing. Using a Taiwan company can provide greater opportunities for financing business activities, as well as an opportunity for local investors to participate in the business.

Sales by a Distributor

Appointing a distributor in Taiwan, rather than a sales agent, provides a more significant presence. Unlike a sales agent, a distributor is an independent contractor that purchases the product for later resale. The relationship between the distributor and the foreign company is to be governed by the Taiwan Civil Code. The distributor bears the cost of warehousing and servicing the product, setting prices and maintaining the sales and service force. Unlike a sales agent, a distributor in Taiwan cannot enter into contracts on behalf of the foreign company, and therefore, the foreign company will not be responsible for the distributor's acts.

Import Licenses

A company desiring to import construction equipment or building products into Taiwan must have a general license for imports, which can be obtained from the Bureau of Foreign Trade (BOFT). Equipment and machinery imported by a company or its direct contractor for use in the construction of a major infrastructure project is exempt from import duties under certain conditions. The BOFT is also the contact agency for such opportunities.

Import Duties: Duties payable on imported items are defined on an ad valorem basis, and the dutiable value of an import is defined as its cost, insurance and freight (c.i.f.) value.

Import and Export Documentation: The supplier's proforma invoice (quotation) is required to apply for an import permit. The documents required for shipment include the commercial invoice, the bill of lading (or air waybill), the packaging list, and the certificate of origin. For imports, the commercial invoice must show the import license number, the f.o.b., c&f or c.i.f. value, insurance, freight and discounts and commissions. The commodity description
and the value shown on the invoice must agree with that on the license. Customs officials do not allow the grouping of marks or numbers on a shipment of mixed commodities.

Income Taxes - A company participating in a major infrastructure project is exempt from business income tax for a maximum period of five years as calculated from the year the project construction commences.

US-TAIWAN BUSINESS COUNCIL

1700 North Moore Street,
Suite 1703 Arlington, Virginia 22209
Phone: (703) 465-2930
Fax: (703) 465-2937
E-mail: Council@us-taiwan.org
URL: www.us-taiwan.org

KEY TAIWAN GOVERNMENT OFFICES

MINISTRY OF ECONOMIC AFFAIRS

15 Foochow Street, Taipei, Taiwan
Tel: (886 2) 2321-2200
Fax: (886 2) 2391-9398

The Ministry of Economic Affairs has overall responsibility within the ROC Government for administering investment policy. Within the above Ministry specific agencies dealing with investment and licensing matters include:

Investment Commission (MOEA)

8Fl, Yumin Building, 7 Roosevelt Road, Section 1, Taipei, Taiwan
Tel: (886 2) 2738-0007
Fax: (886 2) 2735-2656

The Investment Commission approves all inwards and outwards investments according to MOEA guidelines. Foreign companies seeking assistance in making an application may contact the:

Industrial Development & Investment Center (MOEA)

19Fl, 4 Chunghsiao West Road, Sec. 1, Taipei, Taiwan R.O.C
Tel: (886 2) 2389-2111
Fax: (886 2) 2382-0497

Patent and licensing applications should be referred to:

National Bureau of Standards (MOEA)

3Fl, 185 Hsinhai Road, Section 2, Taipei, Taiwan
Tel: (886 2) 2738 0007
Fax: (886 2) 2735 2656

Companies wishing to set up in one of the industry parks should contact:

Industrial Development Bureau (MOEA)

41-3 Hsinyi Road, Section 3, Taipei, Taiwan
Tel: (886 2) 2754-1255Fax: (886 2) 2703-0160

Companies seeking to set up operations in one of the export processing zones should contact:

Export Processing Zone Administration (MOEA)

600 Chiachang Road, Nantze, Kaohsiung, Taiwan
Tel: (886 7) 361-1212
Fax: (886 7) 361 4348

Companies wishing to set up science or technology based manufacturing operations should contact:

Science-Based Industrial Park Administration

2 Hsin An Road, Hsinchu, Taiwan
Tel: (886.35) 773-311
Fax: (886 35) 776-222

All applications for investment or company licensing involving the banking or financial sectors must be approved by the Ministry of Finance:

MINISTRY OF FINANCE

2 Aikuo Road, Taipei, Taiwan
Tel: (886 2) 2322-8000
Fax: (886 2) 2321-1205

Enquiries concerning portfolio investment or qualifications as a foreign equity investor should be made to the:

Securities & Futures Commission

12F, Yangteh Building, 3 Nanhai Road, Taipei, Taiwan
Tel: (886 2) 2341-3101
Fax: (886 2) 2394-0714

Other important government agencies include the:

The Fair Trade Commission (Executive Yuan)

8Fl, 150 TunHua North Road, Taipei, Taiwan
Tel: (886 2) 2545-5501
Fax: (886 2) 2545-0107

Directorate General of Customs

85 Hsinsheng South Road, Taipei, Taiwan
Tel: (886 2) 2741-3181
Fax: (886 2) 2711-4166

GOVERMENT AND DIPLOMACY

Company name	Telephone	Web
Executive Yuan		www.ey.gov.tw/web/english
Legislative Yuan		www.ly.gov.tw
Judicial Yuan		www.judicial.gov.tw/e-index.htm
Examination Yuan		www.exam.gov.tw
Control Yuan	03-5411-0241	www.cy.gov.tw/english_home.htm
Ministry of Foreign Affairs ROC	02-2348-2999	www.mofa.gov.tw/newmofa/emofa/index.htm
Development of the Bureau of Immigration of the Ministry of the Interior	03-5411-0241	www.immigration.gov.tw/E-home.HTM

International Cooperation and Development Fund		www.icdf.org.tw/english/e_index.asp
Ministry of Education		www.moe.gov.tw/english/index.htm
Ministry of Finance		www.mof.gov.tw/english

CITY

Name	Telephone	Web
Chiayi City Government	886-5-2254321	www.chiayi.gov.tw/english.htm
Hsinchu County Government		www1.hchg.gov.tw/html/e2000.htm
Kaohsiung City Government	07-336-8333	sun1.kcg.gov.tw:8080/%7Eintl/index.htm
Keelung City Government		www.klcg.gov.tw/KLCG1/English.nsf/page/introduction?OpenDocument
Penghu County Government		www.phhg.gov.tw/english/intro/intro.htm
Taichung City Council	04-2221-7911	www.tccn.gov.tw/
Taichung County Government	886-4-5263100	www.taichung.gov.tw/english/index.htm
Tainan City Government		www.tncg.gov.tw/eng.htm
Taipei City Government	886-2-2720-8889	www.taipei.gov.tw/English

FOREIGN CHAMBERS & COMMUNITY ASSOCIATIONS IN TAIWAN

American Chamber of Commerce in Taipei

Suite 1012,, Chia Hsin Building Annex
96 Chung Shan N. Rd, Section 2, Taipei 104
Tel: (886 2) 2581-7089
Fax: (886 2) 2542-3376

Australia & New Zealand Business Association

C/- ANZ Banking Group
8F, 44 Chung Shan N. Rd, Section 2, Taipei
Tel: (886 2) 2568-3353
Fax: (886 2) 2511-1232

British Chamber of Commerce in Taipei

7th Floor, Fu Key Building
99 Jen Ai Road, Section 2, Taipei 10625, Taiwan
Tel: (886 2) 2356-0210
Fax: (886 2) 2356-0211

Canadian Society

C/o The Canadian Trade Office in Taipei
13F, 365 Fuhsing N. Road, Taipei
Tel: (886 2) 2547-9500
Fax: (886 2) 2712-7244

European Council of Commerce & Trade

11F, 285 Chung Hsiao E. Rd, Section 4, Taipei Taiwan
Tel: (886 2) 2740-0236
Fax: (886 2) 2772-0530

Community Services Center

No. 25, Lane 290, Chung Shan N. Road, Section 6, Taipei 111, Taiwan
Tel: (886 2) 2836-8134
Fax: (886 2) 2835-2530

INTERNATIONAL PROPERTY FIRMS IN TAIWAN

Colliers Jardine (Taiwan) Limited

7F, Fubon Min Sheng Building
138 Min Sheng East Road, Section 3, Taipei
Tel: (886 2) 2719 6006
Fax (886 2) 2545 0414

Investec (Taiwan) Limited

3F, 147 Chien Kuo Road, Section 2, Taipei
Tel: (886 2) 2501 1908
Fax: (886 2) 2509 0626

Richard Ellis, Taiwan Branch

7F, Cosmos Building, No. 134, Section 3, Min Sheng East Road, Taipei
Tel: (886 2) 2713 2266;
Fax: (886 2) 2712 3065

Major Accounting Firms in Taiwan

Diwan Ernst & Young

9th Fl, 333 Keelung Road Section 1, Taipei
Tel: (886 2) 2720-4000
Fax: (886 2) 2757-6469

KPMG

6th Fl, 156 Min Sheng East Road, Section 3, Taipei
Tel: (886 2) 2715-9999
Fax: (886 2) 2715-9888

Price Waterhouse

27th Fl, 333 Keelung Road, Section 1, Taipei
Tel: (886 2) 2729-6666
Fax: (886 2) 2757-6371

REPRESENTATIVE OFFICES

UNITED STATES REPRESENTATIVE OFFICES

American Institute in Taiwan, Washington Headquarters
Suite 1700, 1700 North Moore Street, Arlington, VA 22209
Tel: 703-525-8474; fax 703-841-1385.

American Institute in Taiwan, Taipei Office
No. 7, Lane 134, Hsin Yi Road, Section 3, Taipei, Taiwan
Tel: 011-886-2-2709-2000; fax 011-886-2-2702-7675

American Institute in Taiwan, Kaohsiung Office
5F, No. 2, Chung Cheng 3rd Road; Kaohsiung, Taiwan 800
Tel: 011-886-7-224-0154; fax 011-886-7-223-8237

TAIWAN REPRESENTATIVE OFFICE

Taipei Economic and Cultural Representative Office (TECRO)
4201 Wisconsin Ave. NW, Washington, DC 20116-2137
Tel: 202-895-1800; fax 202-363-0999.

SELECTED EXPORT-IMPORT AND BUSINESS OPPORTUNITIES

EXPORT POTENTIAL AND OPPORTUNITIES

Taiwan's exports go to almost every corner of the world, and in many cases their high quality and reasonable cost give them a commanding position in global markets. The Taiwan information industry, for example, ranked third among all countries in 1998 in terms of total production value, accounting for 58 percent of the monitors and 84 percent of the image scanners sold around the world

A multitude of other Taiwan-made items also enjoy wide international popularity, including textiles, electronics, machinery, metal products, vehicles, plastic and rubber products, footwear, furniture, chemicals, and processed agricultural products. Just as important, however, are the many other categories of lesser export value that represent the emergence of entirely new industries or product lines. Although not yet leaders in absolute dollar terms, they are pointing the way toward the future and helping to highlight the great strides the ROC has been making in encouraging innovation and the upgrading of industry.

Taiwan's manufacturers offer an enormous array of goods, ranging from traditional standbys such as giftware and sporting goods to the very latest in advanced plastics processing machinery and telecommunication equipment. Exports of these and other goods and services not only help the island sustain high levels of economic growth, but also ensure that consumers everywhere are able to enjoy quality products at the most competitive prices.

COMPUTES EQUIPMENT AND INFORMATION PRODUCTS

Taiwan retained its position as the world's third largest producer of information products in 1998, with total output of computer and information hardware reaching US$33.77 billion for an increase of 11.9% over the previous year. Notebook PCs are the largest contributors to the industry's performance. Sound cards, CD-ROM drives, monitors, desktop PCs, and scanners are, however, the fastest growing product lines.

Taiwan's notebook-PC, desktop-image-scanner, sound-card, and modem manufacturers became the world's largest producers in their lines in 1998. With makers of computer mice, keyboards, motherboards, hand held scanners, monitors, network interface cards, switching power supplies, and graphic cards retaining their leading positions in the world market, Taiwan is now the world's top producer of 14 computer-related products.

As a result of this success, Taiwan has become a leading supplier for the entire global information technology industry in areas ranging from manufacturing and R&D to key components. For instance, Taiwan is currently the most important overseas procurement site for Compaq, the world's largest personal computer company. It purchased US$5.6 billion worth of computer products in 1998 and expects to spend some US$7 billion in 2005, primarily on such items as PCs and semiconductors.

As production costs continue to rise and the labor pool diminishes in Taiwan, more and more companies are focusing on manufacturing abroad. In 1998, overseas operations accounted for about half of total production value. In some lines, the offshore share was even greater. For instance, overseas production of monitors now exceeds that in Taiwan even though control remains on the island. Predictions call for Taiwan's computer industry to continue to grow at an annual rate of about 15 percent, reaching US$50 billion in sales by the year 2011.

MONITORS

Taiwan remains the world's top producer of monitors with an output of 49.98 million units in 1998, a total that accounted for 57.8% of the entire global market. The market share of 14" models dipped from the 1997 level of 43.7% to 41.7% in 1998, while that for 17" models rose from 19.4% to 32.9%.

Compliance with safety and environmental standards is receiving even greater attention from monitor makers. In addition, designs are becoming more ergonomic in an attempt to accommodate the ever-growing home-user market. A further area of development is in multimedia features. Speakers and cameras are already incorporated as standard on some models, and fax and telephone functions are expected to be added to new models. Taiwan is expected to turn out 580,000 monitors in 2005, up some 16%

NOTEBOOK PCS

In 1998, the total number of notebook computers produced in Taiwan was 6.07 million units, up 35.9% over 1997 and accounting for about 40% of the entire global market. Some 90% of Taiwan-made notebook computers are produced either on an OEM or an ODM basis. Acer, FIC, Twinhead, Inventec, Quanta, Clevo, and Compal, are major makers in the line.

Taiwan is expected to produce 8.2 million notebook PCs in 2005, accounting for 46% worldwide and making the island the world's leading producer of the line. 13.3- and 14.1-inch TFT LCD display models will be mainstream items in 2005. In addition, production and demand for mini- and sub-notebooks will also grow as a result of the trend towards quality lightweight units. Taiwan companies, China Picture Tube and Acer, began to turnout LCD panels in the middle of 2005, boosting the island's competitiveness in the industry.

MODEMS

In 1998, Taiwan fax modem production is expected to account for about 52% of world production, making the island the largest supplier in the line. Most makers have seen dramatic growth in the past couple of years, primarily as a result of the growing popularity of Internet applications.

Most major fax-modem makers in Taiwan buy chipsets from multiple sources, diversifying their purchases in order to manage supply risk effectively and provide a variety of cost and performance choices for different customers. Speed for fax-modems has shifted from 33.6Kbps to 56Kbps models.

COMPUTER MOUSES

Taiwan was still the world's top computer mouse supplier in 1998. Production totaled 56.9 million units in 1998, accounting for 60 percent of global production.

To maintain their competitive edge, Taiwan makers are striving to develop higher-end, higher value-added mice. Optical mice, and wireless mice have, for example, become important niche products. Since it is generally accepted that USB will become new industry standard, many makers have already developed USB-compliant models.

SCANNERS

Taiwan is currently the world's largest scanner supplier. The island commanded 84% of the world's market in 1998, turning out 15.24 million units. Current mainstream items are 600dpi models, but 1200dpi units are gaining strength fast. Taiwan's scanner production has reached the economy of scale that ensures competitive quality and prices. As a result, many leading international firms purchase scanners from the island's suppliers on an OEM or ODM basis. Taiwan is expected to command over 90% of global scanner production by the year 2000.

ELECTRONICS PRODUCTS

Electrical and electronics goods remain Taiwan's leading export sectors, with the island's companies shipping some US$35.7 billion worth of goods abroad in 1998. This figure represented a 6.2% decrease over the previous year and accounted for 32.3% of the total value of the ROC's exports for the year. At present, there are approximately 5,300 electronic manufacturers in Taiwan. They are not only major suppliers of simple electronic items such as electronic spare parts, resistors, transistors, capacitors, ICs, calculators, telephones, radio/cassette recorders, but also prime makers of modems, personal computers, workstations, and facsimile machines.

Manufacturers of electronic products are enjoying growing prestige in overseas markets, particularly those turning out mid- to upper-range equipment. Leading products currently include telephone equipment and personal computers. Some makers have already begun to market abroad under their own brand names, while others have just started to accord brand-name development and overseas consumer brand recognition a high priority. Among those with well-established brand names in international markets are such firms as Acer, Tatung, Microtech, and Tecom.

There are a number of supporting industries that provide electronics manufacturers with the solid base of support that enables them to concentrate on technological development and innovation. Many producers are, however, still reliant on key imported components to some extent. As a result, the ROC government organizations has set aside US$555.5 million to promote R&D programs aimed at encouraging the development of key electronic parts and components.

Semiconductors, the foundation technology for electronic products, are one of the most successful areas. Taiwan was the world's fourth largest producer of semiconductors in 1998, with an output of US$9.12 billion, up 3.1% over the previous year. Over US$11 billion is being invested to build 15 eight-inch wafer plants in Taiwan. By the year 2000, it is expected that island's semiconductor industry will account for 10% of world's total.

Three areas of the electronics and electrical industries are deemed to have exceptional potential. These include information products, telecommunications equipment, and consumer electronics. At the same time, items such as 3C products, personal digital assistants (PDAs), wide-screen TVs, multimedia LCD projectors, air purifiers, high-precision screen printers, mobile wireless telephones, digital recorders, and multi-fiber cable components are considered as innovative products with promising futures.

MACHINE TOOLS

Taiwan has approximately 1300 machine tool makers, located primarily in the central part of the island. Among them, about 65 percent produce metal cutting machines. Taiwan makers can produce most of the components for these machines, including ball screws, hydraulic pumps, gears, and PC-based controllers.

In 1998, Taiwan turned out machine tools worth US$1.8 billion, about the same total as in 1997. This ranked Taiwan as the six largest machine tool producer in the world, accounting for 4.8% of world production. Growth was seen in some categories, but it was limited, owing to the impact of the region's financial crisis . Machining centers and lathes are currently the most important lines, followed by metal forming machinery, milling/boring machines, and grinders. Overall, over 50 percent of metal cutting machines turned out are now numerically-controlled, with lathes having the highest ratio of NC units.

Nearly 80 percent of Taiwan-made machine tools are exported. The island is currently the third largest supplier for mainland China, the fourth largest for the US, the sixth largest for Japan and Korea, and overall, the fifth largest for the markets around the world. In 1998, Taiwan machine tool exports fell to US$1.2 billion, down 12.1% over the previous year. The US and Hong Kong were the most important markets, accounting for 49.6% of machine tool exports. Other important markets included Italy, the UK, Germany, Canada, Japan, and Turkey. The US market grew 40%, Italy 30%, Germany 20%, and Belgium 149%. The US regained its position as Taiwan's leading market in 1998, absorbing 26.6% of total exports in the category and topping the Hong Kong-mainland China market. Thailand and Malaysia, which were previously among the top five markets for Taiwan-made machine tools, fell to ninth and eleventh last year, falling 48% and 68% respectively. In general, Taiwan exports to developed countries grew in 1998 while those to developing countries fell.

The Industrial Development Bureau (IDB) of the ROC Ministry of Economic Affairs is working to establish Taiwan as a global center for the OEM production of machine tools. In line with this goal, manufacturers are being encouraged to step up technical cooperation with German firms that have the most advanced machine tool production technology in the world.

LATHES

Lathes are a major item for most of the island's machine tool makers. Taiwan exported lathes worth US$223 million in 1998, about the same amount as in 1997. Companies on the island are currently focusing on turning out NC models. Over 3,000 CNC lathes are produced annually. Products range from simple models with one spindle and one turret to two-spindle, double-turret, seven-axis models. Lathes produced in Taiwan ordinarily have a life cycle of 5-10 years. Typical features include 15-20m/min rapid-traverse rate; 0.2-0.5 sec. turret indexing; 8,000 rpm; automatic bar feed; motorized and controlled tailstocks; swarf converyors; parts catchers; and tool holders.

MACHINING CENTERS

Machining centers are the largest single export category, accounting for 23.8% of Taiwan's total machine tool exports. In 1998 the island Taiwan exported machining centers worth US$284.73 million, up 7.3% over the previous year. Vertical machining centers are the most widely available, but horizontal and horizontal/vertical units are on offer as well. Most designs are based on a stationary column with travelling saddle. CNC machines produced on the island offer high-speed machining. Some units feature high feed rates and heavy-duty machining. Options available include coolant through the spindle, warf conveyors, and NC rotary tables. The control system is normally from Fanuc, Mitsubishi, or Simens. Models with a PC-based control systems are also available.

GRINDERS

Taiwan exported grinders worth US$77.61 million in 1998, down 8% from the previous year. Non-NC models accounted for some 90 percent of this total. Items produced on the island include surface, external cylindrical, universal, tool, hydraulic crank- shaft, and universal cylindrical grinders. Makers have also developed a range of special-purpose machines that offer high efficiency and simplified maintenance.

Wheel-head spindles are usually driven by AC servo motors rated up to 15kW. CNC drives with servo motors and ballscrews in the axes are also available. Features such as automatic wheel dressing, dimensional compensation, rough and fine grinding, and automatic in-process feed are all available. Some also come with double- walled column design to ensure high rigidity and accurate downfeed.

WOODWORKING MACHINERY

The island's exports of woodworking machinery have shown continuous growth over the last five years, reaching US$544 million in 1998, up 11 percent from the previous year. As a result of such growth, Taiwan is now not only the largest exporter in Asia, but also the third largest supplier of woodworking machinery in the world, ranking behind only Germany and Italy.

With total output reaching US$650-US$700 million in recent years, a wide range of woodworking machinery is supplied by the island. In 1998 sawing machines were the largest category in the line, accounting for 46 percent of total exports. Planing, milling, and molding machines ranked second at US$61.9 million, accounting for 11 percent of exports. Grinders and sanders followed at US$54 million, accounting for 10 percent of all overseas shipments by the industry. Other items turned out in Taiwan include drilling, slicing, and bending machines and lathes.

Woodworking machinery has been manufactured on the island for more than two decades. At present, there are about 250 woodworking machinery manufacturers in Taiwan, mainly located in the central part of the island. Eighty percent of them are small- or mid-scale. To a great extent, their success is based upon a subcontracting system that offers superior flexibility and quality, as well as lower costs.

Although Taiwan's exports of woodworking machines have averaged two-digit growth in recent years, only few manufacturers are able to provide whole-plant service. As a result, many of them have entered into manufacturing and marketing alliances. For example, some makers are participating in trade shows together in order to provide more varied lines of machinery, while others are developing common brands and setting up joint after-sales service depots in order to cut marketing costs.

For years, the main destinations for Taiwan-made woodworking machinery have been the US and Southeast Asia, but the latter market has been adversely affected by the regional financial crisis. The US market, however, remains strong. It was still the largest single destination for Taiwan-made units in 1998, purchasing US$302.8 million worth of woodworking machines. This figure represented about 55.6 percent of total exports in the line. Most of the machines shipped to the American market are DIY models. Hong Kong was the second largest market in 1998, with sales of US$132 million, up 45 percent over the previous year. It was followed by Malaysia, Indonesia, and Canada. The UK and Germany were also among the ten leading export markets in 1998. Other markets with great potential include Central and South America, Europe, and South Asia. A large number of buyers in these areas are small- or mid-scale woodworking plants.

Most of the island's woodworking machinery is sold through foreign distributors, trading companies, or directly to the end-users. Some is, however, still produced on an OEM basis. The Taiwan Association of Machinery Industry plays an especially important role in encouraging and supporting woodworking machinery manufacturers. At the same time, domestic makers are working with the government in the area of R&D, striving to develop high-end machines with CNC, CAD, and CAM features.

PLASTICS AND RUBBER PROCESSING MACHINERY

The Taiwan plastics and rubber processing machinery line dates back to the mid-1950s. Its impressive rate of growth over the years is primarily a result of the vigor of the island's petrochemical sector, which in turn has fostered the development of one of the world's most sophisticated plastics and rubber processing industries. And today the island's plastics and rubber processing machinery makers are the second largest suppliers in Asia, ranking behind only Japan.

At present, there are some 240 manufacturers of plastics and rubber processing machinery in Taiwan. Most are small- and medium-scale enterprises. Approximately 77 percent of their production is for export and 23 percent for the domestic market.

In 1998 Taiwan exported US$421.7 million worth of plastics and rubber processing machinery, down 36.7 percent from the previous year. Southeast Asia accounted for 70 percent of total exports in the line. Shipments went primarily to Hong Kong, the US, Vietnam, Japan, and Thailand. Other markets included Turkey, Malaysia, the Philippines, Indonesia, and India. At present, major export items are injection-molding machines, extruders, blow- molding machines, vacuum-molding machines, and other thermo-forming machines.

Plastic injection-molding machines are the leading item in the category, with the bulk of exports coming from approximately 15 firms. In 1998, the export value of such machines reached US$151.3 million. A vast array of different models is available on the island. Items include horizontal, vertical, thermoset, and double- injection units. Thanks to the continuing entry of new manufacturers, the line is highly competitive in terms of price, quality, and innovation.

Extruders are also important export items, with shipments overseas totaling US$19.9 million in 1998. Shipments of blow-molding machines were worth US$22.3 million in 1998.

Owing to a well-developed satellite factory system that integrates the operations of countless small- and medium-scale factories into a sophisticated network, Taiwan's plastics and rubber processing machinery industry is exceedingly flexible in terms of its ability to meet the most exacting specifications. In recent years the industry has, moreover, been highly successful in upgrading levels of technology and diversifying its markets overseas. Public-sector assistance has been particularly important with respect to technological development. In addition, in order to provide a complete line of plastics and rubber processing machinery to buyers, some makers have formed cooperative alliances covering both manufacturing and marketing.

These strategic alliances, the industry's satellite system, and public-sector encouragement of R&D should help guarantee the continued competitiveness of Taiwan plastics and rubber processing machinery in the years ahead. Buyers can expect to see an expanding range of advanced items, as well as pricing substantially below that offered by suppliers in the developed countries.

AUTO PARTS

The Taiwan auto parts industry is highly efficient as a result of the central-satellite system that has emerged over the past decade. Typically, individual concerns specialize in the production of specific parts and components for later assembly in a central factory. This system permits a tremendous degree of flexibility in production and management strategies. In particular, the central-satellite system has enabled Taiwan manufacturers to move into a host of niche markets.

At present, there are some 2,000 auto markers on the island. About 400 of these operations focus on the OEM market, while the remainder concentrate on the after-sales market. Most Taiwan makers have already earned CSA, SAE, CE mark, E/e mark and European safety certifications. Many are also striving to gain ISO-9000 and US's QS-9000 approvals. In addition, to meet the needs of today's consumers, Taiwan makers have installed automated production lines and are cooperating with some of the world's leading auto companies to produce top quality products at very competitive prices. Together, companies on the island exported over US$2.1 billion worth of auto parts in 1998.

Taiwan offers a comprehensive assortment of auto parts and accessories that are noted for precision, durability and safety. Major export items currently include road wheels and parts and accessories, radial tires, pneumatic tires, rear-view mirrors, parts for use in internal combustion piston engines, lead-acid accumulators, radio-broadcast receivers, electrical lighting and visual signaling equipment, bumpers, body parts, ignition wiring sets, brakes and servo-brakes and parts, carburetors, switch, clutches and parts thereof, windscreen wipers, oil or petrol-filters, steering wheels, radiators, and jacks.

In addition, since 1991, the ROC government has been emphasizing the development of the parts sector as a hub or regional center. It wants Taiwan to be more than just a manufacturing base and hopes the island's components industry can become a regional manufacturing and distribution center for Asia, just as Belgium is for Europe.

The total value of auto parts exports exceed US$2.1 billion in 1998.The U.S. has traditionally been Taiwan's largest customer for auto parts, purchasing about 40% of the island's exports. Last year shipments to the US totaled US$818.7 million. OEM business from the US and Japan has grown rapidly in recent years. As Taiwan makers continue to improve the quality and design of their product, they should become ever more successful in international market. Currently, seven domestic automakers have cooperative relations with automakers in Japan. They are, for instance, entering into ventures with international brands for product design and development, contributing to the upgrading of technological levels on the island.

HAND TOOLS

Taiwan exported US$ 1,545.7 million worth of hand tools in 1998. This was a 4.5 % drop from the previous year and the first time that the exports of hand tools have decreased. However the performance of hand tools was not as badly affected by the regional economic crisis as other industries. Nonetheless, shipments to Southeast Asia and Japan fell almost 20%. The largest markets for Taiwan hand tools are the US and Europe, where sales remain strong.

At present, the Taiwan hand tool industry is striving to maintain its position in the face of strong competition from Mainland China, India, South Korea, and Brazil. Manufacturers are upgrading quality and facilities, and improving design and materials in an effort to increase their edge over competitors. They have also moved production of low-end items abroad to take advantage of more favorable labor and land costs. Today, for instance, almost 40% of the jacks made in China are turned out in the factories operated by Taiwan manufacturers.

MANUAL HAND TOOLS

Taiwan offers an extensive choice of tools ranging from those for carpentry, electrical work, plumbing, and painting to those for plastering, measuring, automobile repair and gardening. In 1998, exports of manual hand tools amounted to US$1,292.1 million, a decrease of 3.5 percent over the preceding year. Manual tools are the most important hand tools exported from Taiwan. Major export items include wrenches, pliers, tool kits, hammers and screwdrivers. The US is the largest market for Taiwan-made manual hand tools, accounting for 39.4 percent in 1998, followed by the UK and Japan.

Tool makers in Taiwan are currently developing new manufacturing techniques and installing more sophisticated production equipment. Many are using CAD/CAM systems, CNCs, and EDMs. Others have set up facilities in China to handle bulk orders for lower-end items.

JACKS

Taiwan, once considered one of the world's top suppliers of jacks, has seen a decline each year because of rising labor costs at home. Last year, Taiwan exports were valued at US$25.8 million, down 26.1% from 1997. The largest orders last year came from the US, which accounted for 50% of exports in the line, followed by Germany at 11.6% and Sweden at 6.6%.

ELECTRIC TOOLS

Exports of Taiwan-made electric tools are aimed primarily at the DIY market. In 1998, foreign sales in this category amounted to US$77.9 million, down 23.6? from 1997. The US, the UK and Belgium are the largest markets. Best-selling items include drills, sanders, saws, soldering irons, and heat guns. The current trend is towards the production of more cordless tools that offer multiple functions and longer battery-life.

Most electric tools conform to UL, CSA, GS, SAA, and BS specifications. Manufacturers have also obtained ISO 9000 certifications. Components for electric tools are usually sourced domestically, with only a few key components such as drill chucks and electric motors being imported from the US and Hong Kong.

PNEUMATIC TOOLS

Taiwan's pneumatic tool makers registered an increase of 5.5? in their 1998 shipments abroad, with the total value of exports in the category amounting to US$149.9 million. ROC-made pneumatic tools are selling best in the US, which accounts for 66.7% of the island's pneumatic-tool export sales. ROC air tool makers have been manufacturing more models for professional, industrial, and automobile repair use in recent years. Impact wrenches, air sanders, air grinders, air drills, air screwdrivers, air hammers, and air spray guns are the most important export items in this category.

FURNITURE

In 1998 Taiwan shipped US$1.56 billion worth of furniture abroad, down 7% from the previous year. The island's industry has long enjoyed success in the international marketplace, with exports in 1987 reaching to US$1.7 billion. In the years since, higher labor costs and difficulties in obtaining raw materials have, however, forced manufacturers to employ new strategies and cut costs. Among other things, cross-border division of labor has become a way of life for many in the industry.

Major markets for Taiwan-made furniture include the US, Japan, Germany, Hong Kong, Canada, the UK, Australia, the Netherlands, France, and Saudi Arabia. Shipments to the US in 1998 reached about US$802 million, or 51.3% of total furniture exports. Japan was the second largest market at US$324 million, a figure equal to 20.7% of exports in the line.

Major export items consist of metal furniture, wooden furniture, bamboo and rattan furniture, plastic furniture, and medical furniture. Metal furniture has led in the category since 1993, with exports in 1998 totalling US$780.5 million, or some 50% of total furniture exports. There are several reasons for the boom in Taiwan metal furniture in recent years. First, materials used in metal items are readily available from the domestic China Steel Corporation. Secondly, many makers on the island are automating their manufacturing operations and emphasizing R&D, leading to the development of more innovative metal products at competitive prices.

At the same time, exports of wooden furniture have decreased, falling by 9.0% in 1998. In the past, the wood used by Taiwan's makers was imported primarily from Southeast Asia. However, countries there have recently tightened export regulations on wood and semi-finished products in the last few years. As a consequence, a number of Taiwan makers of wooden furniture have responded by moving production lines to Southeast Asia and mainland China. These companies typically maintain R&D facilities in Taiwan and turn out the vast majority of their higher-end products at home. The policy of handling orders in Taiwan and producing semi-finished products offshore for shipment back to the island for final processing has become popular among wooden furniture makers. In fact, it contributes substantially to mainland China's growing furniture export figures.

In another move to overcome supply problems, some Taiwan wooden-furniture makers have set up wood processing plants in various countries around the world. Still others have gone abroad to gain access to new marketing channels, obtain more detailed market information, and secure advanced technologies. For the most part, such moves have focused on the US.

Taiwan's exports in the bamboo and rattan furniture line grew by 9.4% in 1998. This increase was essentially the result of previous Taiwan investments in the establishment of offshore plants in Indonesia and Vietnam in order to secure access to raw materials. Semi-finished products are shipped back for the final touches. This system has, of course, contributed to the increased volume of Taiwan exports in the line. In addition, the plastic furniture category has also seen an increase, primarily because of Taiwan's leading role in plastics and rubber technologies. Plastic furniture exports were up 7.8% in 1998 .

GIFTWARE

Over the past 20 years, low labor costs, an emphasis on craftsmanship, the availability of a wide range of raw materials, and strong supporting industries have helped to make the Taiwan giftware industry into a world leader. The prevalence of small- and medium-scale manufacturers in the industry has also contributed to this success, providing the high degree of flexibility that has enabled the island to respond rapidly to new trends and opportunities.

Thanks to a well-organized satellite factory system and years of experience, Taiwan's thousands of small giftware firms are able to offer samples, quote prices, and make delivery on almost any item within a very short time. In addition, they are often in a position to make suggestions on how products could be modified or improved.

Taiwan-made giftware can be divided into decorative items and housewares. Products in the first of these categories include Christmas decorations, jewelry boxes, crystalware, porcelain figurines, flower pots and vases, artificial flowers, and photo frames. Of these, Christmas decorations currently rank as the single most important line. The latter category covers such areas as kitchenware, clocks, hair brushes, combs, towels, and a host of other items that depend on Taiwan's well-developed plastics industry and expertise in mold-making.

Availability of raw materials stands out as key factor in production. There is a close relationship between giftware products and the geographic location of manufacturers. For instance, most porcelain and ceramic products come from Taiwan's Miaoli and Yingko regions; bamboo and rattan products from Sanyi, Tungshiao, Hsinchu, and Guanmiao; mineral products from Hualien and Yuli in eastern Taiwan; molded metal products from Sanchung, Changhua, and Tainan; and holiday decorations from Puli and Tsaotun in central Taiwan.

Combinations of materials, such as the use of metal with acrylic and polymer with wood, as well as stronger emphasis on environmental protection and design, are some of the latest trends in the industry. Common design subjects include popular cartoon characters, pets, wild animals, the countryside, the sea, aliens, and nostalgic motifs.

The majority of exports are currently handled by trading houses. These firms not only act as liaisons between foreign buyers and domestic manufacturers, but also help giftware producers keep abreast of international developments in design and materials. Such arrangements are well-suited to the short life cycles and small, diversified orders that are characteristic of the giftware market.

Taiwan exported US$248.7 million worth of decorative gift items and US$964.1 million worth of houseware goods in 1998. The US was the major market, with Japan ranking as the second most important destination for items in both categories.

Overall, Taiwan giftware exports have been declining in recent years, owing to the appreciation of the NT dollar, and a shortage of labor on the island. To cope with these developments, labor-intensive operations are being moved to mainland China and countries in Southeast Asia. At the same time, factories on the island are being upgraded and marketing activities expanded.

Greater attention is also being paid to design and the development of innovative products for export markets, and more and more companies are focusing on original design manufacturing. After years of turning out designs supplied by overseas customers, companies are now emphasizing R&D. Most are, in fact, investing three to six percent of their profits R&D. Taiwan giftware manufacturers have also begun to hire substantial numbers of design personnel, with some even employing free-lance designers from Europe, the US, and Japan to help them gain a better understanding of overseas market preferences.

Manufacturers are promoting their own brand names as well. A good many have established warehouse facilities in Europe, the US, and Southeast Asia to serve these areas more effectively and position themselves to market their own brand-name products. Industry associations, the Taiwan Handicraft Promotion Center, and the China External Trade Development Council are also organizing seminars and training courses covering the latest product designs, production developments, and new material applications in an effort to encourage the development of more high-end items.

TEXTILES AND GARMENTS

Textile manufacturing was one of the first light industries established in Taiwan. As early as 1951, it ranked as the island's largest export sector. Although this position was ultimately lost to the electronics industry, the sector remained a strong second in 1998, with exports of US$14.56 billion, a total equal to 16 percent of the nation's total overseas sales.

The main categories of Taiwan textile exports are fibers, yarns, fabrics, apparel, and accessories. Yarns and fabrics dominate, comprising about 73 percent of the total export mix.

Taiwan is the number three manufacturer of man-made fibers in the world. The export value of these materials in 1998 was US$769.7 million. The vast range of man-made fiber produced in Taiwan includes polyester filament yarn, polyester staple fiber, nylon filament yarn, acrylic staple fiber, rayon filament yarn, and rayon staple fiber.

Exports of fabrics in 1998 declined 12 percent to US$8,918 million. They accounted for 61% of the total textile exports, followed by apparel at 16%, yarns at 12%, fibers at 5%, and accessories at 5 %. Fabrics of man-made fiber are the most important, since Taiwan possesses abundant supplies of competitively-priced synthetic fiber. Woven man-made filament fabrics are of particular importance in terms of exports.

Apparel turned out by the domestic garment industry consists mainly of woven garments, knitted garments, and sweaters. In recent years, mainland China has replaced Taiwan as the world's leading garment manufacturer. Labor and land shortages on the island have caused many manufacturers to move their factories to the mainland and Southeast Asia. As a result, exports in the line have been declining since 1988. In 1998, they totaled US$2.349 billion, down 4 percent from the previous year.

The United States was long the leading export market for Taiwan textiles. However, in 1991 Hong Kong overtook the US to become the island's most important market. In 1998, it accounted for 34 percent of total exports in the category, followed by the US at 18 percent and the Philippines at 3 percent.

Major exports to Hong Kong in 1998 were fabrics and yarns, totaling US$3,619.7 and US$802.6 million respectively. As indirect trade across the Taiwan Strait increases, the Hong Kong market is projected to absorb even more textile products from Taiwan.

Garments and accessories are the most important exports to the US, totaling US$1,992 million in 1998, and accounting for 73% of exports in the line. Exports of fabrics to the US market reached US$502.6 million in the same year.

In the Japanese market, yarns and fabrics are the major Taiwan export items. In 1998 some US$103.2 million worth of yarns and US$168 million worth of fabrics were shipped to Japan.

As a result of increasing investments by Taiwan manufacturers in Southeast Asia in recent years, exports of Taiwan-made yarns and fabrics to that region are growing dramatically. The Philippines is the leading market in the area, purchasing US$ 483.7 million worth of textile products in 1998.

To counter escalating domestic wages and land costs, as well as competition from developing countries, textiles manufacturers in Taiwan are placing more emphasis on production automation, the acquisition of new technologies, the enhancement of design capabilities, and the adoption of small-volume production. Going public to obtain capital for investment and R & D is also widespread among leading textile manufacturers.

BEST PRODUCTS TO EXPORT TO TAIWAN

The import requirements of the ROC are shaped by its relative lack of natural resources and by the technological needs of its advanced export-oriented industrial economy. In order to turn out the countless products that are shipped to virtually every country in the world by Taiwan suppliers, vast quantities of agricultural and industrial raw materials must be imported each year. In addition, increased prosperity and rising living standards are leading to much greater demand among the island's own populace for imported consumer items of all kinds. In 1998, for instance, Taiwan purchased US$66.83 billion worth of agricultural and industrial raw materials abroad, a dollar total equal to 63.8 percent of total imports. The majority were destined for processing and re-export, with major items in the category including raw cotton, lumber, maize, soybeans, wheat, electronic components, chemicals, basic metals, and crude oil.

At the same time, the growth of sophisticated industries on the island has also created a demand for a wide range of advanced equipment and new technologies in such areas as aerospace, advanced mass transportation, precision measuring and testing, industrial automation, and pollution control. Products in this category, which were worth US$24.31 billion in 1998, accounted for 23.2 percent of total imports.

In the area of consumer products the outlook is also promising for foreign suppliers. The people of Taiwan are avid consumers of goods from around the world, with those items carrying internationally-renowned brand names enjoying particular popularity. As the liberalization of the island's economy gains further momentum and per capita income continues to rise, this market for imported goods should become even more lucrative.

AGRICULTURAL PRODUCTS

With only limited arable land, Taiwan is dependent on imports to meet demand for many primary agricultural products and meats. This reality, plus growing prosperity and government efforts to bring its agricultural policies more into line with the WTO rules, has helped transform the island into an exceptionally profitable market for a host of items. In 1998, for instance, agricultural imports amounted to US$7,794 million.

Leading import items currently include cereal grains for human and animal consumption, fruits, cotton, aquatic products, meats, and various other raw materials for food processing. Taiwan's most important agricultural supplier is US, which exported US$3.26 billion worth of agricultural products to the island in 1998. This total amounted to 36.3 percent of the island's total imports in the line. Taiwan has become the fifth largest market for such US agricultural products, as maize, soybeans, fruits, and cotton. Other important suppliers include Malaysia, Australia, Japan, New Zealand, Thailand, and Indonesia.

CEREAL GRAINS

Wheat, maize, barley, sorghum, and soybeans rank as Taiwan's most important cereal imports. In 1998 Taiwan imported US$1.03 billion worth of items in this category, down 22.4 percent over the previous year. Major cereal imports in 1998 included 852,169 tons of wheat, 4,757,910 tones of maize, 225,704 tons of barley, 80,194 tons of sorghum, and 2,002,136 tons of soybeans. The US is traditionally the island's major supplier of maize, wheat, and soybeans, while barley and sorghum come primarily from Australia.

FRUITS

The island's fruit imports are also substantial, both in terms of volume and value. Imported fruit accounts for nearly 10 percent of the domestic consumption. At present, leading imports in the category are apples, grapes, kiwi fruit, plums, peaches, and grapefruit. The US has been the main source for most products in the category, and Taiwan has become the third largest importer for US fruit. In 1998, the island purchased a total of US$387.6 million worth of fresh and dried fruits from abroad.

It should also be noted that the number of species of fruit imported is growing year by year, as foreign growers become more familiar with Taiwan's market potential and the island's consumers increase their taste for exotic items. Major import sources are the US, Thailand, Iran, Australia, New Zealand, Chile, South Africa, Japan, and South Korea.

COTTON

Most of the raw cotton that Taiwan uses comes from abroad. In 1998, the island imported US$618.8 million worth of cotton, up 2.9 percent over the previous year. Pakistan, the US, and India were the island's major suppliers. The cotton spinning industry in the ROC is sizable, and foreign firms that can furnish a steady supply of competitively-priced, quality cotton will find a substantial market for the commodity, which can be imported tariff-free. Taiwan importers usually purchase raw cotton through agents on the island, with only a few seeking out their own overseas suppliers.

AQUATIC PRODUCTS

Imports of primary and processed aquatic products in 1998 reached US$540.63 million. Thanks to growing affluence, a lowering of ROC trade barriers, depleted marine resources in the seas around Taiwan, and an international ban on drift-net fishing, demand on the island for imported seafood of all kinds is strong. Hotels and restaurants tend to be major buyers of higher-end seafood, such as lobster, snapper, and abalone, while lower-priced items find a welcome reception in supermarkets and other outlets catering to the household market. Most countries currently exporting seafood to Taiwan have seen their sales surge in recent years.

DAIRY PRODUCTS

Dairy products are yet another promising area in terms of import prospects. Although Taiwan's domestic diary industry is stable and profitable, it remains relatively small in relation to the size of the island's population and market potential. Processed milk powder was the leading dairy product import in 1998, with imports amounting to US$334.31 million. Opportunities in this area should be particularly outstanding for suppliers from Australia, New Zealand, and possibly France and Denmark.

Demand in Taiwan for liquid pure milk and flavored milk has been increasing steadily in recent years as well. With the probable removal of restrictions in connection with the ROC's application for admittance to the WTO, imports of these products could soar dramatically. In addition, consumption of cheese has been rising in Taiwan as a result of the growth of foreign fast-food chains. As domestic tastes continue to change and the island's residents become more accustomed to cheese products, imports in the line should continue to grow.

MAJOR AGRICULTURAL IMPORTS

Unit: US$ Million

Product	1998	1997	Growth

			Rate(%)
Cereal Products	4,461.13	5,463.67	-18.3
Cereals.	1,034.14	1,331.84	-22.4
Oil Seeds & Flours	551.79	885.29	-37.7
Vegetable	163.97	158.74	3.3
Fruits	387.62	435.04	-10.9
Roots, Tubers	65.51	76.41	-14.3
Plant Medicinal Herbs	88.33	108.12	-18.3
Flowers & Flower Seeds	16.47	16.38	0.5
Sugar & Related Preparations	134.16	155.51	-13.7
Tea	12.50	11.48	8.9
Tobacco	457.26	436.27	4.8
Cotton	532.41	517.29	2.9
Wine	390.12	597.51	-34.7
Others	626.85	733.79	-14.6
Livestock Products	1,600.88	1,928.49	-17.0
Fishery Products	540.64	729.97	-25.9
Forestry Products	1,191.78	1,797.70	-33.7
Total	7,794.41	9,919.83	-21.4

Source: Customs Statistics of the ROC

BASE METALS

Base metals, including ferrous metals and non-ferrous metals such as aluminum, copper, brass, zinc, tin, lead, and nickel, play an indispensable role in Taiwan's economic well-being. They are not only used in the manufacture of a host of export items, ranging from machinery and auto parts to electrical and electronic goods and hardware, but also in countless products for the domestic market. Thanks to continuing economic development, expanding exports, and a rising standard of living on the island, the demand for base metals has been exhibiting a steady increase over the years.

IRON AND STEEL

In 1998 Taiwan imported US$4.7 billion worth of iron and steel products, down 26.3 percent from the previous year. The decline was mainly the result of an expansion in capacity by the island's China Steel Corporation and various private-sector companies rather than of any absolute decline in demand. Overall, import value in this category accounted for 4.5 percent of the total value of Taiwan's imports, reflecting the island's continuing dependence on overseas sources of supply.

China Steel and private-sector steel companies currently import a broad range of iron and steel materials. CSC, for example, imports everything from iron ore to ancillary refining materials, while many private concerns focus on imports of steel scrap, ship plate, and billets and slabs.

In 1998, Taiwan also imported 7,537 thousand tons of crude steel. Import value reached US$1,693 million. Russia, mainland China, Brazil, and Poland were the most important sources. Among rolled steel products, hot steel coil/sheet was the leading import item, with inbound shipments amounting to US$474.9 million. Purchases of galvanized steel have remained substantial as well, with imports reaching US$495.2 million. Zinc plate, steel rod, and H beams were also import major items.

The construction sector was the island's biggest buyer of steel products, accounting for 48 percent of total consumption in 1996. Steel bars and sections were in the most demand. The manufacturing sector consumed 32 percent of all iron and steel products, with fabricated metal products and transportation equipment accounting for 23.8 percent and 5.3 percent of this demand. Steel coil and sheet were the most important items.

Specialty steels are key materials in a wide range of Taiwan's cutting-edge products, including those in such areas as aerospace, automobiles, electronics, and machinery. Some 51 percent of stainless steel and 99 percent of alloy steel are used in the manufacturing sector. Currently, 38 percent of total specialty steel needs are met by imports, and the rapid growth of sophisticated industries should help maintain this strong demand in the years ahead.

In 1998, for example, imports of specialty steels reached 563 thousand tons, valued at US$739.7 million. Import demand was particularly strong for stainless hot-rolled coil and alloy steel. Japanese firms ranked as the leading suppliers of these specialty steels. Germany, South Korea, Italy, and Belgium were important suppliers as well.

NON-FERROUS METALS

Non-ferrous metals are also important in the Taiwan industrial picture, with aluminum, copper, brass, zinc, tin, lead, and nickel all being used in the manufacture of key export products. Imports of copper and copper products, which find extensive application in the production of electrical wire and cable, amounted to US$1,551 million in 1998. Currently, all of the domestic demand for electrolytic copper has to be met by imports. Japan, Chile, the US, Peru, Australia, Zambia, and South Africa are the major sources.

Total imports of aluminum ingots, scrap, plate, foil, and other items amounted US$1,224million in 1998. Except for aluminum extrusion products, a line in which domestic manufacturers were able to meet most of the island's demand, most aluminum for domestic consumption was imported. Aluminum and aluminum alloy ingots were the most important import item. Aluminum foils, which are widely used in the food-packaging, electrical-machinery, electronics, and pharmaceutical industries, were also imported in large quantities. Australia, Japan, US, South Africa, Bahrain, and Russia were the major suppliers.

Both nickel and zinc imports remain substantial. Shipments of nickel and nickel products to Taiwan amounted to US$1243.3 million in 1998. During the same period, imports of zinc products amounted to US$314.7 million. Zinc ingots, alloy ingots, and scrap were the most important items.

SOURCES OF IMPORTED IRON AND STEEL PRODUCTS

Unit: US$ million

Source	1997	1998
Japan	1,831.1	1,579.2
Russia	857.4	590.5
Mainland China	568.8	485.3
South Africa	295.2	247.9
South Korea	283.0	344.6
Ukraine	270.6	174.2
U.S.A	248.6	163.4
Germany	317.0	165.7
Australia	219.4	126.0
Brazil	249.6	108.4

Source: Taiwan Steel and Iron Industries Association

MAJOR BASE METAL IMPORTS

Unit: US$ Million

	1997	1998
Iron and Steel	7,229.0	4,675.0
Copper	2,136.8	1,551.2
Aluminum	1,704.7	1,223.6
Nickel	342.5	243.3
Zinc	394.4	314.9
Lead	88.5	60.7
Tin	75.5	67.4

GARMENTS AND CLOTHING ACCESSORIES

Taiwan's garment and clothing accessory imports can be divided into high-end name-brand products from Japan, Italy, and France and low-priced garments from Southeast Asia. The first of these two categories has grown rapidly in importance, owing to the economic prosperity the island enjoys, a strong demand for exclusive imported goods, and lower import duties. Many importers have obtained agency agreements from world-famous brands, and more high-end foreign companies have been striving to share in Taiwan's lucrative market. At the same time, as the low-end garments traditionally produced by Taiwan manufacturers have lost their competitiveness, domestically-made shirts, underwear, socks, sweaters, and children's wear have been replaced by those from other Asian countries.

There are no special restrictions or regulations covering the import of apparel and clothing accessories. Import duties currently stand at a relatively low 12.5%, and according to ROC Customs statistics for 1998, the import value of garment and clothing accessories increased 1%.

In 1998, Taiwan purchased US$822 million worth of garments and US$123 million worth of clothing accessories from abroad. Major import sources included Hong Kong, Italy, Japan, South Korea, Vietnam, and France, while clothing accessories came mostly from Japan, Italy, the US, Vietnam, and Mainland China.

The value of garments imported from Hong Kong amounted to US$278.8 million, a gain of 14 percent over the previous year. Accounting for 34 percent of Taiwan market, Hong Kong garments are popular with consumers on the island because of their fashionable design and competitive prices.

In terms of sales channels, domestic Taiwan agents either set up booths in department stores or establish their own boutiques. The major Taiwan agents in this line include Chung Hseng Trading, Blue Jones, Silver Benz, Pacific 88 Co., and Emporio Trade Co.

In line with the growing popularity of brand-name fashions in Taiwan, more and more foreign brands sell successfully in Taiwan. For instance, Italy's Prada, Max Mara, Salvatore Ferragamo, Giorgio Armani, E. Armani, and Dolce & Gabana; France's Agnes b, and ET Vous; and SODA, Guess and Anne Klein II of the US have entered the market. Lower-end garments and clothing accessories produced in other Asian countries are usually imported by domestic trading companies and sold in chain stores, discount stores, and ordinary clothing shops.

As a consequence of the popularity of imported high-end apparel and clothing accessories in Taiwan and the ending of export quotas in the year 2011, domestic manufacturers have been adjusting their marketing strategies, putting more emphasis on the potential of the Taiwan market. Some large factories on the island have even obtained authority to produce famous European and US brands, while manufacturers of low-end items are continuing to shift production overseas, with the finished goods then being shipped back to Taiwan for sale.

IMPORT VALUE OF GARMENTS AND CLOTHING ACCESSORIES

Unit: US$ Million

	1996	1997	1998
Woven Garments	466.0	502.8	471.4
Knitted Garments	234.0	259.9	243.0
Sweaters	115.0	132.6	107.7
Clothing Accessories	124.8	129.3	122.8

SOURCES OF IMPORTED GARMENTS AND CLOTHING ACCESSORIES

Unit: US$ Million

Garments	Hong Kong	Italy	Vietnam	Japan	Korea
	277.8	141	67.3	52.5	51.2
Clothing Accessories	Japan	Italy	Vietnam	USA	Mainland China
	33	13	12	9	9

FURNITURE

Taiwan's furniture imports have grown rapidly in recent years, owing to lower import duties, higher capita income, increased consumption, and a widespread desire for more comfortable home and office environments. In 1998, Taiwan purchased US$272.4 million worth of furniture from abroad, a fall of 11.1 percent from the previous year.

Mainland China, Vietnam, Italy, Indonesia, Malaysia, the US, Japan, Germany, Spain, and Denmark are major import sources. Mainland China ranked as the top overall supplier, exporting US$59.85 million furniture products to Taiwan in 1998, mainly wooden furniture and parts. Vietnam shipped US$34.33 million worth of furniture to Taiwan in 1998. The growth in imports of Vietnam-made furniture is a result of the growing popularity of rosewood furniture in the Taiwan market. Some firms on the island are even establishing their own plants in Vietnam to produce such furniture. During the same period, Italy shipped US$27.92 million worth of furniture and parts to the island, mainly wooden furniture and seats, making it Taiwan's second largest supplier.

At the same time, Indonesia supplied US$23.82 million worth of products, including wooden, bamboo, and rattan furniture. Malaysia and the US shipped US$19.18 and US$19.15 million worth of furniture respectively. Exports from these latter two sources consisted mainly of parts, wooden furniture, and upholstered furniture.

Overall, wooden furniture led imports totaled US$105.06 million in 1998 and accounted for 38.6% of all furniture imports. Imports in this category, however, suffered a 19.7% downturn, primarily as a result of restrictions on exports of wood in Malaysia and Indonesia, as well as export limitations imposed upon finished rosewood furniture from Vietnam.

Metal furniture is another category worth noting. Import value of items in the line amounted to US$12.98 million during 1998, down 1.2% from the previous year.

The Taiwan market is attracting not only domestic producers who previously concentrated on exports, but also noted international manufacturers. The world's two leading home furnishing companies from northern Europe, IKEA of Sweden and ID Design of Denmark, are working to dominate the huge Taiwan domestic market. IKEA, for instance, offers one-stop shopping for home needs, including sofas, wardrobes, beds, carpets, lights, fabrics, and children's toys and continues to expand its network of outlets.

ID Design opened its first store on the island in Kaohsiung in December of 1994, and a second store in Taipei in January of 1997. The company plans to open more large-scale outlets in Taichung and other cities as well.

In the domestic market, variety, function, emphasis on interior design, and individualism are major considerations for Taiwan furniture importers. In terms of sofas, leather is still important. However, consumers have begun to turn to lighter colored leathers. At the same time, cloth sofas in floral designs are becoming more popular, at least partly because they are priced at only 50 percent of leather sofas.

Natural wooden furniture is more popular with domestic consumers than glass or coated-metal items. Currently, wooden furniture from Denmark, Sweden, and Spain is especially welcome in the Taiwan market. In addition, sales of children furniture have been growing rapidly in recent years, with beds, desks, cabinets, and play furniture being among the most popular products.

Comfort, color, and modernity are also receiving more emphasis in office furniture. As a result of the growth of service industries, opportunities of this category remain lucrative.

SOURCES OF IMPORTED FURNITURE

Unit: US$ thousand

Country	Import Value	Percentage(%)
Mainland China	59,851.0	22.0
Vietnam	34,328.6	12.6
Italy	27,921.2	10.2
Indonesia	23,822.0	8.7
Malaysia	19,178.8	7.0
US	19,148.9	7.0
Japan	18,668.8	6.9
Germany	15,830.3	5.8
Spain	8,765.3	3.2
Denmark	5,814.4	2.1

TAIWAN FURNITURE IMPORTS

Unit: US$ thousand

	1997	1998	Growth Rate(%)
Wooden Furniture	130,802.9	105,060.7	-19.7
Metal Furniture	13,130.8	12,976.2	-1.2
Bamboo and Rattan Furniture	12,938.3	10,868.0	-16.0
Plastic Furniture	1,067.3	1,325.5	+24.2
Medical Furniture	12,571.9	9,386.8	-25.3
Other	135,776.4	132,807.7	-2.2
Total	306,287.6	272,424.9	-11.1

ENVIRONMENTAL PROTECTION AND POLLUTION CONTROL EQUIPMENT

Environmental-protection and pollution-control equipment has become an extremely promising field for foreign manufacturers and suppliers in recent years, owing to the tightening of environmental regulations and changing attitudes in Taiwan. As rapid economic development takes its toll, technologically advanced solutions are needed to prevent, control, and remedy the impact of pollution. This need has created a multi-billion dollar industry, with some of the world's largest corporations looking to break into the market.

Many government agencies and state-run enterprises have already begun to make very substantial investments in such equipment as part of an effort to implement various national environmental projects. The ROC Environmental Protection Agency (EPA), for example, is placing greater emphasis on waste treatment and water and air pollution control. Its many initiatives include the establishment of solid-waste and waste-to-energy facilities, the tracking and control of the use of toxic chemicals, and the setting up of emission inventory and abatement programs for the Taipei and Kaohsiung areas.

The EPA is currently planning to establish an industrial waste material control center in an attempt to attract both domestic and foreign investors to encourage the development of the waste disposal market. The center will focus on integrating and filing relevant information contributed by the island's state-run and local environmental protection institutions. This data will then be given to interested domestic and foreign recycling companies to facilitate planning for waste-treatment services. At present, the annual volume of industrial waste materials exceeds 15 million tons, but only few Taiwan companies are capable of handling hazardous waste. The government is endeavoring to persuade large- scale domestic and foreign-based waste disposal companies to work together to combat the island's trash problems.

In line with the worldwide trend toward environmental protection, the Industrial Development Bureau proposed a five-year program beginning in 1997. This program is designed help develop the pollution control industry and assist domestic manufacturers in turning out more "green" products. The government also plans to privatize various environmental-related businesses including waste treatment, recycling, and vehicular exhaust testing operations. More incinerators will be built on build-operate-transfer and built- operate-own bases as well. The IDB estimates that with an annual growth rate of 11%, the production value of the island's environmental protection industry should reach US$4.2 billion by 2003. Since the industry in Taiwan, consists of mostly of medium- and small-scaled companies, coopeation with foreign firms will be essential.

Private-sector enterprises are already spending increasing sums on the installation of pollution control equipment in order to bring their operations into conformity with newly enacted rules and regulations such as the Environmental Impact Evaluation Law, the Solid Waste Disposal Act, and the Air Pollution Control Act. Tax breaks, low-interest-financing programs, and incentives given for the import of environmental protection equipment are motivating domestic industries to invest more in pollution control technology and services as well.

According to Taiwan Environmental Industry Association, Taiwan spent US$25 billion on environmental-protection and pollution-control equipment in 1998. Taiwan manufacturers supplied only US$ 300 million worth of this equipment, with most of the market being dominated by foreign manufacturers. The US and Japan were the most important sources, supplying 30% and 24% of imported equipment, respectively.

There is also a growing demand for environmental services. As a result, environmental engineering firms, pollution-control services, and environmental impact assessment and consulting companies should find a lucrative market for their services in the years ahead.

TELECOMMUNICATIONS PRODUCTS

Taiwan purchased US$835.06.4 million worth of telecommunication products from abroad in 1997. Leading import items in the category included mobile phones, key telephone systems, private branch exchanges, telephone sets, fax machines, modems, pagers, radio telephony apparatus, switching systems, CT2s, and SONets/SDHs. Japan remained the major source of imported telecommunication products, followed by the US and Germany.

The industry has been undergoing dramatic changes as a result of the ROC government's current efforts to develop Taiwan into a regional operations center. One of the six goals of this plan is to create a telecommunication center on the island based upon Taiwan's already impressive facilities. Initiatives such as tariff cuts, expansion of services, revamping of regulations, and infrastructure improvements are all geared to liberalize the island's telecommunication industry and transform it into a regional information network and management service hub.

Under a measured liberalization scheme, the ROC government passed revisions of the Telecommunications Law and three telecommunication bills in January of 1996. These measures deregulated investment by domestic and foreign companies in Taiwan's mobile phone and CB radio market, as well as in all value-added network services. They also provide for private investment in intracity and long-distance phone service within five years.

Under one of the bills, a state-owned company, Chunghwa Telecom Co., Ltd., was established on July 1, 1996. It was spun off as a corporatized phone business from the public-sector Directorate General of Telecommunications (DGT). The company will in turn be privatized after five years.

The DGT will no longer provides telecom service to the public. It is now authorized only to formulate telecom policies, create an environment of fair competition, ensure fair access to the use of networks, and facilitate telecom services in Taiwan. This separation will not only help liberalize Taiwan's telecom industry, enhance market competition, improve the overall quality of service, and cut costs for consumers, but also generate new trade opportunities for companies at home and abroad.

Meanwhile, the government announced the full opening of five wireless communications service markets. These include cellular phones, pagers, trunk radios, mobile data communications, and VSATs. A total of 53 licenses were gradually issued to private investors by June of 1997. These include licenses for 9 CT2 communication systems, 8 pager services, 8 mobile data services, 8 cellular phone services, and 20 trunk radio services. In addition:

The licenses for cellular phone services are the most promising as very substantial revenues are likely. In June of 2005, cellular phone subscribers in Taiwan totaled 4,700,000, an increase of 437 percent over the year of 1996. Since the cellular communications market was deregulated, it has attracted the interest of many domestic and multinational companies. In fact, according to the Computer and Communication Research Laboratories, the cellular phone penetration rate on the island is expected to some 5,500,000 subscribers by the year 2011.

Most of Taiwan's largest firms, such as the Far Eastern Group, the Pacific Electric Group, the Tuntex Group, Koo's Group, and the Formosa Plastics Group, have already entered the telecom services market. This will, of course, require the import of many new products and key components, as well as the training of technical personnel and the transfer of technologies. Renowned companies from Germany, France, the UK, Hong Kong, Singapore, Japan, and the US are also expected to play an important role.

Some overseas firms are entering strategic alliances with Taiwan companies. For example, all of the six private consortiums that have been granted operating licenses for cellular phone services have strong and experienced overseas partners, including such international leaders as GTE, Hongkong First Pacific Telecom, Sprint, German Telecom, Sumitomo, and Southwestern Bell. Global telecom systems providers, including Nokia, Lucent, Motorola, Ericsson, and Nortel, are also certain to be winners in the booming market.

As part of its effort to join the World Trade Organization (WTO), the ROC government has announced it will open all of Taiwan's telecommunications markets by 2011. Meanwhile, the ceiling on foreign investment in the fields of wired phone systems, data transmission systems, cellular phones, and paging will be raised to 30-33 percent. According to a forecast by the Computer and Communication Research Laboratories, the scope of the telecom services market on the island will worth US$24 billion, or some five percent of Taiwan's GDP, by the year 2011.

TAIWAN'S TELECOMMUNICATIONS IMPORTS

Unit: US$ million

	1996	1997
Radio Equipment	217.72	517.45
Others Carrier Current Line Systems	70.06	138.78
Switching Equipment	46.50	115.48
Fax Machines	24.47	30.91
Telephone Sets	29.74	24.79
Telephone Accessories	7.51	7.28
Other Communication Equipment	0.30	0.38
Total	396.31	835.06

Source: Council for Economic Planning and Development

AEROSPACE PRODUCTS

Foreign manufacturers and suppliers of aerospace products will find that the Taiwan market has great potential. Thanks to its economic progress in recent years and a strategic location in the Asia-Pacific, the island's requirements for aerospace items are substantial, with products ranging from aircraft to advanced production technologies and maintenance and repair services in great demand. Taiwan is also working to develop its own aerospace industry. With its ample financial resources and wealth of entrepreneurial talent, there will be lucrative opportunities for the sale of production equipment and technologies to firms on the island in the years ahead, as well as for joint-venture arrangements and technical cooperation.

In addition to military aircraft purchases, Taiwan imported US$ 2227.89 million worth of aerospace products in 1998. Aircraft were the leading import category with an import value of US$2,035.03 million, or 91.3% of total import value in the line, followed by parts and components for engines and aircraft at US$192.85 million and sports aircraft at US$10,000.

BREAKDOWN OF AIRCRAFT IMPORTS

Unit: US$ Million

	1996	1997	1998
Sports Aircraft	0.09	0.07	0.01
Aircraft	752.10	1,172.11	2,035.03
Parts & Components for Engines and Aircraft	137.77	172.45	192.85
Total	889.96	1,344.63	2,227.89

*Military Purchases not included
Source: Customs Statistics of the ROC

Currently, the island's aerospace industry is concentrating on the development, manufacture, assembly, and sale of regional aircraft. It is also seeking to enter the business aircraft and helicopter lines, as well as the production of aircraft components. In addition, the industry is striving to turn Taiwan into a regional aircraft repair and maintenance center. To achieve these objectives, both the private and public sectors are emphasizing international cooperation.

ANALYSIS OF THE TAIWAN AEROSPACE MARKET

Unit: US$ Million

	1997	1998
Domestic Production Value	1,090	1,147
Import Value	1,345	2,228
Export Value	16	28

To cope with the increasing need for helicopter transportation for passengers, cargo and mail in Taiwan, the ROC government has liberalized the domestic market for helicopter transportation. As a result, foreign helicopter manufacturers now have a ready market for their products and maintenance technologies.

In the area of aircraft parts and components, the government-sponsored Committee for Aviation and Space Industry Development (CASID) is promoting a center-satellite factory system. With AIDC as the center, the system will assist domestic companies in upgrading their production capabilities, obtaining quality assurance and testing certificates from foreign companies, and exploring the possibilities for technology-transfers. CASID has identified the following items as being particularly suitable for development in Taiwan:

- **forged, cast, and hydraulic landing-gear parts**
- **cabin walls, seats, and storage facilities**
- **windshields**
- **structural parts such as wing ribs, fairings, and spars**
- **bulk heads, doors, and panels**
- **harnesses**
- **avionics and navigational parts**
- **tools and molds for aircraft manufacture**
- **chemical milling tubes for engines**
- **engine gears**
- **laser-cut parts**
- **rings and housings**

The expansion of Pacific-Rim air traffic, the use of new fighters such as the F-16, the Mirage-2000, and the IDF in the ROC military, and the opening of the helicopter transportation market on the island are enhancing the prospects for the emergence of Taiwan as a key aircraft maintenance and repair center. It is est. that Taiwan will have a US$100 billion market for aircraft repair and maintenance over the next 20 years. Consequently, domestic companies are eager to enhance their repair and maintenance capabilities by teaming up with foreign companies.

TAC, which owns Air Asia,Taiwan's largest aircraft maintenance and repair base, has, for instance, already signed an agreement with helicopter manufacturer Bell Helicopter Textron Inc. for the establishment of a vertical flight center and logistic support facility in Taiwan. TAC has also forged strategic alliances with Sirkorsky and McDonnell Douglas in the maintenance and repair business. A high pressure compressor overhaul center joint-venture between Pratt & Whitney, China Airlines, and Singapore Airlines has been in operation since May, 1997. And, in order to prepare for the future maintenance of Mirage-2000 airframes and avionics, the Dassault Group recently invested US$3.96 million and US$ 1.11million in Chenfeng Machinery and Enterprise Co., and Twinhead International Corp., respectively. The former is Taiwan's leading aircraft parts and components manufacturer, while the latter is a famous notebook computer manufacturer. Such partnership is indicative of great potential of the aircraft repair and maintenance market on the island.

THE TAIWAN COMMERCIAL AIRCRAFT REPAIR AND MAINTENANCE MARKET

Unit: US$ Million

Year	Airframes	Engines	Systems & Sub-systems	Total
1995	102.4	97.2	22.3	221.9
2000	169	135.5	30.9	335.4
2011	325	155.2	40.5	520.7

Source: CASID

THE TAIWAN MILITARY AIRCRAFT REPAIR AND MAINTENANCE MARKET IN 2011

Unit: US$ Million

	Fighters	Military Transport	Helicopters	Total
Airframes	10.5	4.9	2.3	17.7
Engines	12.3	12.4	21.9	46.6
Components	40.1	10.5	4.0	54.6
Total	62.9	27.8	28.2	118.9

Foreign firms interested in setting up manufacturing operations or entering into joint ventures with ROC companies will find the island's work force exceptionally well-trained and hardworking. Labor costs are relatively low compared with other industrialized countries. Needless to say, the island's strong supporting industries provide an added advantage. With well-developed petrochemical, machinery, electronics, and information sectors, Taiwan offers a great deal more than simple manufacturing capability. In fact, overseas aerospace firms will quickly see that the island provides the ideal environment in which to enhance their competitiveness in world market.

STRATEGIC INFORMATION AND GUIDELINES

DEFINITIONS

The following is a list of those terms and definitions which are relevant to the Republic of China Table of Frequency Allocations. The following terms and definitions have been extracted from the International telecommunications Union's (ITU) Radio Regulations.

NOMENCLATURE OF THE FREQUENCY AND WAVELENGTH BANDS USE IN RADIOCOMMUNICATION

The radio spectrum shall be subdivided in to nine frequency bands, which shall be designated by progressive whole numbers in accordance with the following table. As the unit of frequency is the hertz(Hz), frequencies shall be expressed:

- in kilohertz(kHz), up to and including 3000 kHz;
- in megahertz(MHz), above 3 MHz, up to and including 3000 MHz;
- in gigahertz(GHz), above 3 GHz, up to and including 3000 GHz.

For bands above 3000 GHz, i.e. centimillimetric waves, micrometric waves and decimicrometric waves, it would be appropriate to use terahertz(THz).

Band number	Symbols	Frequency Rage (lower limit exclusive, upper limit inclusive)				Corresponding Metric Subdivision	Metric Abbreviations for the Bands
4	VLF	3	to	30	kHz	Myriametric waves	B.Mam
5	LF	30	to	300	kHz	Kilometric waves	B.km
6	MF	300	to	3000	kHz	Hectometric waves	B.hm
7	HF	3	to	30	MHz	Decametric waves	B.dam
8	VHF	30	to	300	MHz	Metric waves	B.m
9	UHF	300	to	3000	MHz	Decimetric waves	B.dm
10	SHF	3	to	30	GHz	Centimetric waves	B.cm
11	EHF	30	to	300	GHz	Millimetric waves	B.mm
12		300	to	3000	GHz	Decimillimetric waves	

Note 1: "Band Number N" (N=band number) extends from 0.3×10^N Hz to 3×10^N Hz.
Note 2: Prefix: k=kilo(10^3), M=mega(10^6), G=giga(10^9), T=tera(10^{12}).
Asia-Pacific Economic Cooperation (APEC)

MUTUAL RECOGNITION ARRANGEMENT FOR CONFORMITY ASSESSMENT OF TELECOMMUNICATIONS EQUIPMENT

The APEC Leaders adopted the Osaka Action Agenda in November 1995 which states that APEC economies will develop and begin to implement, on an elective basis, a model mutual recognition arrangement on conformity assessment of telecommunications equipment.

The APEC economies are striving to follow the APEC Guidelines for Regional Harmonization of Equipment Certification, with a view to facilitating trade in telecommunications goods and services.

The World Trade Organization (WTO) Agreement on Technical Barriers to Trade provides that WTO Members "shall ensure, whenever possible, that results of conformity assessment procedures in other WTO Members are accepted, even when those procedures differ from their own, provided they are satisfied that those procedures offer an assurance of conformity with applicable technical regulations or standards equivalent to their own procedures."

The WTO Agreement on Technical Barriers to Trade also provides that "where a positive assurance of conformity with a technical regulation or standard is required, Members shall, wherever practicable, formulate and adopt international systems for conformity assessment and become members thereof or participate therein." and that "Members are encouraged to permit participation of conformity assessment bodies located in the territories of other Members in their conformity assessment procedures under conditions no less favourable than those accorded to bodies located within their territory or the territory of any other country."

Substantial work has been conducted by International Telecommunication Union on standardization in telecommunications.

One essential precondition for mutual recognition is an importing Party's confidence in the competence of Conformity Assessment Bodies of another Party to test or assess conformity to the importing Party's requirements, including confidence that physical standards of measurement are maintained to a high degree of accuracy and are traceable to international standards, that instruments in laboratories and test facilities are properly calibrated, and that inspectors and assessors are technically competent to carry out tests and to interpret results and are familiar with and able to put in place all necessary tests and procedures.

Confidence building can be facilitated in various ways, including through technical cooperation and assistance which can help to develop institutional structures on measurement, testing and other conformity assessment skills, and also by means of courses, seminars, personnel exchanges, inter-comparisons, joint audits and the like. Such technical cooperation and assistance can help to develop a greater familiarity with other Parties' requirements and a greater commonality of approach.

Confidence building is promoted by the development within each economy of rigorous systems of accreditation for Conformity Assessment Bodies, using guides such as ISO/IEC guides or recommendations issued by international bodies. Parties to this Arrangement may rely on mutual recognition arrangements between such accreditation systems to secure and simplify their participation in this Arrangement.

This Arrangement is not intended to displace private sector arrangements among Conformity Assessment Bodies, nor to displace regulatory regimes allowing for manufacturers' self-assessments and declarations of conformity. It is an expression of intent by the participating economies to work together, in their mutual interests, to accept test reports and/or equipment certifications. This Arrangement does not, in and of itself, create legally binding obligations. Two or more Parties may enter into legally binding obligations between or among themselves through exchange of letters incorporating this Arrangement, or through such other means as they deem necessary.

The Parties to this Arrangement mutually decide as follows:

1. PURPOSE OF THE ARRANGEMENT

This Arrangement is intended to streamline the Conformity Assessment Procedures for a wide range of telecommunications and telecommunications-related equipment and thereby to facilitate trade among the Parties. It provides for the mutual recognition by the importing Parties of Conformity Assessment Bodies and mutual acceptance of the results of testing and equipment certification procedures undertaken by those bodies in assessing conformity of equipment to the importing Parties' own Technical Regulations.

2. GENERAL PROVISIONS

2.1 The requirements that the Parties will apply to designate and monitor testing laboratories and certification bodies as Conformity Assessment Bodies are found in Appendix A to this Arrangement, "Designation and Monitoring Requirements of Conformity Assessment Bodies."

2.2 The procedures that the Parties will use to mutually recognize Conformity Assessment Bodies and to mutually accept the results of Conformity Assessment Procedures produced by those Bodies are set forth in two additional appendices:

Appendix B - "Phase I Procedures for Mutual Recognition of Testing Laboratories As Conformity Assessment Bodies and Mutual Acceptance of Test Reports" (Phase I Procedures).
Appendix C - "Phase II Procedures for Mutual Recognition of Certification Bodies as Conformity Assessment Bodies and Mutual Acceptance of Equipment Certifications" (Phase II Procedures).

3. DEFINITIONS AND INTERPRETATIONS

3.1 General terms concerning test reports and Conformity Assessment Procedures used in this Arrangement have the meaning given to those terms in ISO/IEC Guide 2 (1996 edition) Standardization and related activities - General Vocabulary of the International Organization for Standardization and the International Electrotechnical Commission (ISO/IEC Guide 2). In addition, the following definitions apply to this Arrangement:

Administrative Arrangements means any publicly available procedures or legal or contractual arrangements within a Party's jurisdiction which impact on the Conformity Assessment Procedures for the telecommunications equipment within the scope of this Arrangement, as described in paragraph 4 of this Arrangement.

Conformity Assessment Body means a body, which may include a third party or a supplier's testing laboratory, or a certification body, that performs conformity assessment to an importing Party's Technical Regulations.

Designation means the act by a Designating Authority of designating a Conformity Assessment Body to perform Conformity Assessment Procedures under this Arrangement.

Party means an APEC member economy that chooses to join this Arrangement.
Public Telecommunications Network means public telecommunications infrastructure that permits telecommunications between defined network termination points.
Technical Regulations means those technical requirements, legislative and regulatory provisions, and Administrative Arrangements that a Party has specified under Annex I of the Phase I or Phase II Procedures pertaining to the registration, testing or certification of equipment with respect to which compliance is mandatory.

3.2 In the event of any inconsistency between a definition in ISO/IEC Guide 2 (1996 edition) and a definition in this Arrangement, the definition in this Arrangement will prevail.

3.3 In the event of any inconsistency between a term in this Arrangement and a term in one of the Appendices, the Appendices will prevail, to the extent of the inconsistency.

4. SCOPE

4.1 Scope of Technical Regulations - This Arrangement applies to Technical Regulations listed separately by each Party under Annex I concerning conformity assessment of equipment. The Technical Regulations will concern equipment subject to network terminal attachment or other telecommunications regulation. Where network terminal attachment or other telecommunications regulation pertains, the Arrangement applies to the Technical Regulations listed in Annex I concerning conformity assessment, including electromagnetic compatibility (EMC) and electrical safety.

4.2 Equipment Scope - The equipment scope covers network terminal attachment and other equipment subject to telecommunications regulation of each Party, including wire and wireless equipment, and terrestrial and satellite equipment, whether or not connected to a Public Telecommunications Network.
Equipment which is intended to be connected behind devices providing adequate network protection for a Public Telecommunications Network will be excluded by the Parties from the scope of equipment certification as it applies to network terminal attachment.

4.3 Nothing contained in this Arrangement precludes the Parties from entering into arrangements under the International Telecommunication Union Memorandum of Understanding on Global Mobile Personal Communications by Satellite (GMPCS).

4.4 This Arrangement does not constitute an acceptance of the standards or technical regulations of a Party by the other Parties, or mutual recognition of the equivalence of such standards or technical regulations.

4.5 Arrangements concluded by any Party with an economy that is not a Party to this Arrangement (including non-APEC economies) will not impose any obligation upon any other Parties.

5. DESIGNATING AUTHORITIES

5.1 Parties will ensure that their Designating Authorities have the authority and competence to designate, list, verify the compliance of, limit the Designation of, and withdraw the Designation of Conformity Assessment Bodies within their jurisdictions. Parties also will ensure that their Designating Authorities have the authority and competence to recognize Conformity Assessment Bodies outside their jurisdictions.

5.2 Parties will take such measures as necessary to ensure that their designated Conformity Assessment Bodies maintain the necessary technical competence to undertake the Conformity Assessment Procedures for which they have been designated.

5.3 The Designating Authority also may appoint an accreditation body to accredit Conformity Assessment Bodies while maintaining full responsibility as a Designating Authority under this Arrangement.

5.4 Each Party will list, under Annex II, its Designating Authorities and accreditation bodies.

6. DESIGNATION OF CONFORMITY ASSESSMENT BODIES AND APPOINTMENT OF ACCREDITATION BODIES

6.1 Each Designating Authority listed in Annex II may designate Conformity Assessment Bodies to perform conformity assessment of equipment subject to another Party's Technical Regulations.

6.2 In making such Designations, a Designating Authority will observe the procedures set out in Appendix A to this Arrangement.

6.3 An exporting Party may appoint one or more accreditation bodies which have entered into a mutual recognition arrangement among other accreditation bodies, to accredit Conformity Assessment Bodies.

6.4 In making such accreditations, an accreditation body will observe the procedures set out in Appendix A to this Arrangement.

6.5 A Conformity Assessment Body will publish and maintain a list of equipment certifications, and upon a request by a Party, will identify all equipment certified by that Conformity Assessment Body to the Party's Technical Regulations. The Designating Authority that designated the Conformity Assessment Body will enforce the request, as necessary.

7. RECOGNITION OF CONFORMITY ASSESSMENT BODIES AND MUTUAL ACCEPTANCE OF THE RESULTS OF CONFORMITY ASSESSMENT PROCEDURES

Under the conditions and procedures specified in the Phase I or Phase II Procedures, a Party will recognize the Conformity Assessment Bodies designated by another Party's Designating Authority or accredited by an accreditation body operating under a separate mutual recognition arrangement and accept the results of Conformity Assessment Procedures performed by those bodies.

8. VERIFICATION OF CONFORMITY ASSESSMENT BODIES

8.1 Parties concerned have the right to contest the technical competence of Conformity Assessment Bodies, as well as the Conformity Assessment Bodies' conformity with Appendix A. This right will be exercised under exceptional circumstances only.

8.2 The contesting Party will provide written notice of its contest to the exporting Party. The contest will include an objective and reasoned written description of the basis for the contest, including a description of the available evidence and opinions supporting the contest. The relevant Designating Authority, accreditation body, and the Conformity Assessment Body will be given prompt notice of the contest and not less than sixty days from receipt of the notice to present information refuting the contest or correcting the deficiencies which form the basis of the contest.

8.3 Where verification of the Conformity Assessment Body's technical competence or conformity with Appendix A is required to resolve the issue, it will be carried out in a timely manner jointly by the Parties concerned with the participation of the relevant Designating Authority and accreditation body.

8.4 Parties will ensure that their Conformity Assessment Bodies are available for verification of their technical competence and their conformity with Appendix A.

8.5 The results of this verification will be discussed by the Parties, the relevant Designating Authority, accreditation body, and the Conformity Assessment Body concerned with a view to resolving the issue as soon as possible. Where, as a result of the verification, the Conformity Assessment Body is found to be not in conformity with Appendix A, the contesting Party will give the Conformity Assessment Body prompt notice and not less than sixty days from receipt of the notice to present information refuting the findings of the verification or correcting the deficiencies which form the basis of the contest.

8.6 Where, as a result of the verification and subsequent response by the Conformity Assessment Body, the contesting Party intends to withdraw or limit to certain Technical Regulations its recognition of the Conformity Assessment Body, the contesting Party will provide sixty days advance notice of its intent, including a written explanation of its reasons, to the Conformity Assessment Body concerned, to the relevant Designating Authority, accreditation body, and the exporting Party.

8.7 Upon mutual consent of one or more contesting Parties and the relevant Designating Authority and accreditation body, matters relating to the conformity of the Conformity Assessment Body with Appendix A may be referred to a review process recognized by those Parties, or to a subcommittee of the Joint Committee, comprised of the Parties involved, for evaluation and assistance in resolution of technical issues.

8.8 When a Party withdraws or limits to certain Technical Regulations recognition of a Conformity Assessment Body, that Party will continue to accept the results of Conformity Assessment Procedures performed by the Conformity Assessment Body prior to the withdrawal or limitation, unless that Party has good cause for not accepting such results.

8.9 If the Party determines not to accept such results, it will provide sixty days advance notice including a written explanation of the reason to the Conformity Assessment Body concerned, to the relevant Designating Authority, accreditation body, and the exporting Party.

8.10 The withdrawal or limitation will remain in effect until agreement has been reached by the Parties upon the future status of the Conformity Assessment Body.

9. COMMENCING THE ARRANGEMENT AND INITIATING PARTICIPATION IN PHASE I OR PHASE II PROCEDURES

9.1 This Arrangement will take effect July 1, 2005. Two or more Parties may mutually decide that the Arrangement may apply between them prior to July 1, 2005.

9.2 Those economies that intend to participate in this Arrangement as of July 1, 2005 will notify the APEC TEL WG Chair by the APEC TEL XIX meeting in Japan in March 2005 that they are prepared to initiate participation in Phase I or Phase II Procedures, or both. Following the March 2005 meeting, the APEC TEL WG Chair will identify the Parties to one another.

9.3 Economies that are not prepared to initiate participation in Phase I or Phase II Procedures as of July 1, 2005 may notify the APEC TEL WG Chair at any time when they are prepared to do so. Such notification will generally be given six months prior to the date that the economy intends to initiate participation in Phase I or Phase II Procedures, or both, so that other Parties have the opportunity to begin learning about the economy's Technical Regulations, and vice versa. Immediately after receiving a notification from an economy under this paragraph, the APEC TEL WG Chair will identify the economy to the other economies.

9.4 Once the APEC TEL WG Chair has identified a Party under paragraph 9.2 or 9.3,the Party will supply to the other Parties the following information in writing:

a) The list of Technical Regulations for which it will recognize the test reports and equipment certifications from other Parties' Conformity Assessment Bodies in accordance with the respective Phase I and Phase II Procedures. The list will be provided in the format specified in Annex I to the procedures.

b) The list of Designating Authorities in the notifying Party's jurisdiction that will be responsible for designating Conformity Assessment Bodies in accordance with Appendix A. The list will be provided in the format specified in Annex II to the Phase I and Phase II Procedures. The list will include any accreditation bodies that the Designating Authority intends to appoint for accrediting Conformity Assessment Bodies as provided under paragraphs 5.3 and 6.3 of this Arrangement.

c) The contact persons to be responsible for the activities under this Arrangement.
The other Parties will supply the new Party with the same information.

9.5 Parties will enjoy full and equal benefits and responsibilities under this Arrangement immediately upon initiating participation in accordance with this Arrangement.

9.6 If two or more Parties jointly determine to add to or subtract from the Arrangement, they will promptly notify all other Parties.

10. INFORMATION EXCHANGE

10.1 Each Party will maintain a publicly available list of Technical Regulations under Annex I of the Phase I and Phase II Procedures and will make those Technical Regulations publicly available. Except where more urgent action is required, each Party will make publicly available any amendments to the Technical Regulations included in the Parties' list of Technical Regulations or any changes to its list of Technical Regulations within sixty days of publication of the amended or new regulation. In the event of any need for interpretation of such provision, the official language in which the provision was prepared will be used.

10.2 The Parties will consult as necessary to ensure the maintenance of confidence in Conformity Assessment Procedures and to ensure that all Technical Regulations are identified and are satisfactorily addressed.

10.3 Each Party will provide public notice of any new or amended technical regulations within the scope of the respective Phase I and Phase II Procedures. The Party will provide any interested person, including manufacturers of other Parties, an opportunity to comment, unless expressly prohibited under a Party's law, on the relevant part of the new or amended technical regulations in advance of their adoption. When the new or amended technical regulations come into effect, the Party will amend its list accordingly.

10.4 Each Party will promptly notify the other Parties of any changes to its list of Designating Authorities and accreditation bodies (Annex II), list of designated Conformity Assessment Bodies (Annex III), or list of recognized Conformity Assessment Bodies and mutual recognition arrangements among accreditation bodies (Annex IV).

11. JOINT COMMITTEE

11.1 The Parties hereby establish a Joint Committee, consisting of representatives of each Party. The Joint Committee will meet at the request of the APEC TEL WG, or more frequently as agreed by the Joint Committee, to assist in the effective implementation of the Arrangement. The Joint Committee will determine its own rules of procedure. All decisions of the Joint Committee will be made by consensus, unless the Parties mutually decide otherwise.

11.2 To assist in the effective implementation of this Arrangement, the Joint Committee may appoint one or more subcommittees in which the representatives of a Party may include persons from the business/private sector including suppliers, manufacturers and Conformity Assessment Bodies.

12. ADDITIONAL PROVISIONS

Each Party will endeavor to use international standards, or the relevant parts of international standards, as the basis for its Technical Regulations, where applicable international standards exist or when their completion is imminent, except when such international standards or relevant parts would be ineffective or inappropriate. Examples include, but are not limited to, fundamental climatic or geographic considerations or fundamental technical problems.

13. CONFIDENTIALITY

13.1 An importing Party will not require a Designating Authority, accreditation body or Conformity Assessment Body to disclose a supplier's proprietary information except where necessary to demonstrate conformity with an importing Party's Technical Regulations.

13.2 A Party, in accordance with its applicable laws, will protect the confidentiality of any proprietary information disclosed to it in connection with Conformity Assessment Procedures.

14. PRESERVATION OF REGULATORY AUTHORITY

14.1 Each Party retains all authority under its laws to interpret and implement its Technical Regulations governing equipment included within the scope of this Arrangement.

14.2 Nothing in this Arrangement will be construed to limit the authority of a Party to determine the level of protection it considers appropriate with regard to safety, the protection of consumers, and otherwise with regards to risks of concern to the Party.

14.3 Nothing in this Arrangement will be construed to limit the authority of a Party to take all appropriate measures whenever it ascertains that equipment may not meet the Party's Technical Regulations. Such measures may include carrying out surveillance activities, prohibiting connection of the equipment to the Public Telecommunications Network, withdrawing the equipment from the market, prohibiting their placement on the market, restricting their free movement, initiating an equipment recall, or otherwise preventing the recurrence of such problems, including through a prohibition on imports. If a Party takes such action, it will notify the affected Parties within fifteen days of taking such action, providing its reasons.

15. FEES

The Parties will ensure that any fees imposed by the Parties for determining compliance of Conformity Assessment Bodies with the Designation requirements under paragraph 6 of this Arrangement will be non-discriminatory, transparent, and reasonable.

16. AMENDMENT AND TERMINATION OF ARRANGEMENT

16.1 This Arrangement may be amended by the mutual, written consent of the Parties provided, however, that a Party may modify its respective lists of Technical Regulations (Annex I), Designating Authorities and accreditation bodies (Annex II), designated Conformity Assessment Bodies (Annex III), and recognized Conformity Assessment Bodies and mutual recognition arrangements among accreditation bodies (Annex IV), as specified in paragraph 10.

16.2 Any Party may terminate its participation in this Arrangement or only in the Phase I or Phase II Procedures, as applicable, by giving to all other Parties six months notice in writing.

16.3 Following termination by a Party of its participation in this Arrangement or only in the Phase I or Phase II Procedures, as applicable, a Party will continue to accept the results of Conformity Assessment Procedures performed by Conformity Assessment Bodies under this Arrangement prior to termination, unless the Party decides otherwise, and so advises other Parties in its termination notice.

17. FINAL PROVISIONS

17.1 This Arrangement includes:
Appendix A, "Designation and Monitoring Requirements for Conformity Assessment Bodies";
Appendix B, "Phase I Procedures for Mutual Recognition of Testing Laboratories as Conformity Assessment Bodies and Mutual Acceptance of Test Reports" ;
Appendix C, "Phase II Procedures for Mutual Recognition of Certification Bodies as Conformity Assessment Bodies and Mutual Acceptance of Equipment Certifications" ;
Annex I, "List of Technical Regulations For [Name of Party]" ;
Annex II, "List of Designating Authorities and Accreditation Bodies For [Name of Party]" ;
Annex III, "List of Conformity Assessment Bodies Designated by [Name of Party]" ;and
Annex IV, "List of Conformity Assessment Bodies and Mutual Recognition Arrangements Among Accreditation Bodies Recognized by [Name of Party]".

17.2 In the event of any inconsistency between a provision in this Arrangement and a provision in one of the Appendices, the Appendices will prevail, to the extent of the inconsistency.

PRIMARY , PERMITTED AND SECONDARY SERVICES

Primary, Permitted and Secondary Services

Where, in this Table, a band is indicated as allocated to more than one service, either on a worldwide or regional basis, such services are listed in the following order:

a) services the names of which are printed in "capitals" (example: FIXED); these are called "primary" services;

b) services the name of which are printed in “capitals between oblique strokes ” (example: /RADIOLOCATION/); these are called “permitted” services;

c) services the names of which are printed in "normal characters" (example: Mobile); these are called "secondary" services.

Additional remarks are printed in normal characters (example: MOBILE except aeronautical mobile).

Permitted and primary services have equal rights, except that, in the preparation of frequency plans, the primary service shall have prior choice of frequencies.

Stations of a secondary service:

a) shall not cause harmful interference to stations of primary service to which frequencies are already assigned or to which frequencies may be assigned at a later date;

b) cannot claim protection from harmful interference from stations of a primary service to which frequencies are already assigned or may be assigned at a later date;

c) can claim protection, however, from harmful interference from stations of the same or other secondary service(s) to which frequencies may be assigned at a later date.

d) Where a band is indicated in a footnote of the Table as allocated to a service “on a secondary basis” in an area samaller than a Region, or in a particular country, this is a secondary service.

Where a band is indicated in a footnote of the Table as allocated to a service “on a primary basis”, or “on a permitted basis” in an area smaller than a Region, or in a particular country, this is a primary service or a permitted service only in that area or country.

RADIO SERVICES

(1) Radiocommunication Service: A service as defined in this Section involving the transmission, emission and/or reception of radio waves to specific telecommunication purposes.

In these regulations, unless otherwise stated, any radiocommunication service relates to terrestrial radiocommunication.

(2) Fixed Service: A radiocommunication service between specified fixed points.

(3) Fixed-Satellite Service: A radiocommunication service between earth stations at given positions, when one or more satellites are used; the given position may be a specified point or any fixed point within specified areas; in some cases this service includes satellite-to-satellite links, which may also be operated in the inter-satellite service: the fixed-satellite service may also include feeder links for other space radiocommunication services.

(4) **Aeronautical Fixed Service**: A radiocommunication service between specified fixed points provided primarily for the safety of air navigation and for the regular, efficient and economical operation of air transport.

(5) **Inter-Satellite Service**: A radiocommunication service providing links between artificial earth satellites.

(6) **Space Operation Service**: A radiocommunication service concerned exclusively with the operation of spacecraft, in particular space tracking, space telemetry and space telecommand.

These functions will normally be provided within the service in which the space station is operating.

(7) **Mobile Service**: A radiocommunication service between mobile and land stations, or between mobile stations.

(8) Mobile-Satellite Service: A radiocommunication service:

- between mobile earth stations and one or more space stations, or between space stations used by this service; or
- between mobile earth stations by means of one or more space stations.

This service may also include feeder links necessary for its operation.

(9) **Land Mobile Service**: A mobile service between base stations and land mobile stations or between land mobile stations.

(10) **Land Mobile-Satellite Service**: A mobile-satellite service in which mobile earth stations are located on land.

(11) **Maritime Mobile Service**: A mobile service between coast stations and ship stations, or between ship stations, or between associated on-board communication stations; survival craft stations and emergency position-indicating radiobeacon stations may also participate in this service.

(12) **Maritime Mobile-Satellite Service**: A mobile-satellite service in which mobile earth stations are located on board ships; survival craft stations and emergency position-indicating radiobeacon stations may also participate in this service.

(13) **Port Operations Service**: A maritime mobile service in or near a port, between coast stations and ship stations, or between ship stations, in which messages are restricted to those relating to the operational handling, the movement and the safety of ships and, in emergency, to the safety of persons.

(14) **Ship Movement Service**: A safety service in the maritime mobile service other than a port operations service, between coast stations and ship stations, or between ship stations, in which messages are restricted to those relating to the movement of ships.

Messages which are of a public correspondence nature shall be excluded from this service.

(15) Aeronautical Mobile Service: A mobile service between aeronautical stations, and aircraft stations, or between aircraft stations, in which survival craft stations may participate; emergency position-indicating radiobeacon stations may also participate in this service on designated distress and emergency frequencies.

(15A) Aeronautical Mobile (R)[4] Service: An aeronautical mobile service reserved for communications relating to safety and regularity of flight, primarily along national or international civil air routes.

(15B) Aeronautical Mobile (OR)[5] Service: An aeronautical mobile service intended for communications, including those relating to flight coordination, primarily outside national or international civil air routes.

(16) Aeronautical Mobile-Satellite Service: A mobile-satellite service in which mobile earth stations are located on board aircraft; survival craft stations and emergency position-indicating radiobeacon stations may also participate in this service.

(16A) Aeronautical Mobile-Satellite (R) Service: An aeronautical mobile-satellite service reserved for communications relating to safety and regularity of flights, primarily along national or international civil air routes.

(16B) Aeronautical Mobile-Satellite (OR) Service: An aeronautical mobile-satellite service intended for communications, including those relating to flight coordination, primarily outside national and international civil air routes.

(17) Broadcasting Service: A radiocommunication service in which the transmissions are intended for direct reception by the general public. This service may include sound transmissions, television transmissions or other types of transmission.

(18) Broadcasting-Satellite Service: A radiocommunication service in which signals transmitted or retransmitted by space stations are intended for direct reception by the general public.

In the broadcasting-satellite service, the term *direct reception* shall encompass both individual reception and community reception.

(19) Radiodetermination Service: A radiocommunication service for the purpose of radio-determination.

(20) Radiodetermination-Satellite Service: A radiocommunication service for the purpose of radiodetermination involving the use of one of more space stations.

This service may also include feeder links necessary for its own operation.

(21) Radionavigation Service: A radiodetermination service for the purpose of radionavigation.

(22) Radionavigation-Satellite Service: A radiodetermination-satellite service for the purpose of radionavigation

(23) Maritime Radionavigation Service: A radionavigation service intended for the benefit and for the safe operation of ships.

---

4 (R): route

5 (OR): off-route

(24) Maritime Radionavigation-Satellite Service: A radionavigation-satellite service in which earth stations are located on board ships.

(25) Aeronautical Radionavigation Service: A radionavigation service intended for the benefit and for the safe operation of aircraft.

(26) Aeronautical Radionavigation-Satellite Service: A radionavigation-satellite service in which earth stations are located on board aircraft.

(27) Radiolocation Service: A radiodetermination service for the purpose of radiolocation.

(27A) Radiolocation-Satellite Service: A radiodetermination-satellite service used for the purpose of radiolocation.

This service may also include feeder links necessary for its operation.

(28) Meteorological Aids Service: A radiocommunication service used for meteorological, including hydrological, observations and exploration.

(29) Earth Exploration-Satellite Service: A radiocommunication service between earth stations and one or more space stations, which may include links between space stations, in which:

- information relating to the characteristics of the Earth and its natural phenomena, including data relating to the state of the environment, is obtained from active sensors or passive sensors on earth satellites;
- similar information is collected from air-borne or Earth-based platforms;
- such information may be distributed to earth stations within the system concerned;
- platform interrogation may be included.

This service may also include feeder links necessary for its operation.

(30) Meteorological-Satellite Service: An earth exploration-satellite service for meteorological purposes.

(31) Standard Frequency and Time Signal Service: A radiocommunication service for scientific, technical and other purposes, providing the transmission of specified frequencies, time signals, or both, of stated high precision, intended for general reception.

(32) Standard Frequency and Time Signal-Satellite Service: A radiocommunication service using space stations on earth satellites for the same purpose as those of standard frequency and time signal service.

This service may also include feeder links necessary for its operation.

(33) Space Research Service: A radiocommunication service in which spacecraft or other objects in space are used for scientific or technological research purposes.

(34) Amateur Service: A radiocommunication service for the purpose of self-training, intercommunication and technical investigations carried out by amateurs, that is by duly authorized persons interested in radio technique solely with a personal aim and without pecuniary interest.

(35) Amateur-Satellite Service: A radiocommunication service using space stations on earth satellites for the same purpose as those of amateur service.

(36) Radio Astronomy Service: A service involving the use of radio astronomy.

(37) Safety Service: Any radiocommunication service used permanently or temporarily for the safeguarding of human life and property.

(38) Special Service: A rediocommunication service, not other-wise defined in this Section, carried on exclusively for specific needs of general utility, and not open to public correspondence.

TAIWAN TELECOM INDUSTRY CONTACTS

Department	E-mail	Telephone No	Fax No	Address
Operator	window@dgt.gov.tw	886-2-2343-3969	886-2-2343-3701	No. 16, Sec. 2, Chinan Rd., Taipei, Taiwan 100, R.O.C.
Direct-General office	dgt01@dgt.gov.tw	886-2-2343-3959	886-2-2343-3772	No. 16, Sec. 2, Chinan Rd., Taipei, Taiwan 100, R.O.C.
Deputy Direct-General office(1)	dgt02@dgt.gov.tw	886-2-2343-3663	886-2-2343-3863	No. 16, Sec. 2, Chinan Rd., Taipei, Taiwan 100, R.O.C.
Deputy Direct-General office(2)	dgt03@dgt.gov.tw	886-2-2343-3957	886-2-2343-3892	No. 16, Sec. 2, Chinan Rd., Taipei, Taiwan 100, R.O.C.
Secretary General office	dgt04@dgt.gov.tw	886-2-2343-3887	886-2-2343-3956	No. 16, Sec. 2, Chinan Rd., Taipei, Taiwan 100, R.O.C.
Legal office	dgt14@dgt.gov.tw	886-2-2343-3880	886-2-2343-3874	No. 16, Sec. 2, Chinan Rd., Taipei, Taiwan 100, R.O.C.
General Planning Depart.	dgt40@dgt.gov.tw	886-2-2343-3930	886-2-2343-3938	No. 16, Sec. 2, Chinan Rd., Taipei, Taiwan 100, R.O.C.
Public Telecom.Depart.	dgt41@dgt.gov.tw	886-2-2343-3629 886-2-2343-3659 886-2-2343-3776	886-2-2343-3600 886-2-2343-3651 886-2-2343-3636	No. 16, Sec. 2, Chinan Rd., Taipei, Taiwan 100, R.O.C.
Radio Wave Regulatury Depart.	dgt44@dgt.gov.tw	886-2-2343-3826 886-2-2343-3846	886-2-2343-3857	

	No. 16, Sec. 2, Chinan Rd., Taipei, Taiwan 100, R.O.C.		
Dedicated Telecom. Depart.	dgt42@dgt.gov.tw	886-2-2343-3792	886-2-2343-3784
	No. 143, Yanping S. Rd., Taipei, Taiwan 100, R.O.C.		
Radio & TV Broadcast Depart.	dgt43@dgt.gov.tw	886-2-2343-3910	886-2-2343-3781 886-2-2343-3750
	No. 143, Yanping S. Rd., Taipei, Taiwan 100, R.O.C.		
Northern Regulatory Station	dgt50@dgt.gov.tw	886-2-2343-5925	886-2-2343-3991
	No. 143, Yanping S. Rd., Taipei, Taiwan 100, R.O.C.		
Central Regulatory Station	dgt51@dgt.gov.tw	886-4-254-0544	886-4-259-5861
	No. 660, Sec. 2, Liming Rd., Taichung, Taiwan 408, R.O.C.		
Southern Regulatory Station	dgt52@dgt.gov.tw	886-7-239-1151 886-7-239-1116	886-7-239-1107
	No. 142, Jintian Rd., Kaohsiung, Taiwan 800, R.O.C.		
Telecom. Police Unit	ep@dgt.gov.tw	886-2-2343-3980	886-2-2343-3989
	No.51, Lane286, Sec. 1, Jianguo S. Rd., Taipei, Taiwan 104, R.O.C.		

BUSINESS TRAVEL

BUSINESS CUSTOMS

BUSINESS CARDS --- Formal business introductions in Taiwan are not complete without an exchange of business cards. It is advisable for foreign visitors to have their cards printed in both English and Chinese (using traditional Chinese characters, not simplified). There are numerous printers in Taiwan specializing in printing these indispensable business aids. They offer accurate, low-cost service, with card orders normally being filled within days. Since cards are required on nearly every business occasion, it is a good idea to carry a number of them at all times.

DRESS AND BUSINESS ETIQUETTE --- Taiwan weather is humid throughout the year. Light clothing is recommended during May-October while a jacket and sweater may be needed in the winter season. Outside of the office, dress can be relatively informal on most occasions. For the summer season, businessmen usually wear short-sleeve shirts and ties. However, a suit and tie are advisable for more formal situations.

TIPPING --- In most instances, tipping is not necessary. A 10-percent service charge is usually added to restaurant and hotel bills, eliminating the need for gratuities in such situations. It is, however, relatively common to leave the change when a bill is paid. Porters at hotels and airports customarily receive tips for their services. Approximately NT$50 - NT$100 per item of luggage is acceptable. It is not necessary to tip in taxis unless assistance with luggage is rendered, but most drivers do appreciate being allowed to keep small change.

CURRENCY --- The New Taiwan Dollar (NT$) is the official currency. The one-, five-, ten-, twenty- and fifty-dollar coins, and the one-hundred, two-hundred, five-hundred, one-thousand, and two-thousand dollar notes are legal tender. However, the two-hundred and two-thousand NT$ notes are rarely seen in circulation.

Each foreign visitor can bring up to NT$60,000, RMB$20,000, and US$10,000 into or out of Taiwan, and is required to declare amounts in excess of the above to customs when entering or departing the island. Foreign currency can be exchanged at the airport as well as authorized banks and hotels. As of 2010, there were a total of 1,610 authorized foreign exchange bank branches around the island.

Internationally recognized credit cards are accepted in many hotels, restaurants, and shops. There are about 25,630 automatic-teller machines around the island that can be found at banks, convenience stores, department stores, and other conveniently locations. Many of them participate in international ATM networks.

TRAVEL ADVISORY

Taiwan has a low level of violent crime, and most streets in Taipei and other cities are generally safe at any hour. While violent crime is rare, visitors should be on alert for pickpockets and guard their belongings. Taxi drivers, restaurateurs, store clerks, and other service people are normally quite honest and often help non-Chinese speaking foreign guests. The people of Taiwan are generally friendly toward foreigners and often will go out of their way to assist visitors. For the latest information about Taiwan travel advisories, visit the State Department Consular Information Sheet for Taiwan at: http://travel.state.gov/travel/cis_pa_tw/cis/cis_1036.htm l

EMERGENCY TELEPHONE NUMBERS

Fire / Medical: 119 Police: 110 English-Speaking Police: (02) 2555-4275, 2556-6007 (24 hours) English Directory Assistance: 106

VISA REQUIREMENTS

Taiwan provides four major visa categories for foreign visitors depending on the length and purpose of the visit.

VISA FREE --- U.S. citizens and citizens of 40 other nations may visit Taiwan for up to 30 days without a pre-arranged visa, provided they have a passport valid for at least six months upon entry, a confirmed onward/return plane ticket with reservations off the island, and a visa for the next destination. Visa-exempt entry is only applicable to formal passports, not including emergency, temporary, other informal passports or travel documents. Visa-exempt entry cannot be converted to other types of visa. No extensions of stay are permitted under this program.

LANDING VISA --- Holders of U.S. passport with validity less than six months may apply for a Landing Visa upon arrival and may be admitted for up to 30 days. Landing visa cannot be converted to other types of visa. Holders of U.S. passport with validity less than six months applying for visas upon arrival at the ports of entry in Taiwan shall be charged a special handling fee of US$140 plus an additional fee of US$24. No extension of stay is allowed.

VISITOR VISA --- A Visitor Visa is appropriate for tourism, business, or visiting relatives and may be obtained at a Taiwan representative office abroad. It is usually valid for five years and allows multiple entries for stays of up to ninety days. A holder of sixty or ninety days visas that do not bear the stamp "No Extension Will be Granted" may apply for a maximum of 120- or 90-day extensions at the local city/county police headquarters. A flow chart about Visitor Visa application is available at MOFA Bureau of Consular Affairs website at http://www.boca.gov.tw

RESIDENT VISA --- Resident Visas are normally issued if the applicant has a valid work permit or is married to a Taiwan national. When applying for Resident Visas, applicants must submit supporting documents or official letters of approval from a competent authority in Taiwan, together with completed application forms. Normally, foreign nationals submit applications through their domestic Taiwan agents, representatives, or affiliates of their firms. A Resident Visa does NOT automatically convey permission to work in Taiwan. To be eligible to work in Taiwan, a foreigner must possess both a work permit and a Resident Visa.

For additional details about Taiwan visas, including current fees, please visit http://www.boca.gov.tw or http://www.ait.org.tw

U.S. Companies that require travel of foreign businesspersons to the United States should be advised that security evaluations are handled via an interagency process. Visa applicants should go to the following links.

State Department Visa Website: http://travel.state.gov/visa/

The Consular Section of the American Institute in Taiwan: http://www.ait.org.tw

TELECOMMUNICATIONS

Taiwan's telecommunications system is both efficient and convenient. International calls can be made from private cell phones, public International Direct Dialing (IDD) phones, or hotel IDD phones. Cellular phones are very popular, with many operators offering preferential rates or packages. The Global System for Mobile Communications (GSM) is the standard for cellular phone service. Many networking companies provide broadband Internet services to meet growing domestic demand. Internet cafes can be found in Taiwan's cities and towns, and most hotels in Taipei have internet access in their bedrooms. Facsimiles are also widely used in Taiwan. The main office of the Chunghwa Telecom Co., LTD. (CHT) provides 24-hour facsimile service. Most major hotels and business service centers offer facsimile and electronic mail services. Many convenience stores, such as 7-Eleven, also provide facsimile services.

TRANSPORTATION

AIR TRAVEL --- Taiwan has two major international airports: Taoyuan Airport in the north (about 40km from Taipei City) and Hsiaokang Airport in the south (in Kaohsiung City). Taoyuan Airport is the primary gateway to the island. The Kaohsiung airport offers regular flights to major destinations in the region. Taipei Song Shan Airport currently offers direct flights to and from major cities in China and Handeda in Japan. There are also several domestic airports and domestic airlines that provide fast and convenient connecting flights between Taiwan's larger cities as well as outlying islands.

AIRPORT PICKUP --- It generally takes about one hour to travel from the Taoyuan airport to Taipei City. Airport buses to Taipei depart from the airport every 20 minutes and tickets cost about NT$145 (approximately US$4.50) per person. Four bus companies currently provide the service to and from Taipei. Buses from the airport to Hsinchu, Taichung, Changhua, Tainan, and Kaohsiung are also available.

Taxis are available at the airport. A 50 percent surcharge is added to the meter fare for airport pickup (highway tolls not included). The total cost of a taxi ride from the airport to Taipei is about NT$1,000-1,500 (US$34-$52), depending on the destination. Many large hotels offer car or shuttle services from the airport to Taipei. It is, however, necessary to arrange such services when making hotel reservations.

The Hsiaokang Airport is close to the city of Kaohsiung, and it usually takes about 20 minutes to reach downtown and costs about NT$300 (US$9). Metered taxis charge a NT$50 surcharge. Several bus services are available at a low cost as well.

TAXIS --- Taxis are widely available in Taipei and other major cities. For most cities, a meter is used to calculate the fare. The basic charge is NT$70 (about US$2.2) for the first 1.25 kilometers, with an additional NT$5 for every additional 250 meters. In addition, there is an NT$5 charge for every 100 seconds for waiting, and a 20 percent nighttime surcharge is added to fares between 11:00 pm and 6:00 am. Taxi services can also be booked over the telephone. These services are generally considered safer and more reliable than individual taxis.

Taxis have a surcharge of NT$10 for luggage service. There is a surcharge of 20 percent in effect for two days before the eve of the Chinese New Year until the end of the holiday period. While some taxi drivers speak a little English, visitors are strongly advised to present taxi drivers with the address of their desired destination written in Chinese.

RAIL --- Taipei has seven Mass Rapid Transit (MRT) lines in operation with a combined track length of 74.4 kilometers. The MRT lines form a transportation network connecting downtown Taipei with the suburban areas of Muzha, Danshui, Xindian, Tucheng, and Nangang. Kaohsiung has two MRT lines in operation going north-south and east-west respectively.

The Taiwan Railway Administration operates an extensive rail network that is more than 1,000 kilometers in length. Tickets can be conveniently purchased through ticketing kiosks or ordered over the phone or on the Internet.

The Taiwan High Speed Rail (THSR) began operations on January 5, 2007. It uses Japan's Shinkansen technology and runs approximately 355.5 kilometers from north to south. The THSR takes only 96 minutes to travel from Taipei to Kaohsiung, as opposed to 4.5 hours by conventional rail. The one-way fare for Taipei-Kaohsiung is around NT$1,490 (US$46.5). Currently eight stations are in operation on the THSR line along Taiwan's western corridor: Taipei, Banchiao, Taoyuan, Hsinchu, Taichung, Chiayi, Tainan, and Zuoying (Kaohsiung).

BUSES --- Bus services in major cities are extensive and inexpensive, but can be incomprehensible to foreign visitors. Long-distance bus networks around the island also make it possible for people to travel virtually anywhere on the island quickly, comfortably, and at reasonable cost.

CAR RENTAL --- Limousines with drivers may be booked through hotels or car rental companies for about NT$9,000 (US$280) per eight-hour day. Self-drive rental cars are also available at rates that start at around NT$2,000 (US$63) a day. An international driver's license is required, as well as a credit card for a deposit.

LANGUAGE

Mandarin is the official language. The Taiwanese dialect is also commonly spoken, especially in the southern and rural areas. English is by far the most popular foreign language, and large numbers of people speak it fluently. In particular, those working in hotels, business, or public organizations are likely to have a good command of the language. Moreover, many elder people, especially those educated before the Second World War, can also speak Japanese.

HEALTH

As is true of many other tropical and sub-tropical areas, tap water in Taiwan should be boiled before drinking, although water quality is certainly improving in the major cities. Hotels and restaurants do provide drinking water, and bottled mineral water is widely available. Visitors should also take special care to wash all fruits and vegetables before eating and to avoid eating in any of the island's countless street stalls, for at least the first few weeks.

There are several international-standard private and public hospitals and clinics. Taiwan also offers high-quality dental care, with most clinics being privately operated. The majority of doctors and dentists in Taiwan speak English well. Qualified foreign nationals with Alien Resident Certificates (ARCs) and their family members can apply for coverage under the National Health Insurance Program (NHIP).

Many Western brand-name pharmaceuticals are sold in Taiwan, often without prescription. In addition, a wide range of foreign and domestic over-the-counter nonprescription drugs are available. Visitors should, however, bring a sufficient supply of any specific medications that they might require. Emergency medical treatment can be obtained by dialing 119.

LOCAL TIME, BUSINESS HOURS, AND HOLIDAYS

LOCAL TIME --- Taiwan is eight hours ahead of Greenwich Mean Time and 12 or 13 hours ahead of the U.S. Eastern Standard Time depending on the time of year, because Taiwan does not practice daylight savings time.

BUSINESS HOURS --- In general, business hours are 9:00 am to 5:30 pm for office workers and 8:00 am to 5:00 pm for factory workers, with a one-hour lunch break. Banks are open from 9:00 am to 3:30 pm without a lunch break. Most shops and retail stores are open daily from 10:00 am to 10:00 pm. Restaurants generally run from 11:00 am to 10:00 pm.

HOLIDAYS --- There are four national holidays and four festivals celebrated in Taiwan during which corporate and government offices are closed. Dates for the four festivals – Chinese Lunar New Year, Tomb-Sweeping Festival, Dragon Boat Festival, and Mid-Autumn Festival – are based on the lunar calendar and may vary each year.

Temporary Entry of Materials and Personal Belongings

Personal belongings and household articles (excluding controlled or restricted articles) carried by inbound passengers may be granted duty exemption as follows:

Each person, 20 or over in age, may bring in alcoholic beverages (1,000 cc or less without limitation on the number of bottles), plus 200 cigarettes, or 25 cigars or one pound of tobacco.

Articles that are already owned and used by the passenger abroad, and their customs value does not exceed NT$10,000 (about US$312.5) for each piece.

Other articles for personal use (not including the articles mentioned above) if their total customs value does not exceed NT$20,000 (about US$625) for each passenger.

Samples carried by inbound passengers may be granted duty exemption if the total customs value does not exceed NT$12,000 (about US$375). Duty and in some cases the commodity tax and/or value added tax will be imposed on articles imported in excess of the exemption limit. More information is available at the website:
http://eweb.customs.gov.tw/ct.asp?xItem=15227&ctNode=6485

Taiwan uses electric current of 110 volts at 60 cycles, the same as in the United States. Appliances from Europe, Australia or South-East Asia will need an adaptor or transformer. Many buildings have outlets with 220 volts especially for the use of air conditioners.

Web Resources

The Taiwan Tourism Bureau has a wealth of information about traveling in Taiwan on its website at: http://taiwan.net.tw

For the latest information about Taiwan travel advisories, visit the State Department Consular Information Sheet for Taiwan at: http://travel.state.gov/travel/cis_pa_tw/cis/cis_1036.htm l

Business travelers to Taiwan seeking appointments with the Commercial Section of the American Institute in Taiwan should contact the office in advance. The Commercial Section can be reached by telephone at 886-2-2720-1550, fax at 886-2-2757-7162, or by e-mail at Taipei.Office.Box@trade.gov

US STATE DEPARTMENT: SUGGESTIONS FOR TRELERS

COUNTRY DESCRIPTION: Taiwan is a stable democracy and has a strong and well-developed economy. Tourist facilities are widely available.

ENTRY REQUIREMENTS: Passport required. Taiwan previously required that U.S. visitors to Taiwan hold passports valid for at least six months. This is no longer the case: Taiwan now considers U.S. passports valid for return to the United States for six months beyond the expiration date of the passport. For specific information about entry requirements, travelers may contact the Taipei Economic and Cultural Representative Office (TECRO), 4201 Wisconsin Avenue, N.W., Washington, D.C. 20116-2137, via either its main telephone number,(202) 895-1800, or its visa section telephone number,(202) 895-1814. The main fax number at TECRO is (202) 363-0999, and the visa section fax number is (202) 895-0017. There is also an Internet address: http://www.taipei.org/teco.htm. The Taipei Economic and Cultural Office (TECO) also has offices in Atlanta, Boston, Chicago, Guam, Honolulu, Houston, Kansas City, Los Angeles, Miami, New York, San Francisco and Seattle.

INFORMATION ON CRIME AND SAFETY: Although there has been an increase in the crime rate over the last year, due in part to local enforcement reporting methods, the overall crime rate in Taiwan remains relatively low. Nonetheless, there has been intense public concern in Taipei resulting from several violent crime cases in 1996-97. Residential burglaries and thefts are the predominant crimes affecting foreigners in Taiwan, but other more serious crimes do occasionally occur. Generally, U.S. citizen visitors to Taiwan should follow the basic security precautions that would apply in any large city. Women should exercise caution when traveling alone in taxis, especially at night, as there have been incidents reported involving violence directed towards unaccompanied female taxi passengers; calling for a radio-dispatched taxi is an option. Local police departments have foreign affairs sections which are normally staffed by English-speaking officers. Police contact numbers for the major cities in Taiwan are as follows: Taipei (02)2556-6007, Kaohsiung (07) 215-4342, Tainan (06) 222-9704, Taichung (04) 327-3875, Taitung (089) 334-756, Pingtung (08) 733-6283. The loss or theft abroad of a U.S. passport should be reported immediately to the local police, and to the American Institute in Taiwan, at Taipei or Kaohsiung. Useful information on guarding valuables and protecting personal security while traveling abroad is provided in the Department of State pamphlet, *A Safe Trip Abroad*. It is available by mail from the Superintendent of Documents, U.S. Government Printing Office, Washington, D.C. 20402, via the Internet at http://www.access.gpo.gov/su_docs, or via the Bureau of Consular Affairs home page at http://travel.state.gov.

CRIMINAL PENALTIES: When outside the U.S., a U.S. citizen is subject to local laws and regulations, which sometimes differ significantly from those in the United States and do not afford the protections available to the individual under U.S. law. Penalties for breaking the law can be more severe than in the United States for similar offenses. Persons violating the law, even unknowingly, may be expelled, arrested or imprisoned. Criminal penalties for possession, use, or trafficking of illegal drugs are strict, and convicted offenders can expect severe jail sentences and fines. Taiwan law provides for the death penalty for some narcotics offenses.

COMPULSORY MILITARY SERVICE: Taiwan law provides for compulsory military service. Men between the ages of 18 and 45 who were born in Taiwan or who have ever held a Taiwan passport should be aware that they may be subject to compulsory military service in Taiwan, even if they are also U.S. citizens, and even if they have entered Taiwan on U.S. passports. Affected individuals are urged to consult with the nearest office of the Taipei Economic and Cultural Office (TECO) in the United States before visiting Taiwan to determine whether they are subject to the military service requirement.

MEDICAL FACILITIES: Health facilities in Taiwan are fully adequate for routine medical treatment. Doctors and hospitals may expect immediate cash payment for health services, and U.S. medical insurance is not always valid outside the United States. The Medicare/Medicaid program does not provide for payment of medical services outside the United States.

MEDICAL INSURANCE: Serious medical problems requiring hospitalization and/or medical evacuation to the United States can cost from $10,000 to $100,000. Supplemental overseas medical insurance, including coverage for medical evacuation, may prove useful. Check with your own insurance company to confirm whether your policy applies overseas, and whether it includes a provision for medical evacuation. Ascertain whether payment will be made to the overseas hospital or doctor, or whether you will be reimbursed later for expenses you incur. Some insurance policies also include coverage for psychiatric treatment and for disposition of remains in the event of death. Useful information on medical emergencies abroad, including overseas insurance programs, is provided in the Department of State, Bureau of Consular Affairs' brochure *Medical Information for Americans Traveling Abroad*, available via the Bureau's home page and autofax service.

For additional health information, travelers may call the toll-free numbers of the Centers for Disease Control and Prevention's international travelers hotline 1-877-FYI-TRIP (1-877-394-8747), may use the CDC autofax service, 1-888-CDC-FAXX (1-888-232-3299), or may access the CDC home page on the Internet: http://www.cdc.gov.

AVIATION SAFETY OVERSIGHT: The U.S. Federal Aviation Administration (FAA) has assessed the Civil Aviation Authority of Taiwan as Category 1 -- in compliance with international aviation safety standards for oversight of Taiwan's air carrier operations. For further information, travelers may contact the Department of Transportation within the U.S. at 1-800-322-7873, or visit the FAA Internet home page at http://www.faa.gov/avr/iasa/index.htm. The U.S. Department of Defense (DOD) separately assesses some foreign air carriers for suitability as official providers of air services. For information regarding the DOD policy on specific carriers, travelers may contact DOD at 618-256-4801.

TRAFFIC SAFETY AND ROAD CONDITIONS: Roads in Taiwan's major cities are generally congested, and driving conditions are made worse by large numbers of scooters and motorcycles that weave in and out of traffic. Special caution should be taken when driving on mountain roads, which are typically narrow, winding, and poorly banked, and which may be made impassable by mudslides after heavy rains.

REGISTRATION AND PASSPORTS: U.S. citizens are encouraged to register at the American Institute in Taiwan, and to obtain updated information on travel and security. The American Institute in Taiwan does not issue U.S. passports but accepts passport applications and forwards them to the Passport Agency in Honolulu for processing. Processing time takes three to four weeks. In an emergency, the American Institute in Taiwan can issue a travel letter to permit a U.S. citizen who has lost a passport to return to the United States.

CHILDREN'S ISSUES: For information on international adoption of children, international parental child abduction, and international child support enforcement issues, please refer to our Internet site at http://travel.state.gov/children's_issues.html or telephone (202) 736-7000.

AMERICAN INSTITUTE IN TAIWAN: Unofficial relations with the people of Taiwan are conducted through the American Institute in Taiwan, whose offices are authorized by law to perform American citizen services. For assistance, U.S. citizen travelers may contact the American Institute in Taiwan at No. 7 Lane 134, Hsin Yi Road Section 3, Taipei, Taiwan; telephone (886-2) 2709-2000; fax: (886-2) 2709-0908; or the American Institute in Taiwan branch office at No. 2 Chung Cheng 3rd Road, 5th Floor, Kaohsiung, Taiwan, telephone: (886-7) 224-0154; fax: (886-7) 223-8237. In case of emergencies after working hours, the duty officer at the American Institute in Taiwan at Taipei may be contacted at (886-2) 2709-2014.

GETTING THERE

Air

The national airline is *China Airlines (CI)*. *EVA Air* offers flights to destinations throughout Asia, Europe, North America, Australia and New Zealand. Other airlines serving Taiwan include *British Asia Airways*, *Continental Airlines*, *Singapore Airlines* and *Thai Airways*.

Approximate flight time: From Taipei to Los Angeles is 14 hours.

International airports

Chiang Kai-shek–Taipei (TPE) is 40km (25 miles) southwest of the city (travel time – 30 minutes). Airport facilities include an outgoing duty-free shop (0800-2100), post office, car hire, bank/bureau de change (0900-1700), bar/restaurant (0900-2100) and tourist information. Buses depart every 15 minutes for both *Sung Shan* (domestic) airport and the main railway station. Taxis and buses are available to the city centre.

Kaohsiung International (KHH) is 9km (4 miles) from the town centre. Airport facilities include an outgoing duty-free shop (0800-1900), car hire (0900-1900), bank/bureau de change (0900-1900) and bar/restaurant (0900-1900). A regular bus service is available (travel time – 30 minutes). There is a taxi service to the town.

Sea

There are sea links with Macau, Hong Kong and Japan.

GETTING AROUND

Air

China Airlines, *Eva Air*, *Far Eastern Air Transport*, *Formosa Airlines* and five other domestic airlines run services to local destinations from *Sung Shan* airport, Taipei.

Sea

There are reasonable connections from local ports. For details contact port authorities.

Train

Services are provided to destinations all over the island by the *Taiwan Railway Administration*. The main tourist routes are Taipei–Taichung–Chiayi–Tainan–Kaohsiung (a top-class service), Taipei–Taichung–Sun Moon Lake (with the last leg of the journey by bus), Chiayi–Alishan (with spectacular mountain scenery) and Taipei–New Hualian–Taitung (scenic coastal route). Air-conditioned electric trains run at least hourly from Taipei to Kaohsiung; some trains have restaurant cars. Children under three travel free; children aged 3-13 pay half fare. Train tickets can be purchased at many major hotels in Taipei, as well as at the main railway station.

Road

Traffic drives on the right. There is an adequate road system joining all major cities. A highway links Taipei and Kaohsiung. Some main streets have English signs.

Bus

There are both local and long-distance bus and coach services.

Taxi

These are plentiful and inexpensive (metered). The destination must be written in Chinese for the driver.

Car rental

This is available in major towns.

Documentation: An International Driving Permit is required.

Urban

A number of private bus companies provide extensive services in Taipei. Two lines of a Mass Rapid Transit (MRT) system, a monorail train system serving Taipei and its suburbs, opened in 1996. Metered taxis are available in Taipei; tipping is not expected, but it is starting to come into practice.

Travel Times

The following chart gives approximate journey times (in hours and minutes) from Taipei to other major cities/towns.

	Air	Road	Train
Kaohsiung	0.40	5.30	4.40
Tainan	0.40	4.30	4.10
Taichung	0.30	2.30	2.30
Hualien	0.30	7.00	3.00

Taitung	0.50	10.00	5.30
Sun Moon L.	-	4.30	-
Alishan	-	6.00	-
Kenting	-	6.30	-
Makung	0.40	-	-

ACCOMMODATION

Hotels

There are over 398 tourist hotels in the country offering a broad range of accommodation and services. Prices range from US$30-50 a day for smaller hotels with US$90-150 a day being average. For details, contact the Press Division of the Taipei Representative Office in the UK or the Taiwan Visitors Bureau. Many hotels belong to the International Tourist Hotel Association of Taipei, 8th Floor-1, 369 Fu Shing N Road. Tel: (2) 27 17 21 55. Fax: (2) 27 17 24 53.

Grading: Hotels are rated on a scale of 1 to 5 'Plum Blossoms' using a system equivalent to the more familiar 5-star system, with three Plum Blossoms being about average:

4 to 5 Plum Blossoms: 50 hotels (half of which are in Taipei) are in these categories. The hotels are luxury class with a range of services and facilities, eg tennis courts, swimming pools and beauty salons.

2 and 3 Plum Blossoms: The 80 hotels in these categories are clean, comfortable and functional.

Camping

Campsites are available.

Youth Dorms

Dormitory and non-dormitory rooms are available in major cities and in scenic areas.

MONEY

Currency

New Taiwan Dollar (NT$) = 100 cents. Notes are in denominations of NT$1000, 500, 100 and 50. Coins are in denominations of NT$50, 10, 5 and 1, and 50 cents.

Currency exchange

All travelers are required to make a currency declaration in writing together with the baggage declaration. Unused currency can be reconverted on departure, on production of exchange receipts.

Credit cards

Accepted in most hotels, restaurants and shops.

Travelers' checks

Accepted in most hotels, restaurants and shops. To avoid additional exchange rate charges, travelers are advised to take travelers' checks in US Dollars.

Exchange rate indicators against the US Dollar

The following figures are included as a guide to the movements of the New Taiwan Dollar against Sterling and the US Dollar:

Date	Aug'99	Nov'99	May'00	Aug'00
$1.00=	32.17	31.73	30.74	31.10

Currency restrictions

The import and export of local currency is limited to NT$40,000. Free import of foreign currency is allowed, subject to declaration. The export of foreign currency is limited to the equivalent of US$5000 or up to the amount imported and declared. All exchange receipts must be retained.

Banking hours: 9AM-3.30PM Monday to Friday; 9AM-12PM Saturday.

SUPPLEMENTS

STRATEGIC GOVERNMENT AND BUSINESS CONTACTS

Title(Name)	Address	Phone NO.
Atomic Energy Council, EY	Floors 2-8, No. 80, Section 1, Chenggong Road, Yonghe City	886 2 8231 7919
Aviation Police Office	No.27, Hangqin N. RD., Dayuan Shiang, Taoyuan County , 337, Taiwan R.O.C	886-3-3982177
Banking Bureau, Financial Supervisory Commission, Executive Yuan, R.O.C.	7F., No.7, Sec. 2, Sianmin Blvd., Banciao City, Taipei County 22041, Taiwan, Republic of China	886-2-8968-9999
Board of ForeignTrade, MOEA	1 Hu Kou Street,Taipei,Taiwan 100-66, R.O.C.	886-2-23510271
Bureau of Consular Affairs, MOFA	3~5 Fl., 2-2 Chi-Nan Rd., Sec. 1, Taipei , Taiwan, ROC	886-2-2343-2888
Bureau of Food and Drug Analysis	No.161-2, Kunyang St, Nangang District, Taipei City 115-61, Taiwan (R.O.C)	886-2-26531318
Bureau of High Speed Rail	9F, No. 7, Sec. 2,Sianmin Blvd., Banciao City, Taipei County, 220, Taiwan R.O.C	886-2-8072-3333
Bureau of Mine,MOEA	No.2,Jhenjiang St.,Taipei City 10051	886-2-23917341
Bureau of National Health Insurance, ROC	No. 140, Sec. 3, Hsinyi Road, Taipei 10634, Taiwan, R.O.C.	886-2-2706-5866
Bureau of Standards, Metrology and Inspection, MOEA	No.4, Sec.1, Jinan Rd., Taipei City 100, Taiwan(R.O.C.)	886-2-23431700
Central Election Commission	10F, No. 5, Syujhou Rd., Taipei City 10055, Taiwan R.O.C.	886-2-2356548
CENTRAL GEOLOGICAL SURVEY, MOEA	2, Lane 109, Hua-Hsin Street, Chung-Ho, Taipei, Taiwan 235, Republic of China	886-2-29462793
Central Personnel Administration, EY	10th Fl. 2-2 Chinan Road, Section 1, Taipei, Taiwan 10051, R.O.C.	886-2-23979298
Central Weather Bureau	64, Gongyuan Road, Taipei 10048, Taiwan (R.O.C.)	886-2-2349-1000
Changhua County Government	No.416, Sec. 2, Jhongshan Rd., Changhua City, Changhua County 50001, Taiwan (R.O.C.)	886-47-222151
Chiayi City Government		
Chiayi County Government	No. 1 Sianghe 1st Rd, East Section, Sianghe Sincun, Taibao City, Chiayi County 61249, Taiwan	886-5-3620143
Chunghwa Post	Jinshan Building Address : No.55, Sec. 2, Jinshan S. Rd., Da-an District, Taipei City 10603, Taiwan (R.O.C.).	886-2-2392-1310
Civil Aeronautics Administration	No.340, Dunhua N. Rd., Taipei City 10548, Taiwan (R.O.C.)	886-2-2349-6280
Civil Service Development Institute	30, ShinSheng S.Rd. Sec.3, Taipei, Taiwan 10660, R.O.C.	886-2-83691399
Construction and Planning Agency, MOI	342, Sec. 2, Bade Rd., Songshan District, Taipei City, 10556, Taiwan(R.O.C.)	886-2-8771-2345
Consumer Protection Commission, EY	No.12,Jihe Rd, Shihlin District, Taipei City 111, Taiwan(R.O.C)	886-2-2886-3200
Council for Cultural Affairs	No.30-1, Beiping East Road, Jhongjheng District, Taipei City 10049, Taiwan(R.O.C.)	886-2-2343-4000
Council of Agriculture, Executive	37 Nanhai Road, Taipei, Taiwan 10014, R. O. C.	886-2-2381-

Yuan, R.O.C.		2991
Department of Health, EY	No.36, Tacheng St., Datong District, Taipei City 10341, Taiwan (R.O.C.)	886-2-8590-6666
Directorate General of Customs, MOF	13 Ta-Cheng Street, Taipei City	886-2-25505500
Directorate General of Highways,MOTC	No.70, Sec. 1, Jhongsiao W. Rd., Jhongjheng District, Taipei City 100, Taiwan (R.O.C.)	886-2-23113456
Directorate-General of Budget, Accounting, and Statistics, EY	No.1, Sec.1, Jhongsiao E.Rd., Taipei City, Taiwan 10058, R.O.C.	886-2-33566500
Environmental Protection Administration	No.83, Sec. 1, Jhonghua Rd., Jhongjheng District, Taipei City 100, Taiwan (R.O.C.)	886-2-23117722
Fair Trade Commission, Executive Yuan, R.O.C	12-14 F, No. 2-2 Jinan Rd., Sec. 1, Jhongjheng (Zhongzheng) District, Taipei City 100, Taiwan (R.O.C.)	886-2-23517588
Financial Examination Bureau, Financial Supervisory Commission	15th Floor, No. 7, Section 2, Hsien Ming Boulevard, Panchiao City, Taipei County 22041	886-2-89680899
Forestry Bureau	No. 2, Hangchou S. Rd., Sec. 1, Taipei City, Taiwan R.O.C.	886-2-23515441
Government Information Office, EY	2 Tianjin St. Taipei, 10051, Taiwan, R.O.C.	886-2-3356-8888
Hsinchu City Government	No. 120 Zhongzheng Road, Hsinchu City, 30051, Taiwan, ROC	886-3-5216121
Hsinchu County Government	No.10, Guangming 6th Rd., Jhubei City, Hsinchu County 302, Taiwan ROC	0800241111
Hualien County Government	97001, No.17, Fucian Rd., Hualien City, Hualien County 970, Taiwan (R.O.C.)	886-3-822-7171
Hualien Harbor Bureau, MOTC	No.66, Hai-an Rd., Hualien City, Hualien County 970, Taiwan (R.O.C.)	886-3-8325131
Industrial Development Bureau	No. 41-3, Hsin Yi Rd., Sec. 3, Taipei, Taiwan, R.O.C.	886-2-27541255
Institute of Transportation, Ministry of Transportation And Communications	No.240, Dunhua North Road, Songshan District , Taibei City 10548, Taiwan, R.O.C.	886-2-23496793
Insurance Bureau, Financial Supervisory Commission, Executive Yuan, R.O.C.	17F., No.7, Sec. 2, Sianmin Blvd., Banciao City, Taipei County 22041, Taiwan (R.O.C.)	886-2-89680899
Intellectual Property Office, MOEA	185 Hsinhai Rd., Sec. 2, 3F; Taipei 10637, Taiwan, R.O.C	886-2-2738-0007
Investigation Bureau, MOJ	74, Chung-hua Rd. Hsin-tien City Taipei County	886-2-29188888
Investment Commission, MOEA	8F., No.7, Sec. 1, Roosevelt Rd., Jhongjheng District, Taipei City 100, Taiwan (R.O.C.)	886-2-33435700
Kaohsiung City Government	No. 2, Sihwei 3rd Road, Lingya District, Kaohsiung City, Taiwan	886-7-3368333
Kaohsiung County Government	132, Guang Fu Road, Section 2, Fengshan City, Kaohsiung County, Taiwan, R.O.C.	
Kaohsiung Harbor Bureau, MOTC	No.62.Linhai 2nd Road, Gushan District, Kaohsiung, Taiwan 804, R.O.C	886-7-5612311
Keelung City Government	No.1, Yi 1st Rd., Jhongjheng District Keelung City 202, Taiwan (R.O.C.)	886-2-24201122
Kinmen County Government, FPG	No.60, Minsheng Rd., Jincheng Township, Kinmen County 893, Taiwan (R.O.C.)	886-82318823
Lienchiang County Government of Fujian Province	No.76, Jieshou Village, Nangan Township, Lienchiang County 209, Taiwan (R.O.C.)	886-836-25131
Miaoli County Government	No.100, Sianfu Rd., Miaoli City, Miaoli County 36001, Taiwan (R.O.C.)	886-37-322150

Ministry of Economic Affairs	15 Fuzhou St., Taipei, 10015, Taiwan, ROC.	886-2-23212200
Ministry of Education	No.5, Zhongshan S. Rd., Zhongzheng Dist., Taipei City 10051, Taiwan (R.O.C.)	886-2-7736-6051
Ministry of Finance	2, Aiguo W. Road Taipei ,10066 Taiwan , ROC	886-2-23228000
Ministry of Foreign Affairs	2 Kaitakelan Blvd. Taipei, 10048, Taiwan (R.O.C.)	886-2-2348-2999
Ministry of Justice	NO. 130, Chung-Ching S. Rd., Sec. 1, Taipei City, Taiwan.	886-2-23146871
Ministry of Labor MOL	9th Floor, No.83, Second Section, Yianping N. Road, Datong District, Taipei City	886-2-8590-2866
Ministry of National Defense	No. 172. Bo-ai Rd. Jhongjheng District, Taipei City 100, Taiwan(R.O.C) 10048	886-2-2311-6117
Ministry of Science and Technology	No. 106, HoPing E. Road, Sec.2, Taipei 10622, Taiwan (R.O.C.)	886-2-27377992
Ministry of the Interior	10055 No.5, Syujhou Rd., Jhongjheng District, Taipei City 100, Taiwan (R.O.C.)	886-2-2356-5000
Mongolian and Tibetan Affairs Commission	4Fl., No. 5, Shiujou Rd., Jungjeng Chiu, Taipei, Taiwan 100, R.O.C.	886-2-2351-4280
Nantou County Government	No.660, Jhongsing Rd., Nantou City, Nantou County 54001, Taiwan (R.O.C.)	886-49-2222106
National Archives Administration	No.10, Lane 59, Yitong St., Zhongshan District, Taipei City 10486, Taiwan (R.O.C.)	886-2-2513-1888
National Development Council	No.3 Baoqing Road, Taipei City 10020, Taiwan(R.O.C.)	886-2-2316-5300
National Fire Agency of the Ministry of the Interior R.O.C.	8F, NO.200, Sec.3, Beixin Rd., Xindian City, Taipei County, Taiwan 23143 (R.O.C)	886-2-8911-4119
National Institute for Compilation and Translation	No. 179, Heping E. Road, Sec. 1, Da-An District, Taipei City, 10644, Taiwan	886-2-3322-5558
National Palace Museum	221 Chih-shan Rd., Sec. 2; Shih-lin, Taipei, 11143, TAIWAN	886-2-2881-2021
National Police Agency	No.7, Sec. 1, Jhongsiao E. Rd., Jhongjheng District, Taipei City 10058, Taiwan (R.O.C.)	0800-018111
National Security Bureau		886-2-2889-1338
National Youth Commission, Executive Yuan	14F , No.5, XuZhou Road , Taipei 10055, Taiwan	886-2-23566126
National Youth Commission, EY	14F , No.5, XuZhou Road , Taipei 10055, Taiwan	886-02-23566232
Office of the President, Republic of China(Taiwan)	No. 122, Sec. 1, Chongqing S. Rd., Taipei City, 100, Taiwan (ROC).	886-2-2311-3731
Oversea Compatriot Affairs Commission	5 Hsuchou Road, Floors 3, 15-17 Taipei, Taiwan, R.O.C.	886-2-3343-2600
Penghu County Government	No.32, Jhihping Rd., Magong City Penghu County 880, Taiwan (R.O.C.)	886-6-927-4400
Pingtung County Government	No.527,Tzu-yu Rd,Pingtung City, , Taiwan, R.O.C.	886-8-732-0415
Public Construction Commission, Executive Yuan	Public Construction Commission Executive Yuan, 9F., No. 3, Songren Rd., Taipei City, 11010, Taiwan (R.O.C)	886-2-87897500
Railway Reconstruction Bureau, MOTC	20F, No.7, Sec. 2, Sianmin Blvd., Banciao City, Taipei County 220, Taiwan (R.O.C.)	886-2-8969-1900
Regional Civil Service Development Institute, C.P.A.		

Securities and Futures Bureau, Financial Supervisory Commission, Executive Yuan, R.O.C.	85, Sec.1, XinSheng S.Road, Da-an District, Taipei, Taiwan, 106, R.O.C	886-2-8773-5100
Small and Medium Enterprise Administration, MOEA	3rd Fl. No. 95, Sec.2, Roosevelt Rd., Taipei 10646, Taiwan, R.O.C.	886-2-2368-6858
Supreme Prosecutors Office	NO. 235, Sec.1,Guiyang St.,Zhongzheng Dist., Taipei City,100 Taiwan(R.O.C.)	886-2-23167000
Taichung City Government	99, MinQuan Rd., West District, Taichung City 403, Taiwan (R.O.C.)	886-4-22289111
Taichung County Government	36 Yangming St.Fengyuan, Taichung County	886-4-25263100
Taichung Harbor Bureau, MOTC	No.2, Sec. 3, Zhongqi Rd., Wuqi Township, Taichung County 435, Taiwan (R.O.C.)	886-4-26562611
Tainan City Government	No.6, Yonghua Rd.,Sec.2, 70801 Tainan City, Taiwan.	886-6-2991111
Tainan County Government	No.36, Minjhih Rd., Sinying City, Tainan County 73001, Taiwan (R.O.C.)	886-6-632-2231
Taipei City Government	No.1, Shifu Rd., Xinyi District, Taipei City 11008, Taiwan (R.O.C.).	886-2-2720-8889
Taipei County Government	No.161, Sec. 1, Jhongshan Rd, Banciao City, Taipei County 22001, Taiwan (ROC)	886-2-2960-3456
Taitung County Government	N o.276, Jhong shan Rd.,Taitung City.Taitung County , Taiwan 95001, R.O.C	886-89-326141
Taiwan Area National Expressway Engineering Bureau, MOTC	5F., No.1, Ln. 1, Sec. 3, Heping E. Rd., Da-an Dist., Taipei City 10669, Taiwan (R.O.C.)	886-0800-067-567
Taiwan Area National Freeway Bureau	NO. 70,Banshanya,Liming Village,Taishan Township,Taipei County,Taiwan 24303,R.O.C.	886-2-2909-6141
Taiwan Railways Administration, MOTC	No.3, Beiping W. Rd., Jhongjheng District, Taipei City 100, Taiwan (R.O.C.)	886-2-2381-5226
Taoyuan County Government	No.1,Shianfu Rd,Taoyuan City, Taoyuan County 33001 Taiwan.	886-3-3322101
The Central Bank of Republic of China (Taiwan)	2, Sec. 1, Roosevelt Rd., Taipei, 10066, Taiwan, R.O.C.	886-2-2393-6161
The Examination Yuan	No.1, Shiyuan Rd., Wenshan Dist., Taipei City 11601, Taiwan (R.O.C.)	886-2-82366000
The Executive Yuan	No.1, Sec. 1, Zhongxiao E. Rd., Zhongzheng Dist., Taipei City 10058, Taiwan (R.O.C.)	886- 3356-6500
The Judicial Yuan	No. 124, Sec. 1 Chungking S. Rd. Taipei City, 100 Taiwan R.O.C.	886-2-23618577
The Legislative Yuan	No.1, Jhongshan S. Rd., Jhongjheng District, Taipei, 10051, Taiwan , R.O.C.	886-2-23585858
Tourism Bureau Ministry of Transportation and Communications, R.O.C.	9F., No.290, Sec. 4, Zhongxiao E. Rd., Da-an District, Taipei City 10694, Taiwan (R.O.C.)	886-2-2349-1635
Tourism Bureau, Republic of China (Taiwan)	9F., No.290, Sec. 4, Zhongxiao E. Rd., Da-an District, Taipei City 10694, Taiwan (R.O.C.)	0800-011765
Veterans Affairs Commission, EY	No.222, Sec. 5, Jhongsiao(Zhongxiao) E. Rd., Sinyi(Xinyi) District, Taipei City 110, Taiwan (R.O.C.)	886-2-2757-1750
Yilan County Government	No.1, Sianjheng N. Rd., Yilan City, Yilan County 26060, Taiwan (R.O.C)	886-3-9251000
Yunlin County Government	No.515, Sec. 2, Yunlin Rd., Douliou City, Yunlin County 64001, Taiwan (R.O.C.)	886-5-5322154

U.S. & COUNTRY CONTACTS

AMERICAN INSTITUTE IN TAIWAN (AIT)

Commercial Section
Chief: Greg Loose
Suite 3207, 333 Keelung Rd., Sec. 1, Taipei, Taiwan
Tel: 886-2-2720-1550, Fax: 886-2-2757-7162
Website: http://www.buyusa.gov/taiwan/en

Agriculture Trade Office
Director: Hoa Huynh
Suite 704, 7Fl., 136 Jen Ai Rd., Sec. 3, Taipei, Taiwan
Tel: 886-2-2705-6536, ext. 287, Fax: 886-2-2706-4885
Website: http://ait.org.tw

Agriculture Section
Chief: Jonathan Gressel
7, Lane 134, Hsin Yi Rd., Sec. 3, Taipei, Taiwan
Tel: 886-2-2709-2000, ext. 2317, Fax: 886-2-2709-2054
Website: http://ait.org.tw

Economic Section
Chief: William Weinstein
7, Lane 134, Hsin Yi Rd., Sec. 3, Taipei, Taiwan
Tel: 886-2-2709-2000 x2374, Fax: 886-2-2706-3023
Website: http://ait.org.tw

WASHINGTON, D.C.-BASED COUNTRY CONTACTS

AIT/Washington
Trade and Commercial Programs
Director: Rick Ruzicka
Suite 1700, 1700 N. Moore Street
Arlington, VA 22209
Tel: 703-525-8474, Fax: 703-841-1385

U.S. Department of Commerce
Taiwan Desk Officer: Mary-Beth Morgan
Room 2319, 14th and Constitution Ave. NW
Washington, D.C. 20230
Tel: 202-482-3876, Fax: 202-482-3316
Website: http://www.doc.gov

U.S. Department of Commerce
US & Foreign Commercial Service, East Asia Pacific
Regional Director: Ann Bacher
Room 1223, 14th and Constitution Ave. NW
Washington, D.C. 20230
Tel: 202-482-0423, Fax: 202-501-6165
Website: http://www.doc.gov

U.S. Department of Commerce
Trade Information Center
Room 7424, 14th and Constitution Ave. NW
Washington, D.C. 20230
Tel: 1-800-USA-TRADE
Website: http://www.doc.gov

U.S. Department of Agriculture
Foreign Agricultural Service
Trade Assistance and Promotion Office
South Building, 14th and Independence Ave. SW
Washington, D.C. 20250
Tel: 202-720-7420
Website: http://www.fas.usda.gov

AMCHAM AND/OR BILATERAL BUSINESS COUNCILS

US-ROC (Taiwan) Business Council
President: Rupert J. Hammond-Chambers
Suite 1703, 1700 North Moore Street
Arlington, Virginia 22209
Tel: 703-465-2930, Fax: 703-465-2937
Website: www.us-taiwan.org

American Chamber of Commerce in Taipei
President: Gus Sorenson
Suite 1012, Chia Hsin Building Annex
96 Chung Shan N. Rd., Sec 2, Taipei, Taiwan
Tel: 886-2-2581-7089, Fax: 886-2-2542-3376
Website: www.amcham.com.tw

China External Trade Development Council
3-8F, 333 Keelung Rd., Sec. 1, Taipei, Taiwan
Tel: 886-2-2725-5200, Fax: 886-2-2757-6653
Website: http://www.taiwantrade.com.tw

TRADE OR INDUSTRY ASSOCIATIONS

Chinese National Association of Industry & Commerce
Chairman: Theodore M.H. Huang
13F, 390 Fuhsing S. Rd., Sec. 1, Taipei, Taiwan
Tel: 886-2-2707-0111, Fax: 886-2-2707-0977
Website: http://www.cnaic.org

Chinese National Federation of Industries
Chairman: Earle J. S. Ho
12F, 390 Fuhsing S. Rd., Sec. 1, Taipei, Taiwan
Tel: 886-2-2703-3500, Fax: 886-2-2705-8317
Website: http://www.industry.net.tw

PUBLIC AGENCIES

Ministry of Economic Affairs (MOEA)
Minister: Yi-fu Lin
15 Foochow St., Taipei, Taiwan
Tel: 886-2-2321-9273, Fax: 886-2-2391-9398
Website: www.moea.gov.tw

Ministry of Finance (MOF)
Minister: Lin Chuan
2 Aikuo W. Rd., Taipei, Taiwan
Tel: 886-2-2322-8000, Fax: 886-2-2322-8006
Website: www.mof.gov.tw

Board of Foreign Trade (BOFT), MOEA
Director General: Chih-Peng Huang
1 Hukou St., Taipei, Taiwan
Tel: 886-2-2351-0271, Fax: 886-2-2351-3603
Website: www.trade.gov.tw

Ministry of Transportation and Communications (MOTC)
Minister: Lin Ling-san
2 Changsha St., Sec. 1, Taipei, Taiwan
Tel: 886-2-2349-2900, Fax: 886-2-2389-6009
Website: www.motc.gov.tw

Directorate General of Telecommunications, MOTC
Director General: Dr. Jen-Ter Chien
16 Chi-Nan Rd., Taipei, Taiwan
Tel: 886-2-2343-3953, Fax: 886-2-2343-3772
Website: www.dgt.gov.tw

Council of Agriculture (COA), Executive Yuan
Chairman: Lee Chin-lung
37 Nanhai Rd., Taipei, Taiwan
Tel: 886-2-2312-6000, Fax: 886-2-2361-4397
Website: www.coa.gov.tw

Council for Economic Planning and Development (CEPD)
Chairman: Lin Hsin-i
3, Paoching Rd., Taipei, Taiwan
Tel: 886-2-2316-5306, Fax: 886-2-2370-0403
Website: www.cepd.gov.tw

Department of Health (DOH), Executive Yuan
Minister: Chien-Jen Chen
100 Aikuo E. Rd., Taipei, Taiwan
Tel: 886-2-2396-7166, Fax: 886-2-2341-8994
Website: www.doh.gov.tw

Environmental Protection Administration (EPA), Executive Yuan
Minister: Hau Lung-bin
41 Chunghwa Rd., Sec. 1, Taipei, Taiwan
Tel: 886-2-2311-7722; Fax: 886-2-2311-6071
Website: www.epa.gov.tw

OTHER U.S. GOVERNMENT CONTACT NUMBERS

U.S. Department of State
Office of Business Affairs
2201 C Street N.W.
Washington, D.C. 20520
Tel: 202-647-1625, Fax: 202-647-3953

Overseas Private Investment Corporation
1100 New York Avenue, N.W.
Washington, D.C. 20527
Tel: 202-336-8400

BASIC TITLES ON TAIWAN

IMPORTANT!
All publications are updated annually!
Please contact IBP, Inc. at ibpusa3@gmail.com for the latest ISBNs and additional information

TITLE
Taiwan A "Spy" Guide - Strategic Information and Developments
Taiwan A Spy" Guide"
Taiwan Air Force Handbook
Taiwan Air Force Handbook
Taiwan Army Weapon Systems Handbook
Taiwan Army Weapon Systems Handbook
Taiwan Army Weapon Systems Handbook
Taiwan Army, National Security and Defense Policy Handbook
Taiwan Army, National Security and Defense Policy Handbook
Taiwan Aviation and Aerospace Industry Handbook
Taiwan Aviation and Aerospace Industry Handbook
Taiwan Business and Investment Opportunities Yearbook
Taiwan Business and Investment Opportunities Yearbook

TITLE
Taiwan Business and Investment Opportunities Yearbook Volume 1 Strategic Information and Opportunities
Taiwan Business and Investment Opportunities Yearbook Volume 2 Leading Export-Import, Business, Investment Opportunities and Projects
Taiwan Business Intelligence Report - Practical Information, Opportunities, Contacts
Taiwan Business Intelligence Report - Practical Information, Opportunities, Contacts
Taiwan Business Law Handbook - Strategic Information and Basic Laws
Taiwan Business Law Handbook - Strategic Information and Basic Laws
Taiwan Business Law Handbook - Strategic Information and Basic Laws
Taiwan Business Law Handbook - Strategic Information and Basic Laws
Taiwan Business Success Guide - Basic Practical Information and Contacts
Taiwan Clothing & Textile Industry Handbook
Taiwan Clothing & Textile Industry Handbook
Taiwan Company Laws and Regulations Handbook
Taiwan Company Laws and Regulations Handbook - Strategic Information and Basic Laws
Taiwan Constitution and Citizenship Laws Handbook - Strategic Information and Basic Laws
Taiwan Country Study Guide - Strategic Information and Developments
Taiwan Country Study Guide - Strategic Information and Developments Volume 1 Strategic Information and Developments
Taiwan Country Study Guide Volume 1 Strategic Information and Developments
Taiwan Criminal Laws, Regulations and Procedures Handbook - Strategic Information, Regulations, Procedures
Taiwan Customs, Trade Regulations and Procedures Handbook
Taiwan Customs, Trade Regulations and Procedures Handbook
Taiwan Diplomatic Handbook - Strategic Information and Developments
Taiwan Diplomatic Handbook - Strategic Information and Developments
Taiwan Ecology & Nature Protection Handbook
Taiwan Ecology & Nature Protection Handbook
Taiwan Ecology & Nature Protection Laws and Regulation Handbook
Taiwan Economic & Development Strategy Handbook
Taiwan Economic & Development Strategy Handbook
Taiwan Education System and Policy Handbook
Taiwan Electoral, Political Parties Laws and Regulations Handbook - Strategic Information, Regulations, Procedures
Taiwan Energy Policy, Laws and Regulation Handbook
Taiwan Export-Import Trade and Business Directory
Taiwan Export-Import Trade and Business Directory
Taiwan Foreign Policy and Government Guide
Taiwan Foreign Policy and Government Guide
Taiwan Government and Business Contacts Handbook
Taiwan Government and Business Contacts Handbook
Taiwan Healthcare Sector Organization, Management and Payment Systems Handbook - Strategic Information, Programs and Regulations
Taiwan Immigration Laws and Regulations Handbook - Strategic Information and Basic Laws
Taiwan Industrial and Business Directory

TITLE
Taiwan Insolvency (Bankruptcy) Laws and Regulations Handbook - Strategic Information and Basic Laws
Taiwan Intelligence & Security Activities & Operations Handbook
Taiwan Intelligence & Security Activities & Operations Handbook
Taiwan Internet and E-Commerce Investment and Business Guide - Strategic and Practical Information: Regulations and Opportunities
Taiwan Internet and E-Commerce Investment and Business Guide - Strategic and Practical Information: Regulations and Opportunities
Taiwan Investment and Business Guide - Strategic and Practical Information
Taiwan Investment and Business Guide - Strategic and Practical Information
Taiwan Investment and Business Guide - Strategic and Practical Information
Taiwan Investment and Business Guide - Strategic and Practical Information
Taiwan Investment and Business Guide Volume 2 Business, Investment Opportunities and Incentives
Taiwan Investment and Business Profile - Basic Information and Contacts for Succesful investment and Business Activity
Taiwan Investment and Trade Laws and Regulations Handbook
Taiwan Justice System and National Police Handbook
Taiwan Justice System and National Police Handbook
Taiwan Labor Laws and Regulations Handbook - Strategic Information and Basic Laws
Taiwan Land Ownership and Agriculture Laws Handbook
Taiwan Medical & Pharmaceutical Industry Handbook
Taiwan Medical & Pharmaceutical Industry Handbook
Taiwan Military Policy and Defense Strategy Handbook
Taiwan Military Policy and Defense Strategy Handbook
Taiwan Military Service Guide
Taiwan Mineral & Mining Sector Investment and Business Guide - Strategic and Practical Information
Taiwan Mineral & Mining Sector Investment and Business Guide - Strategic and Practical Information
Taiwan Mining Laws and Regulations Handbook
Taiwan National Defense and Security Report
Taiwan National Defense Report
Taiwan National Police Handbook
Taiwan National Police Handbook
Taiwan National Security and Defense Law and Regulations Handbook
Taiwan National Security and Defense Law and Regulations Handbook
Taiwan President Handbook
Taiwan President Handbook
Taiwan Province of China Investment, Trade Strategy and Agreements Handbook - Strategic Information and Basic Agreements
Taiwan Recent Economic and Political Developments Yearbook
Taiwan Research & Development Policy Handbook
Taiwan Space Agency and Programs Handbook
Taiwan Space Agency and Programs Handbook
Taiwan Starting Business (Incorporating) in Taiwan Guide

TITLE
Taiwan Starting Business (Incorporating) in....Guide
Taiwan Tax Guide
Taiwan Tax Guide
Taiwan Tax Guide Volume 1 Strategic Information and Basic Regulations
Taiwan Taxation Laws and Regulations Handbook
Taiwan Telecom Laws and Regulations Handbook
Taiwan Telecommunication Industry Business Opportunities Handbook
Taiwan Telecommunication Industry Business Opportunities Handbook
Taiwan Transportation Policy and Regulations Handbook
Taiwan: Business in Taiwan for Everyone: Practical Information and Contacts for Success
Taiwan: Doing Business and Investing in Taiwan Guide
Taiwan: Doing Business and Investing in Taiwan Guide
Taiwan: How to Invest, Start and Run Profitable Business in Taiwan Guide - Practical Information, Opportunities, Contacts
Taiwan: Investing in Taiwan Guide
Taiwan: Investing in Taiwan Guide: Strategic and Practical Information
Taiwan: Starting Business (Incorporating) in Taiwan Guide

BASIC LAWS AND REGULATIONS AFFECTING BUSINESS[6]

COUTRY	LAW TITLE
Taiwan	Accounting Act
Taiwan	Act For Development Of Small And Medium Enterprises
Taiwan	Act for the Establishment and Administration of the Financial Restructuring Fund
Taiwan	Act Of Military Service System
Taiwan	Administrative Appeal Act
Taiwan	Administrative Penalty Act
Taiwan	Administrative Procedure Act
Taiwan	Agricultural Development Act
Taiwan	Agricultural Finance Act
Taiwan	Agro-pesticide Act
Taiwan	Air Pollution Control Act
Taiwan	Amusement Tax Act
Taiwan	Animal Protection Act
Taiwan	Anti-Corruption Statute
Taiwan	Architects Act
Taiwan	Archives Act
Taiwan	Atomic Energy Law of The Republic of China
Taiwan	Basic Environment Act
Taiwan	Budget Act
Taiwan	Building Code
Taiwan	Business Accounting Act

[6] For ordering tests of specific laws in English or French, Please contact Global Investment Center USA at ibpusa3@gmail.com

Taiwan	Cable Radio and Television Act
Taiwan	Certified Public Accountant Act
Taiwan	Certified Public Bookkeepers Act 2008/1/7
Taiwan	Civil Code
Taiwan	Code of Court Martial Procedure
Taiwan	Commodity Labeling Law
Taiwan	Commodity Tax Act 2004/7/21
Taiwan	Communications Basic Law
Taiwan	Company Act
Taiwan	Computer-Processed Personal Data Protection Law
Taiwan	Construction Industry Act
Taiwan	Controlled Drugs Act
Taiwan	Cooperatives Act
Taiwan	Copyright Act 2007
Taiwan	Copyright Intermediary Organization Act
Taiwan	Credit Union Act
Taiwan	Criminal Code of the Armed Forces
Taiwan	Cultural Heritage Preservation Act
Taiwan	Customs Law
Taiwan	Deed Tax Act
Taiwan	Deposit Insurance Act
Taiwan	Domestic Violence Prevention Act
Taiwan	Drinking Water Management Act
Taiwan	Electronic Signatures Act
Taiwan	Electronic Signatures Act
Taiwan	Employment Insurance Law
Taiwan	Employment Services Act
Taiwan	Energy Management Law
Taiwan	Enforcement Rules of the Income Tax Act 2007/8/10
Taiwan	Enforcement Rules of the Integrated Circuit Layout Protection Act
Taiwan	Environmental Agents Control Act
Taiwan	Estate and Gift Tax Act
Taiwan	Fair Trade Act of 2002
Taiwan	Fair Trade Law
Taiwan	Financial Asset Securitization Act
Taiwan	Financial Holding Company Act
Taiwan	Financial Statement Act
Taiwan	Fisheries Act
Taiwan	Food Administration Act
Taiwan	Foreign Exchange Control Act
Taiwan	Foreign Trade Act
Taiwan	Futures Trading Act
Taiwan	Futures Trading Law Enforcement Rules
Taiwan	Futures Transaction Tax Act
Taiwan	Gender Equality in Employment law

Taiwan	Guide to ROC Taxes
Taiwan	House Tax Act
Taiwan	Immigration Act
Taiwan	Implementing Regulations of the Patent Act
Taiwan	Income Basic Tax Act 2006/3/6
Taiwan	Income Tax Act 2008/5/29
Taiwan	Industrial Group Act
Taiwan	Integrated Circuit Layout Protection Act
Taiwan	Ionizing Radiation Protection Act
Taiwan	Labor Inspection Law
Taiwan	Labor Insurance Act
Taiwan	Labor Pension Act
Taiwan	Labor Safety and Health Act
Taiwan	Labor Standards Act
Taiwan	Labor Union Law
Taiwan	Land Surveying and Mapping Act
Taiwan	Land Tax Act 2005/6/1
Taiwan	Law of Extradition
Taiwan	Law on the Exclusive Economic Zone and the Continental Shelf of the Republic of China
Taiwan	Law on the Territorial Sea and the Contiguous Zone of the Republic of China
Taiwan	Legal Aid Act 2004
Taiwan	Legal Aids Act
Taiwan	Local Government Act
Taiwan	Marine Pollution Control Act
Taiwan	Maritime Act
Taiwan	Meteorological Act
Taiwan	Money Laundering Control Act
Taiwan	Money Laundering Control Act
Taiwan	Name Act
Taiwan	National health insurance Act
Taiwan	National Property Act
Taiwan	National Sports Act
Taiwan	Nationality Act
Taiwan	Noise Control Act
Taiwan	Nuclear Damage Compensation Law
Taiwan	Nuclear Emergency Response Act
Taiwan	Nuclear Emergency Response Act
Taiwan	Nuclear Materials and Radioactive Waste Management Act
Taiwan	Nuclear Reactor Facilities Regulation Act
Taiwan	Oath Act
Taiwan	Occupational Accident Labor Protection Act
Taiwan	Offshore Banking Act
Taiwan	Optical Disk Act
Taiwan	Passport Statute
Taiwan	Patent Act

Taiwan	Patent Attorney Act
Taiwan	Petroleum Administration Law
Taiwan	Pharmacists Act
Taiwan	Plant Protection and Quarantine Act
Taiwan	Plant Variety and Plant Seed Act (2004)
Taiwan	Postal Act
Taiwan	Prevention of Sexual Harassment
Taiwan	Prison Act
Taiwan	Public Nuisance Dispute Mediation Act
Taiwan	Real Estate Securitization Act
Taiwan	Red Cross Society Act of the Republic of China
Taiwan	Referendum Act
Taiwan	Regulations for Implementing Energy Management Law
Taiwan	Regulations for the Collection of Commodity Tax 2004/7/22
Taiwan	Regulations Governing Auditing and Certification of Financial Statements by Certified Public Accountants
Taiwan	Regulations Governing Invention and Creation Awards
Taiwan	Rules for Integrated Circuit Layout Fees
Taiwan	Rules of Patent Fees
Taiwan	Satellite Broadcasting Act
Taiwan	Securities and Exchange Act
Taiwan	Securities Investment Trust and Consulting Act
Taiwan	Securities Investor and Futures Trader Protection Act
Taiwan	Securities Transaction Tax Act 2004/7/22
Taiwan	Sexual Assault Crime Prevention
Taiwan	Shipping Law
Taiwan	Social Education Act
Taiwan	Soil and Groundwater Pollution Remediation Act
Taiwan	Soil and Water Conservation Law
Taiwan	Stamp Tax Act 2004/7/22
Taiwan	State Compensation Law
Taiwan	Statistics Act
Taiwan	Taiwan Code of Civil Procedure
Taiwan	Taiwan Patent Act
Taiwan	Taiwan Relations Act
Taiwan	Tax Collection Act 2007/3/21
Taiwan	Teachers' Act
Taiwan	Telecommunications Act
Taiwan	The Act Governing Bills Finance Business
Taiwan	The Act of Special Education
Taiwan	The Arbitration Law of ROC
Taiwan	The Banking Act of The Republic of China
Taiwan	The Classified National Security Information Protection Act
Taiwan	The Coast Guard Act
Taiwan	The Code Of Criminal Procedure (Article 1 ~ 343)
Taiwan	The Commodity Inspection Act

Taiwan	The Credit Cooperatives Act Of The Republic Of China
Taiwan	The Enforcement Rules of the Statistics Act
Taiwan	The Financial Institutions Merger Act
Taiwan	The Forestry Act
Taiwan	The Freedom of Government Information Law
Taiwan	The Hygiene Standards for Alcohol Products
Taiwan	The Land Act
Taiwan	The Law of Ships
Taiwan	The Motion Picture Law
Taiwan	The Plant Variety and Plant Seed Act
Taiwan	The Regulation for the Implementation of the Offshore Banking Act
Taiwan	The Seafarer Law
Taiwan	The Settlement of Labor Disputes Law
Taiwan	The Ship Registration Law
Taiwan	The Standards Act
Taiwan	The Weights and Measures Act
Taiwan	Tobacco and Alcohol Tax Act 2004/7/22
Taiwan	Tobacco Hazard Prevention Act
Taiwan	Toxic Chemical Substances Control Act Enforcement Rules
Taiwan	Toxic Chemical Substances Management Act
Taiwan	Toxic Chemical Substances Transportation Management Regulations
Taiwan	Trade Secrets Act
Taiwan	Trademark Act 2003
Taiwan	Trademarks Regulations 2003
Taiwan	Trust Enterprise Act
Taiwan	Trust Law
Taiwan	University Act
Taiwan	Urban Renewal Act
Taiwan	Urban Road Act
Taiwan	Value-added and Non-value-added Business Tax Act 2004/7/21
Taiwan	Vehicle License Tax Act Related Laws & Regulations
Taiwan	Vocational Training Act
Taiwan	Waste Disposal Act
Taiwan	Water Act
Taiwan	Water Pollution Control Act
Taiwan	Water Supply Act
Taiwan	Wildlife Conservation Act
Taiwan	Witness Protection Act
Taiwan	Wrongful Imprisonment Compensation Act

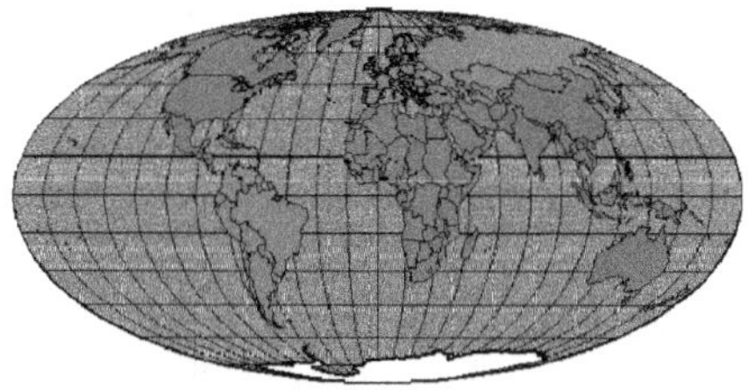

DOING BUSINESS AND INVESTING LIBRARY

World Business Information Catalog, USA: http://www.ibpus.com
Email: ibpusa@comcast.net.

Price: $99.95 Each

TITLE
Abkhazia (Republic of Abkhazia): Doing Business and Investing In...Guide - Practical Informtion, Regulations, Opportunities
Afghanistan: Doing Business and Investing In...Guide - Practical Informtion, Regulations, Opportunities
Aland: Doing Business and Investing In...Guide - Practical Informtion, Regulations, Opportunities
Albania: Doing Business and Investing In...Guide - Practical Informtion, Regulations, Opportunities
Algeria: Doing Business and Investing In...Guide - Practical Informtion, Regulations, Opportunities
Andorra: Doing Business and Investing In...Guide - Practical Informtion, Regulations, Opportunities
Angola: Doing Business and Investing In...Guide - Practical Informtion, Regulations, Opportunities
Anguilla: Doing Business and Investing In...Guide - Practical Informtion, Regulations, Opportunities
Antigua and Barbuda: Doing Business and Investing In...Guide - Practical Informtion, Regulations, Opportunities
Antilles (Netherlands): Doing Business and Investing In...Guide - Practical Informtion, Regulations, Opportunities
Argentina: Doing Business and Investing In...Guide - Practical Informtion, Regulations, Opportunities
Armenia: Doing Business and Investing In...Guide - Practical Informtion, Regulations, Opportunities
Aruba: Doing Business and Investing In...Guide - Practical Informtion, Regulations, Opportunities
Australia: Doing Business and Investing In...Guide - Practical Informtion, Regulations, Opportunities
Austria: Doing Business and Investing In...Guide - Practical Informtion, Regulations, Opportunities
Azerbaijan: Doing Business and Investing In...Guide - Practical Informtion, Regulations, Opportunities
Bahamas: Doing Business and Investing In...Guide - Practical Informtion, Regulations, Opportunities
Bahrain: Doing Business and Investing In...Guide - Practical Informtion, Regulations, Opportunities
Bangladesh: Doing Business and Investing In...Guide - Practical Informtion, Regulations, Opportunities
Barbados: Doing Business and Investing In...Guide - Practical Informtion, Regulations, Opportunities
Belarus: Doing Business and Investing In...Guide - Practical Informtion, Regulations, Opportunities
Belgium: Doing Business and Investing In...Guide - Practical Informtion, Regulations, Opportunities
Belize: Doing Business and Investing In...Guide - Practical Informtion, Regulations, Opportunities
Benin: Doing Business and Investing In...Guide - Practical Informtion, Regulations, Opportunities
Bermuda: Doing Business and Investing In...Guide - Practical Informtion, Regulations, Opportunities
Bhutan: Doing Business and Investing In...Guide - Practical Informtion, Regulations, Opportunities
Bolivia: Doing Business and Investing In...Guide - Practical Informtion, Regulations, Opportunities
Bosnia and Herzegovina: Doing Business and Investing In...Guide - Practical Informtion, Regulations, Opportunities
Botswana: Doing Business and Investing In...Guide - Practical Informtion, Regulations, Opportunities
Brazil: Doing Business and Investing In...Guide - Practical Informtion, Regulations, Opportunities
Brunei: Doing Business and Investing In...Guide - Practical Informtion, Regulations, Opportunities
Bulgaria: Doing Business and Investing In...Guide - Practical Informtion, Regulations, Opportunities
Burkina Faso: Doing Business and Investing In...Guide - Practical Informtion, Regulations, Opportunities
Burundi: Doing Business and Investing In...Guide - Practical Informtion, Regulations, Opportunities
Cambodia: Doing Business and Investing In...Guide - Practical Informtion, Regulations, Opportunities

TITLE
Cameroon: Doing Business and Investing In...Guide - Practical Informtion, Regulations, Opportunities
Canada: Doing Business and Investing In...Guide - Practical Informtion, Regulations, Opportunities
Cape Verde: Doing Business and Investing In...Guide - Practical Informtion, Regulations, Opportunities
Cayman Islands: Doing Business and Investing In...Guide - Practical Informtion, Regulations, Opportunities
Central African Republic: Doing Business and Investing In...Guide - Practical Informtion, Regulations, Opportunities
Chad: Doing Business and Investing In...Guide - Practical Informtion, Regulations, Opportunities
Chile: Doing Business and Investing In...Guide - Practical Informtion, Regulations, Opportunities
China: Doing Business and Investing In...Guide - Practical Informtion, Regulations, Opportunities
Colombia: Doing Business and Investing In...Guide - Practical Informtion, Regulations, Opportunities
Comoros: Doing Business and Investing In...Guide - Practical Informtion, Regulations, Opportunities
Congo: Doing Business and Investing In...Guide - Practical Informtion, Regulations, Opportunities
Congo, Democratic Republic: Doing Business and Investing In...Guide - Practical Informtion, Regulations, Opportunities
Cook Islands: Doing Business and Investing In...Guide - Practical Informtion, Regulations, Opportunities
Costa Rica: Doing Business and Investing In...Guide - Practical Informtion, Regulations, Opportunities
Cote d'Ivoire: Doing Business and Investing In...Guide - Practical Informtion, Regulations, Opportunities
Croatia: Doing Business and Investing In...Guide - Practical Informtion, Regulations, Opportunities
Cuba: Doing Business and Investing In...Guide - Practical Informtion, Regulations, Opportunities
Cyprus: Doing Business and Investing In...Guide - Practical Informtion, Regulations, Opportunities
Czech Republic: Doing Business and Investing In...Guide - Practical Informtion, Regulations, Opportunities
Denmark: Doing Business and Investing In...Guide - Practical Informtion, Regulations, Opportunities
Djibouti: Doing Business and Investing In...Guide - Practical Informtion, Regulations, Opportunities
Dominica: Doing Business and Investing In...Guide - Practical Informtion, Regulations, Opportunities
Dominican Republic: Doing Business and Investing In...Guide - Practical Informtion, Regulations, Opportunities
Ecuador: Doing Business and Investing In...Guide - Practical Informtion, Regulations, Opportunities
Egypt: Doing Business and Investing In...Guide - Practical Informtion, Regulations, Opportunities
El Salvador: Doing Business and Investing In...Guide - Practical Informtion, Regulations, Opportunities
Equatorial Guinea: Doing Business and Investing In...Guide - Practical Informtion, Regulations, Opportunities
Eritrea: Doing Business and Investing In...Guide - Practical Informtion, Regulations, Opportunities
Estonia: Doing Business and Investing In...Guide - Practical Informtion, Regulations, Opportunities
Ethiopia: Doing Business and Investing In...Guide - Practical Informtion, Regulations, Opportunities
Falkland Islands: Doing Business and Investing In...Guide - Practical Informtion, Regulations, Opportunities
Faroes Islands: Doing Business and Investing In...Guide - Practical Informtion, Regulations, Opportunities
Fiji: Doing Business and Investing In...Guide - Practical Informtion, Regulations, Opportunities
Finland: Doing Business and Investing In...Guide - Practical Informtion, Regulations, Opportunities
France: Doing Business and Investing In...Guide - Practical Informtion, Regulations, Opportunities
Gabon: Doing Business and Investing In...Guide - Practical Informtion, Regulations, Opportunities
Gambia: Doing Business and Investing In...Guide - Practical Informtion, Regulations, Opportunities
Georgia: Doing Business and Investing In...Guide - Practical Informtion, Regulations, Opportunities
Germany: Doing Business and Investing In...Guide - Practical Informtion, Regulations, Opportunities
Ghana: Doing Business and Investing In...Guide - Practical Informtion, Regulations, Opportunities
Gibraltar: Doing Business and Investing In...Guide - Practical Informtion, Regulations, Opportunities
Greece: Doing Business and Investing In...Guide - Practical Informtion, Regulations, Opportunities
Greenland: Doing Business and Investing In...Guide - Practical Informtion, Regulations, Opportunities
Grenada: Doing Business and Investing In...Guide - Practical Informtion, Regulations, Opportunities
Guam: Doing Business and Investing In...Guide - Practical Informtion, Regulations, Opportunities

TITLE
Guatemala: Doing Business and Investing In...Guide - Practical Informtion, Regulations, Opportunities
Guernsey: Doing Business and Investing In...Guide - Practical Informtion, Regulations, Opportunities
Guinea: Doing Business and Investing In...Guide - Practical Informtion, Regulations, Opportunities
Guinea-Bissau: Doing Business and Investing In...Guide - Practical Informtion, Regulations, Opportunities
Guyana: Doing Business and Investing In...Guide - Practical Informtion, Regulations, Opportunities
Haiti: Doing Business and Investing In...Guide - Practical Informtion, Regulations, Opportunities
Honduras: Doing Business and Investing In...Guide - Practical Informtion, Regulations, Opportunities
Hungary: Doing Business and Investing In...Guide - Practical Informtion, Regulations, Opportunities
Iceland: Doing Business and Investing In...Guide - Practical Informtion, Regulations, Opportunities
India: Doing Business and Investing In...Guide - Practical Informtion, Regulations, Opportunities
Indonesia: Doing Business and Investing In...Guide - Practical Informtion, Regulations, Opportunities
Iran: Doing Business and Investing In...Guide - Practical Informtion, Regulations, Opportunities
Iraq: Doing Business and Investing In...Guide - Practical Informtion, Regulations, Opportunities
Ireland: Doing Business and Investing In...Guide - Practical Informtion, Regulations, Opportunities
Israel: Doing Business and Investing In...Guide - Practical Informtion, Regulations, Opportunities
Italy: Doing Business and Investing In...Guide - Practical Informtion, Regulations, Opportunities
Jamaica: Doing Business and Investing In...Guide - Practical Informtion, Regulations, Opportunities
Japan: Doing Business and Investing In...Guide - Practical Informtion, Regulations, Opportunities
Jersey: Doing Business and Investing In...Guide - Practical Informtion, Regulations, Opportunities
Jordan: Doing Business and Investing In...Guide - Practical Informtion, Regulations, Opportunities
Kazakhstan: Doing Business and Investing In...Guide - Practical Informtion, Regulations, Opportunities
Kenya: Doing Business and Investing In...Guide - Practical Informtion, Regulations, Opportunities
Kiribati: Doing Business and Investing In...Guide - Practical Informtion, Regulations, Opportunities
Korea, North: Doing Business and Investing In...Guide - Practical Informtion, Regulations, Opportunities
Korea, South: Doing Business and Investing In...Guide - Practical Informtion, Regulations, Opportunities
Kosovo: Doing Business and Investing In...Guide - Practical Informtion, Regulations, Opportunities
Kurdistan: Doing Business and Investing In...Guide - Practical Informtion, Regulations, Opportunities
Kuwait: Doing Business and Investing In...Guide - Practical Informtion, Regulations, Opportunities
Kyrgyzstan: Doing Business and Investing In...Guide - Practical Informtion, Regulations, Opportunities
Laos: Doing Business and Investing In...Guide - Practical Informtion, Regulations, Opportunities
Latvia: Doing Business and Investing In...Guide - Practical Informtion, Regulations, Opportunities
Lebanon: Doing Business and Investing In...Guide - Practical Informtion, Regulations, Opportunities
Lesotho: Doing Business and Investing In...Guide - Practical Informtion, Regulations, Opportunities
Liberia: Doing Business and Investing In...Guide - Practical Informtion, Regulations, Opportunities
Libya: Doing Business and Investing In...Guide - Practical Informtion, Regulations, Opportunities
Liechtenstein: Doing Business and Investing In...Guide - Practical Informtion, Regulations, Opportunities
Lithuania: Doing Business and Investing In...Guide - Practical Informtion, Regulations, Opportunities
Luxembourg: Doing Business and Investing In...Guide - Practical Informtion, Regulations, Opportunities
Macao: Doing Business and Investing In...Guide - Practical Informtion, Regulations, Opportunities
Macedonia: Doing Business and Investing In...Guide - Practical Informtion, Regulations, Opportunities
Madagascar: Doing Business and Investing In...Guide - Practical Informtion, Regulations, Opportunities
Madeira: Doing Business and Investing In...Guide - Practical Informtion, Regulations, Opportunities
Malawi: Doing Business and Investing In...Guide - Practical Informtion, Regulations, Opportunities
Malaysia: Doing Business and Investing In...Guide - Practical Informtion, Regulations, Opportunities
Maldives: Doing Business and Investing In...Guide - Practical Informtion, Regulations, Opportunities
Mali: Doing Business and Investing In...Guide - Practical Informtion, Regulations, Opportunities

TITLE
Malta: Doing Business and Investing In...Guide - Practical Informtion, Regulations, Opportunities
Man: Doing Business and Investing In...Guide - Practical Informtion, Regulations, Opportunities
Marshall Islands: Doing Business and Investing In...Guide - Practical Informtion, Regulations, Opportunities
Mauritania: Doing Business and Investing In...Guide - Practical Informtion, Regulations, Opportunities
Mauritius: Doing Business and Investing In...Guide - Practical Informtion, Regulations, Opportunities
Mayotte: Doing Business and Investing In...Guide - Practical Informtion, Regulations, Opportunities
Mexico: Doing Business and Investing In...Guide - Practical Informtion, Regulations, Opportunities
Micronesia: Doing Business and Investing In...Guide - Practical Informtion, Regulations, Opportunities
Moldova: Doing Business and Investing In...Guide - Practical Informtion, Regulations, Opportunities
Monaco: Doing Business and Investing In...Guide - Practical Informtion, Regulations, Opportunities
Mongolia: Doing Business and Investing In...Guide - Practical Informtion, Regulations, Opportunities
Montserrat: Doing Business and Investing In...Guide - Practical Informtion, Regulations, Opportunities
Montenegro: Doing Business and Investing In...Guide - Practical Informtion, Regulations, Opportunities
Morocco: Doing Business and Investing In...Guide - Practical Informtion, Regulations, Opportunities
Mozambique: Doing Business and Investing In...Guide - Practical Informtion, Regulations, Opportunities
Myanmar: Doing Business and Investing In...Guide - Practical Informtion, Regulations, Opportunities
Nagorno-Karabakh Republic: Doing Business and Investing In...Guide - Practical Informtion, Regulations, Opportunities
Namibia: Doing Business and Investing In...Guide - Practical Informtion, Regulations, Opportunities
Nauru: Doing Business and Investing In...Guide - Practical Informtion, Regulations, Opportunities
Nepal: Doing Business and Investing In...Guide - Practical Informtion, Regulations, Opportunities
Netherlands: Doing Business and Investing In...Guide - Practical Informtion, Regulations, Opportunities
New Caledonia: Doing Business and Investing In...Guide - Practical Informtion, Regulations, Opportunities
New Zealand: Doing Business and Investing In...Guide - Practical Informtion, Regulations, Opportunities
Nicaragua: Doing Business and Investing In...Guide - Practical Informtion, Regulations, Opportunities
Niger: Doing Business and Investing In...Guide - Practical Informtion, Regulations, Opportunities
Nigeria: Doing Business and Investing In...Guide - Practical Informtion, Regulations, Opportunities
Niue: Doing Business and Investing In...Guide - Practical Informtion, Regulations, Opportunities
Northern Cyprus (Turkish Republic of Northern Cyprus) Doing Business and Investing In...Guide - Practical Informtion, Regulations, Opportunities
Northern Mariana Islands: Doing Business and Investing In...Guide - Practical Informtion, Regulations, Opportunities
Norway: Doing Business and Investing In...Guide - Practical Informtion, Regulations, Opportunities
Oman: Doing Business and Investing In...Guide - Practical Informtion, Regulations, Opportunities
Pakistan: Doing Business and Investing In...Guide - Practical Informtion, Regulations, Opportunities
Palau: Doing Business and Investing In...Guide - Practical Informtion, Regulations, Opportunities
Palestine (West Bank & Gaza): Doing Business and Investing In...Guide - Practical Informtion, Regulations, Opportunities
Panama: Doing Business and Investing In...Guide - Practical Informtion, Regulations, Opportunities
Papua New Guinea: Doing Business and Investing In...Guide - Practical Informtion, Regulations, Opportunities
Paraguay: Doing Business and Investing In...Guide - Practical Informtion, Regulations, Opportunities
Peru: Doing Business and Investing In...Guide - Practical Informtion, Regulations, Opportunities
Philippines: Doing Business and Investing In...Guide - Practical Informtion, Regulations, Opportunities
Pitcairn Islands: Doing Business and Investing In...Guide - Practical Informtion, Regulations, Opportunities
Poland: Doing Business and Investing In...Guide - Practical Informtion, Regulations, Opportunities
Polynesia French: Doing Business and Investing In...Guide - Practical Informtion, Regulations, Opportunities
Portugal: Doing Business and Investing In...Guide - Practical Informtion, Regulations, Opportunities

TITLE
Qatar: Doing Business and Investing In...Guide - Practical Informtion, Regulations, Opportunities
Romania: Doing Business and Investing In...Guide - Practical Informtion, Regulations, Opportunities
Russia: Doing Business and Investing In...Guide - Practical Informtion, Regulations, Opportunities
Rwanda: Doing Business and Investing In...Guide - Practical Informtion, Regulations, Opportunities
Sahrawi Arab Democratic Republic : Doing Business and Investing In...Guide - Practical Informtion, Regulations, Opportunities
Saint Kitts and Nevis: Doing Business and Investing In...Guide - Practical Informtion, Regulations, Opportunities
Saint Lucia: Doing Business and Investing In...Guide - Practical Informtion, Regulations, Opportunities
Saint Vincent and The Grenadines: Doing Business and Investing In...Guide - Practical Informtion, Regulations, Opportunities
Samoa (American): Doing Business and Investing In...Guide - Practical Informtion, Regulations, Opportunities
Samoa (Western): Doing Business and Investing In...Guide - Practical Informtion, Regulations, Opportunities
San Marino: Doing Business and Investing In...Guide - Practical Informtion, Regulations, Opportunities
Sao Tome and Principe: Doing Business and Investing In...Guide - Practical Informtion, Regulations, Opportunities
Saudi Arabia: Doing Business and Investing In...Guide - Practical Informtion, Regulations, Opportunities
Scotland: Doing Business and Investing In...Guide - Practical Informtion, Regulations, Opportunities
Senegal: Doing Business and Investing In...Guide - Practical Informtion, Regulations, Opportunities
Serbia: Doing Business and Investing In...Guide - Practical Informtion, Regulations, Opportunities
Seychelles: Doing Business and Investing In...Guide - Practical Informtion, Regulations, Opportunities
Sierra Leone: Doing Business and Investing In...Guide - Practical Informtion, Regulations, Opportunities
Singapore: Doing Business and Investing In...Guide - Practical Informtion, Regulations, Opportunities
Slovakia: Doing Business and Investing In...Guide - Practical Informtion, Regulations, Opportunities
Slovenia: Doing Business and Investing In...Guide - Practical Informtion, Regulations, Opportunities
Solomon Islands: Doing Business and Investing In...Guide - Practical Informtion, Regulations, Opportunities
Somalia: Doing Business and Investing In...Guide - Practical Informtion, Regulations, Opportunities
South Africa: Doing Business and Investing In...Guide - Practical Informtion, Regulations, Opportunities
Spain: Doing Business and Investing In...Guide - Practical Informtion, Regulations, Opportunities
Sri Lanka: Doing Business and Investing In...Guide - Practical Informtion, Regulations, Opportunities
St. Helena: Doing Business and Investing In...Guide - Practical Informtion, Regulations, Opportunities
St. Pierre & Miquelon: Doing Business and Investing In...Guide - Practical Informtion, Regulations, Opportunities
Sudan (Republic of the Sudan): Doing Business and Investing In...Guide - Practical Informtion, Regulations, Opportunities
Sudan South: Doing Business and Investing In...Guide - Practical Informtion, Regulations, Opportunities
Suriname: Doing Business and Investing In...Guide - Practical Informtion, Regulations, Opportunities
Swaziland: Doing Business and Investing In...Guide - Practical Informtion, Regulations, Opportunities
Sweden: Doing Business and Investing In...Guide - Practical Informtion, Regulations, Opportunities
Switzerland: Doing Business and Investing In...Guide - Practical Informtion, Regulations, Opportunities
Syria: Doing Business and Investing In...Guide - Practical Informtion, Regulations, Opportunities
Taiwan: Doing Business and Investing In...Guide - Practical Informtion, Regulations, Opportunities
Tajikistan: Doing Business and Investing In...Guide - Practical Informtion, Regulations, Opportunities
Tanzania: Doing Business and Investing In...Guide - Practical Informtion, Regulations, Opportunities
Thailand: Doing Business and Investing In...Guide - Practical Informtion, Regulations, Opportunities
Timor Leste (Democratic Republic of Timor-Leste): Doing Business and Investing In...Guide - Practical Informtion, Regulations, Opportunities
Togo: Doing Business and Investing In...Guide - Practical Informtion, Regulations, Opportunities
Tonga: Doing Business and Investing In...Guide - Practical Informtion, Regulations, Opportunities
Trinidad and Tobago: Doing Business and Investing In...Guide - Practical Informtion, Regulations, Opportunities

TITLE
Tunisia: Doing Business and Investing In...Guide - Practical Informtion, Regulations, Opportunities
Turkey: Doing Business and Investing In...Guide - Practical Informtion, Regulations, Opportunities
Turkmenistan: Doing Business and Investing In...Guide - Practical Informtion, Regulations, Opportunities
Turks & Caicos: Doing Business and Investing In...Guide - Practical Informtion, Regulations, Opportunities
Tuvalu: Doing Business and Investing In...Guide - Practical Informtion, Regulations, Opportunities
Uganda: Doing Business and Investing In...Guide - Practical Informtion, Regulations, Opportunities
Ukraine: Doing Business and Investing In...Guide - Practical Informtion, Regulations, Opportunities
United Arab Emirates: Doing Business and Investing In...Guide - Practical Informtion, Regulations, Opportunities
United Kingdom: Doing Business and Investing In...Guide - Practical Informtion, Regulations, Opportunities
United States: Doing Business and Investing In...Guide - Practical Informtion, Regulations, Opportunities
Uruguay: Doing Business and Investing In...Guide - Practical Informtion, Regulations, Opportunities
Uzbekistan: Doing Business and Investing In...Guide - Practical Informtion, Regulations, Opportunities
Vanuatu: Doing Business and Investing In...Guide - Practical Informtion, Regulations, Opportunities
Vatican City (Holy See): Doing Business and Investing In...Guide - Practical Informtion, Regulations, Opportunities
Venezuela: Doing Business and Investing In...Guide - Practical Informtion, Regulations, Opportunities
Vietnam: Doing Business and Investing In...Guide - Practical Informtion, Regulations, Opportunities
Virgin Islands, British: Doing Business and Investing In...Guide - Practical Informtion, Regulations, Opportunities
Wake Atoll: Doing Business and Investing In...Guide - Practical Informtion, Regulations, Opportunities
Wallis & Futuna: Doing Business and Investing In...Guide - Practical Informtion, Regulations, Opportunities
Western Sahara: Doing Business and Investing In...Guide - Practical Informtion, Regulations, Opportunities
Yemen: Doing Business and Investing In...Guide - Practical Informtion, Regulations, Opportunities
Zambia: Doing Business and Investing In...Guide - Practical Informtion, Regulations, Opportunities
Zimbabwe: Doing Business and Investing In...Guide - Practical Informtion, Regulations, Opportunities

www.ingramcontent.com/pod-product-compliance
Lightning Source LLC
LaVergne TN
LVHW080033210926
848481LV00011B/3180
* 9 7 8 1 5 1 4 5 2 7 9 4 8 *